T. HAAGSMA

Preface

Nature is comparable to a highly skilled architect, and living things are the products of her designs. Among these plants and animals are many forms that are marvelously fashioned for their lifestyle; however, the most successful design of all is the beetles. The total of nearly 300,000 species of beetles in the world approaches the total for all described species of plants, and represents about $\frac{2}{5}$ of the total number of insects, which themselves make up about 70–80% of the number of animals in the world.

The great adaptability of beetles allows them to live in many different land habitats; in fact, there are few places in which they are not found. They live in bodies of water ranging from small puddles to cold mountain streams, and from the driest of deserts to frigid mountain tops. There are virtually no parts of living or dead land plants that are not fed upon by beetles. For example, the moist, dark recesses of a rotting log may contain hundreds of feather-winged beetles, which, incidentally, are among the smallest of all insects.

Many beetles feed on plants, but most of them are of little direct significance to man. However, those species that feed upon plants that are important to us are often serious pests. Some beetles do tremendous damage each year to crops by feeding on them or by transmitting fungi and other causal agents of plant diseases. Wood-boring beetles can cause a great deal of damage to recently felled trees unless precautions are taken. Their damage pales in significance, though, when compared to the destruction caused by certain bark beetles that are capable of killing many thousands of trees each year, especially in pure stands of western forests.

One of the worst problems faced by agricultural scientists and farmers in this country is control of the cotton boll weevil, which damages hundreds of millions of dollars worth of cotton each year. The indiscriminate spraying of insecticides to control this beetle causes much of the chemical pollution in the southeastern U.S.

Not all beetles that are important to man are injurious, for the lady beetles (which are often called ladybird beetles or ladybugs) are among the most beneficial of all insects. They feed upon aphids and other small sucking insects that are highly injurious to many plants. Some lady beetles are reared artificially and released to control some of these insect pests. Other species of lady beetles have been introduced into this country, often at great expenditure of time and money, to help control insect pests.

Because of the great variety of habitats in which beetles thrive, collecting them is relatively easy. A number of different techniques are highly effective. Mastery of these will not only closely acquaint you with many natural habitats, but will also show you which collecting methods are most productive in your area. You will find in your collecting that exploration of widely different regions will yield the greatest variety of beetles.

The great number of different beetles practically guarantees that you will always be capturing beetles that you have never collected before. As you develop collecting skill, you will find it highly satisfying to collect a beetle that is quite rarely caught. However, because your search for these rare specimens will so often be in vain, you will learn that the designation of a beetle as rare is thoroughly justified.

Many people have assisted me during the preparation of this book. I must first thank my wife, Pun Ye, and my daughter Bonnie for kindly tolerating the work habits required for the project. My wife has also skillfully assisted me with the artwork. I have asked many coleopterists to read portions of the manuscript and offer corrections and suggestions; almost without exception they have agreed. Some of these specialists have also checked over the illustrations. A few noncoleopterists have assisted me by loaning bugs, hoppers, and other insects for illustrations, or by supplying important data. To John Lawrence, who knows our beetle fauna as well as anyone does, go my thanks for numerous suggestions on the treatments of many small families. My thanks also go to Donald Anderson, Fred Andrews, George Ball, Edward Becker, W. A. Connell, Jay Cross, Mignon Davis, Michael Druckenbrod, Henry Dybas, Ginter Ekis, Wilbur Enns, Terry Erwin, Kenneth Fender, Robert Gordon, Jon Herring, Donald Hilton, Henry Howden, John Kingsolver, Jim Kramer, James Lloyd, Frank Moore, Ian Moore, Charles O'Brien, Philip Perkins, Marc Roth, Alex Smetana, Paul Spangler, Ted Spilman, Karl Stephen, Warren Steiner, William Tyson, Barry Valentine, Bob Ward, Rosella Warner, Floyd Werner, Richard Westcott, Donald Whitehead, Stephen Wood, and Frank Wood. My thanks also go to the staff of Houghton Mifflin for their expert assistance.

Richard E. White

Contents

Illustrations

Drawings of families and other groups of insects that appear between pp. 56 and 333 in the text are indicated by page numbers in *italics* in the Index.

Color Plates (*grouped after p. 176*)

A Field Guide to the Beetles

A Field Guide
to the Shells

1

How to Use This Book

General Organization. This guide is similar in plan to *A Field Guide to the Insects* by Borror and White. That Field Guide dealt with all 26 orders and 579 families of insects, but this book focuses specifically on beetles — the Coleoptera, the largest order of insects, with its 111 families. As a result, considerably more information is given here on each family of beetles than was possible in the insect guide. At least 1 species is illustrated for every family, and for the larger families there are drawings of many species. The total number of beetles in North America is less than one-third of the number of insects (about 88,600 species), but it is still necessary to restrict the complete coverage in this guide to just the family level. For the largest families of beetles we extend our detailed coverage to subfamilies, and sometimes to tribes. Selected genera or species, or both, are also frequently discussed, generally as examples of the most common, economically important, or striking beetles.

The sequence of suborders and superfamilies in this guide is phylogenetic; that is, they are arranged according to what scientists believe to be the order of their evolutionary development. In general, families are also arranged in phylogenetic order within superfamilies, as are the subfamilies or tribes of larger families.

Identification. To identify beetles using this guide, you will need to have a specimen in hand. For details on how to collect or rear your own specimens, see pp. 6–31 and check the **Collecting Methods** section under each family description.

The large number and great diversity of beetles can make their identification to just the family level quite challenging, especially if you are not familiar with beetles. This guide is designed to help you accurately identify most of the beetles you will collect to at least the family level. The problems in identifying any other insect are also encountered in attempting to identify a beetle: there is a huge number of species, and the small size of many of them makes distinguishing characters difficult to see. The fact that beetles undergo a great change during their life cycle (termed complete metamorphosis) also complicates any attempt to identify all the stages. In this book the emphasis is on the adult stage of each beetle.

When you first begin to study beetles you usually have to examine a combination of structural characters given in a description or key in order to identify a specimen to family. But as you gain more experience you will gradually come to know just which features to look for in classifying a familiar-looking beetle and will less often be obliged to examine specific parts. Members of a family frequently have a distinctive appearance in common, and with continued study you will be able to use these attributes to identify many families of beetles on sight. In fact, as you become acquainted with the family resemblances, you will be able to group beetles correctly even though you have never seen them before, without ever having to resort to descriptions or a key.

If you wish to identify your beetles to the genus and species level you will generally need references in addition to this guide (see Annotated Bibliography), for such identification can be done with this book alone in only a few cases. Keys for generic and species identification will require considerable study and effort. Should your interest develop to the point where your collection is extensive and you attempt to fully identify your specimens, you will find that even with diligence the process can take many years; in fact, the collection and identification of beetles can easily prove to be a life-long avocation.

To use this book for identifying a beetle, first turn to the pictorial key on the front and back endpapers, where all but a few very rarely encountered families are included. Some means of magnifying your specimen, such as a hand lens, or better still, a dissecting microscope, will be a great aid in using the key. Compare your beetle with the first pair of alternatives — does it have a beak or snout? Next study the form of the antennae and decide which description best fits your beetle. Each alternative description will lead to further alternatives, and, finally, to a list of several families, with page numbers directing you to the part of the text where each one is illustrated and discussed. If at any step along the way you are unsure of which alternative in the key to select, try both. Now compare your beetle with the black-and-white drawings on the text pages, or the color illustrations at the center of the book, for the families that have been keyed to. Note that life-size silhouettes are provided beside each drawing for the smaller beetles, and life-size lines for the larger ones. Next, check the **Identification** section of the text description for each family to which your beetle might belong; here the distinctive characters are stressed, often in *italics*. Then select the proper family by using the diagnostic features that are pinpointed by arrows in the illustrations and described in the text and legend pages.

To verify your selection, check the information in the **Similar families** section. This lists the families most easily confused with the family under discussion and highlights the diagnostic features that separate them.

Thirteen families are excluded from the pictorial key; these are listed at the upper right on the front endpapers. The species in these families are very small, or have obscure habits, or have very limited distribution (or a combination), and it is very unlikely that most collectors will encounter these beetles.

Family format. In preparing the **Identification** and **Similar families** sections of each family account, I have stressed those characters that are relatively easy to use and have avoided or de-emphasized those that are very technical or complicated. In the **Identification** section the most important diagnostic characters for each family are generally given first. The very small beetles will be the most difficult to identify, and you may have to set these specimens aside until greater familiarity with identification sharpens your skills.

Under **Range and numbers** the North American distribution of each family is described. Most beetle families range throughout North America, but some are limited in distribution. Differences in regional abundance are mentioned when this occurs. The numbers of genera and species in North America are also given in this section.

The **Collecting methods** section discusses the best ways to collect specimens of each family, depending on their habits. The members of a family often have very similar habits, and because these habits may differ greatly from those of other beetles, the most effective way to collect members of one family will often be unsuitable for collecting specimens of another. The ease with which species of the family may be collected is noted. These remarks are intended as general guides, and in this country of highly diverse climates and habitats they will not apply equally in all areas. In addition, since most of my collecting experience has been in the eastern U.S., such information often applies more directly to that area than to other parts of North America.

Under **Habits** there are brief summaries of adult and larval feeding preferences, their usual habitats, and adult behavior. If members of the group are economically important as pests, there is a discussion of the damage they do; the beneficial behavior of lady beetles and other insect predators is also described.

Selected genera and species are discussed under **Examples,** with an emphasis on the most common, economically important, or, sometimes, unique beetles. Habits, or body form, or a combination of both are described. Ranges in body length are given for many genera and species, when these data have diagnostic value and have been readily available in beetle literature. Diagnostic characters that will allow you to separate closely related genera or species are sometimes given. Since this guide (like all Field Guides) is intended primarily for non-specialists, if these points of difference are very complicated, they are not included.

Habits and **examples** are discussed together for very small families of beetles. For the 10 largest families selected **Subfamilies** or **Tribes** are also covered as examples.

Illustrations. At least 1 genus or species is illustrated for each family, and the largest and most diverse families are represented by more than 40 illustrated examples. The scale of each beetle is indicated by a life-size silhouette placed beside each full-figure drawing, or, for very large beetles, a life-size line. As in other Field Guides, diagnostic arrows point to major distinguishing features. Close-ups of certain body parts show important or unusual characters. The labels for each illustration give the genus of each specimen shown, or the full scientific name or common name of the species (when available). Small figures portraying unusual beetle behavior (such as a click beetle clicking) have been inserted where appropriate. The most colorful or unusual beetles are shown in the 65 color drawings at the center of the book. You may be surprised to see that over half of the beetles illustrated in color belong to just 5 families. These families have many colorful species, but most beetle families have few or no colorful or highly unusual species.

Common names. The names used in this book for families are generally those accepted by coleopterists. Most of the species common names are from the list approved by the Entomological Society of America. Most common names given in this book for subfamilies and tribes have been newly devised for this Field Guide. For a more complete discussion on common and scientific names, see Classifying and Naming Beetles (Chapter 6).

Terms, measurements, abbreviations, and symbols. The term *beetle* as used in this book refers to both the adult and larva. A reference to a wood-boring beetle, for example, means that during at least 1 stage of its life cycle, the insect (usually the larva) bores in wood. (In some cases, the adult stage of a wood-boring beetle never bores in wood.)

Although technical terms have been avoided whenever possible, you will need to learn the names of parts of beetles that are important for identification. Consult Chapter 4 on the Structure of Beetles, especially Fig. 19 (on p. 47), and the Glossary, which begins on p. 337 of this guide.

Unless otherwise indicated, measurements in this guide refer to body length, and are given in millimeters. However, when the maximum length for members of a family exceeds 1 inch, the millimeter measurement is followed by the equivalent in inches. For example, the length range for the Carabidae (ground beetles) is given as follows: 2–35 mm (up to $1\frac{3}{8}$ in.). The inch measurements are sometimes rounded off to the nearest $\frac{1}{8}$ in.

The number of segments in each tarsus is often useful for identification and is given as a 3-part formula. For example, the tarsal formula 5-5-5 means that there are 5 segments in the tarsus of each of the first pair of legs; 5 segments in the second pair of legs; and 5 in the last pair. Tarsal formulae are provided only for beetles averaging over 5 mm in length, because the tarsi of small beetles can be very difficult to see.

Symbols are used to indicate the sex of a specimen: ♂ indicates the male, and ♀ indicates the female.

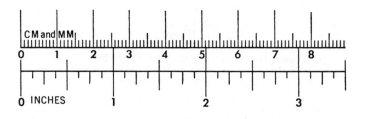

2

Collecting Beetles

Beetles probably live in a greater variety of land habitats than any other group of living things. Because of the diversity of their habitats and behavior, many methods are effective for collecting them. Mastering these methods and learning which ones work best in your area can provide you with many hours of interesting activity.

The 4 collecting methods most likely to yield large numbers and a good variety of species are: sweeping foliage, beating foliage, collecting at lights, and hand-picking. Most other methods (such as bait traps or Berlese funnels) are best suited for collecting particular kinds of beetles that usually cannot be taken by the above methods. Because of the great number of beetles in North America, you need not worry that your collecting will have an adverse effect on beetle populations unless you visit the same collecting site too often.

Some of the collecting sites suggested in this guide (such as animal carcasses and dung) may seem unpleasant at best, but often attract very showy beetles that will be desirable additions to your collection.

Collecting Equipment and Its Use

The following items will prove to be very useful to the beetle collector:

Killing jars (p. 7)
Killing agents (p. 8)
Sweep net (p. 9)
Beating sheet (p. 14)
Beating umbrella (p. 14)
Aerial net (p. 15)
Aquatic net (p. 15)
Portable lights (p. 17)
Backyard light traps (p. 17)
Underwater light trap (p. 17)
Headlamp or flashlight (p. 18)
Pitfall trap (p. 20)

Berlese funnel (p. 20)
Separator (p. 21)
Sifter (p. 22)
Bait traps (p. 23)
Chopping and prying tools (p. 25)
Cardboard rearing box (p. 28)
Forceps and brushes (p. 29)
Aspirator (p. 29)
Hand lens or pocket magnifier (p. 30)
Notebook and pen or pencil

It is generally inexpensive to purchase collecting equipment from a supply house (see p. 345), but if you make your own equipment it will cost even less. Instructions are given below for making many of the items you will need.

Killing jars. This is the single most important piece of collecting equipment, and the only one that can effectively be used by itself in the field. Most insect-killing jars are 3–4 in. in diameter, have a screw-top lid, and contain cyanide as the killing agent. Although this is the kind of jar most collectors use for larger insects, it is not the best kind to use for beetles. The best kind of killing jar for most beetle collecting is a long, cylindrical glass jar plugged with a rubber or neoprene stopper (see Fig. 1) and containing ethyl acetate (discussed below). Olives, Alka-Seltzer, and Polident tablets come in jars of this shape, but they normally have screw-top lids. These jars vary in length from $2\frac{5}{8}$–$5\frac{7}{8}$ in. and in diameter from $1\frac{1}{4}$–$1\frac{3}{4}$ in. Even the largest beetle in North America — the Eastern Hercules Beetle (p. 147) — will fit into a container only $1\frac{1}{4}$ in. in diameter.

Jars of this size are handy to carry; one or more will fit easily in your pocket. When fitted with a rubber or neoprene stopper, they retain a killing liquid very well. You can open the jar with just one hand by forcing the stopper off with your thumb (see Fig. 1) — a

POISON

Killing jar

Lid removal

Fig. 1

great advantage in the field. This type of jar is very durable and is much less likely to be broken than a wide-mouth jar if you drop it by accident, but it is a good idea to cover the bottom of any killing jar with adhesive, masking, or electric tape as a precaution.

For smaller killing jars (about $1\frac{1}{4}$ in. in diameter), use a No. 5 stopper; for larger ones use a No. 6 or $6\frac{1}{2}$ stopper. Cork is not effective; unlike rubber and neoprene, it is porous and allows the volatile killing agent to escape.

Killing agents. Since cyanide is potentially lethal to humans as well as to beetles, beginning collectors should not use it as a killing agent. Ethyl acetate is better than cyanide for a number of reasons: It is much safer to use; it does not discolor a specimen left in it; and it softens muscles rather than hardening them. As a result, appendages (legs or antennae) are not as brittle on beetles killed by ethyl acetate, and it is quite an advantage to be able to adjust those parts of a mounted specimen with little fear of breaking them. You can purchase ethyl acetate by the pint at a drugstore, but you may have to tell the pharmacist what you intend to use it for. Though this chemical is safer than cyanide, avoid getting it on your skin and breathing the fumes.

If ethyl acetate is not readily available for your killing jar, chloroform, fingernail polish remover (acetone), or ether can be used as a killing agent. No matter what chemical is used, all killing jars should be conspicuously labeled POISON, and should be kept away from children.

Making your own killing jars. To make a killing jar, first stuff $\frac{1}{2}$ in. (for a very short jar) to 2–3 in. of cotton or sawdust into the bottom. Next, prepare a small amount of plaster of Paris, using a little extra water so the mixture will pour easily. The plaster should form a smooth layer $\frac{1}{4}$–$\frac{1}{2}$ in. thick on top of the cotton or sawdust. In deeper jars, the plaster layer should be thick enough so that your middle finger can reach it. This will enable you to clean out the jar easily after each use with a moistened cloth wrapped around your finger. Leave the newly prepared jar open (preferably overnight) so it can dry out. It is useful to prepare a number of different sizes of killing jars at one time. After using different jars, you will find out which size is best for your needs; the remaining jars can serve as spares.

Before starting on a collecting trip, pour 1–2 teaspoons of ethyl acetate into the jar and let it stand (stoppered) for about 5 minutes, to allow the liquid to be absorbed. Pour any excess liquid back into the ethyl acetate container. With practice you will learn how much liquid to add to each jar. Because it is very volatile, ethyl acetate evaporates quickly with the stopper off, so keep the jar closed as much as possible. A jar prepared in this way will be effective for several hours. Recharge it before each collecting trip.

To each charged jar add a 4–5-in. square of crumpled tissue paper or strips of tissue with about that much surface area. The tissue will absorb ethyl acetate as well as body liquids from beetles. It will also keep both your jar, and more important, your specimens cleaner. The tissue also keeps beetles separated in the jar and can prevent a large beetle from damaging smaller ones as it thrashes about trying to escape. In addition, the tissue traps beetles as they are added to the jar and makes it more difficult for them to escape each time you remove the lid to add new specimens. After you have removed your specimens from the jar to prepare them for mounting, examine the tissue closely for any beetles that are still lodged in it, then discard it.

Take along a couple of charged killing jars on each collecting trip. One jar is usually enough, but if your collecting is very productive a second jar will be handy. A regular insect-killing jar (3–4 in. in diameter, with a screw-top) can be useful for collecting that is highly successful, such as good sweeping or collecting at lights (see below).

Never use a beetle-collecting jar for butterflies or moths, for the scales covering their wings rub off easily, and will coat any beetles put into the jar. Scale-covered beetles are not very attractive and can be very difficult to identify if the scales obscure their structural features.

Hand-picking. Although some beetles are elusive or have concealed habits, others can be hand-picked off their feeding or resting places and dropped into a killing jar. Many beetles can be picked off flowers and foliage (and should be, if the plant is likely to be damaged by sweeping or beating); others can be found lurking beneath objects on the ground and may aid their capture by feigning death when disturbed. Especially during early spring, when warm days alternate with cool nights, many beetles seek temporary shelter beneath rocks and other objects. If you place a board on the ground in a grassy area where it will not be concealed by other vegetation, you will find a variety of beetles congregated on its bottom surface in the morning.

Sweep net. This is one of the most useful pieces of equipment for collecting a large number and wide variety of beetles. A sweep net, as the name indicates, is swept through foliage, so the handle is comparatively short. The rim is strong, so it will not bend easily when it hits branches or the ground, and the bag material is thick and durable, for it too often takes quite a beating.

You can purchase a sweep net from a biological supply house (see p. 345) or you can make your own at a lower cost. A very serviceable sweep net can be made from the frame of a sturdy fish-landing net (see Fig. 2, bottom). Many of these nets are made of aluminum so they are very light; they are also constructed so the handle can be screwed off the rim frame, which is useful. My

favorite sweep net is made from a fish-landing net with a handle
19 in. long and ¾ in. in diameter that screws into the rim frame.
The rim frame measures 13¾ in. across the opening, 18 in. from
front to back and the rim itself is ⅜ in. in diameter. A minor draw-
back in using a sweep net with an aluminum frame is that the
metal handle will discolor your hand, but this can be prevented by
wrapping some smooth plastic tape (such as electrical tape or duct
tape) around the handle, as shown in Fig. 2.

A sweep net can also be made from a cut-off broom handle and a
wire rim (see Fig. 2, top). The handle should be long enough to
allow you to touch the ground easily with the net rim while standing up. A handle much longer than 2 ft. can be awkward to handle
when you are checking the net for your catch. A long handle does
not give you any real advantage in sweeping either, for most of the
foliage you will sweep will be between ground level and shoulder
height.

The rim of the net should be about 1 ft. in diameter and about
45 in. in circumference. For a rim of this size, you will need a piece
of sturdy but flexible wire (or light metal rod) about 45 in. long and
⅛-¼ in. in diameter. Bend the wire into a circle (step A) and poke
the ends through the holes you have drilled near one end of the
broom handle (steps B and C). Bend both protruding ends of the
wire down against the handle (step D) and secure the wire rim by
binding it to the handle with cord or wire (step E). Make the cloth
bag about 1½-2 ft. long and make the width an inch or so greater
than the circumference of the rim; note the proper shape (step F).
Taper it from the top to the bottom so the bag contents can be held
easily in one hand. Reinforce the rim with 2 or 3 layers of strong
cloth, such as strips of denim or canvas (step G); with regular use a
single layer would soon wear through. Then sew the bag together
using a flat overlapping stitch (step H), to avoid having a crevice
that could trap beetles between the 2 pieces of cloth. If you want
the bag to be semitransparent (and if cost is not important), use a
good grade of organdy or silk.

Sweep your net through grass, weeds, shrubs, or tree branches
with a quick, vigorous motion. Keep the rim vertical or the bottom
slightly ahead of the top, so beetles will be knocked from the foliage into the bag. At the end of a series of strokes, and before you
examine the contents, flip the net so the bottom of the bag swings
around the rim and into its center, so the catch will be trapped
inside.

Fig. 2. Sweep nets. (opposite) A. Rim wire. B. Drill holes near end of
handle. C. Insert wire. D. Bend wire down. E. Bind wire with fine wire
or heavy cord. F. Cut cloth for bag. G. Blue denim or canvas strips for
rim. H. Finished net, showing seam sewn with overlapping stitch.
I. Sweep net made from frame of fish-landing net (note tape around
handle).

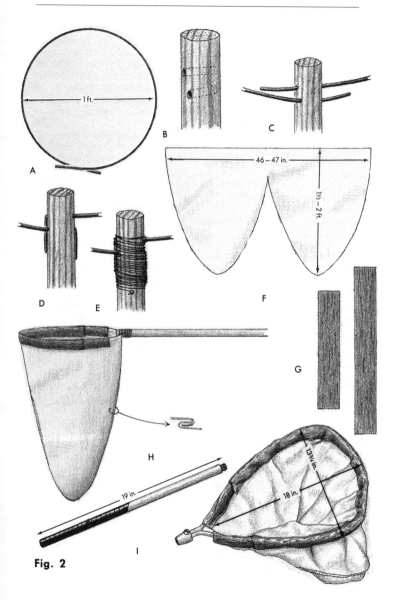

Fig. 2

When you are ready to check the net, hold the handle between your left arm (if you are right-handed) and your body. You will find that bees and wasps are often captured in a sweep net; open the bag briefly and they will nearly always fly out. They are much more intent on escaping than on stinging you. (In many years of collecting with a sweep net, I have never been stung by a bee or wasp in the net.) Only rarely does a beetle take flight as hastily as a bee or wasp, so few specimens will be lost by briefly opening the net. Spiders are also frequently caught in a sweep net; they too will leave readily if given a chance.

When you are sure that any spiders or stinging insects have left the net, grasp the bag with your left hand (or your right hand, if you are left-handed) and slowly push the contents up through the rim. Have the killing jar ready in your other hand to capture the beetles as you expose them. With a little practice you will be able to keep escapees to a minimum. Many beetles play dead when disturbed, so examine the net contents carefully to be sure that you have removed all specimens before discarding the unwanted contents.

Sweeping is a very effective way to catch beetles that feed on plants or prey on plant-eating insects. Examples of families that are commonly found on foliage include leaf beetles (p. 289), weevils and other snout beetles (p. 309), soldier beetles (p. 183), and click beetles (p. 172). Sweeping can also be a good way to collect other beetles that seem to use foliage or flowers only as a convenient resting place.

You can even sweep for beetles from a car. Look for places along an infrequently traveled road where low foliage crowds close to the road's edge. The driver should keep the car's speed very low (not over 5–10 mph) while a passenger holds the net out of a window. Many beetles can be collected using this method, but the net must be emptied frequently. For this or any other collecting that may be highly productive, use a larger (regular) insect-killing jar with a screw-top. You can stuff the entire contents of your net into the jar and examine your "take" after the collecting trip. This will save time normally taken in the field to sort specimens.

Early spring to just past midsummer is usually the best time for sweeping. From late summer into fall the foliage becomes drier and more brittle and fewer beetles will be found on it.

Night sweeping can be a good way to capture beetles that may

Fig. 3. Beating sheets and beating umbrella. (opposite) A. 2 sticks, each about 1 in. sq., with holes drilled for pivot. B. Sticks made to pivot. C. Muslin cloth with tiestrings at corners. D. Finished beating sheet, ready for use. E. Lightweight beating sheet with wire rim. F. Beating umbrella made from old umbrella (note cloth lining sewn in).

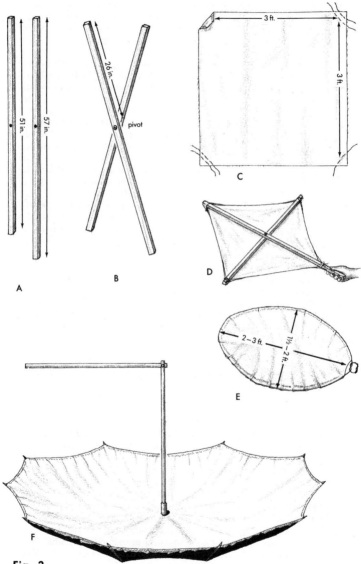

Fig. 3

be active only at night, such as certain long-horned beetles (p. 279), click beetles (p. 172), scarab beetles (p. 138), checkered beetles (p. 208), and leaf beetles (p. 289). This type of collecting can be especially effective in arid regions of the western U.S.

Beating umbrella or sheet. This is another way to capture beetles found on foliage. The sheet or umbrella is held beneath the foliage while the collector strikes it with a stick or club, knocking the beetles into the umbrella or sheet. An umbrella or sheet has more surface area than a sweep net, so the beetles from a large mass of foliage can be knocked into it with one stroke. Fewer specimens will probably be missed this way than with a sweep net. In parts of the western U.S. where the plants are tough and scrubby, an umbrella or sheet works much better than a sweep net. The main disadvantage of a beating umbrella or sheet is that it is more awkward to handle and its openness allows some active beetles to escape.

A very simple beating sheet or umbrella can be made from a 3-ft. square of unbleached muslin and 2 square sticks (each about 1 in. in diameter) — one about 51 in. long and the other about 57 in. long (see Fig. 3, step A). Bolt the 2 sticks together so they can pivot; make the joint at the middle of the shorter stick, and about 26 in. from one end of the longer stick, as shown in step B. Sew tiestrings to opposite corners of the cloth (step C); these will temporarily attach the cloth to the long stick when the sheet is in use. Permanently tie or staple both ends of the shorter stick to the other 2 corners of the cloth so it will be reinforced on both diagonals by the crossed sticks when it is open, as shown in step D. The projecting end of the longer stick serves as the handle for the sheet or umbrella.

You can make a lightweight beating sheet by attaching an oval piece of cloth to a malleable wire rim (see Fig. 3, E). The cloth should measure 2–3 ft. by $1\frac{1}{2}$–2 ft.

A beating umbrella can also be made from an old umbrella. Sew some white cloth (such as a piece of an old sheet) to the inside of the umbrella's frame as shown in Fig. 3, F; this will catch any beetles that are knocked into the umbrella. Make a joint at about the middle of the handle so it can pivot. This will enable you to hold the umbrella away from your body and underneath the foliage.

As with sweeping, the most favorable time for beating foliage is from spring to just past midsummer. You can expect to capture many of the same beetles that can be collected by sweeping (see above), plus some that might be missed by a sweep net.

During the midday heat on summer days beetles are more active than they are during cooler weather. If you notice that many beetles are escaping from your beating sheet or umbrella on a hot day, try collecting them in the early morning when they are less active. This tactic is especially effective in the arid Southwest.

Aerial net. On warm days in early spring and late fall, many beetles fly from one region to another and are common in natural areas. Trying to catch them by hand or with a sweep net can be very frustrating; it is much easier to use an aerial net with a long handle (the kind of net used for butterfly collecting). Since the net is an open-weave bag that will snag and tear easily, avoid sweeping foliage with this type of net.

Aquatic net. This is a very effective way to capture beetles in shallow areas of streams, ponds, and lakes. You can purchase an aquatic net from a supply house (see p. 345) or make your own. Unlike a sweep net, this net has a long handle and a triangular rim that is about 1 ft. long on each side. Wire the rim to the handle as

Fig. 4. Aquatic net. A. Drill holes for wire. B. Bend wire into triangle; insert wire in holes as shown. C. Bend wire and bind with fine wire or cord. D. Muslin cloth for outer bag. E. Inner net of fine mesh — sew inside of muslin bag, about halfway down. F. Finished net with open bottom.

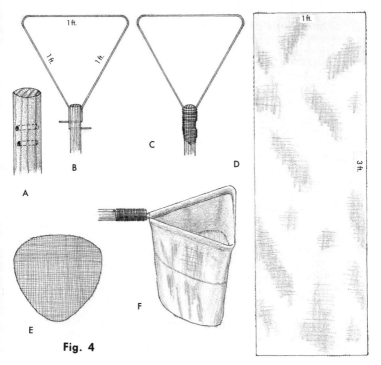

Fig. 4

shown in Fig. 4. Make the outer bag out of durable cloth such as canvas and attach it to the rim so the bag hangs perpendicular from the rim. Leave the bottom open. Sew an inner net of fine mesh to the outer bag, about halfway down (step F). The outer bag will protect this inner net, which will trap beetles while allowing water to pass through.

Skim your aquatic net lightly along the bottom of a stream or pond. Do not dig into the bottom sediment. Hold the open side downward, then pull the net toward you. Lift the net out of the water and dump its contents onto a white surface such as a sheet. Pick through the debris for beetles, using forceps or better yet, an aspirator (see p. 29).

Water scavenger beetles (p. 104), predaceous diving beetles (p. 96), and crawling water beetles (p. 95) are the families most frequently captured with an aquatic net, but riffle beetles (p. 163), long-toed water beetles (p. 162), and other aquatic beetles can sometimes be caught this way. Most of them are found in shallow water where vegetation is abundant. Temporary pools of water can also produce interesting specimens.

Collecting at lights. On warm summer nights, any outdoor light in a good location will attract beetles and other insects. When conditions are ideal, the effectiveness of collecting at lights cannot be surpassed. Warm nights with temperatures above 65° F. (18° C.) and little or no moonlight or wind are usually best. Although these conditions are uncommon, collecting at lights usually will produce a good variety of specimens and is used regularly by nearly all serious beetle collectors. A variety of light sources can be used (see Fig. 5).

The most favorable site for collecting at lights is a natural area with an abundance of weeds, bushes, and trees nearby. Try training the headlights of your car or a portable light onto a white sheet. A portable light with a white 15-watt tube is an ideal lure for beetles and is not expensive. If you set your light in front of a suspended white sheet, it will attract beetles from a wider area and will provide a convenient surface for picking up beetles with an aspirator or forceps (see p. 30). A portable black light (ultraviolet tube) can be used the same way. If your collecting is very successful, more than one killing jar may be essential.

Ground beetles (p. 86), scarab beetles (p. 138), and rove beetles (p. 110) are among the most common beetles attracted to lights. White neon, mercury vapor, and other kinds of white lights may attract different kinds of beetles than black lights do. The most successful collecting may result from using a black light and a white light together.

You can purchase a power converter from a supply house that will allow you to run your collecting light off a car battery (see Fig. 5, B). Alligator clips can be used to connect the converter to the battery terminals. Since the light does not draw much power, it generally can be used for a few hours without running down a car battery excessively. You can also purchase a fluorescent collecting light that will run off a car battery without a converter, or a self-contained battery-operated fluorescent lantern.

If you keep a collecting light on all night, you will find that a succession of different beetles will be attracted to it. Some will come early; others will show up later in the evening. A few beetles may be attracted to the general vicinity of the light but will not fly to the light itself. Examine the ground within 10–15 ft. of the light periodically for these beetles.

Light traps. To make your collecting at lights even more effective, set up a simple trap beneath your light source. Two homemade light traps are illustrated in Fig. 5 (p. 19). The first kind (5, C) uses a regular incandescent lightbulb suspended over a wide-mouth jar; the other trap (5, D) uses a white fluorescent tube suspended over a plastic bucket. The sheet metal around the fluorescent tube intercepts beetles in flight, causing them to fall into the bucket. The celluloid cone over the lightbulb serves much the same purpose.

An even simpler trap (not shown) can be made by suspending a light over a wide shallow pan or tray with water in it. Add a little detergent or alcohol to the water in the pan to make the trap more effective. (The detergent or alcohol will lower the surface tension of the water so beetles will sink more quickly.) You can also set up a light trap with a fan and collecting bag in your backyard. This trap may provide good specimens, but do not try to collect beetles from a backyard ultraviolet trap with an electric grid — any insects that are attracted to it will be damaged.

You can leave your light trap on all night unattended. When you examine your catch in the morning, however, you will probably find that scales from the wings of moths lured to the trap have coated every desirable beetle in it. Any beetles that you plan to keep for your collection must be thoroughly cleaned with alcohol before they can be mounted and identified.

Underwater light trap. This light trap collects many of the same beetles that are caught in an aquatic net, including water scavenger beetles, predaceous diving beetles, and crawling water beetles. It will also attract water bugs and mites and various insect larvae and nymphs. The effectiveness of this trap is based on the fact that light will attract beetles (and of course, other insects) whether they are in the air or under water.

The trap (not shown) is easy to make: It consists of a rectangular boxlike frame with a wooden bottom. The two long sides, the top, and one end (the short side opposite the entrance) are covered with a fine-mesh wire or copper screen. The top should be attached with hinges or some kind of fasteners that can be removed, so the top can be opened to allow access to the trap. To make the entrance, roll up some screen into a broad cone shape, leaving a hole about 1½ in. in diameter at the narrow end of the cone. Attach the broad end of the cone to one of the short sides of the trap, so the narrow end of the cone opens into the trap. Next wire a mason jar, which will hold a small flashlight, to the opposite end of the trap. Make sure that the jar will seal tightly. When the trap is in operation the flashlight should be aimed at the cone entrance, to attract beetles.

This trap will be most effective if you set it in relatively shallow water (1–3 ft. deep). Put rocks or iron weights on the bottom of the trap to hold it under water. If your flashlight batteries are strong enough, you can let the trap run all night and examine it in the morning.

Other night collecting. Many beetles are active at night and can be easily collected by sweeping or beating foliage or by hand-picking them from logs, stumps, or dead trees (see p. 25). A word of warning is essential. Familiarize yourself with a collecting site before venturing into it at night. Unfamiliar territory can hold unwelcome and even hazardous surprises for the unwary collector. Having had the bracing experience of stepping into a drainage ditch during a night collecting trip, I know of what I speak. A flashlight or better yet, a headlamp (which frees both hands), is essential for collecting at night.

Headlamp. A headlamp is not expensive and can be purchased from a supply house. This type of lantern generally uses either 8 D cell batteries or 1 6-volt battery. (A 6-volt dry cell will last longer than the D cell batteries.) To save your batteries as well as your eyesight, use your headlamp only for short periods (1–4 hrs.). A headlamp will cause eyestrain after several hours of use. Keep in mind that it will also create a tunnel vision effect, which may cause you to trip over objects underfoot if you are not careful.

Protect the plastic lens of your headlamp from branches and insect repellent sprays; these will scratch or fog the lens and reduce the amount of light transmitted. Carry extra bulbs in case the one in the lamp wears out. Unhook one of the battery terminals whenever the lamp is not in use; otherwise if you hit the switch by accident you may wear out the battery. The battery case for a headlamp is usually secured with an elastic band, which is not very durable. You will probably want to replace it with a canvas battery case that attaches to your belt.

Fig. 5. Collecting lights and light traps. (opposite) A. Fluorescent collecting light with ballast. B. Fluorescent fixture with power converter and alligator clips for battery. C. Homemade light trap with incandescent bulb. D. Homemade light trap with fluorescent bulb.

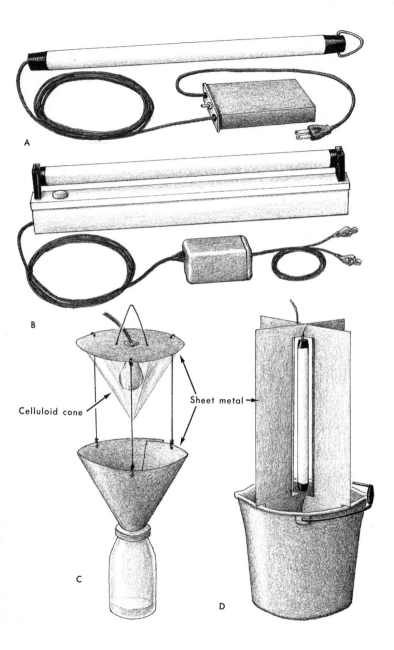

Celluloid cone

Sheet metal

A

B

C

D

Pitfall trap. This kind of trap captures beetles (primarily nocturnal ones) that fall into it as they roam about on the ground. The
trap consists of a wide-mouth jar, can, or plastic container with an
inch or so of a water-alcohol mixture that serves as a killing agent.
Plastic containers usually work best because they come in a variety of useful sizes, are flexible, and do not rust. Set the container in
a hole that is deep enough so that the top edge of the container is
level with the ground. Set up 3 or 4 long strips of wood (1–2 in.
high) in a radiating pattern around the trap, as shown in Fig. 8,
p. 24; these will direct wandering beetles that might otherwise miss
the trap. You may wish to put some kind of loose cover on the trap
that will let beetles fall in but keep the container from filling with
water in a heavy rain.

The location of the trap is critical, for a pitfall trap in a poor area
can be a complete disappointment. A trap in a good area, however,
can capture some very desirable beetles. The edge of an old woods
with many mature or dying trees and decaying logs and stumps
can be a very productive site. The ground should be relatively free
of grass and other vegetation that would discourage beetles from
strolling. Put traps in several different locations until you have
found the best spots. Check your pitfall trap daily. If you find that
it contains only parts of beetles (such as legs or other fragments), a
small mammal such as a shrew has probably collected your beetle
before you arrived.

Berlese funnel. This is an effective way to capture very small
beetles that may never be collected by other methods. Heat and
light are used to force these beetles to leave the rich organic material they inhabit and fall down into a killing jar (see Fig. 6). The
most productive Berlese material is usually moist rotten wood, leaf
litter, fungi, or mosses.

This material is added to the sheet metal funnel, then an incandescent bulb is suspended over it (but not touching it) to generate
light and heat. A loose metal cover traps the heat of the bulb inside
the funnel but allows moisture to escape. (If moisture from the
collecting material cannot escape, it will condense on the sides of
the funnel and trap beetles there, before they reach the killing jar.)
As the material dries out — a process that takes hours — the beetles are forced downward. They eventually drop into the jar containing a water-alcohol mixture, which acts as a preservative as
well as a killing agent. A fine-mesh screen at the bottom of the
funnel keeps the organic material from falling into the jar but
allows beetles to pass through. (Plastic screening works best because it can flex a bit to let slightly larger beetles fall into the jar.)

Families of beetles that are most frequently found in Berlese
material include: feather-winged beetles (p. 126), antlike stone
beetles (p. 128), rove beetles (p. 110), and short-winged mold beetles (p. 118). Other beetles that may be extracted from it are round

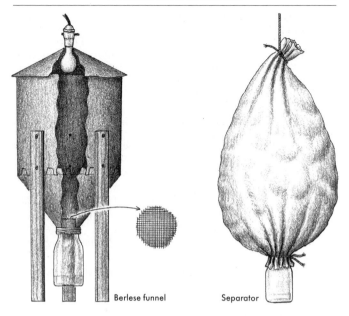

Fig. 6. Berlese funnel (cut away to show construction — note plastic screen) **and Separator** (made of cloth bag tied over a mason jar)

fungus beetles (p. 124), hister beetles (p. 132), small carrion beetles (p. 122), and shining fungus beetles (p. 131). You can capture the greatest variety of beetles by collecting Berlese material from many different habitats, including tree holes, stumps, leaf litter and other accumulations of plant debris, and mammal nests. If you collect too much material to put into the funnel at one time, you can store the rest temporarily in a large plastic bag.

You can pick through decaying plant material and stream-drift debris (see p. 26), then put it into a Berlese funnel to extract smaller specimens. This is a very good way to collect beetles with obscure habits, including many that are not listed above.

Separator. This operates on much the same principle as the Berlese funnel but is easier to make. Open both ends of a cloth sack (such as a burlap feed sack) and attach a strong drawstring to each end. Fasten a screen sieve over the mouth of a mason jar that contains a water-alcohol mixture. Then attach the jar to the bottom of the bag as shown in Fig. 6, by tightening the drawstring around the jar's mouth. Put some relatively light organic matter (such as leaf litter or dry fungi) in the bag and hang it up until the contents have dried out completely. As the material dries out, the beetles in it will move downward and end up in the killing jar.

This method is well-suited for organic material that is relatively light and not moist, but it does not work well with material that is heavy and wet, such as moist rotted wood.

Sifter. A sifter will enable you to collect many of the same beetles you can get using a Berlese funnel or a separator, but much more rapidly. Sifting the top layer of soil or accumulations of organic material in late fall or early spring can be a very good way to collect beetles that overwinter in those conditions, such as leaf beetles (p. 289), snout beetles (p. 309), rove beetles (p. 110), and ground beetles (p. 86). One disadvantage is that by using a sifter you may miss some very small beetles.

You can make your own sifter, as shown in Fig. 7. You will need 2 round wire rims, which will be attached to short handles and will support the top and bottom of a long cloth bag. The lower rim should be covered with wire mesh that has openings from 3–6 mm

Fig. 7. Sifter (portion of bag cut away to show wire mesh inside)

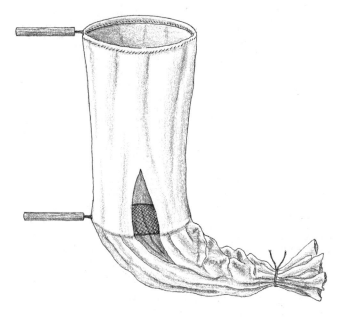

across. Put some relatively light organic material in the upper part of the sifter, shake, and discard the debris. When you have sifted a quantity of material this way, open the bottom of the lower bag, spread the fine substance from it on a white sheet, and pick through it for beetles.

Bait traps. Beetles feed on various plant and animal materials in the wild that can also be used as bait in traps. Molasses, decaying fruit, small dead animals, meat, or dung can be placed in a plastic container (see Fig. 8, p. 24) and set out as a lure for beetles.

For a molasses trap, mix about equal quantities of water and molasses. Let the mixture set for a day or so to enable fermentation to start — the odors of fermentation will attract beetles. Add a little yeast to speed up the process. Put your molasses trap in an area with abundant trees and vegetation, preferably in a protected spot where rain will not fill it and where passersby will not disturb it. Check the trap daily. Beetles that are attracted to the trap will drown, and if they remain in it too long they will decay and be lost. Sap beetles (Nitidulidae, p. 215) are most common in a molasses trap but members of other families may also be captured this way. Decaying fruit can also be used in a bait trap; again, sap beetles are the most common catch.

Decaying animal remains — a small dead mammal, bird, lizard, frog, snake, or fish — can be placed in a small bucket as bait (see Fig. 8). You can also use beef or hog liver, chicken heads, soft fungi, rotting meat, or dung as a lure. If you use this type of bait, cover the container with a wire screen that has openings about 1 in. square; this will admit beetles while keeping out most debris and larger animals that scavenge for food. Fasten the wire top securely or weigh it down. Wrap the bait in cheesecloth or some other kind of open-weave cloth; tie it with a plastic twist tie, a cord, or a piece of wire; then suspend it by the tie from the middle of the wire cover. Put 1–2 in. of water mixed with alcohol in the container to drown any beetles that are attracted to the bait trap.

You will need to add a preservative to your bait trap in warm weather if it is not to be examined and emptied at least once every day or two. The best preservative is a mixture of water with 5% each of chloral hydrate and table salt, and a wetting agent such as a detergent. This solution will keep beetles in the trap from decomposing for a month or so; you can store the solution or carry it around and add the chloral hydrate only when needed. Another solution that is nearly as good and easier to obtain is a 50-50 mixture of ethylene glycol and water. Antifreeze with an ethylene glycol base is a good source; the other ingredients in the antifreeze will not harm beetles, but you should wash your specimens before you handle them.

To set up your bait trap, dig a hole for the container (as in a

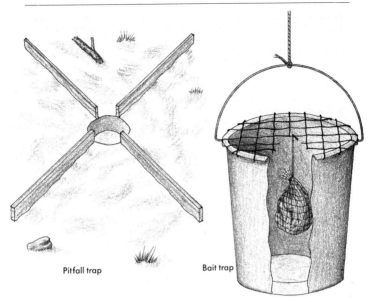

Pitfall trap

Bait trap

Fig. 8. Pitfall trap and bait trap (cut away to show construction and bait).

pitfall trap, above) or hang it from a tree limb. A degree of conceal-ment is highly desirable. If you set your trap in a hole in the ground, you can place a large flat rock over the opening to par-tially conceal the trap and keep out rain while allowing beetles to enter. A carrion trap will be most effective during the first 5 days; after this an accumulation of maggots on the bait will make sort-ing difficult. To sort your beetles, pour the solution from the con-tainer through the sieve and agitate; then rinse any beetles that are left in the sieve.

Good Sources of Specimens

Flowers. These are always a good place to look for beetles. All flowers, though, are not equally attractive to beetles — evidently some are highly attractive, while others are not attractive at all. The best flower collecting in the eastern U.S. is usually on vibur-num in spring. This is an excellent way to collect certain long-horned beetles (p. 279). In the western U.S., look for beetles on *Rhus* and *Ceanothus*.

Dead trees, logs, and stumps. Decaying wood serves as host material for many species of beetles that feed on it as larvae. By examining this material you will find adults of these species as well as other adult beetles that prey on wood-boring insects. You can also raise live specimens of adult beetles from samples of rotten wood containing larvae (see p. 27). Look for dead wood in areas where earth-moving operations such as highway construction have altered normal drainage patterns and killed many trees. Collect from several different areas rather than relying on just one spot; habitats that look identical can provide an interesting variety of specimens.

Night collecting on dead trees, logs, or stumps can be very productive, especially on warm spring or summer nights when the temperature is at least 65° F. (18° C.). Darkling beetles (p. 249), bark-gnawing beetles (p. 207), false darkling beetles (p. 264), click beetles (p. 172), and tumbling flower beetles (p. 266) are among the beetles that can be collected on dead trees at night. These beetles can be hand-picked from the surface at night, but in the daytime you will have to pull off loose bark or use some kind of prying or chopping tool to expose them. Some collectors prefer a small hatchet, for it allows you to chop into rotten logs with authority and to pry off bark effectively. A scout knife or screwdriver can be very useful for prying off loose bark, but neither is of much use for chopping into dead wood. I have found a small meat cleaver to be quite satisfactory, for it has sufficient weight to allow me to swing with power and can be used to pry off bark. It also fits easily into a pocket.

Pulling loose bark off dead trees during the day will reveal many beetles that are normally concealed. Examine the exposed areas very carefully, especially the inner surface of the bark, for many beetles found in these situations are less than 1 mm long. Rather than tossing the loose bark on the ground, tie or nail it back on the tree if possible. This will enable you to check that habitat again and again, instead of destroying it immediately. Fewer beetles will be found on the decaying wood as it dries out, but a series of different species will be attracted to it as it goes through the various stages of decay. Even in midwinter, repeated examination of these collecting sites can provide you with new beetles or rearing material for live specimens. Check the dead wood every week or two; returning to the same site too often will deplete the beetle populations there and result in unproductive collecting trips.

Fungi, mushrooms, mosses, lichens. You may find on these plants good numbers of beetles that you will not find elsewhere. If possible, leave these plants in good condition, to assure that future collecting will be productive and to minimize damage to the habitat. If these plants are very abundant, you can take home some samples to examine for beetles with a hand lens (see p. 30) or to extract specimens with a Berlese funnel or separator.

Stream banks, ocean and lake shores: Some beetles conceal themselves in banks of streams and can be forced out by splashing water onto part of the bank. Ground beetles (p. 86), rove beetles (p. 110), and variegated mud-loving beetles (p. 161) can often be exposed this way. Another way to collect them is to pull small sections of an overhanging bank into the water and take the beetles by hand as they float to the surface.

Piles of fine grasses and other plant debris often wash up on stream banks during a flood. If you check these piles after a storm or a spring thaw with a heavy snowmelt, you may find that many beetles have been carried to shore along with the debris. The beetles may even stay there for a few days during cold weather. Scatter the plant debris on a flat, light-colored surface (such as a sheet) and examine it closely for large beetles; then put it through a Berlese funnel to extract the smaller ones.

When a breeze blows from land to sea or over a large lake, it carries many flying insects with it. Eventually the insects tire and fall into the water, and are carried to shore by waves or currents. Under ideal conditions (which are infrequent) these washed-up insects will form a continuous narrow mound along the shore. The insects are frequently dead or nearly so, and are seldom able to evade the collector. You may have to walk along many shores before you come across such an excellent collecting opportunity, but your patience will be well-rewarded.

Dead animals. Animal carcasses provide food for many scavengers, including beetles and other insects. Various beetles breed in animal remains or feed on other insects attracted to the carcass. A succession of different beetles will be attracted to a dead animal from the time shortly after its death until there is little left but bones and bits of fur. You can leave a carcass in place and examine it at intervals or use it as bait in a trap (see Fig. 8).

In one study of insects that were attracted to pig carrion, rove beetles, hister beetles, and scarab beetles appeared in large numbers. Members of 6 other families — ground beetles, water scavenger beetles, carrion beetles, small carrion beetles, click beetles, and sap beetles — were less numerous; and members of more than 20 other families were attracted in smaller numbers.

Animal excrement. Dung attracts many beetles, primarily scarab beetles (p. 138). If you can overcome a natural reluctance to examine this material, you will find some beetles that are quite desirable for your collection. Use a stick or twig to examine dung closely for specimens. Some beetles burrow into the ground beneath dung; dig carefully into the soil to look for them. If you drop dried dung into a bucket of water, you can skim off the beetles as they rise to the surface. Different species of scarab beetles are found in different kinds of animal dung.

Assorted suggestions. Examine compost piles or other rotting vegetation for very small beetles. Check the bottom of a haystack that has been neglected for some years. Look for beetles near streetlights and other outdoor lights. Look on the inside of windows of open buildings such as garages and outbuildings — insects that fly into such buildings often head for a light source (window) when attempting to escape. Food stored in warehouses and granaries often harbors beetles. The wood at a sawmill can provide interesting specimens. The sap of freshly-cut trees in a woodlot attracts certain beetles — lay wood chips, stones, or other boards on a fresh stump to provide places where beetles can hide and examine them frequently. Dead hollow stems of certain reedlike plants often provide shelter for hibernating beetles.

Beetles will float to the water surface if the material in which they live is dropped into a bucket of water. Try this with dense clumps of grass, fungi, bark, etc. During spring and autumn, on cool mornings before the heat of day drives insects underground, examine ant nests for beetles. Lay stones on the side of an ant nest and look underneath them every few days. Examine mammal nests closely for beetles that may live there.

Rearing Your Own Live Specimens

Rearing live specimens is an excellent way to get specimens that may be difficult to collect otherwise. It also provides beetles in perfect condition, which is especially important for species with fine hair or scale patterns that are easily rubbed off in nature.

Selecting good specimen-rearing material is essential. Look in tree holes for rotted wood of earthlike consistency; this may contain beetle larvae. Chop into logs and stumps in active decay — on occasion larvae, and sometimes pupae as well, will be numerous there. Dead limbs or twigs may also contain larvae. Examine shelf fungi for larvae or signs of their feeding or tunneling.

Late winter to spring is usually the best time to gather rearing material. At that time most larvae are mature and ready to pupate. When they are brought into a warmer environment indoors, their development can be rapid. An absence of foliage and ground cover in the northern U.S. also makes it easier to locate suitable rearing material at that time of year.

The rearing material containing larvae or pupae must be supplied with a little water at times to keep the moisture level fairly constant; it should also be kept from extremes of temperature. A large-mouth glass jar can serve as a rearing container; it has the advantage of allowing you to observe the adult beetles readily when they emerge. Cover the top with fine cloth or netting, as shown in Fig. 9, A — this will allow air to pass through so excess moisture from the rearing material can escape. Secure the cloth or netting with a rubber band.

If you have a greater quantity of rearing material than you can put in a jar, use a cardboard box as a rearing container. Cover the bottom of the box with plastic so the moisture from the rotten wood or other rearing material will not make the cardboard disintegrate. Seal the box tightly so the beetles cannot escape when they emerge from the rearing material. Cut a hole at one end of the box and insert a vial or small jar as shown in Fig. 9, B — just far enough to hold it in place. When a beetle emerges inside the box it will be attracted to light and will end up in the jar or vial. Again, water must be added now and then so the rearing material will not dry out.

Other Useful Equipment

Forceps and brushes. Light-action forceps are very useful for sorting beetles, especially when large numbers are captured in an aquatic net (p. 15) or a light trap (p. 17). Regular forceps can be

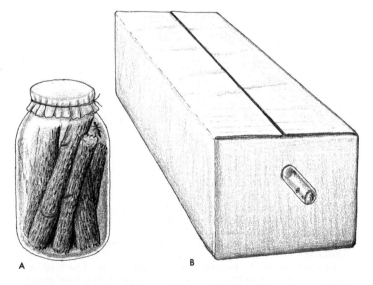

A   B

Fig. 9. Specimen-rearing containers. A. Jar with rearing material. B. Cardboard rearing box with glass vial.

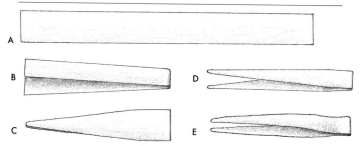

Fig. 10. Light-action forceps. A. Strip of metal for forceps. B. Bend at middle (side view). C. Cut as shown. D. Correct shape (side view). E. Crimp at bend to form forceps.

hard to use because of their stiff action; they make it easy to damage small beetles by applying too much pressure.

You can purchase light-action forceps or make your own (see Fig. 10). To make them you will need a thin, flexible piece of metal, about 2–3 times as thick as a sheet of paper. The aluminum from a pop-top can is excellent for this purpose. Cut a strip of metal 5–7 in. long and ½ in. wide and fold it in half, as shown in steps A and B. Then trim the edges to get the proper forceps shape, as shown in steps C and D. Crimp the folded end of the forceps as shown in step E, then use fine sandpaper to remove any slight burrs of metal from the edges. Make 2 or 3 forceps at a time so you will have extras.

Camel's hair brushes (sizes 0–2) are useful for picking up very small or delicate beetles that could be damaged with forceps. Touch the specimen with the moistened tip of the brush to pick up. If a brush is not available, a moistened fingertip can be used the same way.

Aspirator. This will allow you to pick up very small beetles more easily and safely than any other method. Besides preventing damage to specimens, an aspirator is a convenient way to store small beetles temporarily; they may be very difficult to handle otherwise.

An aspirator can be purchased or made from the same type of glass jar used for a killing jar. The simplest (suction) type of aspirator has a 2-holed rubber stopper and some glass tubing that fits into the holes in the stopper. Insert the longer tube through the

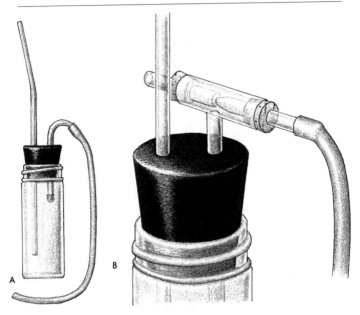

Fig. 11. Aspirators. A. Suction type (note fine screen over end of tube). B. Blow type (detail).

stopper and cover the end that will be inside the jar with a small piece of cloth or fine metal screen (see Fig. 11). Push a piece of rubber tubing over the outside end of the shorter piece of glass tubing. To draw a beetle into the jar, hold the end of the longer glass tube next to the beetle and suck on the rubber tube.

You can also make a blow-type aspirator with a small glass tube that is open at both ends (see Fig. 11). This eliminates the disturbing possibility of sucking a beetle right into your mouth if the fine cloth filter or metal screen comes off the end of the glass tube inside the jar. You can refine the blow-type aspirator further by replacing the rubber tubing with a rubber bulb. Simply squeeze the bulb to draw a beetle into the jar.

Hand lens or pocket magnifier. A hand lens or magnifier can be useful for checking specimens in the field or for examining them at any other time when no dissecting microscope is available. An 8x, 10x, or 15x magnifier will prove most satisfactory.

Notebook and pen or pencil. Use a notebook in the field to record your observations on materials where beetles are found, behavior, or collecting sites. Notes on host material (such as the kind of plant the beetle was swept from or the material it was reared or taken from) can be valuable additions to our knowledge of beetles. Specimen labels that include this kind of data add greatly to the scientific value of a collection, for a great deal remains to be learned about the habits of many of the more obscure beetles.

3

Preparing and
Identifying Beetles

Maintain high standards for accepting beetles into your collection; a damaged or debris-covered specimen may be difficult or impossible to identify. In addition, the distinguishing characters of very small beetles are often hard to see and at best these characters may be, by their very nature, complicated to use for identification. Any specimen that is covered with moth scales or other debris should be washed with an alcohol solution before it is mounted and labeled. A badly damaged beetle is best discarded, unless you are sure that it is hardly ever caught; in that case a damaged specimen of a rare species is better than none.

Temporary storage. Beetles killed in an ethyl acetate jar can be kept there indefinitely until they are mounted. They will remain in a relaxed state, and the liquid will not alter their color or damage them. However, if a specimen is to remain in the jar for a long time, add a slip of paper with the essential collecting data to the jar (see **Labeling,** below), for beetles without data are worthless.

Vials containing a 70% solution of alcohol can be very convenient for storing beetles when they are collected in a Berlese funnel or captured at a light or in any other situation when many beetles are captured at one time. Beetles collected at lights may be put directly into the vial or transferred there from an aspirator (see p. 29). The stoppers of these vials should be rubber or neoprene rather than cork, which is porous and allows evaporation. As with ethyl acetate, beetles kept in alcohol remain relaxed and undamaged, although their color may fade slightly if they are left in the liquid too long. One advantage of alcohol (which may be related to the change of color) is that it removes body oils. When a number of specimens are kept in a relatively small vial, the dissolved oils turn the liquid yellow. Again, add essential collecting data to the vial without fail.

Another method for temporarily storing specimens is to place them between layers of Cellucotton in paper envelopes. They may then be stored in a small, tightly closed box, preferably with naphthalene. The Cellucotton prevents damage and distortion from pressure and keeps the beetles from tumbling about during transport. One disadvantage of this method, however, is that specimens dry out before they are mounted. Drying out can be avoided by adding chlorocresol crystals to the storage box. They keep specimens relaxed and eliminate the need for a moisture chamber (see below). Chlorocresol, with instructions for its use, can be purchased from a supply house. When a fresh beetle is pinned, the soft internal organs act as a glue; a dried-out specimen will not adhere well to the pin, particularly if it is a larger beetle. Before mounting dried-out beetles, it is essential to relax them in a moisture chamber. A large jar or other tight receptacle containing a wet sponge at one side can be used. Add naphthalene to keep down mold.

Mounting beetles. Years of experience in this country have led to rather standardized methods for mounting and labeling beetles. These methods balance the requirement of preparing specimens so that they can be examined without damage, with the necessity of seeing characters needed for identification. Essential collecting data must, of course, accompany each beetle in a form that can be readily understood.

The procedures generally accepted in North American insect museums for mounting and labeling beetles have been developed to satisfy several objectives. Specimens should be mounted securely and neatly (to avoid obscuring diagnostic characters) and should occupy as little space as possible in the collection. A carefully mounted beetle can be examined and identified much more easily than a poorly mounted one. Most directions in this book are based on traditional procedures, but some reflect my personal preference.

Specially made pins are available for mounting beetles. The surface of black insect pins is japanned (coated with varnish) and is therefore nearly rustproof. Some insect pins are stainless steel and light in color. Insect pins are narrow, about 36–38 mm long, and are sharply pointed with a small round head. They come in various sizes (widths), but in general the best ones for beetles are Nos. 2 and 3. Unusually large beetles (see stag beetles, p. 135, and certain scarab beetles, p. 138) are best mounted with No. 4 or 5 pins. Sizes narrower than No. 2 are weak and bend easily, which makes them quite difficult to use, especially on a hard pinning surface. Insect pins are generally sold in packets of 100. Common sewing pins should never be used for mounting; they can damage a specimen because they are too short and thick and corrode readily.

The size of a beetle will determine whether it should be pinned or glued to the tip of a paper point. Beetles longer than 6–7 mm and some very broad-bodied ones with a length of only about 5 mm (see *Valgus* species, p. 147) can generally be pinned without damage. However, some very narrow-bodied beetles up to 8–10 mm long (see lizard beetles, p. 224; cylindrical bark beetles, p. 246; and pinhole borers, p. 325) may be damaged by pinning and are best mounted on a paper point (see Fig. 12, E and F; Fig. 13, A).

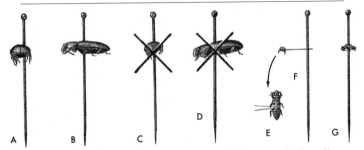

Fig. 12. Pinning and pointing beetles. A, B. Correct pinning alignment. C, D. Poor pinning alignment. E, F, G. Correct alignment of a glued beetle on a point.

Practice will enable you to judge at a glance how to prepare each beetle.

To pin a beetle, grasp it underside down by the thumb and forefinger of your left hand (if you are right-handed) and insert the pin perpendicular to the body, through the right elytron behind its base (see Fig. 12A, B). Be careful not to insert the pin through the base of a leg when the pin pierces the ventral surface, for the leg may be forced off. Push the pin through until about 9–10 mm of it remains above the beetle so that you can handle the pinned specimen without damaging it with your fingers. Compare 9–10 mm with the width of one of your fingernails, which can then be used as a guide. Once the beetle is mounted, move the antennae and legs close to the body to minimize the chance of breaking them during handling. After mounting many beetles, you will be able to position them correctly automatically.

Any beetle less than 6–7 mm long that might be damaged by a pin should be glued to the tip of a paper point. The point should be a narrow, long (about 7–8 mm) triangle. Cut it with scissors or a point punch from white paper about the thickness of an index card. (A point punch can be obtained from a supply house.) Paper much thinner than an index card will bend too easily and will not be satisfactory. If you choose to cut your own points, use strips of paper of the appropriate width and carefully angle each cut slightly so that the point is sharp and the base measures about 2 mm across. Discard any poorly shaped points.

After the point is affixed to the pin, bend the tip of the point down slightly before gluing the beetle on. This will allow the beetle to tilt slightly to its right, with the upperside a little closer to the pin than the underside, as shown in Fig. 12, F.

Fig. 13. Mounting and labeling beetles. (opposite) A, B. Properly mounted and labeled beetles. C–H. Poorly mounted and labeled beetles.

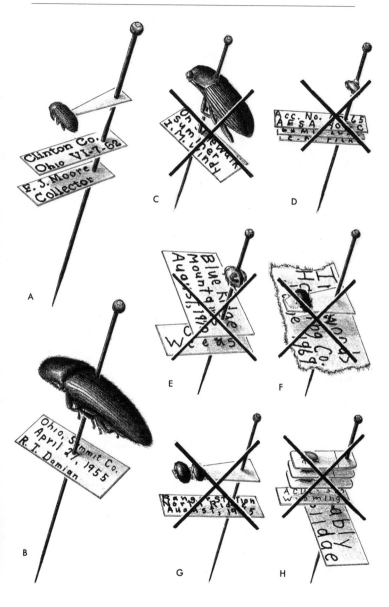

A

Clinton Co.
Ohio VI-7-62

E. J. Moore
Collector

B

Ohio, Summit Co.
April 27, 1955
R. T. Damian

C

Oh. Newark
summer
I. M. Windy

D

Acc. No.
AESA
summer
I. M. Windy

E

Blue Ridge
Mountains
August 1, 1946

Weeds

F

Hall
Co.
Woods
1967

G

Ranger Station
North Ridge
August 1, 1945

H

Acc. No.
Wyoming
probably
...idae

Various types of glue are satisfactory for mounting beetles, but a water-soluble glue is best. Elmer's Glue is convenient, for it comes in a small, squeezable plastic container with a pointed nozzle and is water-soluble. Screw the top down after each use to prevent it from becoming stuck open. Other glues of the same type are available in similar containers. Duco cement may also be used, but it dries out rapidly. If it becomes too thick, use amyl acetate as a thinner. Clear nail polish is another possible cement.

Important diagnostic characters occur on the ventral surface of many beetles. When gluing a specimen to a point, take care that these characters are not concealed. Try to leave the middle and the entire left side of the ventral surface unobscured (Fig. 12, E), so you will be able to examine important structures in the sternal area. Glue the tip of the paper point to the right ventral side of the body, not to the entire ventral surface or to the legs. Legs mired in a blob of glue make it impossible to determine the number of tarsal segments. The smaller the beetle, the greater the care needed to mount it properly without using too much glue.

Lay the beetle on a flat surface, underside down, and tilt it on its left side. Touch the paper point with the glue on it (holding the pin by its point in your right hand) to the right ventral side of the body, at about the middle of the body. Keep the specimen from moving by placing a finger of your left (other) hand against the back of the beetle. If you put your specimen on a surface an inch or so higher than your work table, you will find that mounting it will be a little easier. Once the beetle is on the point, check to be sure that it is at a right angle to the length of the point and that the specimen is tilted to its right. This may have to be done hastily, depending on how fast the glue sets. Unless a beetle is fairly large (5–6 mm long) and has long legs or antennae, it is usually not necessary to move the appendages in against the body. You can expect your first few attempts at mounting on a point to be slow and frustrating, but it will become much easier with practice.

Mounting blocks. A mounting block (Fig. 14) enables you to set points and labels on pins at uniform heights. Mounting blocks can be purchased or can be quite easily made at home, preferably from a hard wood such as oak. To construct a block such as mounting block A, drill holes 28 mm, 19 mm, and 14 mm deep. Drill the holes with the smallest possible bit. Inserting the pin into these holes will allow you to set the paper point at about 9 mm, the 1st label at about 18 mm, and the 2nd label at about 23 mm below the head of the pin. The highest level of mounting block B should be 28 mm from top to bottom, the next level 9 mm below it, and the last level 5 mm lower. Drill the holes completely through the block, then attach a backing of hard composition (particle) board or metal. This block will also enable you to set the point and 2 labels at the appropriate heights. When using a metal-backed block, do not

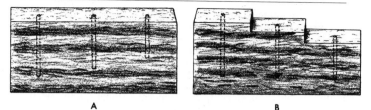

A   **B**

Fig. 14. Mounting blocks.

push the pin into the block too forcefully, for with all but the highest quality pins, the tip will bend. One advantage of this kind of block (over block A) is that the holes will not become deeper with use; in an all-wood block, especially if the wood is soft, the depths of the holes may increase considerably. Do not use a mounting block to adjust a mounted beetle on a pin because the beetles vary too much in body thickness, and the larger ones may end up much too high on the pin.

If you find while using your homemade pinning block that the paper points bend upward, then your pinning holes are too big. Do the following to make them smaller: Insert a common sewing pin most of the way through the middle of a 1-in.-square piece of smooth plastic (or any other material to which glue will not adhere). Put a drop of glue in the oversized hole, then insert the pin in the plastic square into the hole, and carefully set the pinning block upside down, so that it is resting partly on the pin. After the glue has dried, remove the pin and plastic square and sand the surface smooth.

Collectors and researchers who regularly work with many hundreds of specimens find that standardized procedures for mounting and labeling greatly streamline the process. Conversely, poor mounting methods hamper efficient examination of specimens in a beetle collection.

Labeling. Each label must bear the essential, carefully composed data and be arranged on a pin to take up minimum space. The data on a specimen are as important as the specimen itself; to the serious collector and the scientist a specimen without data has little value. The minimum data you should record consist of the place and date of collection and your name (as the collector). First on the label should be the state (in capital letters, abbreviated if long) followed by the collection site (county, town, or city, etc.), the date of collection (month, day, and year), and, last, the collector's name. The collection site must be specified in as much detail as possible so that it can be located on a map. If the site has no name or is unlikely to be labeled on most maps, it may be described in relation to the nearest town or landmark (for example, TEX., 10 mi. e. Amarillo). The essential data will generally fit on the label in 3 or 4 lines, but you can use 2 or more labels if necessary. Other valuable information to record includes the collecting method or equipment used (light trap, sweep net, found under bark), the host material or plant (reared from maple log; in oak stump; on morning glory; reared from shelf fungus), and the altitude, if the specimen was collected on a mountain. The more specific these data are, the more value they have to other collectors and beetle specialists. For example, "on ragweed" is more meaningful than "on weeds," and "in shelf fungus" is more useful than "in fungus." There will be many times when the more specific data are difficult or impossible to provide, but they add greatly to the scientific value of a collection and may even help a researcher find the species in the field and investigate its habits.

If a beetle is pinned, the label should be placed below and parallel to the beetle and the pin should be inserted near the middle of the label (see Fig. 13, B). If a beetle is glued to a point, the label should be parallel to the point and should be pinned near its right edge (see Fig. 13, A).

Ideally, labels should measure about 12–13 mm x 5 mm ($\frac{1}{2}$ x $\frac{1}{5}$ in.). If you have your labels printed professionally, this will give you room for about 15 letters (characters) per line. Oversized labels waste precious space. If you make your own labels, use smooth white paper about as thick as construction paper (thicker than ordinary notebook paper but not as thick as index cards).

If you have a favorite collecting spot and are likely to capture dozens or even hundreds of specimens there, it will pay to have your labels printed by a supply house. Generally, a minimum order for each setup is 100 labels. When you purchase 1000 labels at a time, you can choose a single setup (1000 identical labels) or up to 10 different setups in batches of 100 each. Type the label if possible

A	SC Myrtle Bch. June 20-1955 V. M. Kirk	D	FLA. Bush Key Jan. 14, 1962 H. A. Denmark	G	OHIO, Warren Co. V-18-63 F. J. Moore	J	MD Prince Gge. County, Largo August 20-1974
B	OHIO, Wayne Co. VII-18-57 R. Williams	E	MD. Prince Ggs. Co. VII-10-75 Coll. R. White	H	VA Assateague Isl. VI-20-68 Jay Cross		Light Trap R. E. White
C	ARIZ. Pima Co. Madera Canyon Aug. 14, 1971 W. H. Tyson	F	MISS:HarrisonCo. GulfPark College July 14, 1969 L. H. Williams	I	NEB 5 mi. W. of Lincoln V-10-63 On milkweed R. E. White	K	TEX. Davis Mts. VI-19-68 DJ, JN Knull Collectors

Fig. 15. Well-composed labels. A–I. Properly composed 3- and 4-line labels. J., K. Properly composed 2-part labels.

or print it carefully by hand, for labels are reproduced exactly as submitted to the printer (in a smaller size). Leave the date of collection blank, except for the first 2–3 numbers of the year (*e.g.* 198_); you can fill in the date in ink as you use the labels.

Labels are normally printed by hand when you need only a few, generally no more than 20–30, depending on your tolerance for doing fine printing. A pen with very fine point (such as a crow quill or other fine-tipped dip pen) or a Rapidograph or Unitech pen with a fine 00 or 000 point can be used. The last 2 pens are fairly expensive but have the advantages of holding a large ink supply and producing a smooth line of uniform width. They also come in even finer sizes than 00 or 000, which you may consider using.

Arranging and caring for your collection. A permanent storage box for a collection must be at least 42–50 mm (1¾–2 in.) deep, from bottom to top *with the lid on,* excluding the layer of pinning material. If the box is not deep enough, each time the lid is closed it will knock over or squash your pins, particularly if they are not inserted deeply into the pinning bottom. Inexpensive storage boxes can be made from old cigar or candy boxes or something similar. The pinning material for the bottom should be about 6–10 mm (¼–⅜ in.) thick. The ideal pinning material will accept and support pins readily in an upright position. (The same amount of force should be required to withdraw each pin as was used to insert it.) The best pinning surface is sheet polyethylene, available from supply houses. Cork sheet is also good, or particle board that is not too hard may be used. Sheets of polystyrene — used as molded packing material for many appliances — are useful, but paradichlorobenzene (see **Repellents,** below) must never be added to a box with a polystyrene bottom because the chemical will dissolve it. Cardboard from boxes will work if nothing better can be found, but this may be difficult to force pins into and may not support them well after repeated use. Cut whatever pinning material you use to fit the box snugly and glue it in firmly so that it will not come loose when a pin is pulled out of it.

If you decide to purchase storage boxes for your collection, catalogs from supply houses (see p. 345) display a wide variety of boxes and drawers for an equally wide variety of prices. The cheapest box of all is made of cardboard. The least expensive wooden box is made of redwood, with a particle board bottom, and has no hinges. Other storage boxes, all with hinges, are listed in approximate order of their increasing cost: chipboard box, standard redwood box, economy schmitt box, and schmitt box. A schmitt box is the tightest, most durable box on the market. Glass-topped display cases and drawers of various kinds can be purchased. One of the best bargains is a kit that provides materials and instructions for making insect storage drawers (see BioQuip catalog), but this kit does not include glass tops.

If you live near a natural history or insect museum, you may be able to buy used insect storage boxes, which are occasionally sold at reasonable prices. Museum cases of various sizes with insect storage drawers can be purchased from supply houses; some already have pinning bottoms. However, the cost of these cases makes them impractical for many amateurs.

Repellents. The worst enemies of any insect collection are the larvae of dermestid beetles (p. 192), which are also called carpet beetles. These larvae can reduce a dried insect specimen to a pile of fine dust and fragments. Any collection not protected from these pests can be expected to have a short lifespan. The 2 chemicals most frequently used to ward off these pests are naphthalene (used in mothballs) and paradichlorobenzene (PDB). Naphthalene, though less potent than PDB, is used almost exclusively in large museums; it lasts much longer than PDB. Both chemicals prevent dermestids from entering the collection, but neither will kill larvae once they are present. The fumes of both are mildly toxic to humans, so avoid prolonged exposure. Naphthalene and PDB must never be mixed, for they may interact and break down to produce a liquid.

A small cardboard pillbox or matchbox containing naphthalene crystals can be pinned into a corner of each insect storage box. Remember to replenish the supply of chemical occasionally. If you prefer to use mothballs instead of crystals or flakes, insert a hot sewing pin or small nail — about 35–40 mm (1½ in.) long — into each mothball. (Hold the pin or nail with a pair of pliers as you heat it in a candle flame or the pilot light of a stove.) It will melt its way into the ball, and in just a few seconds the crystals will harden and you can pin the ball into a corner of the insect box, on an angle if the box is shallow. One mothball will suffice for smaller boxes; use 2 in larger ones. *Don't* use insect pins for this because many have plastic heads that will melt in the flame, as will the varnish on japanned pins.

Examine your collection periodically for larvae of dermestid beetles. They obligingly provide a clue to their presence by leaving behind droppings that look like a fine dust. If you see evidence of a larva feeding in a specimen (most often inside), apply a drop of ethyl acetate or alcohol to the beetle specimen to kill the larva.

It is unwise to leave your specimens out in the open overnight. In addition to the danger of becoming infested with dermestids, beetle specimens may be eaten by mice, crickets, or roaches. Store your specimens overnight in a tight box with a fumigant such as naphthalene or PDB.

Identification. Although collecting and mounting beetles is an enjoyable and engrossing pastime, many people who study beetles find that identification is the most rewarding activity of all. Understanding the terms for different parts of beetle anatomy and mastering identification keys are intellectual challenges that require considerable study, but you will find that your efforts will be rewarded by a real feeling of achievement.

The pictorial key on the front and back endpapers and the descriptions and illustrations in the text will help you recognize many beetle families and, in some cases, subfamilies or tribes. However, because of the impossibility of preparing a 4-page pictorial key that covers all the variations in beetle morphology, there will be some beetles (usually the small ones) for which the correct family cannot be identified with this key alone. For much more elaborate keys for family identification, see especially the text by Borror, DeLong, and Triplehorn and the manual by Arnett (p. 343). The Arnett manual will allow the determined student to identify beetles to genus, and it gives references to literature on each family that will permit you to extend your identification to species.

Some means of magnification is essential for examining and identifying beetle specimens. An 8x to 15x hand lens is the minimum needed, but it has marked limitations. A dissecting microscope (sometimes called a stereoscopic or binocular microscope, a stereomicroscope, or a stereoscopic binocular) is mandatory if you have a serious interest in identifying beetles, because you must be able to examine finer structures. Don't confuse the dissecting scope with a compound microscope, which is significantly different. The focal point of the lens system in a compound microscope is a small fraction of an inch below the microscope body; the focal point of a dissecting scope is generally 3–4 inches below the body of the microscope (see Fig. 16, A). This working distance is critical for examining insect specimens. In addition, the magnifications obtained

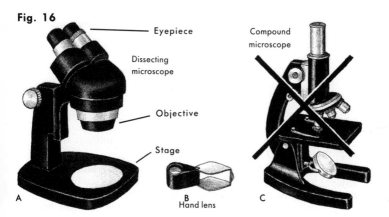

Fig. 16

Eyepiece

Compound microscope

Dissecting microscope

Objective

Stage

A

B
Hand lens

C

with a compound microscope are usually much higher than you will need for work with beetles. A compound microscope also has a light source or mirror below the stage, which generally is not needed in a dissecting scope.

The cost of a dissecting microscope is a serious problem for most amateurs. High quality instruments are quite expensive. However, a serviceable scope can be purchased for less than $100. Bausch and Lomb makes a student scope that is quite inexpensive. Three microscope manufacturers who produce some less costly instruments are listed on p. 345. Write to them for catalogs or the addresses of their nearest dealers. See also the microscopes in biological supply catalogs (p. 345). Larger supply houses (such as Wards, Turtox, or Carolina Biological Supply) stock a good selection of magnifying instruments and dissecting microscopes.

4

The Structure of Beetles

To effectively use the characters that distinguish one beetle family from another, you must understand beetle structure and the terminology used to describe it.

Beetles, like all insects, have an external skeleton called an exoskeleton. This is quite different from our own internal skeleton, but it serves similar functions. The exoskeleton is an outer shell for the body that provides points of attachment for the muscles and protects the internal organs. This outer shell is made of a substance called chitin, is hardened (or sclerotized), and is divided by sutures (usually marked by grooves) into a number of platelike areas, or sclerites.

The body of insects is formed of 3 distinct regions (see Fig. 19): the head, thorax, and abdomen. Each of these parts consists of a number of segments, which are most distinct on the abdomen. The head bears the eyes, the mouth parts, and 1 pair of antennae; the thorax bears 3 pairs of legs, and usually 2 pairs of wings. The abdomen usually has no visible appendages.

Head. The head bears a pair of usually prominent compound eyes, which are made up of many small, individual units. A few beetles also have small, simple eyes called *ocelli*. The region of the head between the eyes is called the *frons*. In front of the eyes are the antennae, which are discussed in detail below. If the head and mandibles are directed forward, the head is described as *prognathous;* if they are directed downward, the head is described as *hypognathous*. The mouth parts are located on the lower front (anteroventrally) of the head. From front to back they consist of: the labrum, which is often likened to the upper lip; the mandibles, or teeth; the maxillae, or second pair of teeth; the hypopharynx, or tongue; and the labium, or lower lip. The maxillae bear a pair of palps, the *maxillary palps,* which are like little fingers. The labium also bears a pair of palps, the *labial palps;* they are smaller than the maxillary palps and are located nearer the middle of the body. Beetles have chewing mouth parts; unlike ours, these work side to side. In the weevils and a few other beetles the head is moderately to greatly prolonged between the eyes and the mouth parts, forming a snout. In all beetles the head is joined to the thorax by a membrane.

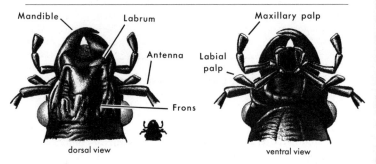

Mandible   Labrum   Maxillary palp

Antenna   Labial palp

Frons

dorsal view   ventral view

Fig. 17. Beetle — head.

Antennae. Beetle antennae function primarily as organs of smell or taste, but also serve as organs of touch. In some groups they may serve other functions; for example, in certain aquatic beetles they help circulate air under the body for use in breathing. The large antennae of some long-horned beetles (p. 279) apparently help them maintain their balance. The antennae are very useful in distinguishing the families of beetles (see pictorial key on front and rear endpapers). Their shape is often very distinctive for groups of families, and, sometimes, for a particular family. In most beetles each antenna consists of 11 segments; in some beetles an antenna consists of fewer segments, and in a few beetles, of more than 11 segments. The most common types of antennae are described below and illustrated in Fig. 18:

Threadlike (filiform). The simplest form of antenna, with segments that are cylindrical and nearly uniform in shape.

Beadlike (moniliform). The segments are rounded and similar from one to another, thus resembling a string of beads.

Sawtoothed (serrate). One side of each segment protrudes slightly, forming a series of points like the teeth of a saw.

Comblike (pectinate). One side of each segment protrudes greatly, forming a series of long sharp points like the teeth of a comb. If both sides of each segment are prolonged, the antenna is called *bipectinate.*

Featherlike (plumose). Similar to bipectinate antenna, with projections on both sides of each segment, but these projections are very long, slender, and flexible, like the vanes of a feather.

Clubbed (clavate). An antenna in which the outer segment or segments are gradually enlarged into a club.

Capitate. An antenna in which the outer segments are abruptly enlarged into a ball-like club.

Lamellate. An antenna in which the outer segments have long projections on one side, which can be brought closely together. *Elbowed* (geniculate). An antenna in which the second segment is attached at an angle to the first, and each following segment is in line with the second.

Beetle antennae vary greatly in form; not all clearly fit into one of these categories. The antennae of some beetles combine features of different kinds of antennae.

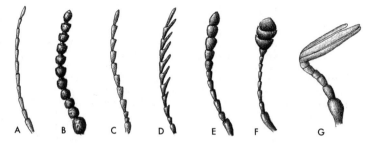

Fig. 18. Types of antennae. A. threadlike B. beadlike C. sawtoothed D. comblike E. clubbed (club weak, gradual) F. clubbed (club abrupt, ball-like) G. lamellate

Thorax. The thorax consists of 3 sections. The first section, the *prothorax,* is quite distinct, but the second and third ones, the *mesothorax* and *metathorax,* are joined and are difficult to distinguish. Each of these 3 sections bears a pair of legs on the lower side (lateroventrally); the mesothorax and metathorax each bear a pair of wings on the upper side (dorsolaterally). The front wings attached to the mesothorax are called the *elytra.* They are prominent (often colorful) and generally conceal the abdomen, but are shorter in some species. The pair of wings on the metathorax are the membranous flying wings, which may be small or absent. They are nearly always concealed beneath the elytra when not in use.

Each thoracic segment consists of 4 sclerites, or platelike areas set off by sutures. The topmost sclerite is the notum (plural — nota), the 2 lateral sclerites are the pleura (singular — pleuron), and the bottom one is the sternum (plural — sterna). Any one of the thoracic sclerites is named by adding the appropriate prefix. For example, the prothorax consists of the pronotum, 2 propleura, and the prosternum. The sclerites of the mesothorax and metathorax are named the same way.

The *pronotum* in beetles is so large and prominent that it may appear to be the entire thorax. The nota of the mesothorax and metathorax are divided into 3 sclerites: the scutum, scutellum, and postnotum. The mesoscutellum (called simply the *scutellum*) in most beetles is conspicuous, and is shaped like a triangle or shield. It is visible at the base of the elytra, before the median suture.

Legs. Starting with the segment closest to the body, each leg consists of the *coxa, trochanter, femur, tibia,* and *tarsus.* Each tarsus consists of 1–5 segments, and the last segment bears a pair of claws at its tip; very rarely there is just 1 claw. The tarsal claws are sometimes useful in distinguishing different groups of beetles. They may be toothed, cleft, serrate, comblike, or bear ventral pads. Most claws, however, are simple, with no modifications. The tarsal formula refers to the number of tarsal segments of each pair of legs. For example, if the front legs each have 5 tarsal segments, the middle legs have 5, and the hind legs have 4, then, in this case, the tarsal formula is 5-5-4. A tarsal formula of 5-5-5 is the most frequent. In some families (such as long-horned beetles and leaf beetles) the 4th tarsal segment is very small and is concealed within the broadened 3rd segment. Thus the tarsi are apparently 4-4-4, but actually 5-5-5. Due to the constancy of the tarsal structure of a group of beetles, and the fact that this structure varies from one group of beetles to another, the tarsi are useful in classification, and are very important in many family keys.

Wings. The front wings, or *elytra* (singular — elytron), of beetles are greatly modified, and mainly provide protection for the membranous flying wings and the abdomen. The elytra are usually relatively hard or horny, but may be soft and pliable, and are nearly always opaque. They are normally held over the abdomen and, with rare exceptions, meet tightly along the midline, forming a straight line or groove (*suture*). In most beetle families the elytra loosely cover the tip of the abdomen; in some families (such as rove beetles, short-winged mold beetles, and others) the elytra are typically short and expose most of the abdomen. Since the elytra are folded back over the body, the morphological front edge of an elytron is actually held along the side of the body, and is called the *lateral margin.* The bent-down portion of the elytron is called the *epipleural fold.* Most beetles have a shoulderlike *humerus* at the base of each elytron. The sculpturing on the elytral surface is sometimes important in distinguishing groups of beetles; for example, in many beetles the elytra bear *striae* — that is, grooves or rows of punctures. The membranous flying wings of beetles are generally not used in distinguishing groups.

Abdomen. This region of the body consists of a series of segments composed of rings or partial rings. At the side of each segment is a spiracle, which is the opening of a trachea, another part of the

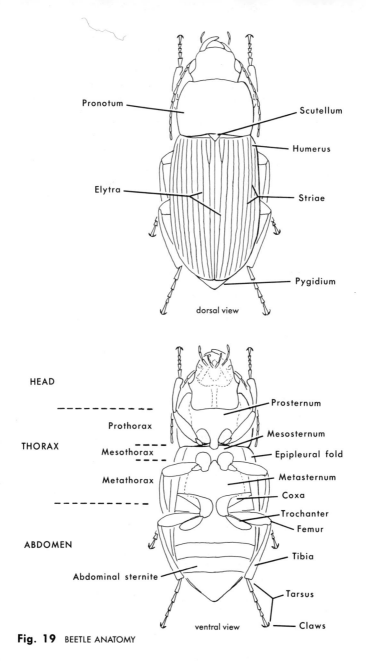

Fig. 19 BEETLE ANATOMY

breathing system. Each abdominal segment has 4 basic sclerites: 1 tergum (dorsally), 2 pleura (1 on each side), and 1 sternum (ventrally). The pleura are normally very small, and are usually hidden. Each spiracle opens on a pleuron. The pleura are frequently fused with the sternum so the spiracle seems to be part of the sternum. The tergum is normally concealed by the wings, so the sternum is the most readily visible part of the abdomen. Most beetles have 9 abdominal segments; these are most easily counted on the tergum. Usually only 5 sternites are visible, for a number of them are small or fused together. The last dorsal segment of the abdomen is the *pygidium*. The reproductive organs are normally concealed within the tip of the abdomen. The genitalia (especially of the male) are often very useful in distinguishing closely related species, but are not used to distinguish genera, subfamilies, or families.

Internal anatomy. Only the most important internal systems are described below.

The breathing system of a beetle is quite different from that of higher animals. Along the sides of the thorax and abdomen are the external openings (called *spiracles*) to the system. These lead to the tracheae, which branch repeatedly to all parts of the body. The oxygen taken in goes directly to the body tissues, and is not carried in the blood as it is in vertebrates.

The blood of beetles varies in color. It is not contained within a closed system of veins. The heart is located dorsally in the thorax, and pumps the blood toward the front of the body, where it simply empties into the body cavity. It flows through the body cavity and reenters the heart through openings called ostia.

The nervous system consists of a simple "brain" or ganglion in the head, a pair of connective nerves passing around the alimentary canal, and a ventral nerve cord that extends to all parts of the body. Beetles have many sense organs; some respond to touch, others to sound, chemicals, light, or other stimuli. The chemical receptors — organs of taste and smell — are located principally on the mouth parts, the antennae, and the feet.

5

The Growth and
Development of Beetles

Beetles, along with flies, moths, wasps, and some other insects, have the most advanced form of insect metamorphosis, called complete metamorphosis or holometabolous development. Great changes occur during this type of development, which includes 4 very distinct stages: egg, larva, pupa, and adult (see Fig. 21).

Egg. The eggs develop in the ovaries of the female and are laid in a sheltered place where the young will have a food supply and favorable conditions for development. Eggs may be laid singly or in masses; hatching usually occurs after several days. The female nearly always goes on her way after egg-laying and leaves the young to care for themselves.

Larva. When the eggs hatch, a wormlike stage called the larva emerges. There is no single general term for beetle larvae comparable to the term caterpillar for moth and butterfly larvae. Beetle larvae are usually called grubs, but some are called worms, or even borers. The larvae of different beetles vary greatly in appearance and habits. Generally they have a distinct head that nearly always has opposable, chewing mouth parts. The thorax consists of 3 segments, each with a pair of segmented legs and a pair of spiracles. The abdomen consists of 8–10 segments that usually have spiracles on each side.

Most larvae have simple eyes (ocelli); others may lack eyes entirely. The skin stretches very little as the larva grows, so it has to be shed periodically to allow for a marked increase in size. This shedding of the skin is called molting. Beetle larvae molt several times as they grow; the stages marked by this molting are called *instars*. The number of instars that a beetle larva passes through varies greatly. Some species have as few as 3 instars, while others have many. As a general rule, the last instar larva is the best-developed and is easiest to recognize.

Several distinct types of body forms are to be found among beetle larvae:

C-shaped (scarabaeiform). The body is distinctly curved and usually soft; the larva is typically inactive and sluggish. Examples are found in the family Scarabaeidae (scarab beetles, p. 138).

Wormlike (vermiform). The body is round (in cross-section), elongate, and legless, like that of a worm.

Campodeiform. Larvae of this type resemble bristletails (a primitive insect) of the genus *Campodea*. The body is elongate and somewhat flattened; the thoracic legs are well-developed; antennae and cerci are usually well-developed; and the larva is usually active. Larvae of many predaceous beetles are of this type.

Wirewormlike (elateriform). The body is elongate and cylindrical, with a hard shell and short legs. Examples are found in members of the family Elateridae (click beetles, p. 172).

Caterpillarlike (eruciform). Larvae of many beetles that live in the open and feed on foliage are of this type. The body is cylindrical and soft and the legs are well-developed. Unlike true caterpillars, beetle larvae of this type do not have abdominal legs.

Most beetle larvae belong to one of the above types, but some are a combination of types or a modification of one type.

Some beetles, especially parasitic species, undergo hypermetamorphosis during their development. This means that the larva exhibits different body types as it develops. For example, in the blister beetles (p. 270) the first instar is active and campodeiform but the following instars are caterpillarlike and the last one is a C-shaped grub.

Most beetle larvae live on land in a wide variety of habitats; others are aquatic. Most beetle larvae feed on or within various parts of plants, both above and below ground. Some live on or within decaying vegetation or animal matter; others feed on stored food (in warehouses), while a few feed on fungi. Many larvae prey on other insects or small animals (*i.e.,* are predaceous) in aquatic or terrestrial habitats. A small number of larvae are parasitic. During

Fig. 20. Beetle larvae (body forms). A. wormlike B. wiremormlike C. caterpillarlike D. C-shaped E. campodeiform

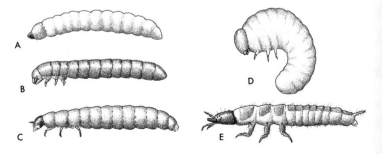

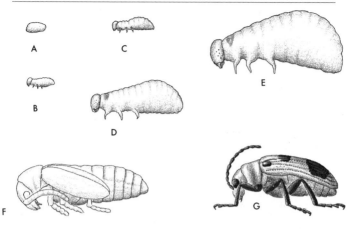

Fig. 21. Stages in development of a beetle. A. egg B.–E. larval instars F. pupa G. adult

its development a *parasitic larva* feeds on or in a single individual, in contrast with a *predaceous larva,* which feeds on more than one individual. In some cases the habits of the adults and larvae of a species are similar, but in most they are not. After the last instar the larva changes into the next stage of development, the *pupa.*

Pupa. The pupa is called the resting stage. The pupa of most species looks like a pale, mummified adult beetle. In a few species the pupa is covered by a cocoon made by the last instar larva. Beetle pupae are of the *exarate* type, that is, the appendages are free and visible and do not cling to the body. Although the pupa is capable of doing little more than wriggling its abdomen, great changes are taking place internally, for larval tissues are breaking down to form adult structures.

Adult. Immediately after the pupa molts to form the *adult,* the beetle is soft-bodied and pale-colored. The wings are small and must expand to their full size; this generally takes a matter of minutes. The hardening of the body and darkening to adult coloration may take many hours. Once the adult exoskeleton hardens, the beetle neither grows nor molts. A beetle that has not yet assumed its full coloration is described as teneral; a recently-emerged specimen in this state should not be put into your collection, for it will give a misleading impression of adult coloration and may shrivel as it dries. Keep such an individual alive until its full coloration has developed.

Life history. One generation per year is typical for beetles, but some, especially in the southern U.S., may have 2 or 3 generations, or rarely more. Seldom does a generation live for more than 1 year. The adult is generally present outdoors for a very limited time; it usually lives for just a few weeks, but some adults may live for several months. Beetles spend the winter in a dormant condition; the overwintering stage is most often the larva or the pupa, but in some species it may be the adult or even the egg. A period of dormancy at low temperatures may be essential for continued development — some species living in northern climates will not complete a generation without exposure to low temperatures.

6

Classifying and Naming Beetles

The scientific classification of all living things is based on their structure (morphology). According to the structural features they have in common, organisms are arranged into categories, which are subdivided further until the species level is reached. Those organisms that share certain characters in common are grouped into one category, and those that share other characters in common are grouped into another category. The very first division of all living things separates them into the plant or animal kingdoms. Each kingdom is divided into major groups called phyla (singular — phylum), each phylum is divided into classes, each class into orders, each order into families, each family into genera (singular — genus), and each genus into species. Other categories are also used. For example, similar families are often grouped into superfamilies. Families can be subdivided into subfamilies; and a subfamily is often subdivided into tribes.

The classification of the **Colorado Potato Beetle** is given below:

Kingdom — Animalia   Phylum — Arthropoda   Class — Insecta
       Order — Coleoptera   Family — Chrysomelidae
      Genus — Leptinotarsa   Species — decemlineata

The names of families and other categories above the genus level have characteristic endings; for example, in the animal kingdom a subfamily ends in *-inae,* and a family in *-idae.* The insects make up the Class Insecta, and, along with spiders, crabs, and other animals, belong to the Phylum Arthropoda. Class Insecta is divided into 25 or so orders, including the Coleoptera — the beetles. In North America the Coleoptera are divided into about 111 families. The number of genera in each family can vary from 1 genus to hundreds, depending upon the size and diversity of the family. A genus may contain just 1 species or hundreds. The species is the most fundamental of all the groups, for scientists can verify whether a species exists by determining if the members of the species population can interbreed successfully with each other. Classification into other groups from the genus level on up often cannot objectively be proven to be valid; these groupings are largely arbitrary. In other words, the opinion of the expert who has done the most research on that group will determine the limits of the category. Though these limits are set as a matter of judgment, the differences of opinion between different researchers are generally minor.

Common names. Animals are given 2 kinds of names — common (or vernacular) names and scientific names. The common name of the beetle in the example above is the **Colorado Potato Beetle;** its scientific name is *Leptotinarsa decemlineata.* Each higher animal, such as a bird or a mammal, generally has its own common name, but comparatively few insects have been given common names. For example, only 9 of 310 described species of the deathwatch beetles (family Anobiidae, p. 199) in North America have common names. The common names that apply to beetle species are nearly always given just to injurious species (such as the **Spotted Cucumber Beetle**); to large, unique species (such as the **Eyed Click Beetle**); or to very common beetles (such as the **Two-spotted Ladybird Beetle**). Some of the species selected for discussion and illustration in this book have common names. Many of the beetle families discussed in this book have common names that have been approved by the Entomological Society of America. These usually consist of 2 or more parts, such as ground beetles (Carabidae), rove beetles (Staphylinidae), leaf beetles (Chrysomelidae), long-horned beetles (Cerambycidae), or water scavenger beetles (Hydrophilidae).

To facilitate communication among researchers all over the world, scientists refer to animals (and plants) by their scientific names, which are much more precise than common names. Several beetles may be known as "potato beetles," but *Leptotinarsa decemlineata* will be recognized by scientists everywhere as the name of 1 certain species.

Scientific names. Every animal that has been described by scientists has a scientific name, which consists of both a genus and species name. The names of insects often include the name of the scientist who proposed the species name. These names are latinized according to the rules governing their use. A species name often refers to the color or morphology of the animal, or may have been proposed to honor a certain individual. The genus name is capitalized and given first, and the species name is given next, as in the combination *Leptinotarsa decemlineata* (Say), the **Colorado Potato Beetle.** The third part, (Say), is the name of the scientist who first described this species in print. The parentheses around his name indicates that the species is now in a genus different from the one in which it was originally described — had Thomas Say originally described this species in *Leptinotarsa,* there would be no parentheses around his name. The species name, *decemlineata,* means 10 lines; this refers to the 10 dark stripes on the elytra (front wings) of this beetle.

When a species consists of populations that are slightly different from each other and occur in different areas, these are called subspecies. A subspecies name is written as follows: *Diabrotica undecimpunctata howardi* Barber. The author name in this case is the name of the scientist who first named the subspecies.

It sometimes happens that 2 researchers describe the same species; when this occurs, the older of the 2 names proposed is the correct name for the species, and the more recent name is considered a synonym.

Beetles: Order Coleoptera

Introduction to Beetles

The following characters identify an insect as a beetle: Elytra (front wings) *horny* or *leathery* and of *same texture* throughout; usually covering entire abdomen — sometimes short and exposing 1 or more abdominal segments, rarely absent (as in larviform adult). Elytra nearly always *meet in a straight line* down back; flight wings membranous, nearly always longer than elytra, concealed beneath elytra in most species, small or absent in a few species. Each antenna usually has 11 segments, rarely more, sometimes 8–10 segments, rarely as few as 2 segments. Antennae highly variable in form — often threadlike, sometimes sawtoothed, or with terminal segments variously enlarged. Mouth parts chewing. Tarsi usually have 3–5 segments. Abdomen usually has 5 segments visible ventrally, sometimes as many as 8. Length highly variable, 0.4–62 mm.

Habits. Beetles live in a great variety of habitats on land and feed on many different plant and animal materials. Few plants or parts of plants are not eaten by some kind of beetle. Many are abundant on vegetation in daytime, some are found on vegetation at night. Beetles often occur under bark or in rotting wood or plant materials; some are common on the ground or beneath objects on the ground. Some occur in fungi, dung, or carrion; some are aquatic; and a few are parasitic on various animals. Many beetles fly at night and are attracted to lights.

Number of species. This is the largest order of living things. World — about 290,000; N. America — about 27,000.

Importance. Many species that feed on plants (usually the foliage) are highly injurious and cause millions of dollars worth of damage yearly to crops, trees, and wood. Some beetles damage a variety of stored foods, including meats, dairy products, flour, meal, cereals, stored grain, nuts, and fruits. Others are very beneficial and feed on insects that are harmful to plants. Many beetles are of significance as scavengers on dead animals and plants, and as a result of these activities, are very important in helping to maintain ecological balances.

Insects Similar to Beetles

Early in your study of beetles it will be easy to confuse a few other insects with beetles. Those that are most similar are the Dermaptera (earwigs), and certain members of the Orthoptera (roaches), Hemiptera (true bugs), and Homoptera (hoppers). These other insects are sufficiently distinctive so that in time you will learn to recognize nearly all of them at a glance, with only some true bugs possibly causing prolonged confusion. Below are characters and illustrations that will aid in distinguishing these other insects. The bugs and hoppers that are illustrated have been chosen for their similarity to beetles; in some cases other members of the same groups look much less like beetles.

BUGS Order Hemiptera

Bugs of various families strongly resemble beetles; a few are so difficult to distinguish that microscopic examination may be needed. Many bugs are common on foliage, so of all insects similar to beetles, these are most often confused with them. Some bugs that resemble beetles live in water.

Distinguishing characters. All bugs have *sucking* mouth parts, in contrast with the *chewing* mouth parts of beetles. A bug's beak is generally very elongate, and is held back beneath the body. The wing covers (short to absent in some bugs) are *membranous* near the tips, and overlap there. The scutellum is generally *large* to *very large,* and in some bugs it conceals the membranous portion of the wings. Each antenna has 5 *or fewer* segments and in some bugs is very short.

Examples: Pleid water bugs. These bugs are very small (1.6–2.3 mm) and are easily confused with beetles because the dorsal surface of the body is strongly *arched.* **Velvet shore bugs.** These bugs are 4–5 mm long; they live along shores of quiet streams and ponds and are infrequently collected. Body is dark and *velvety.* **Creeping water bugs.** These bugs share with many beetles the broadly oval form; they are 9–12 mm long, and brownish. They swim or crawl about vegetation in quiet water. Handle them carefully, for they will bite. **Leaf bugs.** The largest family of bugs, with several hundred species in N. America. Many are common on vegetation, and some are plant pests. Most range from 2–9 mm long; many are brightly colored. Only a few of these bugs (such as *Halticus* species) strongly resemble beetles. **Negro bugs.** Often common on vegetation and flowers. Without close examination, these bugs are readily mistaken for oval, black beetles; they are

3-6 mm long. Note the *enlarged scutellum*. **Shield-backed bugs.** Generally 6-10 mm long. These bugs live on woodland vegetation; they are uncommon. Similar to negro bugs in having an extremely *large scutellum*.

HOPPERS Order Homoptera

Certain species of various families in this order resemble beetles. All live on foliage and are rarely over 10 mm long. Some are quite common, others are uncommon.

Distinguishing characters. These insects have *sucking* mouth parts, short *bristlelike* antennae, and generally hold the *wings like a roof* over the abdomen. Most have a distinct pattern of veins on the wings. As implied by their common name, these insects hop. Their body form alone (rooflike wings and short antennae) will allow them to be distinguished from beetles.

Examples: Treehoppers. Note the greatly *enlarged pronotum* that extends back over the abdomen. Adults generally occur on trees and shrubs; many are humpbacked in appearance, some look like thorns. Most are 4-10 mm long; they are moderately abundant. **Froghoppers.** Usually brown or gray, sometimes with an indistinct pattern. Typically broader-bodied than leafhoppers, which they resemble; 3-12 mm long. Often common on shrubs and herbs. **Leafhoppers.** Color varies, but body is nearly always narrow and elongate (infrequently stout, as in *Penthimia* species); 3-12 mm long. These insects are generally very common and live on trees, shrubs, grasses, and crops; some are injurious. **Planthoppers.** This group includes 11 families; members are rarely as abundant as froghoppers or leafhoppers. The wings are generally semi-transparent, with distinct *veins;* in a few species the wings are quite short. Most are 3-11 mm long. Planthoppers occur on a wide variety of plants. Most are easily distinguished from beetles, but *Bruchomorpha* and *Phylloscelis* species are markedly beetlelike.

EARWIGS Order Dermaptera

Members of all 4 families resemble many rove beetles (p. 110). Earwigs are generally 4-26 mm long. Usually nocturnal — most hide during the day in crevices, under bark, or beneath objects on the ground. Some earwigs have scent glands on the 3rd and 4th abdominal segments from which they squirt a foul-smelling liquid. Generally uncommon.

Distinguishing characters. The hard, pincerlike *abdominal cerci* readily distinguish earwigs from beetles. (When present in rove beetles, the cerci are short and flexible.) Earwigs do not bite, but can inflict a painful pinch with their cerci; larger earwigs can break the skin. Handle them carefully.

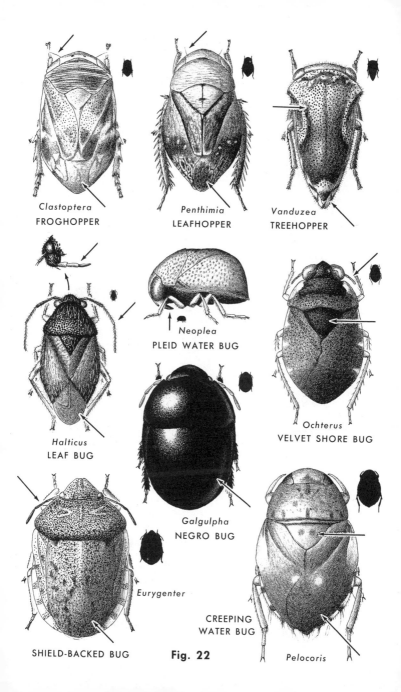

Clastoptera
FROGHOPPER

Penthimia
LEAFHOPPER

Vanduzea
TREEHOPPER

Halticus
LEAF BUG

Neoplea
PLEID WATER BUG

Ochterus
VELVET SHORE BUG

Galgulpha
NEGRO BUG

Eurygenter
SHIELD-BACKED BUG

Fig. 22

CREEPING
WATER BUG

Pelocoris

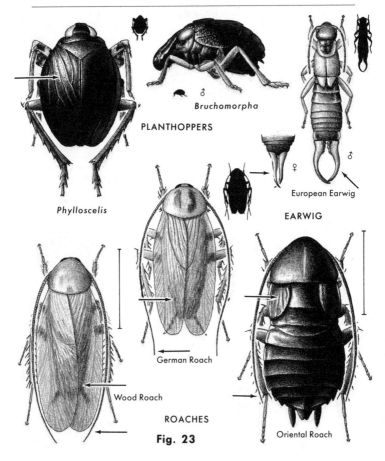

Bruchomorpha ♂

PLANTHOPPERS

Phylloscelis

European Earwig ♂

♀

EARWIG

German Roach

Wood Roach

ROACHES

Fig. 23

Oriental Roach

ROACHES Order Orthoptera, Suborder Blattaria
The best-known roaches are those that invade homes or buildings;
some are major pests. They are generally 10–40 mm long, active,
fast runners that seldom fly. Most abundant in s. U.S., where
many overwinter outdoors. Even in the n. U.S. certain species
(wood roaches) occur beneath bark or under dead logs.
Distinguishing characters. The *veined,* broadly *overlapping*
wings and very *long, tapered antennae* best distinguish these in-

sects from beetles. In a few roaches the wing covers are very small. In nearly all beetles the elytra meet in a straight line; no beetle elytra bear the veins characteristic of roach wing covers. Also, no beetles have antennae as elongate and tapered.

Classification of Beetles

Four suborders of beetles are recognized: Archostemata, Adephaga, Myxophaga, and Polyphaga. Archostemata contains only 2 primitive families; members are infrequently collected. Adephaga contains 8 families; members of these families are common to uncommon and are predaceous. In these beetles the first abdominal segment is divided by the hind coxae. Myxophaga contains 2 families; these species are small and uncommon. Most beetles (99 of the 111 families) belong to Suborder Polyphaga; they vary greatly in form and habits. Families and superfamilies can be distinguished by characters of the antennae, legs, elytra (front wings), pronotum, head, and other parts.

Synopses of distinguishing characters of beetle families (including range and habitat information) appear on the next few pages; a pictorial key to beetle families is located on the front and rear endpapers of this guide.

Family	N. American species	Range
Alleculidae, p. 256 (comb-clawed beetles)	177	throughout N.A.; ⅔ in w. U.S.
Amphizoidae, p. 94 (trout-stream beetles)	4	mts. in w. U.S.
Anobiidae p. 199 (death-watch beetles)	310	throughout N.A.; many in w. U.S.
Anthicidae, p. 276 (antlike flower beetles)	140	throughout N.A.; ⅔ in w. U.S.
Anthribidae, p. 307 (fungus weevils)	81	throughout N.A.
Biphyllidae, p. 240 (biphyllid beetles)	4	in e. & sw. U.S.
Bostrichidae, p. 202 (branch-and-twig borers)	60	throughout N.A.; most in sw. U.S.
Brachypsectridae, p. 159 (texas beetles)	1	Tex. to Calif.
Brathinidae, p. 130 (grass-root beetles)	3	in ne. U.S. & Calif.
Brentidae, p. 308 (primitive weevils)	6	in e. U.S., Tex., & Calif.
Bruchidae, p. 304 (seed beetles)	107	throughout N.A.
Buprestidae, p. 165 (metallic wood-boring beetles)	718	throughout N.A.; many in w. U.S.
Byrrhidae, p. 155 (pill beetles)	42	throughout N.A.; many in w. U.S.
Byturidae, p. 240 (fruitworm beetles)	5	throughout N.A.
Cantharidae, p. 183 (soldier beetles)	455	throughout N.A.

Abundance	Where found	Length	Antennae
fairly common to common	dead bark, vegetation, flowers	4–15 mm	threadlike, sawtoothed
uncommon to rare	cold mountain streams	11–16 mm	threadlike
uncommon to fairly common	foliage, wood, fungi	1.1–9 mm	clubbed, sawtoothed
uncommon to fairly common	on ground, foliage	1.7–4.3 mm	threadlike
fairly common	fungi, foliage	0.8–15 mm	clubbed
uncommon	fungi, under bark	2–3.5 mm	clubbed
uncommon to fairly common	at lights, on fungi	2–52 mm	clubbed
rare	under bark	4.6–6 mm	sawtoothed
rare	roots of grasses near water	3.4–6 mm	threadlike
uncommon	under bark, in wood	5.2–42 mm	beadlike
fairly common to common	foliage, flowers, seeds	1–8 mm	sawtoothed, clubbed
fairly common to common	foliage, trees, flowers	2–40 mm	sawtoothed, threadlike
uncommon	on ground, foliage	1.5–10 mm	clubbed, threadlike
fairly common	foliage of berry plants	2.7–4.4 mm	clubbed
fairly common to common	foliage, flowers	1–15 mm	threadlike, sawtoothed

Family	N. American species	Range
Carabidae, p. 86 (ground beetles)	1700	throughout N.A.
Cebrionidae, p. 171 (cebrionid beetles)	17	se. U.S. to sw. U.S.
Cephaloidae, p. 248 (false long-horned beetles)	10	e. & w. U.S.
Cerambycidae, p. 279 (long-horned beetles)	1100	throughout N.A.
Cerophytidae, p. 177 (rare click beetles)	2	e. U.S. & Calif.
Cerylonidae, p. 228 (cerylonid beetles)	18	throughout N.A.
Chelonariidae, p. 159 (chelonariid beetles)	1	se. U.S. & Ark.
Chrysomelidae, p. 289 (leaf beetles)	1474	throughout N.A.
Cicindelidae, p. 83 (tiger beetles)	119	throughout N.A.
Ciidae, p. 243 (minute tree-fungus beetles)	85	throughout N.A.; many in se. U.S.
Clambidae, p. 149 (minute beetles)	8	throughout N.A.
Cleridae, p. 208 (checkered beetles)	261	throughout N.A.; many in sw. U.S.
Coccinellidae, p. 231 (lady or ladybird beetles)	400	throughout N.A.
Colydiidae, p. 246 (cylindrical bark beetles)	92	throughout N.A.

Abundance	Where found	Length	Antennae
common	beneath objects on ground, foliage	1.2–35 mm	threadlike
uncommon	dead bark, ground, foliage	13.5–25 mm	sawtoothed
uncommon	flowers, foliage	8–20 mm	threadlike
fairly common to common	foliage, flowers, wood	2–60 mm	threadlike, very long
rare	bark, foliage, wood	5.5–8.5 mm	comblike, sawtoothed
fairly common	dead bark, ant nests	1.2–3 mm	clubbed
rare	foliage	6.5–7.2 mm	sawtoothed
common	usually on foliage of weeds	1–16 mm	threadlike, clubbed
fairly common	open, sunny areas	6–40 mm	threadlike
uncommon to fairly common	mostly on polypore fungi	0.5–6 mm	clubbed
rare to uncommon	rotting plants, ant nests	0.8–1 mm	clubbed
fairly common	foliage, flowers, wood	1.8–24 mm	variable
common	foliage	0.8–10 mm	clubbed
uncommon	under dead bark	1.7–13 mm	clubbed

Family	N. American species	Range
Corylophidae, p. 229 (minute fungus beetles)	61	throughout N.A.; ⅔ in e. U.S.
Cryptophagidae, p. 222 (silken fungus beetles)	166	throughout N.A.
Cucujidae, p. 219 (flat bark beetles)	88	throughout N.A.
Cupedidae, p. 80 (reticulated beetles)	4	e. & w. U.S.
Curculionidae, p. 309 (snout beetles)	2432	throughout N.A.
Dascillidae, p. 152 (soft-bodied plant beetles)	16	throughout N.A.; most in w. U.S.
Dermestidae, p. 192 (dermestid beetles)	123	throughout N.A.
Derodontidae, p. 190 (tooth-necked fungus beetles)	9	ne. & w. U.S.
Dryopidae, p. 162 (long-toed water beetles)	15	throughout N.A.; many in w. U.S.
Dytiscidae, p. 96 (predaceous diving beetles)	476	throughout N.A.
Elateridae, p. 172 (click beetles)	800	throughout N.A.
Elmidae, p. 163 (riffle beetles)	93	throughout N.A.
Endomychidae, p. 237 (handsome fungus beetles)	35	throughout N.A.; ⅔ in e. U.S.

Abundance	Where found	Length	Antennae
uncommon	rotting plants, foliage	0.5–2.2 mm	clubbed
uncommon to fairly common	fungi, decaying vegetation	0.8–5 mm	clubbed
uncommon to fairly common	bark, decaying vegetation	1.3–14 mm	beadlike, threadlike
uncommon to rare	rotting wood	7–20 mm	threadlike
common	foliage	0.6–35 mm	clubbed
uncommon to rare	foliage in moist areas	3–40 mm	threadlike, sawtoothed
fairly common to common	flowers, carcasses, indoors	1–12 mm	clubbed
uncommon	dead bark, shelf fungi, foliage	2–6 mm	clubbed
uncommon	in streams, at lights	4–8 mm	comblike
fairly common	fresh water, at lights	1.2–40 mm	threadlike
fairly common to common	foliage, bark, in rotten wood	1.5–45 mm	sawtoothed
uncommon	in streams, lakes, at lights	1–8 mm	threadlike, clubbed
uncommon	fungi, rotten wood, decayed fruit	1–10 mm	clubbed

Family	N. American species	Range
Erotylidae, p. 226 (pleasing fungus beetles)	50	throughout N.A.; ⅔ in e. U.S.
Eucinetidae, p. 151 (eucinetid beetles)	8	e. U.S., Calif.; most in e. U.S.
Eucnemidae, p. 179 (false click beetles)	67	throughout N.A.; most in e. U.S.
Euglenidae, p. 278 (antlike leaf beetles)	39	throughout N.A.; ⅔ in e. U.S.
Georyssidae, p. 109 (minute mud-loving beetles)	2	Nebr.–Calif.
Gyrinidae, p. 101 (whirligig beetles)	51	throughout N.A.; most in e. U.S.
Haliplidae, p. 95 (crawling water beetles)	60	throughout N.A.; many in e. U.S.
Helodidae, p. 149 (marsh beetles)	34	throughout N.A.; most in e. U.S.
Heteroceridae, p. 161 (variegated mud-loving beetles)	28	throughout N.A.
Histeridae, p. 132 (hister beetles)	359	throughout N.A.
Hydraenidae, p. 108 (minute moss beetles)	33	throughout N.A.; most in w. U.S.
Hydrophilidae, p. 104 (water scavenger beetles)	225	throughout N.A.
Hydroscaphidae, p. 103 (skiff beetles)	1	sw. U.S.

Abundance	Where found	Length	Antennae
fairly common to uncommon	fungi	2.5–22 mm	clubbed
uncommon	dead bark, rotting wood, fungi	2.5–4 mm	threadlike
uncommon	dead bark, foliage	2–18 mm	sawtoothed, threadlike
uncommon to fairly common	foliage, flowers	1.5–3 mm	threadlike, clubbed
rare	stream shores	1.5–3 mm	clubbed
fairly common	fresh water	3–15.5 mm	clubbed, short
uncommon to fairly common	fresh water	1.7–4.5 mm	threadlike, short
uncommon to fairly common	on foliage in marshy areas	2–5 mm	threadlike
fairly common	stream & pond shores, at lights	1–8 mm	sawtoothed, short
fairly common	carrion, dung, fungi, dead bark	0.5–20 mm	clubbed, elbowed
uncommon	stream, lake, & pond shores	1.2–2.5 mm	clubbed
fairly common to common	fresh water; some in dung & humus	1–40 mm	clubbed, short
uncommon	filamentous algae in streams	1–1.5 mm	threadlike

Family	N. American species	Range
Lagriidae, p. 256 (long-jointed bark beetles)	21	throughout N.A.
Lampyridae, p. 188 (lightningbugs or fireflies)	136	throughout N.A.; many in e. U.S.
Languriidae, p. 224 (lizard beetles)	17	throughout N.A.; many in s. U.S.
Lathridiidae, p. 239 (minute brown scavenger beetles)	108	throughout N.A.
Leiodidae, p. 124 (round fungus beetles)	126	throughout N.A.
Leptinidae, p. 125 (mammal-nest beetles)	5	throughout N.A.
Leptodiridae, p. 122 (small carrion beetles)	81	throughout N.A.
Limnichidae, p. 161 (minute marsh-loving beetles)	32	throughout N.A.
Limulodidae, p. 128 (horse-shoe crab beetles)	4	e. U.S. to Ariz.
Lucanidae, p. 135 (stag beetles)	30	throughout N.A.; $\frac{2}{3}$ in w. U.S.
Lycidae, p. 186 (net-winged beetles)	78	throughout N.A.; most in w. U.S.
Lyctidae, p. 205 (powder-post beetles)	11	throughout N.A.
Lymexylonidae, p. 214 (ship-timber beetles)	3	e. U.S.

Abundance	Where found	Length	Antennae
uncommon	foliage, dead bark	6–15 mm	threadlike
fairly common to common	foliage, flying at night, on ground	4.5–20 mm	threadlike, sawtoothed
fairly common	foliage, flowers	3–16 mm	clubbed
fairly common	moldy plant & animal materials	1–3 mm	clubbed
uncommon	fungi, slime molds, humus, under bark	1–6.5 mm	clubbed
uncommon	mammal fur & nests, bee & wasp nests	2–5 mm	clubbed,
uncommon to rare	carrion, humus, dung, fungi	1.7–6 mm	clubbed
uncommon	in streams or along edges	0.7–2.5 mm	sawtoothed, clubbed
rare	ant nests	0.7–0.9 mm	clubbed
uncommon to fairly common	logs, stumps, on ground, at lights	8–60 mm	comblike
fairly common to uncommon	foliage, flowers, tree trunks	3–19 mm	threadlike, sawtoothed
fairly common to uncommon	seasoned wood	1–7 mm	clubbed
rare	logs, stumps, under bark	10–13.5 mm	fan-shaped

Family	N. American species	Range
Melandryidae, p. 264 (false darkling beetles)	95	throughout N.A.; most in e. U.S.
Meloidae, p. 270 (blister beetles)	335	throughout N.A.; most in w. U.S.
Melyridae, p. 211 (soft-winged flower beetles)	502	throughout N.A.; many in w. U.S.
Micromalthidae, p. 81 (micromalthid beetles)	1	e. U.S.
Monommidae, p. 245 (monommid beetles)	5	se. to sw. U.S.
Mordellidae, p. 266 (tumbling flower beetles)	204	throughout N.A.
Mycetophagidae, p. 242 (hairy fungus beetles)	26	throughout N.A.; $\frac{2}{3}$ in e. U.S.
Nitidulidae, p. 215 (sap beetles)	177	throughout N.A.
Nosodendridae, p. 192 (wounded-tree beetles)	2	ne. U.S.; Pacific Coast
Noteridae, p. 100 (burrowing water beetles)	17	e. U.S. to Tex.
Oedemeridae, p. 262 (false blister beetles)	53	throughout N.A.
Othniidae, p. 260 (false tiger beetles)	5	Va.; Nebr. to Calif.

Abundance	Where found	Length	Antennae
fairly common to common	bark, foliage, fungi, flowers	2–20 mm	threadlike, clubbed
fairly common to uncommon	foliage, flowers	3–30 mm	threadlike, beadlike
fairly common to common	foliage, flowers	1.5–7 mm	threadlike, sawtoothed
uncommon to rare	decaying oaks, pines, chestnuts	1.5–2.5 mm	beadlike
uncommon	foliage, debris	5–12 mm	clubbed
common to fairly common	flowers, foliage	1.5–15 mm	threadlike, sawtoothed
fairly common to uncommon	fungi, humus	1–6.3 mm	clubbed
common to fairly common	rotting fruit, fungi, sap flows, flowers	1–12 mm	clubbed
uncommon	oozing tree wounds	4–6 mm	clubbed
uncommon	weedy ponds & lakes	1.2–5.5 mm	threadlike
uncommon	decaying wood, foliage, flowers	5–23 mm	threadlike, slightly sawtoothed
rare	humus, cacti, bark	5–9 mm	clubbed

Family	N. American species	Range
Passalidae, p. 137 (passalid beetles)	3	e. U.S., Tex.
Pedilidae, p. 274 (pedilid beetles)	57	throughout N.A.; most in w. U.S.
Perothopidae, p. 179 (perothopid beetles)	3	e. U.S., Calif.
Phalacridae, p. 225 (shining mold beetles)	122	throughout N.A.
Phengodidae, p. 182 (glowworms)	25	e. & w. U.S.
Platypodidae, p. 325 (pinhole borers)	7	throughout N.A.
Pselaphidae, p. 118 (short-winged mold beetles)	500	throughout N.A.
Psephenidae, p. 156 (water-penny beetles)	13	ne. & w. U.S.; most in w. U.S.
Ptiliidae, p. 126 (feather-winged beetles)	111	throughout N.A.; most in e. U.S.
Ptilodactylidae, p. 158 (ptilodactylid beetles)	10	e. U.S. to Ariz.
Ptinidae, p. 196 (spider beetles)	50	throughout N.A.; many in sw. U.S.
Pyrochroidae, p. 260 (fire-colored beetles)	15	throughout N.A.
Rhipiceridae, p. 153 (cedar beetles)	6	e. to sw. U.S.

Abundance	Where found	Length	Antennae
fairly common	logs, stumps	28–40 mm	clubbed
uncommon to fairly common	flowers, foliage	4–15 mm	threadlike, sawtoothed
rare	beech, apple, oak trees	10–25 mm	threadlike
common to fairly common	flowers, foliage; some under bark	1–3 mm	clubbed
rare	at lights	4.5–20 mm	featherlike
uncommon	in wood, at lights	2–8 mm	clubbed
uncommon to fairly common	bark, under objects, tree holes, nests	0.5–5.5 mm	clubbed
uncommon	in or near streams	3–7 mm	threadlike, sawtoothed
fairly common to uncommon	rotten organic material, dung, nests	0.4–1.5 mm	clubbed
uncommon	foliage	4–10 mm	comblike, sawtoothed
uncommon	in animal & vegetable material	1–5 mm	threadlike, clubbed
uncommon	at night on dead trees, logs, stumps	4.5–19 mm	sawtoothed, featherlike
uncommon to rare	tree trunks, foliage	11–24 mm	sawtoothed to lamellate

Family	N. American species	Range
Rhipiphoridae, p. 268 (wedge-shaped beetles)	50	throughout N.A.
Rhizophagidae, p. 217 (rhizophagid beetles)	56	throughout N.A.
Rhysodidae, p. 82 (wrinkled bark beetles)	8	most in e. U.S., Calif., Ore.
Salpingidae, p. 259 (narrow-waisted bark beetles)	34	most in n. or sw. U.S.
Scaphidiidae, p. 131 (shining fungus beetles)	50	throughout N.A.; most in e. U.S.
Scarabaeidae, p. 138 (scarab beetles)	1375	throughout N.A.
Scolytidae, p. 326 (bark-and-ambrosia beetles)	476	throughout N.A.
Scydmaenidae, p. 128 (antlike stone beetles)	181	throughout N.A.; most in e. U.S.
Silphidae, p. 120 (carrion beetles)	46	throughout N.A.
Sphaeriidae, p. 102 (minute bog beetles)	3	e. U.S., Tex., Calif., Wash.
Sphaeritidae, p. 133 (sphaeritid beetles)	1	Alaska to Calif.

Abundance	Where found	Length	Antennae
uncommon to rare	on flowers	3.5–15 mm	sawtoothed, comblike
uncommon	dead bark, rotting wood, ant nests	1.5–3 mm	clubbed
fairly common to uncommon	under dead bark, on dead bark at night	5.4–8.1 mm	beadlike
uncommon to rare	bark of conifers, humus, flowers	2–21 mm	threadlike, beadlike
fairly common to common	on fungi & rotten wood, under bark	1.2–7 mm	clubbed
common to fairly common	foliage, dung, flowers, fungi, humus	2–62 mm	lamellate
uncommon to fairly common	in trees, at lights	0.6–9 mm	clubbed
uncommon to rare	bark, humus, tree holes, under objects	0.6–2.5 mm	clubbed
fairly common to uncommon	carrion, decaying vegetation	3–35 mm	clubbed
rare	in mud, under objects near water	0.5–0.8 mm	clubbed
rare	in fungi, dung, under bark, on moss, in sap flows	3.6–5.6 mm	clubbed

Family	N. American species	Range
Sphindidae, p. 219 (dry-fungus beetles)	6	e. U.S. to Colo.; Calif.
Staphylinidae, p. 110 (rove beetles)	3100	throughout N.A.; many in e. U.S.
Stylopidae, p. 269 (twisted-winged parasites)	56	throughout N.A.; most in e. U.S.
Telegeusidae, p. 181 (telegeusid beetles)	2	Ariz., Calif.
Tenebrionidae, p. 249 (darkling beetles)	1300	throughout N.A.; most in w. U.S.
Throscidae, p. 177 (throscid beetles)	27	throughout N.A.
Trogositidae, p. 207 (bark-gnawing beetles)	55	throughout N.A.; most in w. U.S.

Abundance	Where found	Length	Antennae
uncommon	slime molds, shelf fungi, logs, stumps	1.5–3 mm	clubbed
common to fairly common	under objects, on carrion, fungi, bark	0.7–25 mm	threadlike to clubbed
uncommon to rare	on or inside host (wasps, other insects)	0.5–4 mm	fan-shaped, comblike
rare	at lights	5–8 mm	threadlike, short
common to fairly common	under objects, on fungi, under bark, on foliage	2–35 mm	threadlike, clubbed
uncommon	foliage, flowers	1.6–5 mm	clubbed
fairly common to uncommon	in dead wood, fungi, vegetable material	2.3–22 mm	clubbed

Suborder Archostemata

The most primitive of all living beetles belong here, including the only paedogenic beetle (see p. 81). Antennae threadlike or beadlike.

RETICULATED BEETLES:
Family Cupedidae

This is regarded as the most primitive of beetle familes. Fossil cupedids from upper Permian deposits (about 200 million years ago) are the oldest known remains of beetles that belong to a living family. Extensive fossils and present widely scattered world populations indicate an ancient group that was once more common and widely distributed than it is now.

Identification. Shape and characters distinctive: body elongate, *flattened.* Elytra nearly parallel-sided, strongly *sculptured* with rows of punctures between lengthwise ridges. Pronotum narrow; head about as wide as pronotum. Body covered with *scales.* Antennae long, threadlike. 7–20 mm. Tarsi 5-5-5.

Similar families. The only beetles with similarly sculptured elytra are: (1) Leaf beetles (Subfamily Hispinae, p. 302) — antennae short, usually clubbed. Head narrow. 3–8 mm. (2) Net-winged beetles (p. 186) — head not clearly visible from above.

Range and numbers. Only 2 genera and 4 species in N. America; 2 in e. U.S., 2 in w. U.S.

Habits. Larvae feed in moist, rotting softwoods and hardwoods, and sometimes in moist timbers of buildings. Because they eat decaying wood they are not injurious. Adults normally occur in same habitat as larvae.

Collecting methods. Rarely captured in most collecting. Adults may be exposed by chopping infested logs and stumps; they are infrequently found on vegetation or flying in sunlight near infested material. Males of 1 species in w. U.S. are attracted to odor of laundry bleach (see below).

Examples. Three of the 4 species in this family belong to genus *Cupes. C. concolor* West., 10–13 mm, is the most common species in the e. U.S.; found in rotten oak, chestnut, and apple trees. Males of *Priacma serrata* (LeC.), 10–20 mm, may be attracted to laundry bleach because it is chemically similar to ♀ sex attractant. This speculation is bolstered by behavior of males attracted to bleach; they appear agitated and attempt to mate with one another.

MICROMALTHID BEETLES:
Family Micromalthidae

Identification. Antennae, form, and size distinctive: antennae *short, beadlike,* each with 11 segments. Pronotum widest *at front,* with no lateral margin. Head *wider* than pronotum. Elytra *short,* exposing part of abdomen. Brown to black; antennae and legs yellow. 1.5–2.5 mm.

Similar families. (1) Certain small soldier beetles (p. 183) are similar but have long, threadlike antennae. (2) Checkered beetles (p. 208) never have beadlike antennae, are also covered with long, erect hairs. (3) Soft-winged flower beetles (p. 211) have a lateral margin on pronotum. (4) In rove beetles (p. 110), elytra are generally shorter; antennae not beadlike.

Range and numbers. Only 1 species, which is native to e. U.S. but has been introduced into other areas accidentally (in lumber).

Habits and examples: *Micromalthus debilis* LeC. is one of the most unusual beetles, for its larvae are capable of reproducing (paedogenic). Development is extremely complex, with larvae giving birth to living larvae, or laying eggs from which larvae develop. Larvae occur in decayed oak, chestnut, and pine logs or stumps, and sometimes in rotting telephone poles. Because they feed in wood that is already in an advanced stage of decay, these beetles

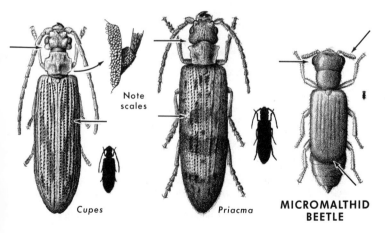

Note scales

Cupes

Priacma

MICROMALTHID BEETLE

Fig. 24   RETICULATED BEETLES

are of no economic importance. Adults are rarely collected, for they are in the open only briefly, when they emerge in mass and (it is believed) fly immediately to a new breeding site.

Collecting methods. Since adults are rarely captured during normal collecting, the best way to obtain specimens is to rear adults from larvae found in rotten wood. In e. U.S. look for an oak, chestnut, or pine log or stump that is moist but not wet, and has reached the red-rotten stage of decay. Larvae are abundant in suitable material; they are quite small and whitish, with a body that is slightly expanded toward the front. If rearing material is collected in late winter or early spring and kept indoors, adults will emerge in 1–3 months.

Suborder Adephaga

Distinctive for having first abdominal segment *divided by hind coxae.* Nearly always predaceous. Antennae threadlike; rarely beadlike or clubbed.

WRINKLED BARK BEETLES: Family Rhysodidae

Identification. Body shape, antennae, and pronotum distinctive: Body *elongate, narrow;* widest at about *middle* of elytra. Antennae *beadlike.* Pronotum with 1 or 3 deep, lengthwise *grooves.* Head *grooved,* with a *neck.* Dark reddish brown to nearly black, and shiny. Tarsi 5-5-5. 5.4–8.1 mm.

Similar families. (1) Primitive weevils (p. 308) — head with a distinct, broad or narrow beak; pronotum not grooved. (2) Flat bark beetles (p. 219) — some similar but pronotum not grooved. (3) Cylindrical bark beetles (p. 246) — some similar but each antenna ends in a 2- or 3-segmented club.

Range and numbers. 2 genera and 8 species in N. America; 6 occur primarily in e. U.S., 2 from Calif. to B.C.

Habits and examples. Adults and larvae live in wood that is already partially decayed and moist so they are not economically important. Groups of adults sometimes hibernate in this kind of wood.

Clinidium sculptile Newm. (e. U.S.; 5.5–7.5 mm) has 1 deep lengthwise groove down the middle of the pronotum and a depression on each side of it, at the base; elytra are grooved and lack punctures. *Rhysodes americanus* Lap. (e. U.S.; 6–7.5 mm) has 3 deep lengthwise grooves on pronotum; elytra have rows of punctures.

Collecting methods. Look beneath loose bark of dead trees, logs, and stumps. Most readily captured at night with a flashlight. Moderately common to uncommon.

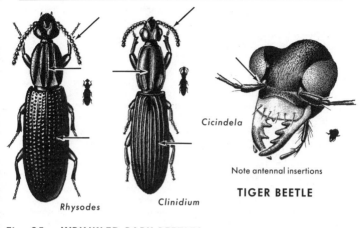

Cicindela

Note antennal insertions

TIGER BEETLE

Rhysodes   Clinidium

Fig. 25   WRINKLED BARK BEETLES

TIGER BEETLES: Family Cicindelidae
(Figs. 25, 26; see also Pl. 1)

Identification. Form distinctive: Elytra usually widest *behind middle,* sometimes nearly parallel-sided. Pronotum *narrower* than base of elytra. Eyes large, bulging; head (at eyes) as *wide* as or *wider* than pronotum. Antennae threadlike; each one inserted above base of mandible. Legs *long, slender.* Body usually brown or black above, often with characteristic pattern of light markings. Most are iridescent blue or green below. Tarsi 5-5-5. 6–40 mm (most 10–20 mm).

Similar families. (1) Some ground beetles (especially *Elaphrus* species, p. 88) have elytra with broad shallow depressions. (2) False tiger beetles (p. 206) — each antenna ends in a 3-segmented club; body smaller, 5–9 mm.

Range and numbers. 4 genera and 119 species; about 75% occur in w. U.S.

Habits. Common name refers to predaceous habits of adults. They feed on other insects, and sometimes pounce on their prey quite suddenly; they also run and fly rapidly. Most are found (sometimes in good numbers) in sunlight in open sandy areas, on beaches, on open paths or lanes, or on mud flats. Larvae construct vertical burrows in hard-packed ground; they wait at top of burrow, and seize any insect that passes by. The 5th abdominal segment of each larva bears curved hooks that dig into side of burrow, and make it difficult to pull the larva from its burrow if it grabs an insect too large to overcome.

Collecting methods. Tiger beetles have long been favorites with collectors, due to their attractive color patterns and the challenge of capturing these elusive beetles. Some tiger beetles (*Cicindela* species) can be quite abundant in the right situations, but are very elusive. They are active on hot sunny days in open, sandy areas; on shores of streams and lakes; or on relatively undisturbed roadsides or paths. Trying to collect these beetles by creeping up on your hands and knees and then lunging with a cupped hand is too often an exercise in frustration. When approached closely, these beetles usually fly off and alight facing their pursuer. They are one of the few beetles best collected with an aerial net. Even with this aid they will often evade capture, for you must approach carefully and swing the net rapidly to catch them. In certain situations an aerosol insecticide is an effective aid in collecting them. If the wind is low, the beetles are numerous, and you creep up carefully, you may spray them before they fly off, then grab them as the insecticide takes effect. A few desert species are easily captured by hand. Some w. U.S. species (mainly *Omus* species) are nocturnal; a few *Omus* species are attracted to lights.

Examples. Note the light markings on the elytra of many *Cicindela* species (90 species, most in w. U.S.), which provide a good example of evolutionary development of color pattern (Fig. 26). These light markings seem to have arisen from a basic pattern similar to that of *C. repanda* Dej. (1). The basic pattern is enlarged in *C. hirticollis* Say (2), more so in *C. tranquebarica* Herbst (3), and even more so in *C. limbata* Say (4). The pattern is reduced in *C. oregona* LeC. (5), more so in *C. scutellaris* Say (6), and even more so in *C. splendida* Hentz (7). Few examples of similar color patterns in closely related beetles are as clear-cut as this. The 25 *Omus* species are black, wingless, and nocturnal. They are 12–18 mm long, and are common in w. U.S.; they resemble certain ground beetles (below). Larvae live in smooth round holes in hard soil, typically on slopes and foothills of mountain ranges. *Megacephala carolina* (L.), 15–17 mm, is one of the most colorful members of the family (Pl. 1); it occurs from Va. south to Fla. and west to Tex. Adults are active at dusk and at night and hide in the daytime. Larvae live in burrows in soil, always near fresh water. *Amblycheila cylindriformis* (Say) is large (over 1 in.) and nocturnal; it occurs from Kans. to Colo. It resembles the *Omus* species.

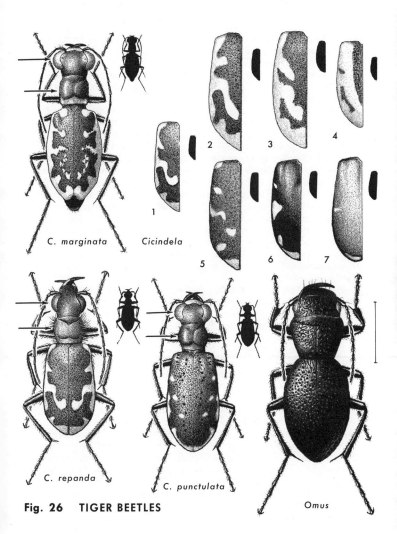

C. marginata   Cicindela

1 2 3 4

5 6 7

C. repanda   C. punctulata   Omus

Fig. 26   TIGER BEETLES

GROUND BEETLES: Family Carabidae
(Figs. 27-31; see also Pl. 1)

Identification. Variable in form, with few distinctive characters. Hind coxae *divide* first abdominal segment. Antenna inserted *between* eye and mandible; *threadlike,* beadlike in a few species. Most species are all or partly *black;* a few are brightly colored. Nearly always long-legged. Body usually shiny; elytra nearly always striate. Tarsi 5-5-5. 1.2–35 mm (up to $1\frac{3}{8}$ in.); most 4–20 mm.
Similar families. (1) Tiger beetles (p. 83) — head (at eyes) wider than pronotum; elytra often patterned. (2) Darkling beetles (p. 249) — tarsi 5-5-4; antennae often end in gradual club. (3) Long-jointed bark beetles (p. 256) — last segment of each antenna elongate. (4) Comb-clawed beetles (p. 256) — tarsi 5-5-4, with finely toothed claws. (5) False darkling beetles (p. 264) — tarsi 5-5-4; first tarsal segment of hind leg very long. (6) Trout-stream beetles (p. 94) — found in or beside streams in w. U.S. (7) Crawling water beetles (p. 95) resemble some ground beetles (*Omophron* species) but head small; body 1.7–4.5 mm long (not 5–8 mm). (8) Some narrow-waisted bark beetles (p. 259) are similar but tarsi 5-5-4.
Range and numbers. The 3rd largest family of beetles in N. America, behind rove beetles (Staphylinidae) and snout beetles (Curculionidae); about 150 genera and 1700 species, widely distributed.
Habits. As the common name implies, these beetles occur on the ground, often in large numbers; some are among the most common beetles. Most of them (larvae and adults) are active at night, and can generally be found beneath objects during the day. Adults and larvae are omnivorous or predaceous, and often feed on dead or dying insects. Some species feed on living insects, such as cutworms, caterpillars, beetle larvae, and maggots, and may be beneficial in controlling pests. A few, such as the **Seedcorn Beetle** (below), eat vegetable matter such as fungi, pollen, seeds, decayed fruits, or berries, and may be injurious. A few larvae are parasitic. A few adults will climb trees in search of prey such as caterpillars; some occur on foliage in the daytime.
Collecting methods. Many species are quite abundant and readily collected. Collecting at lights is very productive, or examine their habitats (beneath stones, boards, logs, debris, etc.) in daytime or at night with a flashlight. These beetles are not common where the ground is very dry. Most run rapidly when disturbed. Those that occur along banks of streams or rivers can be forced to the surface by pouring or splashing water over the ground. Where a stream has undercut a bank, pull some sod down into the water, and wait for beetles to float to the surface; many ground beetles live in such situations. Some found on mud flats and foliage are active during the day.

Subfamilies and tribes. N. American ground beetles are divided into 4 subfamilies, with less than 15 species belonging to 3 of the subfamilies; these smaller subfamilies are excluded from this guide. The vast majority belong to Subfamily Carabinae, which is divided into 40 tribes; 18 of these tribes are covered below.

ROUND SAND BEETLES Tribe Omophronini
The 11 *Omophron* species are distinctive for their *oval, convex body* and *dark markings* on a yellowish background. 5–8 mm. They live in damp sand along lakes, rivers, and streams.

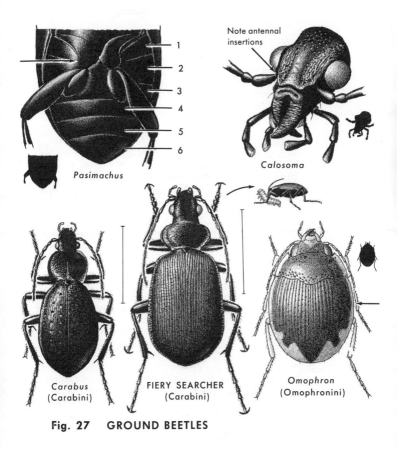

Note antennal insertions

1
2
3
4
5
6

Pasimachus

Calosoma

Carabus
(Carabini)

FIERY SEARCHER
(Carabini)

Omophron
(Omophronini)

Fig. 27   GROUND BEETLES

SEARCHERS Tribe Carabini

Our largest ground beetles (17-35 mm — up to 1⅜ in.). Some are brightly colored. *Carabus nemoralis* Muller, one of 13 N. American *Carabus* species, has been introduced from Europe and occurs in e. U.S. to Midwest and on West Coast. May be common around houses; most active in spring. An important predator on slugs in coastal areas of B.C. Genus *Calosoma* contains 24 species (Fig. 27; see also Pl. 1), including some of the most attractive of all ground beetles. *C. sycophanta* (L.) was imported from Europe to aid in control of the Gypsy Moth in ne. U.S. Both adults and larvae climb trees in search of prey; adults eat much more than larvae do. **Fiery Searcher,** *C. scrutator* Fab., 25-35 mm, is black with a bluish pronotum and green elytra; found nearly throughout N. America; adults eat caterpillars.

SNAIL-EATING GROUND BEETLES Tribe Cychrini

Head, mouth parts, and sometimes pronotum are *narrow,* allowing these beetles to feed on snails through the opening of a snail shell; they also eat insects, myriapods, and berries. Most species (50 of 63) belong to the genus *Scaphinotus;* these occur in cool, damp woods and ravines, and are active at night, running over ground or climbing on logs and tree trunks.

MARSH and BOG GROUND BEETLES Tribe Elaphrini

The 19 *Elaphrus* species (largest of 3 genera) are notable for their resemblance to tiger beetles, but have *punctate depressions* on their elytra. They are widely distributed; 6-8.5 mm. Most occur on mud or sand flats on sunny days; some inhabit marshes and bogs and can be forced to the surface by treading on wet ground.

PEDUNCULATE GROUND BEETLES Tribe Scaritini

In these beetles the body is narrow between the pronotum and elytra. The *large mandibles* typical of the 14 *Pasimachus* species (21-30 mm) give them a fearsome appearance. They live in dry open woodlands, pastures, cultivated fields, or on prairies with sparse vegetation, and feed on caterpillars and other larvae. The 3 *Scarites* species (15-30 mm) are common and distinctive for their body shape; they are found beneath objects near cultivated fields and are beneficial for killing many other kinds of insects. The 25 or so *Clivina* species (4.8-8.5 mm) may be abundant at lights; they usually live in damp soil near streams or in wet places in woods.

STINK BEETLES Tribe Psydrini

Nomius pygmaeus (Dej.) is sometimes known as the **Stink Beetle.** It is frequently attracted to lights, but is unwelcome indoors, for its odor is strong, like overripe cheese, and slightly nauseous. Occurs in Canada and into U.S. along both coasts and Rocky Mts. About 7 mm long.

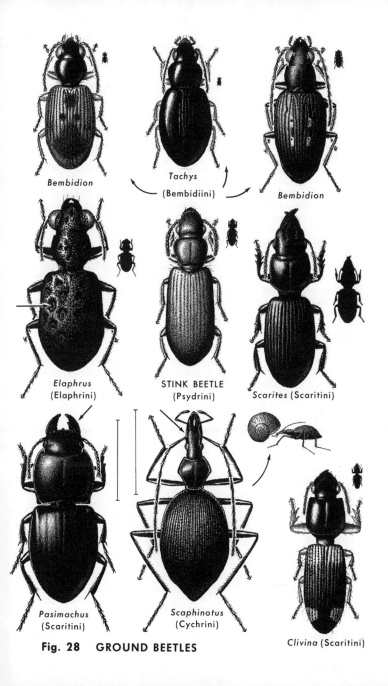

Bembidion

Tachys
(Bembidiini)

Bembidion

Elaphrus
(Elaphrini)

STINK BEETLE
(Psydrini)

Scarites (Scaritini)

Pasimachus
(Scaritini)

Scaphinotus
(Cychrini)

Clivina (Scaritini)

Fig. 28   GROUND BEETLES

MINUTE GROUND BEETLES Tribe Bembidiini
A large tribe with over 150 species; some are quite common. They
are 1.2–7.5 mm long, and widely distributed. *Bembidion* species
(about 50 in N. America) are 2–7.5 mm; their elytra often bear
light markings. They occur in a variety of habitats from Arctic
tundra to streambanks in arid sw. U.S. and marshes in Fla. Typically each species is adapted to a narrow range of conditions and is
intolerant of variation. At 1.2–3.2 mm, the 115 *Tachys* species are
as small as any ground beetles; some are abundant under bark;
others are common in sand or clay near water.

WOODLAND GROUND BEETLES Tribe Pterostichini
These beetles live in a variety of habitats and under a variety of
cover. Many belong to the genus *Pterostichus* (over 150 species;
7–24 mm); they often occur in moist, rotten logs, or on wet ground,
and are found from the frigid tundra to the semitropical s. U.S.
Agonum species (about 150 in N. America; 5–15 mm) also occur in
a wide variety of habitats — some species live only in dry forests,
others only in marshes, bogs, or wet woodlands. Four species have
the unusual habit of being attracted to freshly burned wood. *A.
bogemanni* Gyll. flies to forest fires and runs around in ashes that
are still warm.

SEED-EATING GROUND BEETLES Tribe Amarini
Consists of just 1 genus — *Amara,* which includes over 200 species;
body length is 5–12 mm. As with many large genera of ground
beetles, it is extremely difficult for even the practiced taxonomist
to identify species. Habits of these ground beetles are poorly
known.

DINGY GROUND BEETLES Tribe Harpalini
One of the largest tribes in the family; members occur throughout
N. America. Over 60 species belong to the genus *Harpalus.* Most
are 5–15 mm, but some reach 25 mm (up to 1 in.). Some species are
abundant at lights. A few feed on seeds and so are harmful.
Bradycellus species (66 in N. America, 4–8 mm) are typically
smaller than *Harpalus* species. Like those beetles, they are often
numerous at lights, especially in s. U.S. The **Seedcorn Beetle,**
Stenolophus lecontei (Chaudior), is one of our most harmful
ground beetles for it feeds on germinating seeds. It lives in the cen.
and s. U.S. and is very abundant at lights during April and May.
Geopinus incrassatus Dej., the only member of that genus (e. to
cen. U.S.; 13.5–15 mm), lives in sandy river banks. At first glance it
looks more like a scarab beetle than a ground beetle, but is readily
distinguished from scarabs by its threadlike antennae.

NOTCH-MOUTHED GROUND BEETLES Tribe Licinini
Tip of labrum *deeply grooved.* Some members of the genus
Dicaelus (29 species) reach 25 mm (up to 1 in.). Certain species are

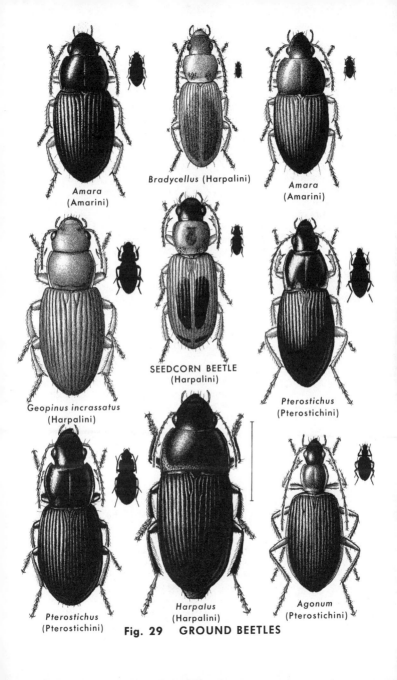

Amara
(Amarini)

Bradycellus (Harpalini)

Amara
(Amarini)

Geopinus incrassatus
(Harpalini)

SEEDCORN BEETLE
(Harpalini)

Pterostichus
(Pterostichini)

Pterostichus
(Pterostichini)

Harpalus
(Harpalini)

Agonum
(Pterostichini)

Fig. 29 GROUND BEETLES

iridescent and are among our most attractive carabids. These ground beetles often live in woodland areas, where they feed on snails.

HAIRY GROUND BEETLES Tribe Panagaeini
Unlike other ground beetles, the 10 *Panagaeus* species (7.5–11 mm) are covered with bristly hairs. They generally live in dry leaf litter but are rarely collected.

VIVID METALLIC GROUND BEETLES Tribe Chlaeniini
A large and varied group, including many of the ground beetles found in the tropics. The 40 or so *Chlaenius* species are 8-23 mm long, foul-smelling, and often brightly colored. They are covered with hairs that lie flat. Most species are found in moist areas; some are semiaquatic and live in marshes. Some species lay eggs in mud cells that are usually placed on the underside of leaves or twigs; egg cells of each species have a distinctive shape.

LONG-NECKED GROUND BEETLES Tribe Odacanthini
The 5 *Colliuris* species are readily recognized by their greatly *elongate head* and *prothorax*. *C. pennsylvanicus* (L.), about 7.5 mm, occurs in much of N. America and may be common at lights. It lives on vegetation in wet areas.

COLORFUL FOLIAGE GROUND BEETLES
Tribe Lebiini   **(see also Pl. 1)**
During the summer many of these beetles are active in daytime on foliage and flowers — an unusual habit for ground beetles. The largest genus, *Lebia,* contains 24 species (3–10 mm), including some that are quite colorful (see Pl. 1). Adults feed on plant lice and other insects. Some larvae are parasites on leaf beetle pupae. Early stage larvae are typical in form for ground beetles but later stages undergo body changes characteristic of a parasitic life. Larvae pupate near remains of host. The 21 *Cymindis* species (9–15 mm) usually live in open, dry grasslands.

FALSE BOMBARDIER BEETLES Tribe Galeritini
Unlike bombardier beetles (below), which these otherwise resemble, these beetles have a black head. Most of the 11 *Galeritula* species are found in s. U.S; some reach nearly 1 in. (25 mm). Typically black and orange; pronotum much narrower than elytra. Some are abundant beneath cover; many are attracted to lights. These beetles are valuable for destroying caterpillars such as cankerworms; examination of stomach contents has shown that most of their food consists of these pests.

FLAT-HORNED GROUND BEETLES Tribe Helluonini
The 7 *Helluomorphoides* species, 13–17 mm, are found in s. and

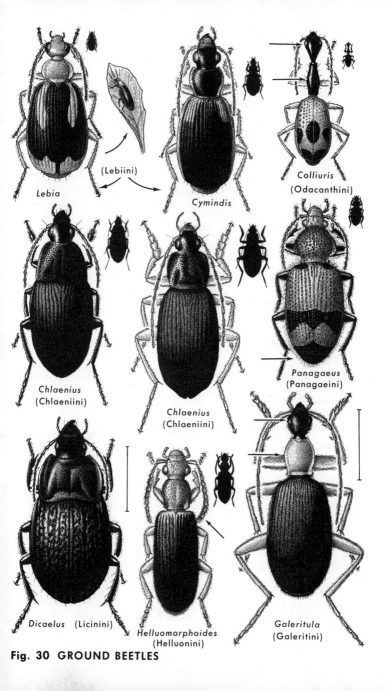

Lebia
(Lebiini)

Cymindis

Colliuris
(Odacanthini)

Chlaenius
(Chlaeniini)

Chlaenius
(Chlaeniini)

Panagaeus
(Panagaeini)

Dicaelus (Licinini)

Helluomorphoides
(Helluonini)

Galeritula
(Galeritini)

Fig. 30 GROUND BEETLES

cen. U.S., and are collected infrequently. Virtually all other ground beetles have antennae of uniform width; in these beetles the *outer segments* are *flattened.*

BOMBARDIER BEETLES Tribe Brachinini
The only genus, *Brachinus* (4–15 mm), contains about 40 species, which occur over much of N. America. All have a narrow *head* and *prothorax;* legs are reddish yellow; elytra bluish or black. Common name refers to their unique means of defense — when threatened they raise the end of their body and fire a few rounds of a chemical gas with a popping sound and smokelike puffs (see *Brachinus,* Fig. 31). This effectively repels enemies such as toads, for the chemical produced is acidic and very irritating. This can be so disconcerting to the collector that the beetle escapes. Larvae of these species are parasitic.

TROUT-STREAM BEETLES:
Family Amphizoidae

Identification. Body shape and habitat distinctive: *Elongate-oval,* dorsal surface moderately *convex,* somewhat *flattened* ventrally. Semiaquatic in w. U.S. streams. Antennae *short, threadlike.* Elytra not striate. Tan or brown to black. Tarsi 5-5-5. 11–16 mm.
Similar families. (1) Some ground beetles (p. 86) are similar but have striate elytra. (2) Certain darkling beetles (p. 249) are similar, but tarsi 5-5-4.
Range and numbers. All 4 species of the single genus occur in w. U.S.
Habits. In daytime adults and larvae cling to floating debris (twigs, catkins, needles, etc.) in eddies of cold mountain streams, or occasionally in warm lowland streams or lakes. In daytime both larvae and adults appear sluggish, and adults swim feebly or not at all. At night, however, they are quite active and predaceous; larvae forage for naiads of stoneflies and mayflies in water, while adults run along shore in search of prey. When handled, adults emit a yellowish fluid that smells like overripe canteloupe.
Collecting methods. Collected only in w. U.S. streams — usually in mountain streams at 1000–4000 feet. Sift through debris in foam-covered eddies where water level remains fairly constant. Rarely collected in sluggish water or in lakes; look in masses of pine needles that accumulate along shore. Trout-stream beetles are highly regarded as collector's items largely due to their restricted habitat. In a mountain stream of w. Wyo. I spent about 1 hour searching for each of 11 adults that I collected of *Amphizoa lecontei.*
Examples. The night activities of larvae and adults described above under **Habits** refer to those of *Amphizoa lecontei* Matth.; other species probably have similar habits.

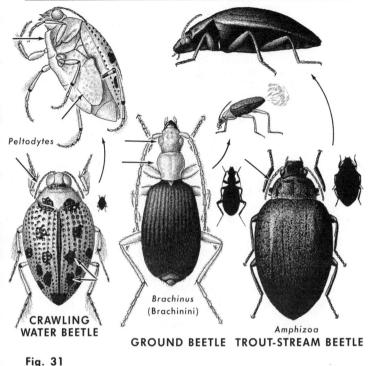

Peltodytes

Brachinus
(Brachinini)

Amphizoa

**CRAWLING
WATER BEETLE**

GROUND BEETLE TROUT-STREAM BEETLE

Fig. 31

CRAWLING WATER BEETLES:
Family Haliplidae

Identification. Shape, size, and hind coxae distinctive: Body oval,
tapered at each end, *convex* above; *1.7–4.5 mm.* Hind coxae greatly
enlarged, concealing 2 or more abdominal segments. Yellow or
brownish with *black spots.* Head small. *Antennae short,* threadlike. *Prosternum with a keel.* Elytra striate.

Similar families. (1) Some ground beetles (*Omophron* species,
p. 87) — head large; body length 5–8 mm. (2) Some predaceous
diving beetles (p. 96) are as small, but their hind coxae are
never enlarged.

Range and numbers. Most of the 60 species occur in e. U.S.;
there are 4 genera.

Habits. Though the common name suggests otherwise, these beetles do swim in quiet water, but do not swim as well as predaceous diving beetles (next family). Long hairs on legs of these beetles help them swim. Crawling water beetles are most numerous in ponds, lakes, and streams, and are found near shore in both running and still water, especially on vegetation. Adults eat algae, along with insect larvae and small aquatic animals. Adults store air in their expanded coxae and come to the surface of the water to replenish their air supply. Larvae are elongate, slender, and aquatic; they also feed on algae. Larvae breathe through their skin. When a larva is mature, it crawls up on shore, digs a pupal chamber (often under a stone or log), and pupates. Probably all species spend the winter as adults; some are also known to overwinter in larval stage, commonly in damp soil. Sometimes adults are active underneath ice.

Collecting methods. Use an aquatic net in shallow weedy areas of streams, ponds, and lakes. Most common in algae; collected in moderate numbers in appropriate habitat.

Examples. *Haliplus* is the largest genus with 40 species, most in e. U.S. *H. confluentus* Rob., 2.7–3 mm, ranges from S.C. to Fla. Most common in canals, ditches, large springs, and brackish pools. Dark elytral markings may be so extensive that beetle appears black. *H. punctatus* Aubé, 3.7–4 mm, is more typical in color, with fewer dark markings. Members of the genus *Peltodytes* (15 species) are widely distributed; most are 3.5–4 mm. The 2 genera differ as follows: In *Haliplus* species, hind coxal plates are not bordered by a groove and reach only tip of 3rd abdominal sternite; in *Peltodytes* species, hind coxal plates are bordered by a groove and reach base of last abdominal segment (Fig. 31).

PREDACEOUS DIVING BEETLES:
Family Dytiscidae

Identification. Form and legs distinctive: Body *elongate-oval* and *streamlined; convex* both above and below. Hind legs *flattened* and fringed with *hairs.* Antennae *threadlike.* Hind tarsi have 1 or 2 claws; tarsi nearly always 5-5-5. Front tibiae lack spines. Scutellum usually visible. Usually black or brown, often with indistinct yellow or light markings. 1.2–40 mm (nearly $1\frac{5}{8}$ in.); few over 20 mm.

Similar families. (1) Burrowing water beetles (p. 100) — scutellum is hidden; front tibiae nearly always have a curved spine or hook. (2) Water scavenger beetles (p. 104) — antennae clubbed; maxillary palps nearly always elongate; ventral surface flat. (3) Whirligig beetles (p. 101) — eyes divided; antennae clubbed. (4)

Crawling water beetles (p. 95) — head narrow; hind coxae expanded. (5) Ground beetles (especially *Omophron* species, p. 87) — scutellum concealed; hind legs not flattened or fringed with hairs.

Range and numbers. Throughout N. America in fresh water; 41 genera and 476 species.

Habits. All adults are aquatic and good swimmers. They prefer small shallow bodies of water with little or no current, rich vegetation, and many minute animals (prey). Many predaceous diving beetles live in small ponds and along the edges of lakes and streams; others live in a variety of habitats ranging from hot springs to cold mountain streams or even small temporary pools. Adults use their hind legs exclusively in swimming and move them together like oars; in contrast, adult water scavenger beetles swim by moving their legs alternately. Adults are active in daytime and spend most of their time under water; they breathe air trapped beneath their elytra. Periodically they come to the surface to renew their air supply, and hang head down to expose their elytra while doing so (Fig. 32, p. 98).

Most species can fly, and may migrate from pond to pond, usually during the spring and fall. These beetles are very clumsy on land. After a migratory flight adults close their wings and plunge into whatever appears to be water. Due to a slight miscalculation, sometimes this may be the roof of a dark-colored car, a greenhouse, the sashes of a cold frame, or a similar object of low reflectivity. Eggs are laid in wet places just out of water, or on plants under water.

Adults and larvae are carnivorous and feed on dragonfly and damselfly nymphs and other aquatic animals, including larvae and adults of aquatic insects, shrimps, worms, leeches, snails, tadpoles, and even small fish. Larvae and adults of larger species can disrupt fish hatcheries by eating small fish in culture ponds. In larvae, mandibles are long, curved, and sometimes hollow, for sucking blood of their prey. Larvae are voracious and will eat each other if confined in aquariums. Like adults, they must come to the water surface to breathe. When mature, larvae leave water to pupate in damp soil or sand. These beetles overwinter primarily as adults, but some also overwinter as larvae, or in both forms. A few are active during winter under ice.

Collecting methods. Many predaceous diving beetles are easily attracted to light traps near water. Some fly long distances and may be collected far from bodies of water. Use an aquatic net in shallows of ponds and other bodies of water to capture a good variety. An underwater light trap (p. 17) will pull in some species.

Examples. The 14 *Laccophilus* species (2.5–6 mm) are widely distributed. They often have light markings on a black or brown background or brown or black markings on a light background. *L. proximus* Say (3.4–4.5 mm) is found from e. U.S. to Mexico in newly formed ponds, puddles, and other bodies of water, including flooded furrows of fields, and rain collected in rain barrels, tin cans, or even old auto tires. The 24 *Bidessus* species are widely distributed and — at 1.2-2 mm — are among our smallest predaceous diving beetles. They have 2 small impressions at the base of the pronotum, and usually 2 similar impressions at the front of the elytra. Frequently found in or near submerged sphagnum moss or algal mats. *B. flavicollis* (LeC.) (1.5-1.8 mm) is found from e. U.S. west to Minn., usually in filamentous algal mats in standing water.

Hydroporus is easily the largest genus, with over 100 species occurring in streams, springs, marshes, and lakes (widely distributed; 2.5-6 mm). In *Hydroporus* species, the 4th segment of fore and middle tarsi is minute and partially concealed by the 3rd segment. *H. vittatipennis* G. & H. (2.6-2.9 mm) occurs from e. U.S. west to Kans. and Tex. This beetle is often found burrowing in sand along banks of streams — over 100 specimens have been taken from less than a quart of sand and water collected at the edge of a stream. Most active at night and can be collected in large numbers at lights. In the 22 *Agabus* species (widely distributed; 6-11 mm) the hind tarsal claws are equal in length and the tarsal segments are lengthened. Labial palps are as long as maxillary palps. Many have light stripes on a black background; in some, the stripes are wider than the dark areas. The 10 *Rhantus* species (9-16 mm) are widely distributed. *R. calidus* (Fab.), 11.5-13.5 mm, is found in a variety of aquatic habitats — usually in swamps — from e. U.S. to Mexico.

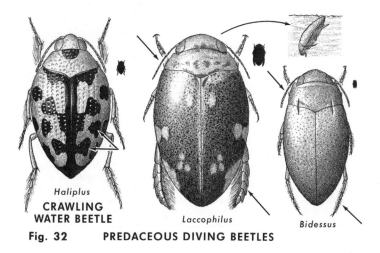

Haliplus
**CRAWLING
WATER BEETLE**

Laccophilus

Bidessus

Fig. 32   PREDACEOUS DIVING BEETLES

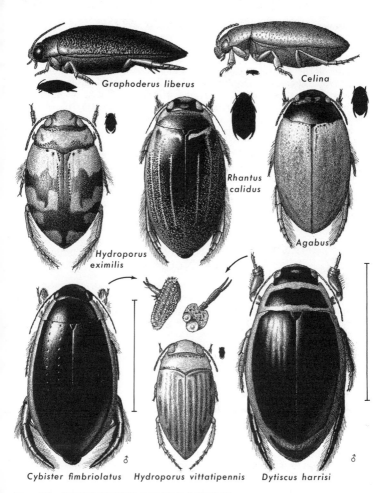

Graphoderus liberus

Celina

Rhantus calidus

Agabus

Hydroporus eximilis

Cybister fimbriolatus   *Hydroporus vittatipennis*   *Dytiscus harrisi*

Fig. 33 PREDACEOUS DIVING BEETLES

Our largest predaceous diving beetles fly to lights and thus may be readily noticed. They belong to 2 genera: *Cybister* (5 species, in e. U.S. and Cal.) and *Dytiscus* (13 species, widely distributed). Most are over 25 mm (over 1 in.) long and 1 grows to 40 mm (nearly $1\frac{5}{8}$ in.). In *Cybister* species, the body is broadest behind the middle, while in *Dytiscus* species the body is broadest near the middle. Species of both genera are most common in deeper parts of ponds and ditches. They are voracious predators — both larvae and adults feed on a variety of organisms and even kill small fishes. Adults fly to lights. *Cybister fimbriolatus* (Say), at 23–33 mm, is one of the larger species; it typically occurs in deeper parts of ponds, ditches, and similar situations, but is most frequently collected at lights. *Dytiscus harrisi* Kirby (ne. U.S.), at 38–40 mm (nearly 1⅝ in.), is our largest predaceous diving beetle. In certain species of *Cybister* and *Dytiscus* the front tarsi of ♂ are modified into suction disks (see Fig. 33) that hold onto the slippery back of ♀ during mating.

In the 3 *Celina* species (3–5.5 mm; e. U.S.), the body is elongate with nearly parallel sides. These beetles characteristically live in the bottom debris of ponds. The 5 *Graphoderus* species (11–15 mm) are widely distributed. *G. liberus* (Say), 10–12 mm, is typically found in deeper parts of well-shaded woodland ponds from Ont. and Que. south to Fla.

BURROWING WATER BEETLES:
Family Noteridae

Identification. Body broadly oval to elongate-oval, *streamlined.* Scutellum *hidden.* Tarsal segments nearly *parallel-sided;* hind tarsi have 2 slender *curved claws.* Front tibiae usually (in 12 of 14 species) have a strong *hook* or curved *spine.* Antennae sawtoothed to threadlike. Black to reddish brown; usually smooth and shiny. 1.2–5.5 mm.

Similar families. (1) Predaceous diving beetles (p. 96), at 1.2–40 mm, are often larger, usually with a visible scutellum; tarsi rarely parallel-sided. (2) Water scavenger beetles (p. 104) have clubbed antennae and elongate maxillary palps.

Range and numbers. 4 genera, 17 species in N. America; most in e. U.S. west to Tex.

Habits. All species live in weedy ponds and lakes. Adults are predaceous; larval eating habits are not known. Adults are strong swimmers and, like predaceous diving beetles, swim by moving their legs in unison. Common name of these beetles refers to burrowing habits of larvae, which have strong legs and dig rapidly through wet mud.

Collecting methods. Burrowing water beetles can be collected at lights near water or by using an aquatic net; they are moderately common.

Example. The 5 *Suphisellus* species (under 3 mm) generally live along the East Coast; dorsal surface is moderately shiny with distinct rows of punctures. *S. puncticollis* Crotch, 2.7–3 mm, lives in ponds, marshes, swamps, and on edges of lakes from Mass. and Mich. south to Fla. In the 4 *Hydrocanthus* species (e. and s. U.S.; 3.7–5.5 mm) the dorsal surface is weakly punctured and shiny. *H. oblongus* Sharp, 3.7–4.6 mm, lives in se. U.S.

WHIRLIGIG BEETLES: Family Gyrinidae

Identification. Eyes and legs distinctive: Each eye is *divided into 2* parts. Front legs *long;* middle and hind legs *short* and *flat.* Body elongate-oval, flattened. Antennae *short, clubbed.* Usually black, rarely dark metallic green. Tarsi 5-5-5. 3–15.5 mm.

Similar families. The eyes, legs, and habits of whirligig beetles are so distinctive that no other beetles will be confused with them.

Range and numbers. 3 genera, 51 species; most occur in e. U.S.

Habits. Whirligig beetles are also known as waltzing beetles or scuttle bugs because the adults rapidly whirl and gyrate on the water surface. They are the only aquatic beetles that regularly use the film on the water surface for support. The ventral surface of the body is not waterproof, but the flattened sides of the body support the beetle on the surface film. When surface tension is reduced by a detergent, these beetles cannot stay afloat. Double compound eyes are an adaptation for aquatic life — the upper pair is suited for vision above, in the air; the lower pair is used for

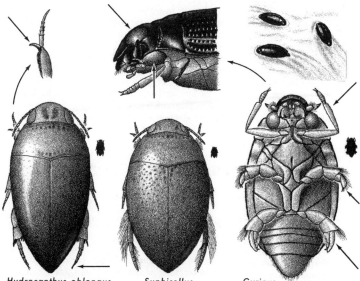

Hydrocanthus oblongus   *Suphisellus*   *Gyrinus*
Fig. 34   BURROWING WATER BEETLES   **WHIRLIGIG BEETLE**

underwater vision. Whirligig beetles are also skillful divers. When a beetle dives, it carries a bubble of air with it, which looks silvery under water. When disturbed, these beetles secrete a liquid; that of *Dineutus* species smells like apples, while that of *Gyrinus* species is quite unpleasant.

Adults live in streams, rivers, ponds, and lakes, rarely far from shore. They often congregate in large swarms or schools, most frequently in late summer or fall. Schools usually form near shore in a sheltered spot. Most whirligig beetles are active in the daytime but may be nocturnal in hot dry localities (such as arid sw. U.S.). Whirligig beetles fly well and often fly from one body of water to another. Adults are scavengers on animal and plant material; larvae usually prey on aquatic insect larvae. Larvae are slender and have featherlike gills on the abdomen.

Collecting methods. Sweep an aquatic net rapidly through groups of these beetles in lakes, streams, or ponds; many will elude the net but you may catch some. Attempting to capture these beetles by hand can be frustrating, for they are skilled at avoiding the collector, both on the water surface and beneath it.

Examples. *Gyrinus* is by far the largest genus, with 35 species (3.4–7.5 mm); they are widely distributed, and most common on lakes and ponds. The scutellum is *exposed,* and each elytron has *11 rows of punctures.* Many species are adapted to local habitats — different whirligigs may be found in quiet pools, eddies of streams, or any puddle large enough to swim in. *G. rockinghamensis* LeC. (3.4–4.3 mm) occurs from Mass. to Fla., usually in small groups. However, on Lake Wauberg near Micanopy, Fla., a dense swarm of these beetles was observed in an area of about 100 by 50 ft. and was estimated to contain over 1 million individuals. Genus *Dineutus* contains 13 species (8.5–15.5 mm), which are widely distributed. Scutellum concealed; elytra are smooth or have 9 faint shallow grooves. They typically live in streams. *D. emarginatus* Say, 8.5–10 mm, is found throughout the e. U.S. and commonly occurs near the mouth of streams, or in lakes where there is some wave action.

Suborder Myxophaga

Small and uncommon; antennae weakly clubbed.

MINUTE BOG BEETLES:
Family Sphaeriidae

Identification. Body broadly *oval, shiny,* and hairless; dorsal surface strongly *convex;* ventral surface nearly *flat.* Head partly visible from above. *Minute* — 0.5–0.8 mm. Dark brown. Each antenna ends in a weak club.

Similar families. Few families with this body shape have members as small, but see: (1) Minute fungus beetles (Fig. 97, p. 230). (2) Minute beetles (p. 149) can partially roll themselves up. (3) Some lady beetles (p. 231) are nearly as small. (4) In feather-winged beetles (p. 126) pronotum is not as narrow.

Range and numbers. Only 1 genus, containing 3 species, which occur in e. U.S., Tex., s. Calif., and Wash.

Habits and examples. Found in mud or under objects near water, or among roots or moss in boggy areas. The 3 *Sphaerius* species are hard to distinguish from minute fungus beetles.

Collecting methods. Examine their habitat closely, or sift material through a Berlese funnel. Rarely collected.

SKIFF BEETLES: Family Hydroscaphidae

Identification. Similar to rove beetles (p. 110) in that elytra are *short*, truncate, and expose 3–5 abdominal segments; abdomen *conical*. Body oval and widest at base of elytra. Hind coxae small, widely separated. Head narrower near tip. Tan to brown. Each

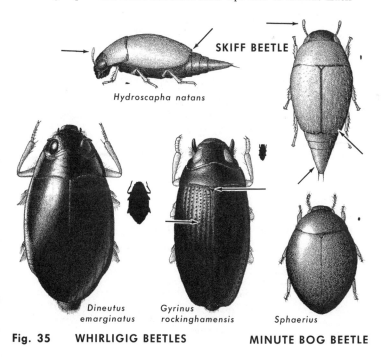

SKIFF BEETLE

Hydroscapha natans

Dineutus emarginatus

Gyrinus rockinghamensis

Sphaerius

Fig. 35 **WHIRLIGIG BEETLES** **MINUTE BOG BEETLE**

antenna has 8 segments; last segment elongate and widened. 1–1.5 mm.

Similar families. (1) In rove beetles (especially Subfamily Tachyporinae, p. 116) each antenna usually has 11 segments. (2) Feather-winged beetles (p. 126) — each antenna has a club of 2 or 3 segments. (3) Horse-shoe crab beetles (p. 128) — each antenna has a club with 3 segments. (4) Minute moss beetles (p. 108) — abdomen less exposed.

Range and numbers. Only 1 species — found in s. Calif., Nev., and Ariz.

Habits and examples. *Hydroscapha natans* LeC. is aquatic and lives among filamentous algae. Both adults and larvae are abundant in suitable streams, especially on algae-covered rocks in shallows. This species is highly tolerant of temperature variations — it has been found in both icy rivers and hot springs. Adults carry a supply of air beneath their elytra; larvae apparently breathe by means of abdominal appendages that function as gills. Larval mouth parts are adapted for feeding on algae. ♀ egg production is quite unusual for beetles — only 1 egg develops at a time. It is laid on algae.

Collecting methods. Closely examine algae-covered rocks at shallow edges of streams in s. Calif., Nev., and Ariz. If you can find these beetles, they can sometimes be collected in good numbers.

Suborder Polyphaga

These beetles differ from those in Suborder Adephaga in that the first abdominal segment is not divided by the hind coxae. This suborder includes all remaining beetle families and the great majority of species.

Superfamily Hydrophiloidea

Antennae clubbed; generally aquatic or semiaquatic.

WATER SCAVENGER BEETLES: Family Hydrophilidae

Identification. Antennae *short,* often *concealed;* each with a club of 4 segments — first segment *enlarged* and nearly always more or less *enclosing* following segment. Maxillary palps *elongate,* each one often *longer* than an antenna. Metasternum sometimes *extended* at rear into a sharp *spine.* Body generally oval or elliptical; convex above, usually flat below. Hind tarsi often flattened and fringed with hair. Usually smooth, black, and shiny, sometimes brown or even yellow; some species patterned. Tarsi nearly always 5-5-5 or 5-4-4; 1st segment often short. Five abdominal segments. 1–40 mm (nearly 1⅝ in.).

Similar families. (1) Predaceous diving beetles (p. 96) — antennae threadlike; maxillary palps not as elongate. (2) Minute moss beetles (p. 108) — 6 or 7 abdominal segments. (3) Shining mold beetles (p. 225) are similar to some water scavenger beetles but their palps are short; body length 1–3 mm. (4) Riffle beetles (p. 163) are similar to some water scavenger beetles, but their legs are long and claws are large.

Range and numbers. 34 genera and about 225 species; widely distributed.

Habits. Larvae and adults of many are aquatic or semiaquatic, but some live in fresh mammal dung, humus-rich soil, or decaying leaves. Adults of both aquatic and terrestrial species are largely herbivorous, but will eat dead animal tissue; a few prey on other insects. All larvae are carnivorous and cannibalistic; about 25% are terrestrial. Aquatic species live in quiet pools, quiet areas of lakes or streams with an abundance of vegetation, or brackish or strongly saline water. Some prefer mineral-rich water, others running water where algae grow. Most adults come up for air *head first* and break surface film with their antennae; predaceous diving beetles (easily confused with water scavenger beetles) come up for air *tail first*, as do larvae of both families. Members of the 2 fami-

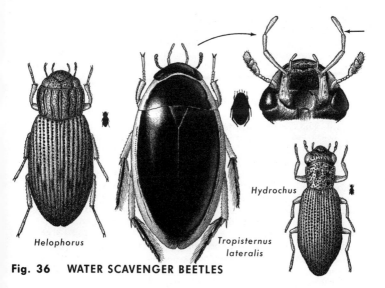

Helophorus

Hydrochus

Tropisternus lateralis

Fig. 36   WATER SCAVENGER BEETLES

lies can also be distinguished by their swimming motions: Predaceous diving beetles move both legs in unison but water scavenger beetles move them alternately, as in walking. The under surface of water scavenger beetles appears silvery in water, for it is covered by a film of air, which is trapped by the pile of fine hairs.

Collecting methods. Use an aquatic net in shallow areas of ponds, lakes, and streams, especially where there is much vegetable material. Also try woodland pools or puddles; even flooded tire tracks can hold these beetles. Terrestrial species are found in plant debris at edges of lakes, ponds, streams, or roadside ditches, but also in dung or in carcasses in advanced decay. Adults are often common in appropriate habitats. Many species are attracted — sometimes in large numbers — to lights near bodies of water.

Examples. The members of the genus *Tropisternus* (15 species; widely distributed) are generally 8–12 mm; their appearance is nearly uniform. *T. lateralis* (Fab.) is common from Canada to Fla. and west to the Rockies. It is common in brackish or temporary pools but also in permanent pools. It is one of the first water scavenger beetles found in newly formed bodies of water, such as rain-filled buckets, washtubs, and wheelbarrows. Unlike other water scavenger beetles, the species of *Helophorus* and *Hydrochus* resemble riffle beetles (p. 163). They have striate elytra and their body surfaces are generally rough and dull-colored, often with a brassy tinge. Also, their maxillary palps are not markedly elongate. The 18 *Helophorus* species (3–7 mm) occur in n. U.S. and Canada. They are distinctive for the 5 lengthwise grooves on their pronotum. Most of the 19 *Hydrochus* species are found in e. U.S., but 2 species live in Calif. They are similar to *Helophorus* species, but pronotum is much narrower than elytra and usually has depressions; body length is 2–6 mm. Most cling to vegetation and debris in ponds or lakes. Some are readily collected in their habitat.

To the genus *Hydrophilus* belong our largest water scavenger beetles; they are usually over 25 mm (1 in.) and reach about 40 mm (nearly 1⅝ in.). The 3 species in this genus occur in e. U.S. and Calif. The **Giant Water Scavenger Beetle,** *H. triangularis* Say, is our largest water scavenger beetle. It is common in weedy ponds where there is deep water. It is sometimes common at lights during spring and fall flights. Its antennal club is quite unusual (see Fig. 37). Members of the genus *Berosus* (17 species; widely distributed) are typically light with dark markings. They have large bulging eyes, striate elytra, and their middle and hind tarsi are fringed (on the inner side) with *long swimming hairs.* Body length is 2–6 mm. Some are most common in shallow, quiet water.

The 9 *Paracymus* species (widely distributed; 1.5–3 mm) are distinctive for their size and the metallic luster of their dorsal surface. *P. subcupreus* (Say), 1.5–2 mm, occurs nearly throughout N. America. It is common in debris around pond edges. The 20 species of *Enochrus* (widely distributed) are 2–8 mm long, have confused

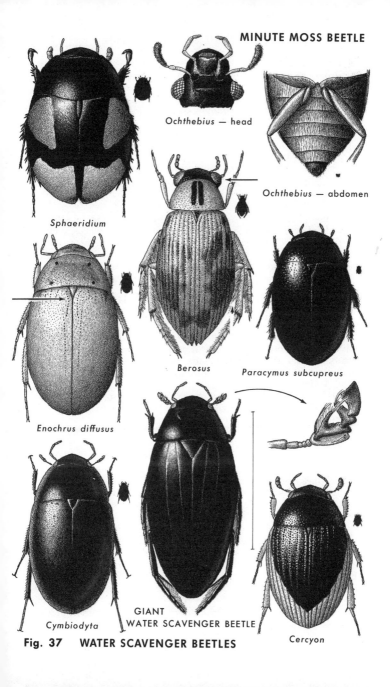

MINUTE MOSS BEETLE

Ochthebius — head

Ochthebius — abdomen

Sphaeridium

Berosus

Paracymus subcupreus

Enochrus diffusus

Cymbiodyta

GIANT
WATER SCAVENGER BEETLE

Cercyon

Fig. 37   WATER SCAVENGER BEETLES

elytral punctation, usually sutural striae, and their front and middle tarsi are 5-segmented. Many are typical of muddy ponds and some are common. *E. diffusus* (LeC.), 4–6 mm, occurs nearly throughout N. America; in parts of e. U.S. it is found in nearly every pond. The 24 *Cymbiodyta* species (widely distributed; 2.6–7.5 mm) superficially resemble members of *Enochrus,* but their front and middle tarsi are 4-segmented. Many occur in springs or streams; they are less common than *Enochrus* species.

The genus *Sphaeridium* contains 3 species (widely distributed; 5.5–7 mm), all introduced from Europe. Adults and larvae are common in fresh cow dung. Adults are often mistaken for hister or scarab beetles; but are readily distinguished by their antennal form. The 38 *Cercyon* species (widely distributed; usually 1.2–3.5 mm) make this the largest genus in the family. These beetles are terrestrial or semiaquatic. Many are found in damp places, such as in rotting vegetation beside ponds, lakes, streams, or roadside ditches. They may be common on dead animals in advanced decay or in dung. Because they are small, they are easily overlooked.

MINUTE MOSS BEETLES:
Family Hydraenidae

Identification. Similar to water scavenger beetles (above) but with 6 or 7 abdominal segments (not 5). Maxillary palps *elongate.* Each antenna has 8 or 9 segments, ending in a 4- or 5-segmented club. Some are streamlined in form. Last tarsal segment elongate. 1.2–2.5 mm.

Similar families. (1) Water scavenger beetles (p. 104) differ as described above, and are often larger at 1–40 mm. (2) Riffle beetles (p. 163) — maxillary palps not elongate.

Range and numbers. 3 genera and 33 species in N. America; most in w. U.S.

Habits. All adults are aquatic or semiaquatic and largely herbivorous; larvae are semiaquatic and carnivorous. Larvae live on land or at edges of ponds, lakes, streams, and rivers, especially where algae grows. Adults of some species tunnel in damp sand or soil at water's edge. Other adults cling to stones and waterlogged wood in streams; a few live in brackish water, and a very few in the intertidal zone. The dense hairs on the ventral surface of these beetles trap a bubble of air to allow breathing underwater.

Collecting methods. Closely examine banks of lakes, ponds, and streams; look, especially on partially submerged stones or debris.

Examples. The 20 *Ochthebius* species (widely distributed) resemble some riffle beetles (p. 163) and water scavenger beetles of the genus *Hydrochus* (p. 106), but in *Hydrochus* species the palps are longer than the antennae. *Ochthebius* species are common in and around ponds, lakes, and saline water. Some are sculptured and show metallic colors. Nearly all have a thin, transparent pronotal border, and base of pronotum is narrower than elytra. One species, *O. bruesi* Darl., lives in hot springs in Nev. The 6 *Hydraena* species are widely distributed along streams and rivers. Species of *Hydraena* have a different body shape than species of *Ochthebius* (Fig. 38), and their maxillary palps are longer than their antennae; in *Ochthebius* species the palps are shorter than the antennae (Fig. 37). *H. marginicollis* Kies. occurs in Fla.; though common, it is rarely collected because its habitat (in debris and roots beside lakes and streams) is usually overlooked. The 7 *Limnebius* species (Calif., Tex., Vt.) resemble streamlined water scavenger beetles; they are common on sandy banks of streams.

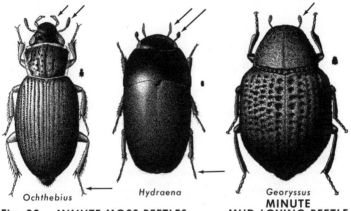

Ochthebius   *Hydraena*   *Georyssus*
                                          MINUTE
Fig. 38   MINUTE MOSS BEETLES   MUD-LOVING BEETLE

MINUTE MUD-LOVING BEETLES:
Family Georyssidae

Identification. These resemble small snout beetles, but lack a snout. Body *broad;* head *concealed* from above by pronotum, pronotum *narrowed* at front. Each antenna is 9-segmented and short; last 3 segments form a *lamellate club.* Distribution limited to Nebr., Idaho, and Calif. Black, lusterless. Elytra striate. 1.5–3mm.
Similar families. (1) Snout beetles (p. 309) are often as small but have a snout. (2) Fungus weevils (p. 307) have a snout. (3) Seed beetles (p. 304) have a snout and a pygidium. (4) Riffle beetles (p.

163) — legs long, claws large. (5) Some pill beetles (p. 155) are similar — see Figs. 60 and 61.

Range and numbers. Only 2 species (1 genus); 1 (*Georyssus pusillus*) occurs in Nebr.; the other in Idaho and Calif.

Habits and examples. Larvae are not yet known. Adults live in banks of streams and often become coated with mud or sand.

Collecting methods. Rarely encountered. In Nebr., Idaho, and Calif. look in sand or mud along streams or other bodies of water. Their small size and habit of coating themselves with mud or fine sand makes these beetles difficult to spot.

Superfamily Staphylinoidea

Some of these have short elytra that expose the abdomen. Except for rove beetles and carrion beetles, most live in concealed habitats.

ROVE BEETLES: Family Staphylinidae
(Figs. 39–42; see also Pl. 2)

Identification. Form of most is characteristic: Body *elongate-slender,* nearly *parallel-sided;* elytra *short,* exposing *3* to (usually) *5 or 6* abdominal segments, rarely concealing abdomen. Abdomen *flexible,* sometimes held upward in life. Antennae threadlike to clubbed. Tarsi variable — usually 5-5-5. Brown or black, a few brightly colored; often shiny. 0.7–25 mm (usually 1–10 mm).

Similar families. (1) Short-winged mold beetles (p. 118) — abdomen short and wide, not elongate; prothorax and head narrower; body not over 5.5 mm long. (2) Horse-shoe crab beetles (p. 128) lack eyes; antennal club 3-segmented. (3) Skiff beetles (p. 103) — last segment of each antenna elongate. Some beetles of other families have short elytra but they can nearly always be easily separated by their appearance alone; see figures for: (4) checkered beetles (Fig. 87, p. 209); (5) long-horned beetles (Fig. 123, p. 284); (6) soft-winged flower beetles (Fig. 89, p. 213); (7) sap beetles (Fig. 90, p. 216); (8) soldier beetles (Fig. 75, p. 185); (9) glowworms (Fig. 74, p. 183); (10) wedge-shaped beetles (Fig. 116, p. 269); (11) micromalthid beetles (Fig. 24, p. 81); and (12) telegeusid beetles (Fig. 74, p. 183).

Range and numbers. The largest N. American beetle family, with about 313 genera and nearly 3100 species; widely distributed.

Habits. Adults occur in a great variety of habitats. They are found under stones and other objects on ground, along shores of streams and lakes (some live along ocean shores), on carrion, in manure, on fungi, on flowers, in ant and termite nests, under bark, in soil or soil litter, and in caves. A few live in nests of mammals or birds. Rove beetles are among the most proficient fliers of all beetles. Many species run with the tip of the abdomen raised, which may cause the beginning collector to wonder if these beetles might sting, but none can actually sting. Larvae usually occur in the same habitat as adults; most prey on small animals such as other insects, but some eat decaying vegetation. No species are harmful; rove beetles may be considered beneficial for feeding on other insects.

Collecting methods. For larger species (and many others) look on carrion, also beneath bark, in fungi, under objects on ground, and along shores of streams and lakes. Sweeping flowers or foliage will produce some specimens. Sifting leaf litter and detritus is also productive. Many rove beetles are very common; in e. U.S. only ground beetles are more numerous beneath objects on the ground. Many fly to lights.

Subfamilies. 17 subfamilies; 6 that are very small or local in distribution are excluded from this guide.

FLAT ROVE BEETLES Subfamily Piestinae
Only 18 species in N. America; most in w. or s. U.S., 1 in ne. U.S. Body is elongate, slender, nearly parallel-sided, and flattened. The common species live under bark of conifers. Largest genus is *Trigonurus* (W. Coast; 7 species).

SPINY-LEGGED ROVE BEETLES Subfamily Oxytelinae
The 280 or so species (widely distributed) differ from all other rove beetles in having 7 ventral abdominal segments; other rove beetles have 6. The 78 *Carpelimus* species are all small (1.8-3.2 mm) and live in wet places. They are elongate and slender and the 2nd tarsal segment has a slender spine (on the ventral surface) that extends as far as the 3rd segment. The 16 *Anotylus* species (widely distributed) are about 1.5-4.5 mm long, black, and usually have a head that is as wide as the thorax. Each front tibia has a row of spines. Species of *Bledius* (easily the largest genus, with about 100 species) have front tibia with 2 rows of fine spines on the outer margin, and head narrower than thorax; most species are 2-7.5 mm long. These rove beetles burrow into moist sand or mud along shores of oceans, lakes, rivers, streams, or in salt flats or temporarily moist soil; they feed on algae and diatoms. Each burrow is marked by a mound of dry sand or mud. To collect these beetles, place soil containing burrow into a bucket of water; beetles will float to the surface.

OCELLATE ROVE BEETLES Subfamily Omaliinae
The 190 or so species differ from nearly all other rove beetles in having a *pair of ocelli* near the rear edge of the eyes (Fig. 40). Many of the 38 genera contain only a few species of limited distribution. The 20 *Omalium* species (widely distributed; 2.3-4.5 mm) have elytra that are comparatively long, reaching middle of abdo-

men or beyond. In *Eusphalerum* species (27 species; most in w. U.S.) the elytra are even longer, reaching tip of abdomen or beyond.

UNMARGINED ROVE BEETLES Subfamily Osoriinae

The 32 or so species (widely distributed) in this group differ from most other rove beetles in lacking a lateral margin on the abdomen. Many are found on sandy shores of streams, some in rotting wood, others in leaf litter. In the 9 *Osorius* species (ne. U.S. to Ariz.; most 4–8 mm) head is nearly as wide as thorax, eyes are small, antennae short, and front tibiae are enlarged and spiny.

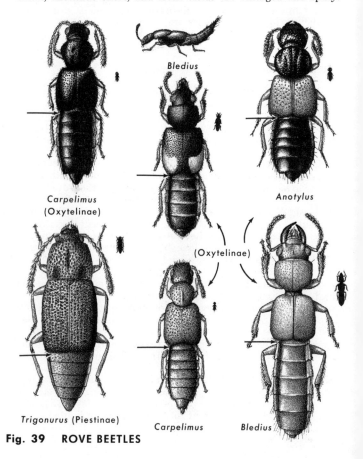

Bledius

Carpelimus
(Oxytelinae)

Anotylus

(Oxytelinae)

Trigonurus (Piestinae)

Carpelimus

Bledius

Fig. 39   ROVE BEETLES

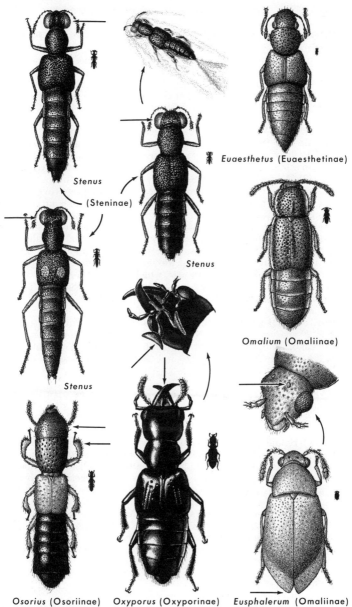

Stenus
(Steninae)

Stenus

Stenus

Euaesthetus (Euaesthetinae)

Omalium (Omaliinae)

Osorius (Osoriinae) *Oxyporus* (Oxyporinae) *Eusphalerum* (Omaliinae)

Fig. 40 ROVE BEETLES

CROSS-TOOTHED ROVE BEETLES (see also Pl. 2)
Subfamily Oxyporinae
The single genus, *Oxyporus* (Pl. 2), contains 11 species. They occur from e. U.S. to Pacific N.W. They feed on fleshy fungi. Body length is 6–9 mm; head is large (usually wider than thorax); the mandibles are *long* and *cross* each other (Fig. 40); and the last segment of each labial palp is large and *crescent-shaped*.

WATER SKATERS Subfamily Steninae
All but 2 of the nearly 200 species belong to the genus *Stenus* (widely distributed). Water skaters have *large, bulging eyes;* most are 3–5 mm long. Their general appearance is quite distinctive (see Fig. 40). As with species of Subfamily Aleocharinae (below), the antennae are inserted between the eyes. Typically these rove beetles occur in sunny spots along muddy or sandy shores of lakes, ponds, and streams; all are believed to be carnivorous. If a beetle falls or is blown into water, it normally paddles its way to shore, but if it is threatened (by a predaceous water insect, for example) it secretes a chemical (from glands at the tip of its abdomen) that breaks the surface tension of the water (the way a detergent does). It dips these glands into the water, which reduces the surface tension and makes the beetle scoot along the water surface. This scooting motion helps these beetles escape predators.

PSELAPHID-LIKE ROVE BEETLES Subfamily Euaesthetinae
The 20 species (e. U.S. to N. Mexico) are difficult to distinguish from short-winged mold beetles (members of Family Pselaphidae, p. 118). *Euaesthetus* species (18, e. U.S. to N.M., most 1–1.5 mm) live in wet areas.

PAEDERINE ROVE BEETLES (see also Pl. 2)
Subfamily Paederinae
A large group with about 430 species (widely distributed); sometimes difficult to distinguish from large rove beetles (Staphylininae, below). Small- to medium-sized, with a head that is narrowed behind into a *distinct neck*. The 28 *Sunius* species (widely distributed) are mostly 3–5 mm, and run rapidly when disturbed; they are sometimes common beneath objects or in vegetable debris. *Lathrobium* is the largest genus, with 79 species (widely distributed); most are 4–11 mm long. Front tarsus is *dilated* and clothed beneath with pads of dense hairs. Genus *Lobrathium* (56 species) is similar, but in those beetles the elytra bear a longitudinal fold above the side margin. Some of the 36 *Homaeotarsus* species have dull, rather densely punctured and sculptured surfaces; most are 8–11 mm.

LARGE ROVE BEETLES (see also Pl. 2)
Subfamily Staphylininae
Over 300 species, including our largest rove beetles. They live in

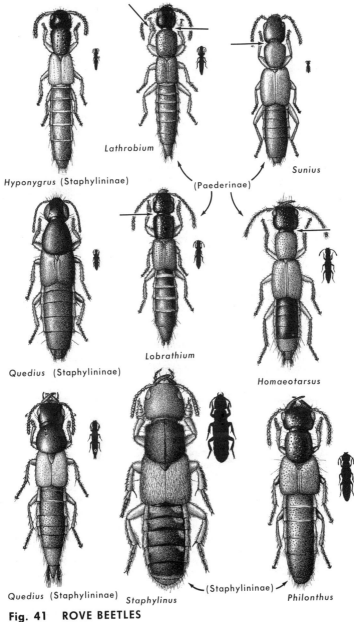

Hyponygrus (Staphylininae)

Lathrobium

Sunius

(Paederinae)

Quedius (Staphylininae)

Lobrathium

Homaeotarsus

Quedius (Staphylininae) Staphylinus

(Staphylininae)

Philonthus

Fig. 41 ROVE BEETLES

decaying fungi, carrion, dung, and rotting organic material. The 24 *Hyponygrus* species (widely distributed) are very slender; 4–8 mm. The middle of each elytron has a series of punctures. Most of the 140 or so *Philonthus* species (widely distributed) have a double row of punctures in middle of thorax; these allow species to be separated into groups. Length is 4–15 mm. In males of some species front tarsi are enlarged and hairy beneath. Many *Philonthus* species live on manure, fungi, and carrion. The 32 *Staphylinus* species (see Pl. 2) are usually brown or black and are large (most 12–20 mm). Head is as wide as thorax or sometimes wider; thorax is hairy. Some species are common on carrion, fungi, or beneath cover of various sorts. Those found on carrion were once assumed to feed on carrion, but are now known to prey on other insects attracted to carrion, primarily maggots. The 96 *Quedius* species (widely distributed) are most common on organic debris, such as ground litter, moss, grass piles, compost, carrion, and dung. A few occur in very moist areas, such as marshes, swamps, or in wet moss; a few live in mammal nests. Most are medium to large (4–21 mm).

CRAB-LIKE ROVE BEETLES Subfamily Tachyporinae
Many of the 150 or so species in this subfamily are unusual-looking for rove beetles: Generally broad and convex with a rather conical body; abdomen pointed, often bordered by long hairs. Most are 1–6 mm, but a few reach 8–9 mm. Some are very common under dead bark. The widely distributed genus *Sepedophilus* contains 22 species, all of which exhibit the crablike shape typical of this subfamily. Genus *Tachinus* has 58 species (widely distributed); most are 3–9 mm long. Species in this genus are difficult to identify unless specimens of both sexes are present. In males front tarsi are dilated and last ventral segment is deeply divided.

OBSCURE ROVE BEETLES Subfamily Aleocharinae
This is easily the largest subfamily, with over 1200 species. It is probably the most poorly known group of beetles in N. America; genera are difficult to distinguish and badly need study. Most species are small; some are among the smallest members of the family. Even so, they are often numerous in a variety of habitats — under stones, on carcasses, in dung, in mushrooms, in decaying vegetation, under bark, in oozing sap, or in moss. Some live in mammal, ant, or termite nests; a few are found on flowers. The 70 *Gyrophaena* species (most 1–2.5 mm) are broad-bodied; head flat, eyes prominent. These beetles typically live in fungi and are gregarious. Genus *Atheta* contains brown or black beetles that are usually 1.5–3.5 mm long. The great size of this genus (540 or so species) and the similarity of its species make their study exceptionally difficult. *Atheta* species are most common on vegetable debris or fungi. The 90 *Oxypoda* species are clothed with silky hair; abdomen usually narrowed behind middle; legs elongate; body generally 1.8–

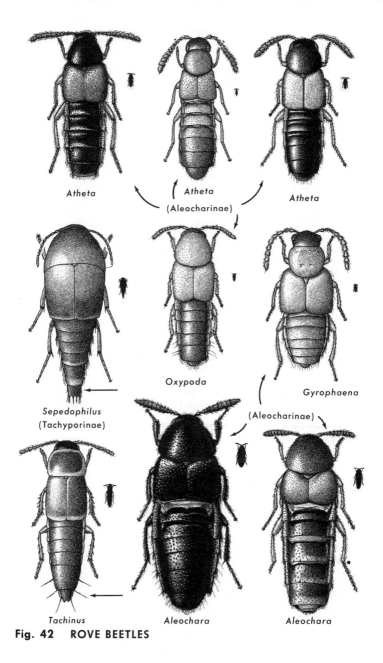

Atheta

Atheta
(Aleocharinae)

Atheta

Sepedophilus
(Tachyporinae)

Oxypoda

Gyrophaena

(Aleocharinae)

Tachinus

Aleochara

Aleochara

Fig. 42   ROVE BEETLES

3.2 mm. The 93 species of *Aleochara* (most 2.5–7.5 mm) are broad-bodied with a small head, large eyes, and usually with short, stout antennae. They are most common on carrion, fungi, and dung.

SHORT-WINGED MOLD BEETLES:
Family Pselaphidae

Identification. Elytra and form distinctive: elytra *short, closely applied to body,* leaving much of abdomen *exposed;* body nearly always *widest* at the abdomen or tip of elytra, with pronotum and head *narrower;* maxillary palps often *modified.* Antennae often beadlike, with last 1–4 segments *enlarged.* Nearly always orange to reddish brown, rarely black. Legs long and thin. 0.5–5.5 mm.
Similar families. (1) Some rove beetles (p. 110) are very similar, but body usually parallel-sided, not widest at abdomen; generally black or dark brown; antennae usually threadlike, not clubbed. (2) Grass-root beetles (p. 130) and (3) antlike stone beetles (p. 128) are of similar size and form, but elytra are longer and do not expose abdomen.
Range and numbers. 71 genera and over 500 species in N. America: widely distributed.
Habits. Most species feed on various molds. They are nocturnal, and generally are found in concealed moist places, such as under bark, in logs, under stones, in leaf mold, on the ground, in soil, in tree holes, in caves, in ant or termite nests, or in mammal nests. Some feed on small organisms such as mites or earthworms. Their preference for dark moist places restricts the habitats for which they are suited. Some that live in ant nests secrete a fluid on which ants feed.
Collecting methods. Though this family is large, its members are not often collected because of their small size and concealed habits. The best method for collecting these beetles is automatic extraction with a Berlese funnel (see p. 20). Collect organic material from tree holes, rotten logs (especially those protected by bark), clumps of moss, mammal nests, and piles of plant debris, such as leaf mold and grass piles or sawdust. These beetles are most common in wooded areas and may occasionally be captured by hand. In spring, lay boards on ground to provide cover and check beneath them for beetles in early morning. Some species fly to lights, but most do not.
Examples. *Euplectus* species (30 species, most in e. U.S.) are more elongate than most pselaphids; body length is 1.2–1.5 mm. Like species of related genera, these have a 3- or 4-segmented antennal club. One species, *E. confluens* LeC., comprises 80% of the short-winged mold beetles in moist tree holes near Chicago; few beetles are found in dry cavities. Most of the 22 *Actium* species occur in

sw. U.S. These species have a curved *groove* at base of pronotum.
Antennal club consists of 1 segment that is as long as 4 or more
preceding segments. Species of closely related genera have similar
antennae. The 71 *Reichenbachia* species are 0.9–1.7 mm long, and
widely distributed. They have wings and many fly to lights, which
makes them easier to collect than most beetles in this family. (Species of many genera in this family are wingless and are never collected at lights.) Little is known of the habits of *Reichenbachia*
species, but some have been collected in association with ants; others have been captured in moist habitats, such as meadows and

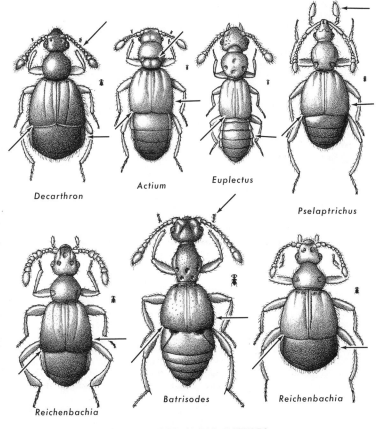

Decarthron

Actium

Euplectus

Pselaptrichus

Reichenbachia

Batrisodes

Reichenbachia

Fig. 43   SHORT-WINGED MOLD BEETLES

bogs. In this genus, the intermediate antennal segments of many males (and a few females) are enlarged, and sometimes lopsided.

In most short-winged mold beetles, each antenna has 11 segments, but the 27 *Decarthron* species (most in e. U.S.; usually 1.4–1.6 mm) have only *10 segments* in each antenna. The 31 *Pselaptrichus* species are more restricted in distribution than are members of most other large genera; all occur in w. U.S. In the 56 *Batrisodes* species (most in e. U.S.; 1.7–2.7 mm) the tarsal claws are markedly unequal in size — 1 claw is normal, the other is short and thin. These species typically occur in 2 types of habitats — in moist organic debris (rotting leaves or wood) on the forest floor, and in ant nests. A few also occur in meadows, in termite nests, or in caves. Some short-winged mold beetles live in caves in Ala. and Tenn.; these are predominantly 9 species of *Batrisodes*. Their eyes are typically very small (in some other cave-dwelling pselaphids eyes are absent). Usually only 1 species of *Batrisodes* is found in each cave. The apparent ability of a species to exclude other species of the genus from its cave habitat is not fully understood.

CARRION BEETLES: Family Silphidae
(Fig. 44; see also Pl. 2)

Identification. Large size, body shape, and antennal club usually distinctive: Body 3–35 mm (up to $1\frac{3}{8}$ in.), usually 10–35 mm. Elytra broad toward rear, either loosely *covering* abdomen or short, *exposing* 1–3 segments. Antennae clubbed; club *gradual* or *abrupt,* last 3 segments dull (lusterless), often hairy. Black, often with red, yellow, or orange markings on elytra or pronotum. Tarsi 5-5-5.

Similar families. Rarely confused with other beetles, see only: (1) sphaeritid beetles (p. 133) — surfaces shiny; W. Coast only.

Ranges and numbers. 10 genera and 46 species; widely distributed.

Habits. Most common on carrion, but sometimes found on decaying vegetation or living plants. Some dig beneath a small animal and bury it; eggs are then laid on carcass so larvae will have a ready food supply. Because host is buried, fly larvae will not compete with beetle larvae for food, and material will not dry out. Though there are reports that adults feed on carrion, close investigations show they feed on maggots and are the chief agents for reducing numbers of fly larvae at carrion. Though most carrion beetle larvae feed on various dead animals, some prey on snails, and a few eat plants and may damage spinach, beets, and other garden crops.

Collecting methods. Examine dead animals or rotting vegetable material. Sometimes beetles must be cleaned in soapy water to remove encrusted material in which they are found. Traps baited

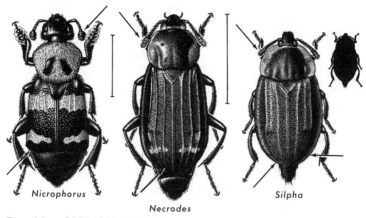

Nicrophorus

Necrodes

Silpha

Fig. 44   CARRION BEETLES

with dead animals of various sorts will attract carrion beetles. Different species are attracted to different kinds of animals; some to mammals, some to birds, some to snakes, some to fish. A few species are attracted to a variety of dead animals. One species comes most readily to carrion suspended in the air, as in a bait can. Some fly to lights.

Examples. The 19 *Nicrophorus* species (widely distributed) are known as sexton or burying beetles. They are typically black, with red markings on truncate elytra; large — 15-35 mm (up to 1⅜ in.); and 2nd antennal segment is very small, making antenna appear 10-segmented. A pair (♂ and ♀) typically digs beneath a small dead animal and buries it under soil to serve as larval food; working together, the two can bury the animal very rapidly. *N. americanus* (Oliv.), 27-35 mm, occurs in e. U.S. and is generally found on larger animals; it flies to lights. *N. marginatus* Fab., 20-27 mm, occurs from e. to sw. U.S. and is most common on dead snakes. Unlike other species of this genus, *N. tomentosus* Web. is attracted primarily to small dead animals suspended in air; its body length is 15-20 mm. The 2 *Necrodes* species (E. and W. Coasts of U.S.) are about the same size as members of *Nicrophorus* but their elytra have few or no red markings and are *rounded* at tip, not truncate; 2nd antennal segment is normal in size and each antenna is clearly 11-segmented. The 9 *Silpha* species (widely distributed; see also Pl. 2) are broad and flattened, and have elytra covering or nearly covering abdomen; they are 9-24 mm long. They are dull black and may have yellow or orange on their pronotum (see Pl. 2). Found primarily on dead mammals, snakes, fish, frogs, or other cold-blooded animals; *Silpha* species also occur on rotting vegetable material or rotting fungi and may damage crops. *S. inaequalis* Fab. (e. to cen. U.S., 10–14 mm) may be found on a variety of carrion nearly all year long. *S. lapponica* Herbst (Can. and w. U.S.) is most common on dead frogs, toads, and snakes; it is 9–13 mm long. *S. bituberosa* LeC. (cen. and n. U.S.) is called the **Spinach Carrion Beetle,** for larvae and adults sometimes damage spinach, beets, squash, pumpkins, and other vegetables. The **Garden Carrion Beetle,** *S. ramosa* Say (w. U.S.; 12–17 mm), generally feeds on decomposed vegetation, but also on garden and field crops, grasses, and weeds.

SMALL CARRION BEETLES:
Family Leptodiridae

Identification. Shape and antennae distinctive: Body *elongate-oval, narrowed* toward rear, often *widest* at pronotum, head *partly* visible from above; antennae with *loose, gradual,* usually 5-segmented club, 8th segment nearly always *very small.* Elytra usually with fine cross *striations.* Dull, rarely shiny. 1.7–6 mm.

Similar families. No other beetles have exactly this form and antennal structure, but families with at least some similar species include: (1) dermestid beetles (p. 192); (2) silken fungus beetles (p. 222); (3) marsh beetles (p. 149); (4) mammal-nest beetles (p. 125); (5) eucinetid beetles (p. 151); (6) throscid beetles (p. 177); (7) false darkling beetles (p. 264); and (8) round fungus beetles (p. 124).

Ranges and numbers: 10 genera and 81 species; widely distributed in N. America.

Habits. These are scavengers that live primarily in moist forests and are generally found in decomposing material such as carrion, humus, dung, and fungi. Some are found in forest litter, in soil, beneath bark, or in nests or burrows of small mammals, owls, tortoises, and ants; a few live in caves.

Collecting methods. The secretive habits of these beetles make them difficult to collect. They are best collected with traps or a Berlese funnel. Look for carrion or dung in the field or use it as bait in traps; check each trap often. Dung is usually better bait than carrion; bait placed in a cave can be effective. Put samples of leaf litter from forest floor, old stumps, and log debris through a Berlese funnel.

Examples. The 10 *Catopocerus* species occur in ne. U.S. and along the Pacific Coast. Unlike all other small carrion beetles, their hind coxae are widely separated or not touching. The 23 *Ptomaphagus* species (widely distributed; 2–3.5 mm) typically live in forest litter, but also in nests of small mammals, burrows of gopher tortoises, and ant nests. Some are specialized for life in caves, where they may be abundant — hundreds of specimens may be attracted to appropriate bait. In this genus there is a tendency for the eyes to be reduced according to habitat: Free-living species have large eyes; those in nests and burrows have smaller eyes; those in litter and humus have even smaller eyes; and those in caves have eyes that are greatly reduced or absent. The 8 *Catops* species (widely distributed) eat fungi and carrion; sometimes they live in mammal nests or on living animals and may be parasitic. *Colon*, with 26 species (1.5–3 mm), is the largest genus; its members are widely distributed.

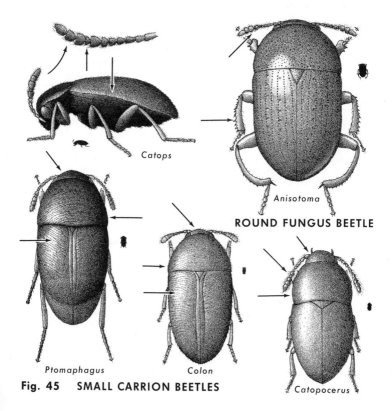

Catops

Anisotoma

ROUND FUNGUS BEETLE

Ptomaphagus   *Colon*

Fig. 45   SMALL CARRION BEETLES

Catopocerus

ROUND FUNGUS BEETLES:
Family Leiodidae

Identification. Body *oval* to nearly *spherical; convex* above, *flat* to *concave* below. Nearly half of the species are able to *roll into a ball* (Fig. 46). Dorsal surface hairless; *shiny,* usually *black,* sometimes brown, rarely with red. Each antenna ends in a 3- to 5-segmented *club;* when club is 5-segmented, 8th segment is often small. Tibiae often expanded and *spiny.* Hind coxae close together or touching. Elytra often striate. 1–6.5 mm.

Similar families. (1) Lady beetles (p. 231) are often similar but antennae short, club weak. (2) Shining mold beetles (p. 225) — antennal club always 3-segmented; tibiae not expanded. (3) Minute beetles (p. 149) — antennal club 2-segmented; hind coxae greatly expanded. (4) Pill beetles (p. 155) — dorsal surface usually sculptured and/or hairy; ventral surface usually convex. (5) Some pleasing fungus beetles (p. 226) are similar but hind coxae separated; many have red or orange elytral markings. (6) Wounded-tree beetles (p. 192) and some (7) sap beetles (p. 215) are similar but antennal club nearly round. (8) Minute fungus beetles (p. 229) — 0.5–2.2 mm long, with widely separated hind coxae.

Range and numbers. 17 genera and 126 species; widely distributed in N. America.

Habits. Adults and larvae most common on fungi, but also live on slime molds, in decaying vegetation, or under bark. Adults of several other beetle families are able to roll themselves up, but none can roll up as tightly as certain round fungus beetles.

Collecting methods. Collected fairly often in their habitats. Examine fleshy fungi and slime molds closely, sift or examine rotting vegetation, and look beneath dead bark. Just before sunset these beetles sometimes climb up foliage in woods or at edge of woods and may be captured with a sweep net.

Examples. The 29 *Leiodes* species (2–3.5 mm) and the 14 *Anisotoma* species (1.5–4 mm) have a 5-segmented antennal club with a very small 2nd club segment. They are not able to roll body up; members of both genera are widely distributed. *Leiodes* species occur on subterranean fungi while those of *Anisotoma* live in powdery fungi found on logs and dead trees. Species of *Anisotoma* bear antennal grooves on the ventral surface of their heads, which are not present in *Leiodes* species. The 46 *Agathidium* species (widely distributed; 2–4 mm) are black and shiny, have a 3-segmented antennal club, and are moderately to highly contractile. Nearly all of the highly contractile round fungus beetles you will encounter belong to this genus. When rolled up, some species form a solid, nearly spherical ball with their appendages completely concealed. They are most common on fungi beneath dead bark.

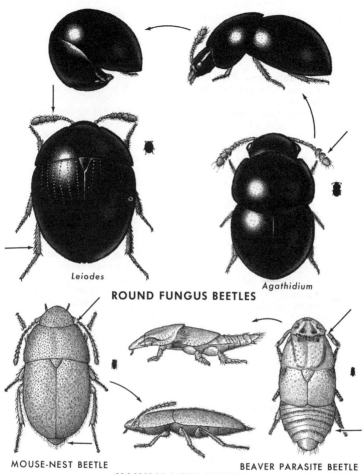

Leiodes

Agathidium

ROUND FUNGUS BEETLES

MOUSE-NEST BEETLE

BEAVER PARASITE BEETLE

MAMMAL-NEST BEETLES

Fig. 46

MAMMAL-NEST BEETLES:
Family Leptinidae

Identification. Form and habits distinctive: Body *flattened;* eyes *reduced* or absent; tip of abdomen exposed (4 species), or 4 segments *exposed* beyond elytra (1 species). These beetles live *in* *mammal nests.* Orange. Antennae long, each with a weak 3-segmented club (4 species), or short and highly modified (1 species). 2–5 mm.

Similar families. Few other beetles can be confused with these — see: (1) small carrion beetles (Fig. 45, p. 123) and (2) hairy fungus beetles (Fig. 103, p. 242).

Range and numbers. 3 genera and 5 species; widely distributed.

Habits. Found as parasites in nests and fur of beavers and rodents; also occur in nests of wasps and bees; sometimes these beetles live outside of mammal, wasp, and bee nests. They cannot fly.

Collecting methods. Usually collected only if you examine fur or nests of host mammals, or nests of ground-nesting bees and wasps. Sometimes found in large numbers in mammal nests, especially those of beavers. Infrequently captured away from hosts or nests.

Examples. Beaver Parasite Beetle, *Platypsyllus castoris* Rits., is an ectoparasite on beavers, and is adapted for life solely on this mammal. Occurs from cen. U.S. to Calif. and Alaska. Larvae and adults live in fur of host; larvae feed on particles from fur and skin. When grown, larvae crawl into the soil and pupate; after emerging, adults enter fur of host. The 2 *Leptinus* species (2–2.5 mm) usually live in nests and fur of mice, shrews, and moles. The **Mouse-nest Beetle,** *L. testaceus* Mull., has also been found with ground-nesting bees and wasps, but perhaps only after bees and wasps have taken over an old mammal nest. May be found outside of nests; occurs in e. U.S. to B.C. The 2 *Leptinullus* species live with beavers. The **Beaver-nest Beetle,** *L. validus* (Horn), is a parasite of the American beaver; it lives in Hudson Bay Territory. It can be very abundant — over 1000 individuals have been collected in a single beaver lodge.

FEATHER-WINGED BEETLES:
Family Ptiliidae

Identification. Size and characters often distinctive: Body is *minute* — 0.4–1.5 mm long, usually 0.6–1 mm. Flight wings *featherlike,* fringed with long hairs, often exposed beyond elytra; elytra often short. Body usually oval to elongate-oval. Antennae *long,* each with a club of 2–3 segments bearing long *hairs;* head usually visible from above. Scutellum often *large.* Usually hairy. Usually brown.

Similar families. (1) Minute beetles (p. 149) are able to partly roll themselves up. (2) Minute fungus beetles (p. 229) — pronotum usually conceals head. (3) Minute bog beetles (p. 102) — broadly oval with narrow pronotum. (4) Horse-shoe crab beetles (p. 128) — abdomen narrowed at tip.

Range and numbers. 19 genera and 111 species in N. America; most in e. U.S.

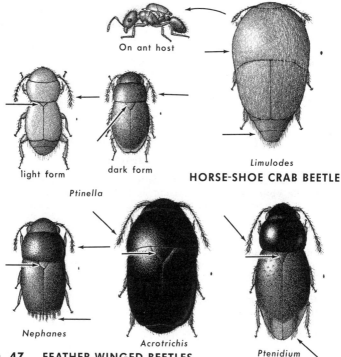

On ant host

Limulodes
HORSE-SHOE CRAB BEETLE

light form   dark form

Ptinella

Nephanes

Acrotrichis

Ptenidium

Fig. 47   FEATHER-WINGED BEETLES

Habits. The smallest of all beetles, nearly as small as any insect. Although common, they are not usually collected due to their small size and nocturnal habits. They live in moist, rotting organic material where they eat molds and fungi. Feather-winged beetles are abundant in forest floor litter, under bark, in tree holes, dung, moss, compost, dead fungi, etc.

Collecting methods. Habitat is similar to that of short-winged mold beetles (p. 118), and antlike stone beetles (p. 128), but feather-winged beetles are easily the most common family of these three. Species from this family can be collected by the same methods suggested for these other groups. Look closely when removing dead bark or examining rotten organic matter. Large numbers can be collected from good Berlese samples.

Examples. The 37 *Acrotrichis* species make this the largest genus; about ⅔ live in e. U.S. In these beetles the pronotum is widest at the base and the elytra are short and truncate. In the 12 *Ptenidium* species elytra cover abdomen and pronotum is widest before base and closely applied to sides of elytra; usually reddish to black and shiny. In the 6 species of *Nephanes* (e. U.S. to Iowa) the pronotum is widest before base with rectangular hind angles; elytra short. *Ptinella* species show extreme variation in form: Both sexes occur in a normal (dark) form and a vestigial (light) form, in which eyes are reduced to absent and wings are reduced (Fig. 47).

HORSE-SHOE CRAB BEETLES:
Family Limulodidae

Identification. Form and eyes distinctive: Body *oval,* widest at *middle,* elytra short and *exposing* tip of *tapering* abdomen; eyes much *reduced* or *absent.* Head inserted in prothorax. Legs short, stout. Each antenna has a long, 3-segmented club. 0.7–1 mm.
Similar families. (1) Some rove beetles (Tachyporinae, p. 116) similar but have eyes; antennal club weak if present; most 1–6 mm long. (2) Feather-winged beetles (p. 126) — never exactly this form. (3) Skiff beetles (p. 103) — no antennal club.
Range and numbers. 2 genera and 4 species in N. America; from e. U.S. to Ariz.
Habits and examples. Found in ant nests, including those in soil, tree stumps, or hollowed twigs. Adults feed on liquids secreted by ant larvae, pupae, and adults. These beetles frequently ride on their ant hosts (see Fig. 47). The *Limulodes* species are compact with retractile appendages; the body is protected, with few vulnerable areas. In the early history of these beetles, this body form is believed to have allowed them to withstand attack from ants. These adaptations may no longer be needed, for study shows that the beetles are accepted in ant nests and coexist peacefully with ants.

ANTLIKE STONE BEETLES:
Family Scydmaenidae

Identification. Form, size, and characters distinctive: Body *antlike.* Elytra *oval,* covering entire abdomen, widest near *middle,* often flattened at base. Humeri *rounded.* Pronotum a little *wider* than head; head with a distinct *neck.* Body minute to small (*0.6–2.5 mm*). Antennae *long,* hairy, each with a loose, 3- or 4-segmented *club.* Body shiny. Dorsal surface usually covered with long hairs. Legs long, femora enlarged at tip. Light brown to black. Maxillary palps often enlarged.

Similar families. (1) Grass-root beetles (p. 130) — larger at 3.5–6 mm; no antennal club. (2) Antlike flower beetles (p. 276) have threadlike antennae; usually larger at 1.7–4.3 mm. (3) Spider beetles (p. 196) — antennae threadlike or with a l-segmented club. (4) Short-winged mold beetles (p. 118) have short elytra.

Range and numbers. 22 genera and 181 species in N. America; most in e. U.S.

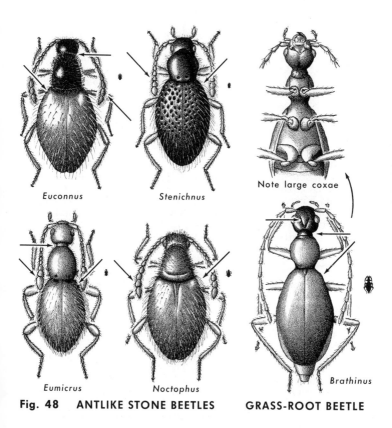

Euconnus

Stenichnus

Note large coxae

Eumicrus

Noctophus

Brathinus

Fig. 48   ANTLIKE STONE BEETLES   GRASS-ROOT BEETLE

Habits. Nocturnal in concealed, humid places, such as under bark, in rotting plant material, under objects on ground, in moss, in tree holes, or in ant or termite nests. Sometimes large numbers fly at dusk, but otherwise they are rarely observed.

Collecting methods. Habits and habitats are similar to those of short-winged mold beetles (p. 118), so a Berlese funnel is also useful for extracting specimens. When collecting under bark or in rotting plant material, look closely for these tiny beetles. Collect small flying insects at dusk. In early spring look underneath objects on ground.

Examples. *Noctophus* is easily the largest genus, with 84 species (most in e. U.S.); length is 0.8–2 mm. As in several other genera, pronotum usually widest at base. Some *Eumicrus* species (12 species; most in e. U.S.) reach 2.5 mm. Thorax is widest at middle, often has 2 depressions at base. Some of the 19 *Stenichnus* species (most in e. U.S.) bear elytral punctures; in these species pronotum is widest at middle. The 25 *Euconnus* species (0.7–1.6 mm) occur east of Rocky Mts.; in some the elytra are hairless or nearly so.

GRASS-ROOT BEETLES:
Family Brathinidae

Identification. Shape and characters distinctive: Body *antlike.* Head prominent, with a *neck* and a V-shaped *groove.* Pronotum somewhat *circular,* about as wide as head. Elytra *oval,* widest at middle, humeri *small.* Legs long, thin. Coxae large, *touching.* Antennae long, threadlike. Orange-brown to dark red brown. Dorsal surface smooth and shiny, may have sparse hairs. 3.4–6 mm.

Similar families. (1) Antlike flower beetles (p. 276) lack head groove, have dense hairs, and are 1.7–4.3 mm long. (2) Pedilid beetles (p. 274) have fine, dense hairs; elytra nearly parallel-sided; 4.5–15 mm long. (3) Spider beetles (p. 196) — head more or less concealed from above; body covered with dense hair. (4) Antlike stone beetles (p. 128) have a 3- or 4-segmented antennal club; 0.6–2.5 mm long. (5) Short-winged mold beetles (p. 118) have short elytra; body 0.5–5.5 mm long.

Range and numbers. Only 1 genus and 3 species in N. America; 2 in ne. U.S., 1 in Calif.

Habits and examples. Found among roots of grasses growing near water; larvae are unknown. The 2 e. U.S. species differ as follows: *Brathinus nitidus* LeC. is 4.2–5.2 mm long and the tip of each antenna is brownish, whereas *B. varicornis* LeC. is 3.3–3.6 mm long and tips of its antennae are white. Scientists believe that species of this family are most closely related to Subfamily Omaliinae of Staphylinidae (rove beetles).

Collecting methods. Rarely collected. Closely examine grasses growing in moist areas or put grass through a Berlese funnel.

SHINING FUNGUS BEETLES:
Family Scaphidiidae
(Fig. 49; see also Pl. 2)

Identification. Body form and elytra distinctive: Broadest near *middle,* each end *tapering.* Elytra *short,* tip nearly always *straight* across, usually *exposing pointed abdomen.* Dorsal and ventral surfaces *convex. Shiny, black* to *brown,* some with red or yellow spots. Legs long, slender. Each antenna usually ends in a gradual to abrupt club of 2–6 segments. Tarsi 5-5-5. 1.2–7 mm.

Similar families. These beetles are so distinctive that few other

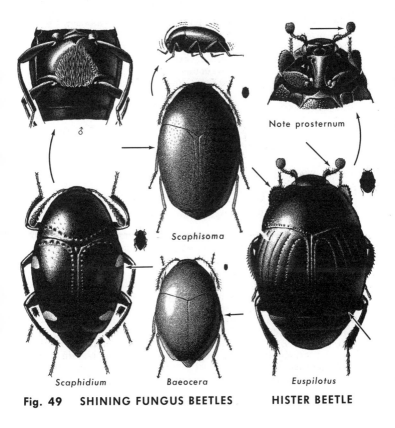

Note prosternum

Scaphisoma

Scaphidium   *Baeocera*   *Euspilotus*

Fig. 49   **SHINING FUNGUS BEETLES**   **HISTER BEETLE**

beetles are confused with them — see only hister beetles (p. 132) — tibiae enlarged; abdomen not pointed; antennae elbowed, with broad club.

Range and numbers. 6 genera and 50 species in N. America; most in e. U.S.

Habits. Adults and larvae are generally associated with fungi; they may be found on fungi, under dead bark, in rotten wood, or in rotting organic material. Adults run with a distinctive staggering gait when trying to escape.

Collecting methods. Examine fungi carefully, for some are very tiny and most run rapidly. Look in rotten wood, under bark, and in organic material. Examine fungi at night; some are active then. Collected with moderate frequency.

Examples. Most large species (usually 3.8–4.5 mm) belong to the genus *Scaphidium* (3 species, e. U.S. to Rocky Mts.) They are typically black and shiny but may have yellow or red spots (see Pl. 2); their pronota and elytra have rows of punctures, their eyes are notched, and the last 5 segments of each antenna form a club. ♂ has yellow hair on metasternum (Fig. 49). Most small species (usually 1.2–3 mm) belong to the genus *Baeocera* (15 species, 11 in ne. U.S.) or *Scaphisoma* (27 species, most e. U.S.). In both of these genera, the last 2–6 segments of each antenna form a slight club; members of these two genera differ by obscure antennal characters.

Superfamily Histeroidea

Nearly always black and shiny; only 2 families — 1 is common.

HISTER BEETLES: Family Histeridae
(Figs. 49, 50, see also Pl. 1)

Identification. Unique for antennal form and short elytra: Each antenna *short, elbowed,* with an *abrupt* 3-segmented club, usually inserted in a *cavity* on underside of prothorax. Elytra *short, exposing* tip of abdomen (rarely covering abdomen). *Prosternum expanded.* Body *hard;* nearly always *shiny* and *black,* sometimes brown, rarely with red or metallic green; usually hairless; round, oval, or cylindrical. Head withdrawn. Front tibiae *expanded,* often spiny. Tarsi 5-5-5 or 5-5-4. 0.5–20 mm (most 1–10 mm).

Similar families. Easily separated from similar groups by the antennae, elytra, and prosternum. See only: (1) sphaeritid beetles (p. 133); (2) shining fungus beetles (p. 131); and (3) certain water scavenger beetles (p. 104).

Range and numbers. 53 genera and 359 species in N. America; widely distributed.

Habits. Adults and larvae feed almost exclusively on insects and other small animals. Most occur in carrion, dung, decomposing plant materials (such as fungi), and tree wounds. Some live under loose bark or in galleries of wood-boring insects, where they prey on other organisms. The greatly flattened species live under bark of dead or dying trees; cylindrical species occur in tunnels of bark beetles and other wood-boring insects. Most species are neither flattened nor cylindrical and are abundant in the early stages of decay of carcasses; they typically eat fly maggots.

Collecting methods. Readily collected. Examine dead animals, dung, rotting vegetation, tree wounds, and bark of recently killed trees. Examine wood infested with borers.

Examples. *Euspilotus* species (28; widely distributed) have the typical hister beetle form. They are most common on animal carcasses — often fish, but also mammals, birds, and reptiles. Sometimes they are found in rotting vegetation. The 9 *Plegaderus* species (widely distributed; 1.3–1.5 mm) are unique for the *lengthwise groove* on each side of pronotum, which may connect with a transverse groove. Larvae and adults are beneficial for feeding on eggs and young of bark beetles. In *Paromalus* species (11 species; widely distributed) the scutellum is not visible. These beetles (most 2–3 mm) occur beneath bark or in rotting plant material. *Cylistix* species (5, e. U.S. to Tex.) are examples of the few cylindrical hister beetles. Unlike most hister beetles, the 6 *Onthophilus* species (widely distributed) have dorsal surfaces that are *heavily sculptured* with ridges and often with coarse punctures. The 30 species of *Margarinotus* and the 22 species of *Hister* (see Pl. 1) are mostly 3–7 mm and are widely distributed; their bodies are oval to oblong or cylindrical. Species of the 2 genera usually live on carrion, in mammal nests, and in rotting plant material. The 6 *Hololepta* species (widely distributed) are large (7–10 mm) and flattened. They are moderately common beneath bark of recently killed hardwoods; larvae and adults eat other insects. The 20 *Hetaerius* species (most w. U.S.) are unusual for bearing a *lobe* on each side of pronotum. They live in ant nests.

SPHAERITID BEETLES:
Family Sphaeritidae

Identification. *Black, shiny;* elongate-robust; dorsal surface *convex.* Head largely *concealed* from above. Elytra *striate, truncate,* loosely covering abdomen, exposing tip. Antennal club 3-segmented. Tibiae spiny. Tarsi 5-5-5. 3.6–5.6 mm.

Similar families. All similar families live throughout entire U.S. (1) Scarab beetles (p. 138) have a lamellate antennal club. (2) Hister beetles (p. 132) — antennae elbowed; elytra tight against abdomen. (3) Carrion beetles (p. 120) — surfaces nearly lusterless.

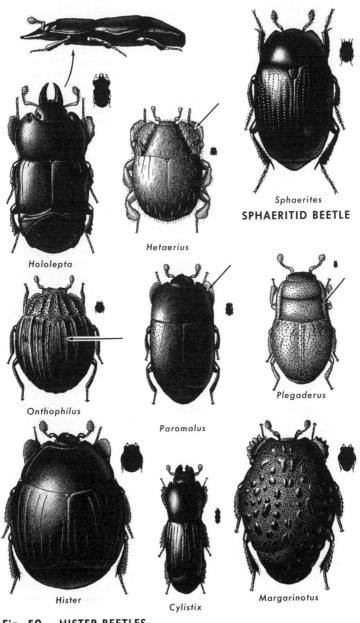

Hololepta

Hetaerius

Sphaerites
SPHAERITID BEETLE

Onthophilus

Paromalus

Plegaderus

Hister

Cylistix

Margarinotus

Fig. 50   HISTER BEETLES

Range and numbers. The single species, *Sphaerites glabratus* (Fab.), occurs on the W. Coast only, from Alaska to Calif.

Habits and examples. Associated with fungi; eat fungi or rotting plant material. *Sphaerites glabratus* (Fab.) resembles certain scarab beetles but is readily distinguished by form of its antennal club. Habits of this species are poorly known.

Collecting methods. Look in decayed fungi, dung, or under bark.

Superfamily Scarabaeoidea

Terminal segments of each antenna expanded sideways; often medium-sized to large.

STAG BEETLES: Family Lucanidae
(Figs. 51, 52; see also Pl. 7)

Identification. Antennae distinctive: each 10-segmented, with a *comblike* club of 3 or 4 segments that *cannot* be held together, antennae often *elbowed*. Mandibles of ♂ often *large* to *very large,* sometimes branched. Body elongate-robust; medium-sized to very large — 8–60 mm (up to $2\frac{5}{8}$ in.). Redbrown to black. Tarsi 5-5-5. Elytra may be striate.

Similar families. Beetles of similar size and antennal form are: (1) passalid beetles (p. 137) — antennae not elbowed; elytra distinctly striate. (2) Scarab beetles (p. 138) — segments of antennal club *can* be held tightly together.

Range and numbers. 10 genera and 30 species in N. America; about $\frac{2}{3}$ in w. U.S.

Habits. Larvae of all species bore in dead or decaying wood of logs or stumps, so are of little economic importance. Stag beetles usually occur in wooded areas. They lay their eggs in cracks of bark on stumps or logs. One species is found on sandy ground, especially along beaches of lakes or oceans. Adults are believed to feed on honeydew and sap from trees or leaves.

Collecting methods. Those that fly to lights in midsummer are most readily collected; they may remain beneath lights after sunrise. In wooded areas look around or chop into hardwood stumps and logs. One species is found along sandy shores of lakes and oceans. Stag beetles are infrequently collected, but are well worth looking for.

Examples. *Pseudolucanus capreolus* (L.) is often called the **Pinching Bug** for the ♂ has enlarged and fearsome-looking mandibles. When disturbed, it rears back with its head high and its mandibles open. Despite its threatening appearance it can be handled with little fear of injury, for it can do little more than give you a mild pinch. Actually, ♂ Pinching Bugs with large mandibles have less leverage for biting than do other stag beetles with short,

stout mandibles. It is reported that ♂ Pinching Bugs with large
mandibles will battle over a female. The Pinching Bug is 1 of 4
species (widely distributed) in this genus and occurs in ne. U.S.; it
is reddish brown and 22–40 mm long. It is often the most easily
collected stag beetle in its range, for it flies to lights in midsummer
and remains on ground after daylight. *P. placidus* (Say), not
shown, occurs from Penn. west to Kans. and is the most common
stag beetle in Kans. It is reddish brown, 19–32 mm, and has fine
silky hairs between pronotum and elytra and on ventral surface.
The **Giant Stag Beetle,** *Lucanus elaphus* Fab., Pl. 7, is our largest
stag beetle at 28–60 mm; it occurs from Va. and N.C. west to Okla.
Its size and appearance (especially of ♂) guarantee it will attract
attention. The **Antelope Beetle,** *Dorcus parallelus* Say (1 of 3
species in genus, all in ne. U.S.), is 15–26 mm long and dark brown
to black. Larvae feed in decaying stumps and logs of elm and other
trees. The 5 *Platycerus* species (widely distributed) are small (8–15
mm); the mandibles vary only slightly in males and females. *P.
virescens* (Fab.), 10–12 mm, occurs throughout N. America east of
Rocky Mts.; sometimes common in rotting logs. Of the remaining
species of *Platycerus,* 3 occur in w. U.S. and 1 in ne. U.S. The 7

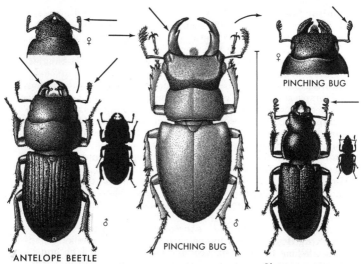

PINCHING BUG

♂

PINCHING BUG

♂

ANTELOPE BEETLE

Platycerus virescens

Fig. 51   STAG BEETLES

Platyceroides species occur from Calif. north to Wash., and are also small (8-15 mm). Sexual differences in mandibles are slight, but in ♀ front half of pronotum is more curved than in ♂. The **Oak Stag Beetle,** *Platyceroides agassizi* (LeC.), is 9-11 mm long and black; it breeds in dead stumps and logs of live oak, madrona, and tanbark oak in Calif. and Ore. The 3 species of *Diphyllostoma* occur in Calif.; they have prominent eyes and *long bristles* on sides of pronotum and elytra. Of the 4 *Ceruchus* species, 2 occur in ne. U.S. and 2 in w. U.S.; 10-16 mm. In these species the sexes differ in the shape of the mandibles. *C. piceus* (Web.) is found in rotting logs in ne. U.S.; it is dark brown. The **Rugose Stag Beetle,** *Sinodendron rugosum* Mann., the only member of the genus, occurs from Calif. to B.C.; it is 11-18 mm long and its head bears a short, backward-directed horn that is much more prominent in males than in females.

PASSALID BEETLES: Family Passalidae

Identification. Size, form, and color distinctive: *28-40 mm* (about $1\frac{1}{8}$-$1\frac{5}{8}$ in.); body elongate-robust, nearly *parallel-sided*. Head with a forward-directed *horn*. Body *black* and *shiny*. Elytra with lengthwise *grooves*. Pronotum with a median *groove*. Antennae not elbowed; each as a 3-segmented club with segments that *cannot* be held together. Pronotum and elytra *not touching* at sides. Tarsi 5-5-5.

Similar families. The only families similar in size and form of antennae are: (1) stag beetles (p. 135) — antennae nearly always elbowed; head never has a horn. (2) Some scarab beetles (p. 138) are as large as passalids, but segments of their antennal club can be held together.

Range and numbers. Only 2 genera and 3 species; 1 occurs throughout e. U.S., 2 in Tex.

Habits. Larvae and adults live in poorly organized colonies in logs. They feed on rotting wood containing microorganisms — newly hatched larvae will not reach maturity if fed only wood in which all microorganisms have been killed. Adults help larvae feed by prechewing wood. Logs in which these beetles feed are always rotted to some extent, so this group is not economically important. Though the adults have powerful mandibles that allow them to chew through solid oak, they can be handled safely, for they are docile and do not normally bite. Both larvae and adults produce sound by stridulating — rubbing their body parts together.

Collecting methods. These beetles do not fly to lights. Common in e. U.S. in large rotting logs — usually oak, but also other hardwoods (including hickory, gum, and sourwood) and sometimes softwoods. Large galleries with coarse frass indicate their presence. It is worth the effort to chop them out, for the **Horned Passalus** is

the largest showy beetle that collectors can find readily in e. U.S.
Examples. The **Horned Passalus** or **Bess-beetle,** *Odonto-taenius disjunctus* (Illig.), lives in e. U.S.; 2 species live in Tex.

SCARAB BEETLES: Family Scarabaeidae
(Figs. 52-57; see also Pls. 7 and 8)

Identification. Antennae distinctive, each with last 3-4 segments (rarely up to last 7) *lamellate* (rarely fan-shaped) — segments expanded laterally into oval or elongate lobes that can be *closed tightly;* each antenna consists of a total of 8-11 segments. Body form variable — usually stout and heavy-bodied, oval to elongate. Tarsi 5-5-5. 2-62 mm (nearly $2\frac{1}{2}$ in.), most 2-20 mm.
Similar families. Only those with similar antennae follow: (1) Stag beetles (p. 135) — antennae usually elbowed, with club segments that cannot be closed. (2) Passalid beetles (p. 137) — antennal club segments cannot be closed.
Range and numbers. 120 genera and about 1375 species in N. America; widely distributed.
Habits. Many are economically important and their habits are comparatively well known. Larvae of most of the injurious species live in soil, where they feed on roots; they are called white grubs. Adults usually eat leaves or fruit. A few larvae and adults live in nests or burrows of mammals. Adults and larvae of some species feed in humus or fungus. Larvae may feed in rotten wood, dry carrion, or skins; some live with termites. Some larvae that live in soil feed on animal dung; in some cases they live in a dung ball prepared by the adult beetle. Adults of certain tribes feed on pollen and sap. (For greater detail, see group treatments below.)
Collecting methods. Many scarab beetles are common and readily collected. The best collecting is generally at lights. Smaller humus- or dung-feeding beetles are in the air in great numbers in early spring, and, to a lesser extent, in fall. Examine dung (especially cow dung) and dig beneath deposits to find tumblebugs and various kinds of dung beetles (Scarabaeinae and Aphodiinae, and occasionally Geotrupinae). Some dung beetles are active at night, including some that are deep in burrows during day. *Geotrupes* species are attracted to bait cans containing water and small amounts of isoamylamine, butyric acid, propionic acid, asafoetida, or amyl acetate. Carrion will attract dung beetles and tumblebugs (Scarabeinae) and earth-boring dung beetles (Geotrupinae); hide beetles (Troginae) are attracted to the last stages of decay. Traps baited with fermenting malt or molasses with yeast attract some scarabs; dung or carrion may also be used as bait. Some species may be found on foliage, particularly at night. Flowers attract

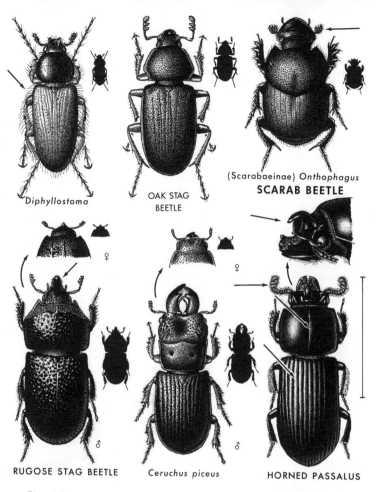

Diphyllostoma

OAK STAG BEETLE

(Scarabaeinae) *Onthophagus*
SCARAB BEETLE

♀

♀

RUGOSE STAG BEETLE

Ceruchus piceus

♂

♂

HORNED PASSALUS

Fig. 52   STAG BEETLES

PASSALID BEETLE

many species of flower beetles (Cetoniinae). A few species are found in leaf litter or decaying vegetation.
Subfamilies. Specialists recognize 13 subfamilies in N. America; 10 are included below.

DUNG BEETLES AND TUMBLEBUGS   (see also Pl. 7)
Subfamily Scarabaeinae
Members of this subfamily and the next subfamily (aphodiine

dung beetles, below) have hind legs situated *far back* on body, nearer tip of abdomen than middle legs or about midway between; antennal club is usually hairy. (In other subfamilies hind legs are nearer middle legs than tip of abdomen, and antennal club is smooth or sparsely hairy.) Unlike aphodiine dung beetles, these dung beetles (Scarabaeinae) have a pygidium that is partly exposed and a small scutellum that is usually not visible. Dung beetles and tumblebugs are robust, 2–30 mm long (nearly 1¼ in.), and generally dull black; some are colorful (see Pl. 7). Adults provide larvae with a stored food supply of a fecal pellet; larvae feed on this exclusively.

The 37 *Onthophagus* species (widely distributed) are 2.8–14 mm long; their middle and hind tibiae are dilated at the tips. *Onthophagus* species dig a burrow beneath fecal supply for their larvae. Members of the genus *Canthon* (18 species; widely distributed) are called tumblebugs. They are similar to *Onthophagus* species but they do not have dilated tibiae. Generally 10–22 mm and black. A pair of adults forms a mass of dung into a ball and rolls it to a suitable site, where they dig an underground chamber and bury the ball; ♀ lays an egg on it. *C. laevis* (Drury), 11–19 mm, occurs in much of U.S.; it is typically dull black with a coppery tinge, but in s. and w. U.S. it is deep blue or bright green.

Dichotomius carolinus (L.) (1 of 9 species in this genus), at 20–30 mm, is our largest dung beetle. This beetle is so powerful that it is difficult to hold in a tightly clenched fist. Its habits are similar to those of *Onthophagus* species. The 9 *Phanaeus* species (cen. and s. U.S.) often have green and red iridescence (see Pl. 7). Length is 12–22 mm; ♂ sometimes has a horn on head, ♀ does not.

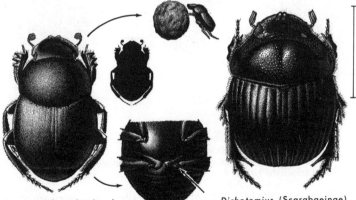

Canthon (Scarabaeinae)   Dichotomius (Scarabaeinae)

Fig. 53   SCARAB BEETLES

APHODIINE DUNG BEETLES Subfamily Aphodiinae
In these beetles elytra cover pygidium and scutellum is well-developed. Hind legs are closer to tip of abdomen than to middle legs. Generally 3–10 mm long, dark, and more elongate than dung beetles and tumblebugs. Most adults tunnel and form a dung ball underground for larva; some larvae live in soil or sand, feeding on organic matter or roots of plants. *Aphodius*, with 189 species (widely distributed), is one of the largest genera of the family. *Aphodius* species feed on humus or dung of higher animals and are abundant in cow dung. They are usually black, often with brown, yellow, or red; 3–12 mm long. They differ from members of the genus *Ataenius* (below) in having keel-shaped *ridges* on their middle and hind tibiae (Fig. 54). *Ataenius* contains 63 species, most in e. and s. U.S. Middle and hind tibiae lack transverse ridges or have only a trace of them; body is generally black and 2.5–6.5 mm long. Larvae feed in dung or in soils rich in organic matter; adults are common in spring flights and at lights.

EARTH-BORING DUNG BEETLES Subfamily Geotrupinae
In these 54 species each antenna is 11-segmented; in members of all other subfamilies each antenna has 8 to 10 segments. These beetles are quite stout-bodied and usually black or dark brown; a few are colorful. Adults are very secretive, spending most of their lives in deep burrows, sometimes beneath carrion or dung on which larvae feed. Burrows are generally marked by a low mound of dirt. Adults may feed on dung or fungi, but some species do not feed at all as adults. *Geotrupes* (9 species, e. U.S. to Rocky Mts.; 10–17 mm) is the best-known genus in this subfamily. In *Geotrupes* species the middle and hind tibiae have a pronounced transverse ridge; body color varies from iridescent blue or green to brown or black. Burrows of these dung beetles are generally shallow (only 1 ft. deep vs. 3–4 ft. in other genera) and larvae are provided with dung or humus.

CONTRACTILE SCARABS Subfamily Acanthocerinae
Only 3 species (e. U.S.; 3–6 mm); 2 belong to the genus *Cloeotus*. Beetles of this subfamily can *roll into a ball;* tips of their middle and hind tibiae are *greatly dilated.* They live under bark and in rotten logs and stumps, and may be found on dead trees at night. Larvae feed in decayed sapwood.

HIDE BEETLES Subfamily Troginae
41 of the 49 species belong to the genus *Trox* (widely distributed). They are 4–19 mm long; dorsal surface nearly lusterless, often with *ridges and tubercles.* Adults and larvae are among the last inhabitants of carcasses of fish, amphibians, reptiles, birds, and mammals. When these beetles are attracted to remains, there is generally little left but skin, fur, or scales, and bones. *Trox* species also

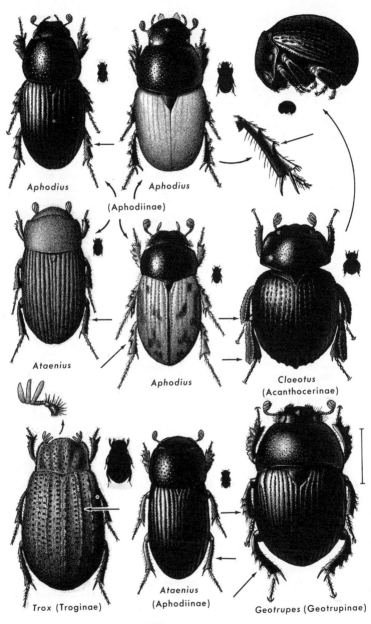

Aphodius

Aphodius

(Aphodiinae)

Ataenius

Aphodius

Cloeotus
(Acanthocerinae)

Trox (Troginae)

Ataenius
(Aphodiinae)

Geotrupes (Geotrupinae)

Fig. 54   SCARAB BEETLES

occur in nests of birds and burrows of mammals, especially those with masses of fur or feathers. Adults remain motionless when disturbed and are generally so encrusted with the material in which they live that they are easily mistaken for a piece of debris. Hide beetles are especially attracted to carcasses after a heavy rain — probably due to increased odor.

JUNE BEETLES, CHAFERS, AND OTHERS
Subfamily Melolonthinae   **(see also Pl. 7)**
A very large group (24 genera, nearly 500 species) all of which feed on plants; some are very serious pests. Tarsal claws often *toothed or double;* bases of antennae usually concealed from above. Larvae live in soil, where they feed on roots or humus. Adults are typically active at night and feed on foliage, flowers, and sometimes fruit.

Larvae of the genus *Serica* (73 species, widely distributed) prune roots of assorted plants near ground surface. Adults are usually 5–11 mm long, robust, and brown to black; they have faintly *striate* elytra, and often bear fine silky hairs. Some species have iridescent surfaces. In s. Calif. some species damage fruit-tree foliage. Larvae of the 120 *Diplotaxis* species (most in w. U.S., about a dozen in e. U.S.) eat roots or humus. Adults are nocturnal and feed on foliage of weeds, bushes, and trees, and rarely on crops. They are larger (6–14 mm) than *Serica* species; the 2 genera are separated by obscure characters. *D. popino* Casey (not shown) is one of the few harmful species. It is reddish brown to nearly black and its upper surface bears many fine, erect hairs. Adults may defoliate apple, peach, rose, walnut, and pear plants; some also eat green fruit. The adult **Asiatic Garden Beetle,** *Maladera castanea* (Arrow), may damage foliage and flowers of various plants; larvae feed on grass roots. It lives in much of ne. U.S.

Phyllophaga is a very large (131 species; widely distributed) and highly injurious genus. Adults are generally orange-brown to dark brown and 8–25 mm long; most have little or no hair on dorsal surfaces. Members of this genus are commonly known as may beetles or june beetles; they are leaf chafers that feed on foliage of various trees and bushes. When weather is cool and wet until late spring, then suddenly warm and dry, adults may emerge in hordes and cause heavy defoliation of trees. If spring warming is gradual, however, they emerge over a sufficient time span so damage caused by their feeding habits is negligible. Larvae are white and C-shaped, with the end of the body dark and broadened. Larvae are as harmful as adults and sometimes more so; they feed on roots of bluegrass, timothy, corn, soybeans, and other crops, and soil humus. The most severe crop damage occurs when crops are planted following removal of grass. Larval populations of *Phyllophaga* can be reduced by planting foods that are less appealing to larvae, such as alfalfa and clover, in rotation with more susceptible crops. This may starve the larvae, for the life cycle of some species takes 3 years. In late spring the ♀ lays pearly white eggs 1–8 in. deep in soil. Larvae feed throughout summer and in fall crawl downward and remain inactive in cool weather. Greatest damage occurs the following spring, when they move up to feed on roots and emerge as adults. Adults are attracted to lights in large numbers. *P. rugosa* (Melsh.) is a common and injurious species in e. U.S.; it feeds on a variety of trees, bushes, and even on grass.

The 28 *Dichelonyx* species (7–13 mm; widely distributed) are neither common nor economically important as pests. Larvae feed on tree roots; adult habits vary. The best-known species, *D. albicollis* (Burm.), feeds both day and night on pine needles, primarily those of jack pine, in e. U.S.

The 3 *Macrodactylus* species (widely distributed) are long-legged, tan, and 8–11 mm long. They are called rose chafers but in mating season they may be found in great numbers on other flowering plants besides roses. Rose chafers typically emerge as adults suddenly and in swarms that congregate on the nearest flowers. The **Rose Chafer,** *M. subspinosus* (Fab.), also feeds on grape, raspberry, blackberry, strawberry, peony, iris, dahlia, hollyhock, and other plants. It occurs from e. U.S. to Rocky Mts., and is most abundant in areas with light sandy soil; larvae feed on roots of various grasses and weeds. Adults emerge in late May and early June.

The 25 *Polyphylla* species (most in w. U.S.) include the **Ten-lined June Beetle** (see Pl. 7); members of this genus are distinctive for the greatly enlarged antennal clubs with many segments. They are 20–35 mm long (up to $1\frac{3}{8}$ in.) and most bear stripes of white hairs. Larvae feed on roots of shrubs and trees and can kill plants. Adults come to lights. The 16 *Hoplia* species (6–9 mm) are widely distributed; some western species are pests. The **Grapevine Hoplia,** *H. callipyge* LeC., eats blossoms, young leaves, and fruit of grapes, peaches, and almonds, as well as flowers of other plants.

SHINING LEAF CHAFERS   (see also Pl. 8)
Subfamily Rutelinae
Adults feed on foliage and fruit; larvae feed on roots. Some species are very colorful, and a number are serious pests. Members of this subfamily are distinctive for having tarsal claws of *unequal length,* especially on the hind legs.

The **Japanese Beetle,** *Popillia japonica* Newm., is probably the most injurious species of the family. It causes far more damage in this country than in Japan, its native habitat. First found in N.J. about 1916, it has since spread to much of ne. U.S. Its larvae feed on roots of many different plants, and are especially destructive in lawns, parks, golf courses, and pastures. Adults feed on foliage, flowers, and fruit of many different plants; damage is often severe when these beetles feed in groups. They are most active on

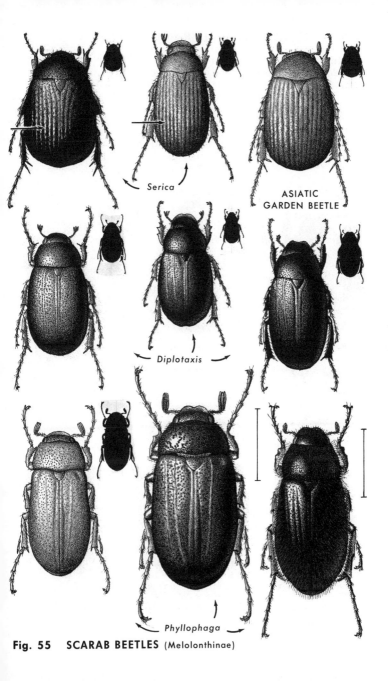

Serica

ASIATIC
GARDEN BEETLE

Diplotaxis

Phyllophaga

Fig. 55   SCARAB BEETLES (Melolonthinae)

warm sunny days. There are 2 species of *Pelidnota* (generally 20–25 mm). The **Spotted Pelidnota,** *P. punctata* (L.), is common in e. U.S. and occurs west to the Rocky Mts. Larvae feed in decaying roots and stumps of trees. Adults feed on foliage and fruit of grapes in midsummer and may damage vines.

The 4 strikingly attractive species of *Plusiotis* (sw. U.S.; see Pl. 8) are among the beetles that are most sought-after by collectors. *P. gloriosa* LeC. is the most common and colorful species. It feeds on juniper leaves at elevations above 4000 ft. and is found from the

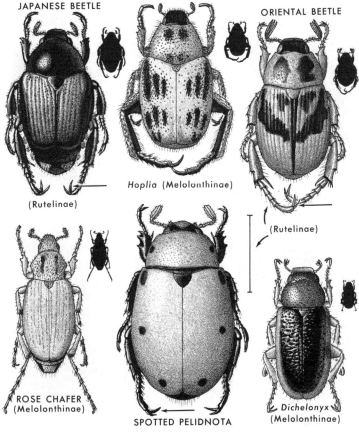

JAPANESE BEETLE

ORIENTAL BEETLE

Hoplia (Melolonthinae)

(Rutelinae)

(Rutelinae)

ROSE CHAFER
(Melolonthinae)

SPOTTED PELIDNOTA

Dichelonyx
(Melolonthinae)

Fig. 56   SCARAB BEETLES

Davis Mts. in Tex. to Pena Blanca, Ariz. *P. woodi* Horn is known only from the Davis Mts. and along the Rio Grande in Tex.; it feeds on walnut leaves. The other 2 species are similar to *P. woodi;* 1 has striate elytra. Larval habits of these species are not known. Most of the 31 *Anomala* species (6–15 mm; widely distributed) are of little economic importance, but larvae of the **Oriental Beetle,** *A. orientalis* Water., damage lawns in N.J. and N.Y. Damage to foliage and flowers by adults is minor.

RHINOCEROS BEETLES, HERCULES BEETLES, AND ELEPHANT BEETLES (see also Pl. 8)
Subfamily Dynastinae

Some of these are among our largest beetles; tropical species are among the largest of all insects. Males may reach nearly $2\frac{1}{2}$ in., and usually have *horns* on the *head* and/or *pronotum.* Tarsal claws are simple and usually equal in size; dorsal surface more or less convex. The largest species in N. America are the 2 of the genus *Dynastes.* The **Eastern Hercules Beetle,** *D. tityus* (L.) (40–62 mm; see Pl. 8), occurs in se. U.S.; ♂ bears an arching horn on both head and pronotum while ♀ has none. Larvae feed in decaying logs and stumps; adults fly to lights in spring and summer. The 9 *Bothynus* species are widely distributed; the **Carrot Beetle,** *B. gibbosus* (DeG.), 11–16 mm, occurs over much of U.S. **Carrot Beetle** larvae eat roots of carrots, celery, corn, potatoes, parsnips, sugar beets, and sweet potatoes; adults feed on foliage. The 5 *Strategus* species (mostly s. U.S.) always have depressions and tubercles on pronotum; males of some species have strongly developed *horns.*

FLOWER BEETLES AND OTHERS (see also Pl. 8)
Subfamily Cetoniinae

Many are found on flowers, where they feed on pollen; some live under bark or in rotting wood; a few live in ant nests. Tarsal claws are simple and equal in size; front coxae are conical; body is more or less flattened above. None of these beetles has horns. Larvae feed on roots, organic material in soil, or decaying trees. The 8 *Trichiotinus* species, most 9–12 mm, live primarily in e. U.S. to Rocky Mts. Adults are found on flowers; larvae feed in decaying hardwoods. *T. piger* (Fab.), 9–11 mm, is common on flowers of Jersey tea and wild hydrangea. The 2 *Trigonopeltastes* species (se. U.S.; see Pl. 8) have a distinctive triangular or V-shaped indentation on the pronotum. Adult habits are like those of *Trichiotinus.*

Cremastocheilus species (32 species; widely distributed) are unique among scarab beetles for living in ant nests. Adults are 9–15 mm long; mouth parts are *uniquely modified* (Fig. 57). The 3 *Valgus* species (ne. U.S., La., and Calif.) have *scales* on the dorsal surface, and widely separated rear coxae; body length is 4–8 mm. Adults are found on spring flowers. The **Green June Beetle,**

Cotinis nitida (L.), is 20–23 mm long (s. U.S.; see Pl. 8). Larvae feed on humus and roots in lawns and gardens; they have the habit of crawling on their backs. Adults eat foliage, flowers, and sometimes fruit and are active in daytime. The 3 other *Cotinis* species

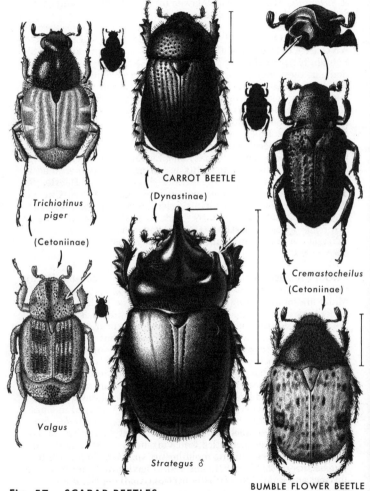

*Trichiotinus
piger*

(Cetoniinae)

CARROT BEETLE

(Dynastinae)

Valgus

Strategus ♂

Cremastocheilus
(Cetoniinae)

BUMBLE FLOWER BEETLE

Fig. 57   SCARAB BEETLES

occur in cen. and s. U.S. The **Bumble Flower Beetle,** *Euphoria inda* (L.), 13–16 mm long, is 1 of 26 species in its genus. In flight it looks and sounds like a bumblebee. Adults feed on fruit and flowers. Larvae develop in dung, rotten wood, and humus.

Superfamily Dascilloidea

These beetles are generally small and are often found on vegetation near water.

MINUTE BEETLES: Family Clambidae

Identification. Capable of *partially* rolling themselves into a *ball* (Fig. 58). Hind coxae *expanded.* Very small — *0.8–1 mm.* Each antenna has 8–10 segments; last 2 enlarged into a club. Body distinctly oval from above; orange to brown to black.
Similar families. (1) In round fungus beetles (p. 124) that roll up this capability is more developed; antennal club is 3–5 segmented. Other beetles similar in size and shape cannot roll up; see: (2) minute fungus beetles (p. 229); (3) shining mold beetles (p. 225); (4) pill beetles (p. 155); (5) feather-winged beetles (p. 126); (6) minute bog beetles (p. 102); and (7) certain sap beetles (p. 215).
Range and numbers. The 8 species belong to 3 genera; they are widely distributed.
Habits and examples. As is typical for very small beetles of no economic importance, habits are poorly known. Minute beetles are generally found in rotting plant material; they feed on molds. 6 species belong to *Clambus;* they are widely distributed.
Collecting methods. Collected infrequently. May be found in rotting vegetation, or flying in wooded areas at dusk; occasionally fly to lights.

MARSH BEETLES: Family Helodidae

Identification. Pronotum *short,* nearly always *concealing head,* sometimes *expanded* at front. Body *elongate-oval* to nearly *round.* Tarsi with 4th segment *lobed* beneath. Hind femora sometimes thickened (in 10 of 34 species). Black or brown, some with orange or red. Antennae threadlike or weakly sawtoothed, rarely featherlike. 2–5 mm.
Similar families. (1) Ptilodactylid beetles (p. 158) — 4–6 mm; scutellum heart-shaped. (2) Soft-bodied plant beetles (p. 152) — 3–40 mm; tarsal segments 2, 3, and 4 often lobed. (3) Hairy fungus beetles (p. 242); (4) shining mold beetles (p. 225); (5) minute fungus beetles (p. 229); and (6) dermestid beetles (p. 192) all have a distinct antennal club. (7) Lady beetles (p. 231) — slight antennal club. (8) Eucinetid beetles (p. 151) — hind coxae expanded. (9)

Small carrion beetles (p. 122) — 5-segmented antennal club. (10)
Sap beetles (p. 215) — abrupt 3-segmented antennal club. (11)
Some leaf beetles (Alticinae, p. 298) are also similar — see Figs. 130, 131.

Range and numbers. The 7 genera contain 34 species; most occur in e. U.S.

Habits. Adults are usually found in marshy areas or near water; larvae are associated with water or very damp places such as tree holes. Larvae are aquatic and feed on microorganisms that they filter out of the water with their mouth parts. Larvae have elongate, many-segmented antennae.

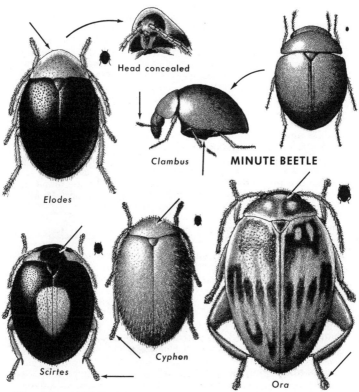

Head concealed

Clambus   **MINUTE BEETLE**

Elodes

Scirtes   Cyphon   Ora

Fig. 58   MARSH BEETLES

Collecting methods. Adults are most numerous near water in which larvae live (streams, springs, very damp areas, tree holes) and may be swept from foliage or captured on objects near water. Look in debris in rotting stumps. They fly to lights, and a light trap near larval habitat may be productive.

Examples. Adults of the genus *Elodes* (7 species; e. U.S., Tex., s. Calif.) live along streams, around springs, or under stones and debris near water; most are 2.5–5 mm long. *E. aquatica* Blaisdell lives under objects that project into water. When these beetles fall into water, some gyrate the way whirligig beetles do; others dive beneath the surface and swim rapidly. Species of *Cyphon* (13 species, widely distributed; 2–4 mm) and *Scirtes* (7 species, e. U.S., Ariz., and Calif.; 2.5–3.5 mm) are usually found on vegetation near water or in damp places where larvae occur. Larvae of *Cyphon* live among dead leaves in ponds, in wet moss around edges of springs, or under stones in a spring; some have been found in tree holes. Adults sometimes occur on flowers. Like flea beetles (p. 298), *Scirtes* species have greatly enlarged hind femora and can jump.

The only other marsh beetles with enlarged femora are the 3 species of *Ora* (Fla. and Tex.; up to 5 mm). Adults of the 2 *Prionocyphon* species (3.5–4.5 mm) hide under dead leaves or are found on fallen branches in woods in e. U.S. Larvae live in standing water in tree holes. Larvae of *P. limbatus* LeC. eat dead leaves. ♂ has featherlike antennae (Fig. 59, p. 153).

EUCINETID BEETLES:
Family Eucinetidae

Identification. Form and hind coxae distinctive: Body *elongate-oval*, narrowed *toward rear;* head *concealed* from above and *resting against front coxae;* hind coxae greatly *expanded* and oblique, *concealing* much of first abdominal segment. Tibiae *enlarged* at tips. Each antenna is 11-segmented, long, and *threadlike.* Elytra often have fine *cross-striations.* Brownish yellow to black, sometimes with tip of elytra reddish. Tarsi 5-5-5. 2.5–4 mm.

Similar families. Members of numerous families are similar in appearance, but none have hind coxae so expanded, and many have clubbed antennae. See: (1) marsh beetles (p. 149); (2) chelonariid beetles (p. 159); (3) small carrion beetles (p. 122); (4) false darkling beetles (p. 264); (5) throscid beetles (p. 177); (6) dermestid beetles (p. 192); and (7) pleasing fungus beetles (p. 226).

Range and numbers. 2 genera and 8 species; 6 in e. U.S., 2 in Calif.

Habits and examples. Adults and larvae occur under bark, in logs, or in fungi; scientists assume that they eat fungi. Adults can jump. There are 6 *Eucinetus* species in e. U.S. Three of these species have punctures on elytra: *E. oviformis* is black and its elytra are weakly striate near tips; *E. testaceus* is brownish yellow; and *E. punctulatus* is brown to black. In the other 3 *Eucinetus* species, the elytra have punctures and fine transverse striae. Of these last 3, *E. morio* LeC. has 2 hind tibial spurs and is nearly black; *E. terminalis* LeC. has 1 tibial spur and reddish tips on its elytra; *E. strigosus* LeC. has 1 tibial spur and is black.

Collecting methods. Collected infrequently. Look beneath bark, in rotting logs, or in fungi. These beetles sometimes fly to lights.

SOFT-BODIED PLANT BEETLES:
Family Dascillidae

Identification. Similar to many other beetles and often difficult to distinguish. Tarsi 5-5-5; segments 1-4 *lobed* beneath. Elytra nearly parallel-sided, *striate*. Pronotum usually narrowed at front, often with nearly straight sides. Head usually concealed from above. Antennae long, threadlike, or sawtoothed. Usually hairy. Most are brown to black. 3-40 mm long (up to $1\frac{1}{2}$ in.).

Similar families. (1) Click beetles (p. 172) — prothorax freely movable. (2) Comb-clawed beetles (p. 256) — tarsi 5-5-4, with comblike claws. (3) Rare click beetles (p. 177) — hind trochanters very long. (4) Click beetles (p. 179) — hind angles of pronotum extended. (5) Perothopid beetles (p. 179) — claws comblike. (6) Ptilodactylid beetles (p. 158) — antennae often comblike. (7) False darkling beetles (p. 264) — tarsi 5-5-4. (8) Texas beetles (p. 159) — each antenna expanded and sawtoothed from 5th segment. (9) Fruitworm beetles (p. 240) — tarsal segments 2 and 3 lobed. (10) Marsh beetles (p. 149) — 2-5 mm.

Range and numbers. Most of the 16 species (8 genera) occur in w. U.S.

Habits. Larvae live in soil (sometimes very moist) or are aquatic; some feed on roots of bushes or trees, others eat grass roots or leaf mold. Adults are generally found on foliage in moist areas; some eat plants, others are carnivorous.

Collecting methods. Sweep or beat foliage beside streams or other bodies of water. In Calif. look on fruit trees in early spring for *Dascillus* species. Most are uncommon.

Examples. Davidson's Beetle, *Dascillus davidsoni* LeC., is the largest soft-bodied plant beetle, reaching 10-40 mm (up to $1\frac{1}{2}$ in.). Larvae feed on roots of snowberry, acacia, apple, and cherry. Adults appear in early spring and feed on fruit trees. Both species of *Dascillus* occur in Calif.; their tarsi have distinct lobes underneath. The 3 *Anorus* species occur in Ariz. and Calif. These beetles differ from *Dascillus* species in that the front coxae of *Anorus* species are prominent and touch each other.

The 3 *Macropogon* species (not shown) occur in ne. U.S., west to

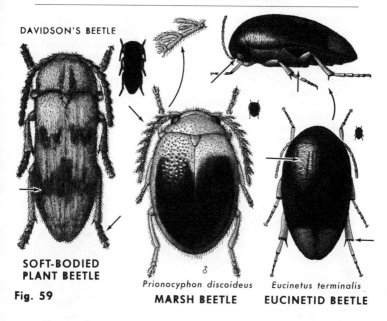

DAVIDSON'S BEETLE

SOFT-BODIED
PLANT BEETLE

Fig. 59

Prionocyphon discoideus
MARSH BEETLE

Eucinetus terminalis
EUCINETID BEETLE

Calif. and north to Canada. Their antennae are slender; segments 2-4 are very short, so their combined length is not longer than that of the 5th segment. *M. rufipes* Horn is black with reddish brown legs and antennae; body about 5.5 mm long. *Eurypogon* contains 4 species; 3 in ne. U.S. to Kans., 1 in Calif. They differ from *Macropogon* species in that antennal segments 2 and 3 are short and their combined length equals that of the 4th segment.

CEDAR BEETLES: Family Rhipiceridae

Identification. Size, form, antennae, and tarsi distinctive: *11–24 mm;* body elongate; sides of elytra *nearly parallel;* pronotum *narrowed* at front. Antennae *short; sawtoothed* to *lamellate. Lobe* present between tarsal claws (Fig. 60). Humeri prominent. Reddish brown to black. Tarsi 5-5-5. Scutellum semicircular.

Similar families. (1) Some long-horned beetles (p. 279) are similar but their antennae are always threadlike. (2) Cebrionid beetles (p. 171) — mandibles prominent; antennae threadlike.

Range and numbers. Just 2 genera and 6 species in N. America; 4 in e. U.S. to Tex. and 2 in sw. U.S.

Habits and examples. Larvae of 1 species live in decayed wood; those of the other 5 are parasitic on cicada nymphs. Adults generally are found on tree trunks or foliage. *Sandalus niger* (Knoch) is the most frequently collected e. U.S. species and ranges as far west as Tex.; length is 21–24 mm. On one day in late September, near Bloomington, Ind., 12 specimens were collected on hickory trunks or in flight in just 1 hour. Collecting at the same time in the same place during previous years had yielded no specimens. It is likely that these beetles were parasites of the brood of periodical cicadas which had emerged the previous year.

Collecting methods. Look on tree trunks in spring or fall, or sweep foliage of trees. Species are infrequent to rare.

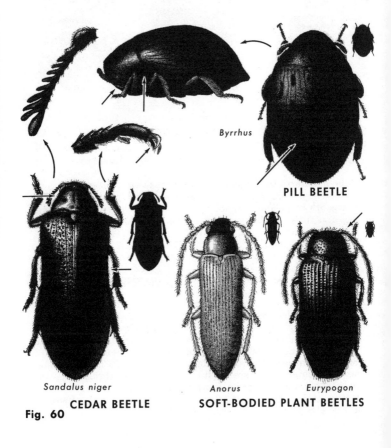

Byrrhus

PILL BEETLE

Sandalus niger
CEDAR BEETLE

Anorus   *Eurypogon*
SOFT-BODIED PLANT BEETLES

Fig. 60

Superfamily *Byrrhoidea*

Includes a single family of small beetles.

PILL BEETLES: Family Byrrhidae

Identification. Body broadly *oval;* dorsal surface *convex,* ventral surface usually convex. Head directed *downward,* usually *concealed* from above. Body often has *depressions* into which legs fit; surface usually dull. Each antenna 11-segmented — usually clubbed, with the last 3–7 segments gradually enlarged; sometimes threadlike. Gray, brown, or black. Usually with *hairs* (sometimes bristles) or *scales* on dorsal surface. 1.5–10 mm.
Similar families. (1) Dermestid beetles (p. 192) that are similar have ocelli on head and abrupt antennal club. (2) Seed beetles (p. 304) nearly always have a short beak and pygidium showing beyond tip of elytra. (3) Some death-watch beetles (p. 199) are similar but antennal club is always lopsided. (4) Fungus weevils (p. 307) nearly always have a short, broad beak and an exposed pygidium. (5) Wounded-tree beetles (p. 192) have an abrupt antennal club, tibiae broadened toward tip, and head directed forward. (6) Monommid beetles (p. 245) have no hairs or scales on dorsal surface, an abrupt antennal club, and head directed forward. (7) Minute fungus beetles (p. 229) have a flat ventral surface; body length 0.5–2.2 mm. (8) Round fungus beetles (p. 124) — dorsal surface hairless and shiny. (9) Sap beetles (p. 215) — abrupt 3-segmented antennal club. (10) Certain darkling beetles (p. 249) are similar but base of each antenna is concealed from above.
Range and numbers. The 14 genera and 42 species occur throughout N. America but most in w. U.S.
Habits. When adults are disturbed they pull in their appendages and remain motionless, which makes them look like pills (and gives them their common name). Both larvae and adults are plant-feeders, and are generally found in moist soil or sand, in moss, under bark, or under objects on ground. A few species may be minor pests of young trees in nurseries or plantations. Some feed on roots of wild grasses, weeds, oats, and clover. One species damages various vegetables and lilies.
Collecting methods. Members of this family are collected infrequently. They are most common beneath objects on ground, in moss, under bark, or near roots of grasses — especially grass growing in very sandy areas. *Byrrhus* species sometimes occur on young trees in nurseries or in plantations; some are most common along lake beaches. Certain species fly to lights.
Examples. Some of the 6 *Byrrhus* species (n. U.S. and Canada) occasionally injure young trees or seedlings and may be common in areas with sandy soil. Their body length of 5–10 mm makes

them among the largest pill beetles. Though most of our pill beetles have scales or hairs on dorsal surface, the 3 *Amphicyrta* species (length 5.8–9.3 mm; all in w. U.S.) lack these features. The **Pasture Pill Beetle,** *A. dentipes* Er. (Calif.; 6–8 mm), lives in holes in the ground and emerges to feed on wild grasses, clovers, oats, and weeds; it is sometimes common. The largest genus is *Curimopsis* (8 species), which occurs nearly throughout U.S. and into Canada; it includes the smaller pill beetles. *Curimopsis* species have striate elytra and may have bristles on the dorsal surface (Fig. 61). The 2 *Cytilus* species are more common than other pill beetles in e. U.S.; their range extends into Canada and to the Rocky Mts. They typically live on moss in sandy areas.

Superfamily Dryopoidea

Nearly all are aquatic, semiaquatic, or live on foliage beside streams. They often have long legs with stout claws.

WATER-PENNY BEETLES: Family Psephenidae

Identification. Body *oval, flattened.* Elytra often broadened *toward the rear, loosely* covering *broad, flat* abdomen. Found in or beside *streams.* Base of pronotum *sinuate* (with an arched margin) or finely *toothed.* Antennae threadlike, sawtoothed, comblike, or fan-shaped. Dorsal surface sparsely hairy; ventral surface covered with fine dense hairs. Head partly to completely concealed from above. Maxillary palps sometimes elongate. Scutellum often large. Brownish to black. Tarsi slender, 5-5-5. 3–7 mm.
Similar families. (1) Marsh beetles (p. 149) — 4th tarsal segment lobed beneath. (2) Soft-winged flower beetles (p. 211) — often bear bristles. (3) Leaf beetles (especially Subfamily Galerucinae, p. 296) — tarsi broad, apparently 4-4-4. (4) Riffle beetles (p. 163) and (5) long-toed water beetles (p. 162) live in similar habitats but look different (see Figs. 64 and 65).
Range and numbers. 5 genera and 13 species; 3 in ne. U.S., 10 in w. U.S.
Habits. Larvae cling to stones in clear streams with rocky or gravel bottoms. Their common name is derived from the shape of their broad, flat, nearly round bodies; this body form is unique among beetles. Larvae feed on microscopic plants and small animals. Adults are believed to eat plants and are found beside streams, usually on rocks at stream edges. ♀ enters water to attach eggs to submerged stones; a film of air held by the dense hairs on her body allows her to breathe underwater.
Collecting methods. Look carefully on rocks that are partially

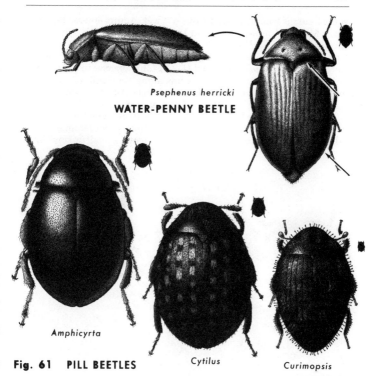

Psephenus herricki
WATER-PENNY BEETLE

Amphicyrta

Fig. 61   PILL BEETLES

Cytilus

Curimopsis

submerged in riffles of shallow streams with rocky or gravel bottoms. In w. U.S. also sweep vegetation adjacent to such streams.
Water-penny beetles are difficult to see when they are motionless,
but periodically run back and forth along rocks. They are rarely
collected unless you look in their habitats but are sometimes numerous in appropriate habitats.

Examples. The genus *Psephenus* contains 7 species — 1 in ne.
and 6 in w. U.S. Unlike other water-penny beetles, in this group
the head is visible from above. Adults are sometimes abundant on
stones or objects protruding from riffles or rapids. Females creep
about on underwater stones looking for egg-laying sites, so females
collected may be in poor condition. Males cling to the surface of
stones and other partially submerged objects, and are more likely
to be collected. Mature larvae crawl out of water and pupate along

shore in areas where it is moist but not wet. Adults emerge between early May and mid-August and live for about a week. The single species in ne. U.S., *P. herricki* (DeKay), and *P. falli* Casey (Calif., Ore., and Idaho) are markedly similar in appearance and habits. Larvae of *Eubrianax edwardsi* (LeC.) (only species in genus) live on rocks in small freshwater streams along the Calif. coast. They pupate underwater in their old larval skin. Adult beetle is 3.5–5 mm long and brown to black; ♀ antennae are threadlike, those of ♂ are *comblike.* The 3 *Acneus* species (Calif. and Ore.; not shown) have fan-shaped antennae; antennae of males and females of all other water-penny beetles are threadlike, sawtoothed, or comblike.

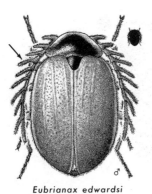

Eubrianax edwardsi
WATER-PENNY BEETLE

Fig. 62

Ptilodactyla
PTILODACTYLID BEETLE

PTILODACTYLID BEETLES:
Family Ptilodactylidae

Identification. Distinctive for scutellum, tarsi, and antennae: Scutellum *heart-shaped.* 3rd tarsal segment distinctly *lobed* beneath. Antennae of ♀ *sawtoothed;* of ♂ *comblike,* with most segments having a long, thin projection at the base. Body elongate-oblong, sides nearly parallel, head largely concealed from above. Body covered with moderately dense hairs. Elytra striate. Orange-brown to dark brown, sometimes partly or mostly black. Tarsi 5-5-5, 4th segment small to minute. 4–10 mm.

Similar families. The few other beetles that can be confused with these beetles do not have the above combination of characters — see: (1) soft-bodied plant beetles (p. 152); (2) comb-clawed beetles (p. 256); and (3) death-watch beetles (p. 199).

Range and numbers. Only 4 genera and 10 species in N. America; from e. U.S. to Tex. and Ariz.

Habits and examples. Larvae live in moist rotting logs of deciduous trees; some have gills for breathing underwater. Adults are found on leaves in or near wooded areas near water. *Ptilodactyla serricollis* (Say), 4–6 mm, has the widest distribution of any species (much of e. U.S.), and is collected with some frequency. There are 6 species in *Ptilodactyla*.

Collecting methods. Sweep or beat vegetation near lakes, ponds, marshes, or swamps. Adults of most species are uncommon.

CHELONARIID BEETLES:
Family Chelonariidae

Identification. Antennae and pronotum distinctive: Base of each antenna fits into a *groove* in middle of sternum; 1st segment small, 2nd and 3rd segments *enlarged,* 4th segment small, segments 5–10 *sawtoothed,* 11th segment broad. Pronotum with *lateral margin extending* over head, concealing it from above; pronotum with series of *teeth* at base (Fig. 63). Front tibiae broad and flat. Elytra with patches of white hair, not striate. Body elongate-oval. Red-brown to dark brown. Tarsi 5-5-5, 3rd segment lobed. 6.5–7.2 mm.

Similar families. Similar beetles never have antennae and pronotum as described above; see: (1) monommid beetles (p. 245); (2) wounded-tree beetles (p. 192); (3) dermestid beetles (p. 192); (4) pleasing fungus beetles (p. 226); (5) death-watch beetles (p. 199); (6) pill beetles (p. 155); (7) eucinetid beetles (p. 151); and (8) ptilodactylid beetles (p. 158).

Range and numbers. Our only species is known from se. U.S. west to Ark. and e. Tex.

Habits and examples. The only species, *Chelonarium lecontei* Thom., is found infrequently on foliage; larvae occur in leaf litter. Adult is able to draw in its head and appendages close to body where they fit into depressions.

Collecting methods. Usually swept from foliage; rare.

TEXAS BEETLES:
Family Brachypsectridae

Identification. Form and characters distinctive: Body clearly *flattened;* hind angles of pronotum *extended* backward and *ridged.* Each antenna has 11 segments, *expanded* and *sawtoothed* from

5th segment to tip. Yellow-brown. Elytra *striate,* sides nearly parallel. Dorsal surface sparsely covered with bristly hairs. Tarsi 5-5-5. 4.6–6 mm.

Similar families. (1) Click beetles (p. 172) — pro- and mesosterna produced into a clicking mechanism; body rarely clearly flattened. (2) False click beetles (p. 179) — antennae sawtoothed with teeth from 3rd or 4th segment to tip. (3) Rare click beetles (p. 177) — antennae sawtoothed from 3rd segment to tip in ♀, comblike in ♂. (4) Perothopid beetles (p. 179) — antennae threadlike; occur in e. U.S. and Calif. (5) Soft-bodied plant beetles (p. 152) — antennae not as above.

Range and numbers. The single species has been collected in Tex., Utah, Ariz., and Calif.

Habits and examples. Adults of *Brachypsectra fulva* LeC. have been collected under bark; larvae feed on spiders. Larvae secrete a liquid that attracts spiders and disables them; larvae then pin spiders down and eat them. These beetles pupate in a silken cocoon.

Collecting methods. Very rarely collected — look beneath bark.

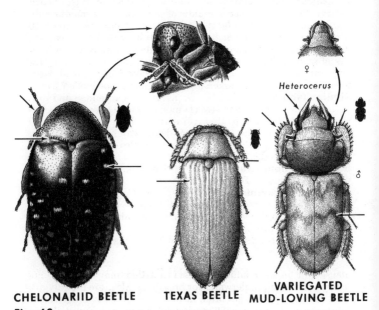

CHELONARIID BEETLE   **TEXAS BEETLE**   **VARIEGATED MUD-LOVING BEETLE**

Fig. 63

VARIEGATED MUD-LOVING BEETLES:
Family Heteroceridae

Identification. Form and often color distinctive: Body *robust.* Elytra nearly parallel-sided. Pronotum *broad.* Tibiae *flattened, spiny.* Antennae *short, sawtoothed.* Mandibles *large,* especially in ♂. Usually light to dark brown; elytra usually marked with *wavy* dark bands. Covered with *dense silky* hair. 1–8 mm.

Similar families. None duplicate the form, tibiae, antennae, and color of these beetles; those most similar are: (1) fruitworm beetles (p. 240); (2) some silken fungus beetles (p. 222); and (3) a few hairy fungus beetles (p. 242).

Range and numbers. Though there is little diversity within this family, there are 10 genera for the 28 species; widely distributed.

Habits and examples. Adults and larvae dig burrows in mud, clay, or sand along streams, ponds, or lakes. Adult burrows are usually marked by chimneys. Some adults scavenge on animal material; larvae feed on either plant or animal materials. *Heterocerus pallidus* Say, 3.8–6.7 mm, is widely distributed and occurs in e. U.S. to Ariz. and north into Canada. Markings vary from distinct to vague or absent.

Collecting methods. Sometimes common. Splash water along shores of streams, ponds, or lakes to force these beetles from their burrows. They may fly readily. May fly to lights in good numbers.

MINUTE MARSH-LOVING BEETLES:
Family Limnichidae

Identification. Similar to long-toed water beetles, but small (0.7–2.5 mm); antennae *sawtoothed* or *clubbed.* Clothed with dense short hairs. Legs long, claws often large; legs often fit into body grooves.

Similar families. (1) Long-toed water beetles (p. 162) — 1–8 mm; antennae comblike. (2) Riffle beetles (p. 163) — 1–8 mm; antennae threadlike or clubbed, rarely hairy.

Range and numbers. The 4 genera and 32 species are widely distributed.

Habits and examples. Adults and larvae occur on banks of streams, in leaf litter, in wet rotten wood, or in moss. The fine dense hair on some adults suggests that they may submerge and carry a film of air underwater for breathing. Most are broadly oval and convex; appendages often fit into body grooves. Some species of the genus *Limnichus* (26 species; 1.2–2 mm; widely distributed) can retract head into thorax so even their eyes are concealed. *L. tenuicornis* (Casey) occurs in wet, springy hillsides. A species of

Throscinus (3 species; Tex. and s. Calif.) lives in mud flats near San Diego that are covered at high tide. The 2 *Lutrochus* species occur in e. U.S. to Tex.; antennal segments 3–11 are sawtoothed.
Collecting methods. Closely examine sandy or muddy banks of streams or other typical habitats. Throwing water over a bank may force these beetles to the surface.

LONG-TOED WATER BEETLES:
Family Dryopidae

Identification. Form, antennae, and coxae distinctive: Elytra more or less *cylindrical,* usually *striate.* Pronotum not as wide as elytra, sides *arched,* front tips of pronotum *pointed.* Antennae

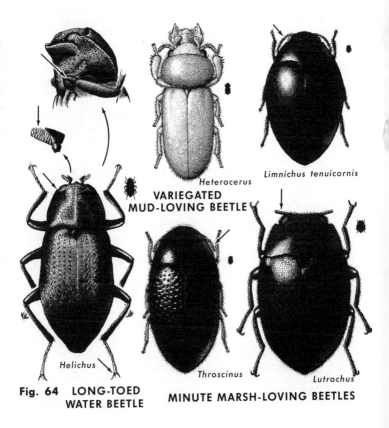

Limnichus tenuicornis

Heterocerus
**VARIEGATED
MUD-LOVING BEETLE**

Helichus

**Fig. 64   LONG-TOED
WATER BEETLE**

Throscinus

Lutrochus

MINUTE MARSH-LOVING BEETLES

short, comblike, often *concealed.* Front coxae *transverse* (not round). Hairs fine, dense, often *silky,* sometimes (in 2 species) bristly. Black, brown, or dull gray. Legs and claws *large.* 4–8 mm.

Similar families. (1) Riffle beetles (below) — antennae usually longer and threadlike, front coxae nearly always round (not transverse). (2) Water-penny beetles (p. 156) — elytra loosely cover abdomen. (3) Minute marsh-loving beetles (p. 161) — 0.7–3 mm long; antennae moderately long and weakly clubbed.

Range and numbers. The 3 genera and 15 species are widely distributed, most in w. U.S.

Habits. Adults are semiaquatic to fully aquatic, though none can swim. They cling to vegetation or debris in well-aerated streams or live beneath objects in water. Adults eat vegetation; larvae eat roots or very small plants and animals in water. Dense hairs of most adults trap air for breathing underwater; oxygen that diffuses in is enough for their unhurried life. Riffle beetles (below) respire the same way.

Collecting methods. Remove vegetation and debris from riffle areas of streams and examine it closely. Aquatic nets in streams, ponds, and lakes may catch some specimens. These beetles fly to lights, sometimes in good numbers.

Examples. The 2 *Pelonomus* species occur primarily in sw. U.S.; their hair is bristly. *P. obscurus* LeC. lives in lakes and ponds; it may come to lights in large numbers. The 11 *Helichus* species (5–6 mm) are widely distributed. They differ from *Pelonomus* species in that their hair is not bristly and the 2nd antennal segment is enlarged into an earlike projection (Fig. 64). *Helichus* species are typically found clinging to logs or debris in riffle areas of streams.

RIFFLE BEETLES: Family Elmidae

Identification. Form, legs, and habitat distinctive: body *oval* to nearly *cylindrical.* Legs *long;* claws *large.* These beetles nearly always live in stream *riffles.* Antennae moderately long and *slender* or short and clubbed. Black to gray, some with light markings; surfaces often dull. Coxae usually rounded (not transverse). Tarsi 5-5-5. 1–8 mm.

Similar families. (1) Long-toed water beetles (p. 162) — antennae short, width of most segments greater than length. (2) Water-penny beetles (p. 156) live in similar habitat but differ in form — compare Figs. 61 and 65. (3) Minute marsh-loving beetles (p. 161) — clothed with short, dense hair; body 1–2 mm long. (4) Minute mud-loving beetles (p. 109) — legs short, claws small; found in Nebr., Idaho, Calif. (5) Minute moss beetles (p. 108) — maxillary palps elongate.

Range and numbers. The 26 genera and 93 species are widely distributed.

Habits. Larvae and most adults are aquatic but do not swim — they crawl about slowly on underwater plants or debris. Adults typically live in riffle areas of streams. Their stout legs and large claws allow them to grip effectively. Rarely found in streams with seasonal variations in flow, heavy sediment, muddy or sandy bottoms, or low oxygen content; few live in lakes or ponds. 4 species (Tex., Calif., and Wash.) live under objects at edges of streams. Those that live in water are inactive and will move only as mate-

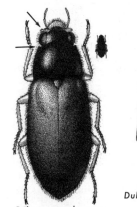

Pelonomus obscurus
LONG-TOED WATER BEETLE

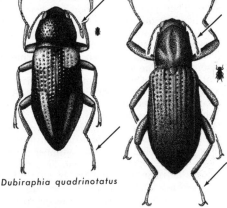

Dubiraphia quadrinotatus

Stenelmis fuscata

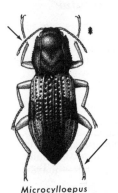

Microcylloepus

Lara

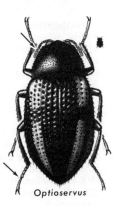

Optioservus

Fig. 65 RIFFLE BEETLES

rial to which they cling dries out. Adults and larvae feed on algae, moss, and other plant material, including roots.

Collecting methods. Most specimens are found by removing and examining vegetation and debris from riffle areas of relatively sediment-free streams. These beetles are camouflaged by their dull colors and are often seen only when they move. An aquatic net used in streams, ponds, and lakes may capture some. A few fly to lights.

Examples. The 3 *Lara* species are among our largest riffle beetles; they are found under debris beside streams in w. U.S. Genus *Dubiraphia* contains 5 widely distributed species. *D. quadrinotatus* (Say) is common in lakes, ponds, and streams from Canada to Fla.; it is about 2.3 mm long. The 27 species of *Stenelmis* make it the largest genus in this family. Only 1 species occurs west of the Rocky Mts. *Stenelmis* is one of the few genera in which adults have no patches of hair on their tibiae. *Stenelmis* species are common in streams; many live in sand-bottomed, relatively clear streams; some are found in lakes and ponds. *S. fuscata* Blatchley, 3.2–3.4 mm, occurs just in Fla. and is characteristic of small sand-bottomed streams, but also occurs in lakes with considerable wave action or in canals with some water movement. *Microcylloepus* species are found in e. N. America, Ariz., Nev., and Calif. Adults in this genus look like small versions of *Stenelmis* species, but are readily distinguished by the patches of fine, dense hair on their tibiae. The 11 species of *Optioservus* and the 6 of *Microcylloepus* are more widely distributed than other riffle beetles. *Optioservus* species have a broad pronotum with finely sawtoothed lateral margins.

Superfamily Buprestoidea

Only 1 family; most members have metallic surfaces.

METALLIC WOOD-BORING BEETLES: Family Buprestidae
(Figs. 66–68; see also Pl. 4)

Identification. Most distinctive for coloration — nearly always *metallic* or *bronzed,* especially on *ventral* surface. Dorsal surface frequently *metallic,* usually *shiny,* with or without hairs, sometimes spotted with yellow. Elytral tip often *pointed,* sides nearly parallel, making body somewhat bullet-shaped. Antennae usually *short, sawtoothed;* threadlike or comblike in some species. Tarsi 5-5-5. 2–40 mm (nearly $1\frac{5}{8}$ in.); most 5–20 mm.

Similar families. Beetles of similar form are rarely metallic — see: (1) Click beetles (p. 172) have a movable prothorax. (2) False

click beetles (p. 179). (3) Lizard beetles (p. 224) — antennae clubbed. (4) Throscid beetles (p. 177) — antennae usually clubbed.
Range and numbers. 39 genera and 718 species in N. America; widely distributed, but most in w. U.S.
Habits. All larvae are plant-feeders, and most bore in wood, usually sapwood. Feeding habits of larvae make many species economically important as pests — this family ranks just behind long-horned beetles in amount of damage they cause to wood. Thoracic segments of larvae are flat and broad (thus the name flat-headed borers). This shape distinguishes them from other wood-boring larvae; not surprisingly, these larvae produce distinctive flattened galleries. They do the most damage by feeding in sapwood of recently felled logs. Some larvae are leaf or stem miners of herbs and woody plants; others produce galls on trees; a few feed in pine cones. Adults are often brightly colored; they are most active in full sunlight on trunks, limbs, leaves, and flowers, where they eat pollen, foliage, or tender bark. These beetles are generally quite alert and fast-moving.
Collecting methods. Moderately common and collected in good numbers by a variety of techniques. Some species, especially those that feed on leaves, can be captured by sweeping or beating foliage. When beating foliage, move quickly to catch specimens that fall into the umbrella (see p. 14). Most are found in sunlight on dead or dying trees or limbs. Approach them carefully, for many are elusive. On cloudy days they conceal themselves and are rarely seen. Some, especially *Acmaeodera* species, frequent flowers. Rearing specimens from infested material (dying or recently dead wood) will sometimes provide you with numbers of a species you will not ordinarily find in the wild. The bright colors of many of these beetles and the challenge of capturing them make this family quite popular with collectors.
Subfamilies. All 4 in N. America are described below.

ABERRANT BUPRESTIDS Subfamily Schizopinae
Members of this subfamily are stout-bodied and distinctive for the *deeply bilobed* 4th tarsal segment (Fig. 66). The 8 species (4 genera, including *Dystaxia*) occur in Ariz. and Calif. Some taxonomists would split this group into a new family because of their relationships to other beetles, such as those in Superfamily Dascilloidea (p. 149).

SCULPTURED BUPRESTIDS   (see also Pl. 4)
Subfamily Buprestinae
There are about 250 species in N. America, some quite injurious. The 22 N. American *Buprestis* species are the most *brilliantly colored* of our buprestids (see Pl. 4). Most are primarily metallic green — some have blues, golds, reds, yellows, or oranges; their colors have made these beetles much sought-after by collectors. The

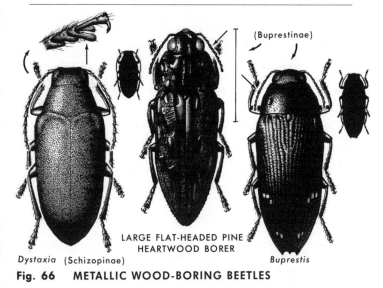

LARGE FLAT-HEADED PINE
HEARTWOOD BORER

Dystaxia (Schizopinae)   (Buprestinae)   *Buprestis*

Fig. 66   METALLIC WOOD-BORING BEETLES

Turpentine Borer, *B. apricans* Herbst, at *30 mm,* is one of our larger pest species; it lives on longleaf and other pines throughout the coastal regions from N.C. to Tex. It is a major pest in orchards where it attacks pine trees cut for turpentine. Larvae mine sapwood and heartwood, reducing pitch flow and rendering trees useless for timber.

The 6 *Chalcophora* species (see Pl. 4) are generally 20–32 mm long, and most of them have shiny ridges on their elytra. The **Large Flat-headed Pine Heartwood Borer,** *C. virginiensis* (Drury) (23–33 mm), occurs nearly throughout e. U.S. Adults are conspicuous in early summer as they fly about with a distinct buzz. ♀ lays eggs on living trees at fire scars and blazes. Larvae mine trees for several years, and many can convert wood to sawdust with little but outer shell remaining. The **Sculptured Pine Borer,** *C. angulicollis* LeC., at 25–28 mm, is the largest buprestid in w. U.S.; larvae feed in dead pines and firs. The **Flat-headed Apple Tree Borer,** *Chrysobothris femorata* (Oliv.), 7–16 mm, is 1 of about 135 species in this genus; they are widely distributed in N. America. This species attacks virtually all fruit, shade, and forest trees, and is one of the best-known members of the family. It occurs throughout N. America to Mexico. Young, recently transplanted trees are particularly susceptible to injury, and older, unhealthy trees are frequently hosts to these pests. Adults are active, alert, and wary when approached. Larvae bore beneath bark and can completely girdle and kill a tree. Trunks of transplanted trees are often wrapped with burlap or paper to keep females from laying eggs there. The **Australian Pine Borer,** *C. tranquebarica* (Gmelin), also called the **Mangrove Borer,** attacks red mangrove and Casuarina trees ("Australian Pine") planted as ornamentals in s. Fla. The **Cedar Flat-headed Borer,** *C. nixa* Horn, injures incense cedar, Sierra juniper, and cypress trees in Pacific Coast states.

Dicerca species (generally 10–20 mm long) usually have finely sculptured elytra with elongate tips. *D. divaricata* (Say) is bronze above, bluish beneath, and 17–22 mm long. Like many of the other 27 members of the genus, it breeds in dead and dying hardwoods. Larvae often mine through a tree until the heartwood is completely riddled; greatest damage follows tree injuries that allow the beetles to enter. The 22 *Anthaxia* species (widely distributed; see Pl. 4) are small (usually 3–7 mm) and have fine elytral sculpturing. They bore beneath bark — some in softwoods, others in hardwoods.

A few of the 20 *Melanophila* species (widely distributed; 4.5–13 mm) are attracted to fires. Pits at base of their middle legs appear to detect the infrared radiation of fires. The **Hemlock Borer,** *M. fulvoguttata* (Harris), occurs throughout e. U.S., where it injures hemlock and occasionally spruce trees; it attacks weakened trees and may hasten a tree's death. The **California Flat-headed Borer,** *M. californica* VanDyke (not shown), is most destructive to ponderosa and Jeffrey pines; it generally attacks pines growing on slopes, in fringe stands, or where soil is dry. Old or unhealthy trees are usually killed, but healthy ones may die also.

YELLOW-MARKED BUPRESTIDS
Subfamily Acmaeoderinae
About 180 species occur in N. America; there are 6 genera. The roughly 150 species of *Acmaeodera* (most in sw. U.S.; usually 5–11 mm) are similar in shape and nearly all have *yellow elytral markings;* many are attracted to flowers. The **Flat-headed Baldcypress Sapwood Borer,** *A. pulchella* (Herbst), occurs in e. U.S. and bores in baldcypress and related trees. It frequently attacks baldcypress killed in lumbering operations. Lumbermen have learned to avoid damage by girdling baldcypress from October to December, after the flight period of this beetle. These seasoned trees are removed from the woods the following spring before beetles emerge to ensure that no eggs will be laid in them.

BRANCH-AND-LEAF BUPRESTIDS Subfamily Agrilinae
Agrilus species (166; widely distributed) are 3–14.5 mm long and elongate-narrow, with elytra that taper at tip. A number harm trees and shrubs by boring in bark and wood of roots, trunks, and

branches. These buprestids attack some healthy trees and shrubs as well as dead or injured ones. Certain species produce galls or deformities in host plants; others make spiral girdles in twigs and branches of oak, birch, willow, and other broadleaved trees. Adults are very active and are good fliers. Adults generally feed on the foliage of the larval host, but damage they cause is minor. The **Two-lined Chestnut Borer,** *A. bilineatus* (Weber), is probably the most harmful and best-known species of the genus. The adult is 6–10 mm long and blackish blue with more or less distinct yellow stripes. Larvae construct characteristic tunnels in wood of various

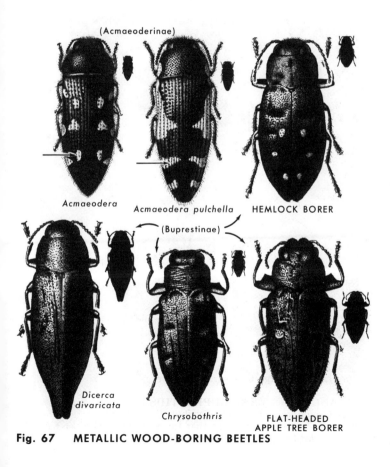

(Acmaeoderinae)

Acmaeodera   *Acmaeodera pulchella*   HEMLOCK BORER

(Buprestinae)

Dicerca divaricata   *Chrysobothris*   FLAT-HEADED APPLE TREE BORER

Fig. 67   METALLIC WOOD-BORING BEETLES

oaks, beech, ironwood, and chestnut trees. This beetle is most injurious in e. and cen. U.S. to trees that have been weakened by disease, insect damage, or other factors. Attack by this beetle usually starts at topmost branches, which may be killed the 1st year; larger limbs are killed the 2nd year, and the entire tree may die the 3rd year. Adults emerge from characteristic D-shaped holes in May or June, feed on foliage, and lay eggs beneath bark of weakened trees.

The **Bronze Birch Borer,** *A. anxius* Gory (not shown) is 7.5–

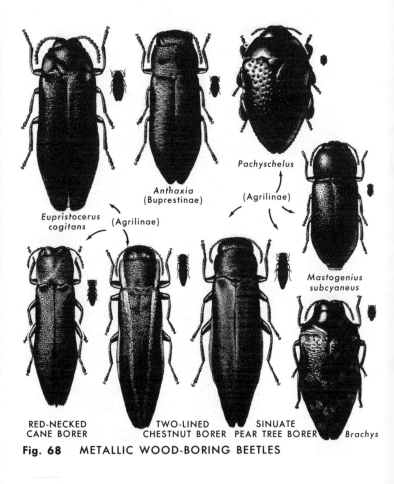

Eupristocerus cogitans

Anthaxia
(Buprestinae)

(Agrilinae)

Pachyschelus

(Agrilinae)

Mastogenius subcyaneus

RED-NECKED
CANE BORER

TWO-LINED
CHESTNUT BORER

SINUATE
PEAR TREE BORER

Brachys

Fig. 68 METALLIC WOOD-BORING BEETLES

11 mm long. It is similar to the Two-lined Chestnut Borer, but does not have yellow stripes. This beetle occurs on dying or weakened birches from ne. and n. cen. U.S. to Wash. and Ore. Its habits are very similar to those of *A. bilineatus*. Pruning infested branches and stimulating growth of birches with fertilizer and water may keep them from dying. The **Sinuate Pear Tree Borer,** *A. sinautus* (Oliv.), is a local pest on pear trees, mountain ash, cotoneaster, and hawthorn trees in ne. U.S. The **Red-necked Cane Borer,** *A. ruficollis* (Fab.), 5.5–7 mm, is distinctive for its rusty-red pronotum. It is widely distributed in e. N. America but is rarely injurious. Larvae produce galls on canes of raspberry, blackberry, and dewberry. *Brachys* species (11 species, most e. U.S.; 3–7 mm) cause minor damage as leaf miners of deciduous trees; hosts include elm, oak, linden, blueberry, alder, ironwood, poplar, and beech trees. These beetles have a distinctive stout body with sinuate (arched) margins.

The 6 *Pachyschelus* species are 2–4 mm long and may be very common in e. U.S. They mine leaves of clover, cranesbill, and ticktrefoils. ♀ usually inserts egg in a little pocket made on the underside of a leaf. Larvae feed between upper and lower surfaces, and overwinter in flat, parchmentlike cocoons. They pupate in spring. There are 7 *Mastogenius* species, most in e. U.S. *M. subcyaneus* (LeC.), 2–2.5 mm, has been reared from dead oak branches. *Eupristocerus cogitans* (Weber) forms galls on alder in e. N. America; it is 2–2.5 mm long. It lays eggs in rough spots on bark; larvae mine through bark into stem, causing a gall.

Superfamily Elateroidea

All are plant-feeders — some are pests. Rear of prosternum is often elongated into a lobe that fits into mesosternum. These beetles are usually medium-sized.

CEBRIONID BEETLES: Family Cebrionidae

Identification. Mandibles and pronotum distinctive: Mandibles *prominent,* strongly *curved,* with *pointed* tips. Hind angles of pronotum distinctly *elongate.* Head prognathous. Each antenna 11-segmented, more or less sawtoothed. 13.5–25 mm (up to 1 in.). Elytra nearly parallel-sided (in 12 species), or widest at base (in 5 species). Legs moderately long. Light to dark brown. Union of prothorax and mesothorax flexible — can be moved. Tarsi 5-5-5. **Similar families.** Characters of mandible and pronotum distinguish this family. Groups otherwise similar include: (1) longhorned beetles (p. 279); (2) click beetles (p. 172); (3) false click beetles (p. 179); (4) false long-horned beetles (p. 248); (5) rare click beetles (p. 177); and (6) cedar beetles (p. 153).

Range and numbers. 2 genera and 17 species in s. U.S.; most in sw. U.S.

Habits. Larvae live in ground and feed on roots; they are not economically important. Adults normally live beneath debris or loose bark. They are good fliers, with wasplike flight.

Collecting methods. Attracted to lights. Look beneath debris or loose bark; some are captured in flight. In sw. U.S. mating flights are associated with heavy rains.

Examples. Genus *Selonodon* contains 12 species that occur from se. U.S. west to Utah and Ariz. The 5 *Scaptolenus* species occur from Tex. to Calif.; these species differ from those of *Selonodon* in that body is widest at humeri; in *Selonodon* species elytra are nearly parallel-sided. 2 *Scaptolenus* species have mating flights during heavy rains. A collector and his family captured 121 males and 2 females of *S. fuscipennis* Fall at 5500 ft. in the Huachuca Mts. in Ariz. after a July rain. Most males were clustered about the 2 females.

CLICK BEETLES: Family Elateridae
(Figs. 69–71; see also Pl. 4)

Identification. Form distinctive: Front of body *loosely* joins back of body and can be *moved.* Hind angles of pronotum nearly always *extend* backward. Body elongate-narrow, often nearly parallel-sided or with elytra tapering at tip; each end of body rounded, often with bluntly pointed elytra. Prosternum has an elongated *lobe* that fits into a depression in mesosternum and allows beetle to click; front edge of prosternum nearly always *lobed.* Antennae close to eyes, nearly always *sawtoothed,* sometimes comblike. Usually brown or black, sometimes with light markings. Tarsi 5-5-5. 1.5–45 mm (up to $1\frac{3}{4}$ in.) — most 3–20 mm.

Similar families. (1) False click beetles (p. 179) — front edge of prosternum straight; union of prosternum and mesosternum not as flexible; antennae not close to eyes; body often widest at pronotum. (2) Throscid beetles (p. 177) — antennae nearly always clubbed, rarely sawtoothed; prosternum and mesosternum fused; 2–5 mm. (3) Rare click beetles (p. 177) — middle and hind trochanters very long; body length 6–8.5 mm. See distribution. (4) Perothopid beetles (p. 179) — antennae not close to eyes; claws comblike. (5) Metallic wood-boring beetles (p. 165) — nearly always with metallic luster, especially on ventral surfaces. (6) Certain false darkling beetles (p. 264) are similar, but tarsi 5-5-4. (7) Soft-bodied plant beetles (p. 152) — prothorax not movable. (8) Texas beetles (p. 159) — prothorax not movable. (9) Cebrionid beetles (p. 171) — mandibles enlarged and prominent.

Range and numbers. 60 genera and about 800 species; widely distributed in N. America.

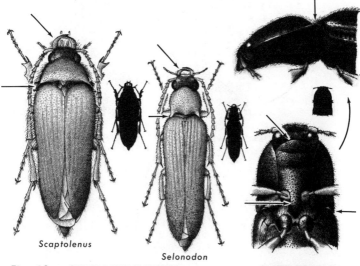

Scaptolenus

Selonodon

Fig. 69   CEBRIONID BEETLES   CLICK BEETLE

Habits. Adults are well-known for their ability to click. If one is placed on its back, it arches its body, then suddenly snaps its prosternal lobe into the mesosternal depression, causing the beetle to recoil into the air (see Fig. 70). The performance is repeated if the beetle lands on its back again. Smaller click beetles are more proficient at flipping than large ones. Adults live on foliage of trees and bushes, or sometimes under bark or in rotten wood. Most elaterid larvae are true wireworms (see p. 50) — long, narrow, and hard-bodied; a few are soft-bodied. Larvae usually live in loam, clay, and sandy soils where they eat roots, underground stems, tubers, bulbs, and corms. They may be very destructive to garden crops. Some live in decaying vegetation; a few of these prey on larvae of other insects.

Collecting methods. Adults are common on leaves of trees and shrubs, and can be collected by sweeping or beating; others occur in rotting logs or stumps, under dead bark, or beneath cover on ground. Many fly to lights.

Examples. The size and appearance of the **Eyed Click Beetle,** *Alaus oculatus* (L.), assure that it will attract attention when encountered — at 25–45 mm (1–1¾ in.) it is the largest click beetle. It is found from e. U.S. to Tex. Larvae live in logs and eat larvae of other insects. The 14 *Lacon* species (most 11–18 mm) are widely

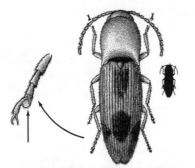

TOBACCO WIREWORM   *Aeolus*

Lacon discoideus   PACIFIC COAST WIREWORM   *Ampedus nigricollis*

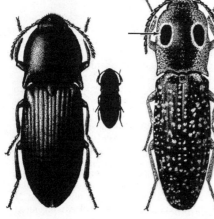

PRAIRIE GRAIN WIREWORM   EYED CLICK BEETLE   *Melanotus communis*

Fig. 70   CLICK BEETLES

distributed; larvae are predaceous. Adults bear flattened, *scalelike hairs;* some feed in groups under bark of dead trees. *L. discoideus* (Weber) is common beneath bark of dead trees and in rotten wood in e. U.S. The 14 *Conoderus* species (most 6–10 mm) occur in ne. and s. U.S.; some are economically important as pests. The **Tobacco Wireworm,** *C. vespertinus* (Fab.), is 7.5–10 mm long and causes serious damage to tobacco, cotton, potatoes, corn, beans, and other truck crops. The **Southern Potato Wireworm,** *C. falli* Lane (not shown) is a pest of potatoes, tobacco, and vegetable crops in se. U.S. In *Conoderus* species the 4th tarsal segment is lobed but not heart-shaped. In the 14 *Aeolus* species (widely distributed; 4–10.5 mm) the 4th tarsal segment is broadened and heart-shaped.

The 46 *Melanotus* species (7–21 mm) occur throughout U.S. but few live in w. U.S. Larvae often feed in seeds and roots of corn, small grains, grasses, and root crops. Adults are generally brown and hairy, with *comblike* claws. *M. communis* (Gyll.) is common in e. U.S.; larvae injure potatoes and other crops. *Ampedus* contains 68 species (widely distributed); 3–16 mm long. *A. nigricollis* (Herbst), 8.5–10 mm, is common under bark and in decayed wood in e. U.S. It is black with dull yellow elytra. *Limonius* is one of the most harmful genera of the family. Most of its 60 species are northern; 4.5–17 mm long. Adults of the **Pacific Coast Wireworm,** *L. canus* LeC. (w. N. America), feed on buds and blossoms of apple, cherry, pear, plum, and other fruit trees. *Ctenicera* (6–20 mm) is the largest genus with 146 species; most occur in n. U.S. Most *Ctenicera* species are entirely black, but a few are light with dark markings. Pests include the **Great Basin Wireworm,** *C. pruinina* (Horn), (Fig. 71, p. 176), and the **Prairie Grain Wireworm,** *C. aeripennis destructor* (Brown), which destroys grains and field crops in w. U.S. The 55 widely distributed *Dalopius* species are typically elongate and narrow; 4.3–9 mm long. The 35 *Cardiophorus* species (widely distributed), 4–12 mm, have *heart-shaped* scutella, as do members of closely related genera. *C. fenestratus* LeC., about 6 mm, occurs in much of n. U.S. to Calif.; it sometimes injures buds and blossoms of fruit trees in ne. U.S. In *Athous* species tarsal segments 2, 3, and sometimes 4 have a *membranous lobe* beneath (Fig. 71); most of the 50 species (5.5–22 mm) occur in w. U.S. Adults emerge in July and August; most click beetles emerge earlier. *A. brightwelli* (Kirby) is 11–18 mm long and is found throughout much of the U.S. east of the Rocky Mts. Members of *Negastrius* (21 species; 2–10 mm) and *Hypolithus* (15 species; 4.3–10 mm) are often found near water; some live beneath rocks near streams. Both genera are widely distributed. *Negastrius* species are especially good at leaping (flipping).

(*text continues on p. 177*)

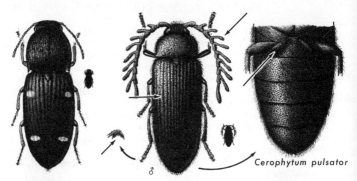

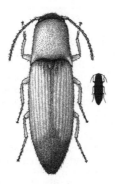

Negastrius

RARE CLICK BEETLE

♂

Cerophytum pulsator

Cardiophorus fenestratus

Dalopius

Hypolithus

GREAT BASIN WIREWORM

Ctenicera triundulata

Athous brightwelli

Fig. 71   CLICK BEETLES

Color Plates

PLATE 1

Ground Beetles, Tiger Beetles, Hister Beetle

GROUND BEETLES, Family Carabidae   **p. 86**
A large family with few distinctive characters; species variable in form. Hind coxae *divide* first abdominal segment. Antennae threadlike, rarely beadlike; each antenna inserted *between* eye and mandible. Most species all or partly *black*; a few brightly colored. Nearly always long-legged. Usually shiny; elytra striate. Tarsi 5-5-5. 2–35 mm (most 4–20 mm).

    SEARCHERS, Tribe Carabini   p. 88
    Large to very large; some species brightly colored. All are pre-
    daceous.
    Calosoma calidum (Fab.). Lake Superior region.

    COLORFUL FOLIAGE GROUND BEETLES,
    Tribe Lebiini   p. 92
    Small to medium-sized; often active during day on foliage.
    Lebia furcata LeC. Much of N. America.

    Tribe Lachnophorini
    A small tribe of just 6 species, found in w. and s. U.S.
    Lachnophorus elegantulus Mann. Ore. to sw. U.S.

TIGER BEETLES, Family Cicindelidae   **p. 83**
Form distinctive: elytra usually widest *toward end,* sometimes nearly parallel-sided; pronotum *narrower* than base of elytra; head (at eyes) as *wide* or *wider* than pronotum. Legs *long, slender.* Antennae threadlike; each one inserted above base of mandible. Dorsal surface usually brown or black, often with a characteristic pattern of light markings. Ventral surface iridescent blue or green in most species; dorsal surface iridescent in some (as shown). Tarsi 5-5-5. 6–40 mm (most 10–20 mm).

    Cicindela scutellaris Say. Cen. U.S.
    Megacephala carolina (L.). Va. south to Fla. and west to Tex.

HISTER BEETLES, Family Histeridae   **p. 132**
Form of antennae and shortened elytra distinctive. Antennae *short* and *elbowed,* each with an *abrupt* 3-segmented club; usually retracted into *cavities* on ventral surface of prothorax. Elytra *short, exposing* tip of abdomen; often striate. Body *hard,* nearly always *shiny* and *black,* sometimes with red. Tibiae *expanded,* often spiny (as shown). 0.5–20 mm (most 1–10 mm).

    Hister sellatus LeC. Calif.

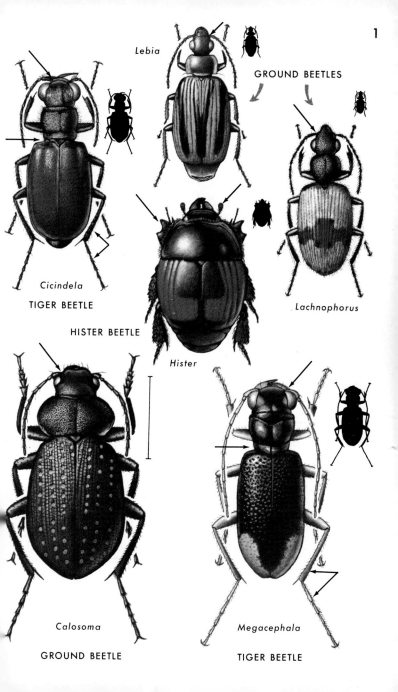

1

Lebia

GROUND BEETLES

Cicindela
TIGER BEETLE

HISTER BEETLE

Hister

Lachnophorus

Calosoma
GROUND BEETLE

Megacephala
TIGER BEETLE

PLATE 2

Rove Beetles, Shining Fungus Beetle, Carrion Beetle, Soldier Beetle

ROVE BEETLES, Family Staphylinidae   **p. 110**
Form of most species characteristic: Body *slender, elongate,* nearly *parallel-sided;* elytra *short, exposing* 3–6 (usually 5–6) abdominal segments, rarely concealing whole abdomen. Abdomen *flexible,* sometimes held upward. Antennae threadlike to clubbed. Brown or black; a few brightly colored. 0.7–25 mm (usually 1–10 mm).

CROSS-TOOTHED ROVE BEETLES,
Subfamily Oxyporinae   **p. 114**
Head large — usually wider than thorax. Mandibles long and crossing; last segment of labial palp large, crescent-shaped. 6–9 mm.
Oxyporus vittatus Graven. Ne. U.S.

PAEDERINE ROVE BEETLES, Subfamily Paederinae   **p. 114**
Head narrowed at rear into a distinct neck. Small to medium-sized. Similar to large rove beetles (Staphylininae).
Paederus grandis Aust. Ariz.

LARGE ROVE BEETLES, Subfamily Staphylininae   **p. 114**
Our largest rove beetles; found in decaying fungi, carrion, dung, and rotting organic material.
Staphylinus fossator Graven. Ne. U.S. and Wash.

SHINING FUNGUS BEETLES, Family Scaphidiidae   **p. 131**
Body broadest near *middle, tapered* at each end. Elytra *short,* usually exposing *pointed* abdomen. Shiny; black to brown, sometimes with red or yellow (as shown). Antennae *clubbed.* 1.2–7 mm.
Scaphidium ornatum Casey. Colo.

CARRION BEETLES, Family Silphidae   **p. 120**
Size, form, and antennal club distinctive: Large—usually 10–35 mm. Elytra broad *toward rear,* often *loosely* covering abdomen. Antennae *clubbed;* last 3 segments of each *hairy.* Black, often with red, yellow, or orange.
Silpha americana L. E. U.S.

SOLDIER BEETLES, Family Cantharidae   **p. 183**
Body elongate, soft, and somewhat *flattened,* with nearly parallel sides. Legs and antennae *long,* slender; antennae threadlike. Elytra *loosely* covering abdomen, sometimes short. Usually black or brown with red, orange, or yellow. 1–15 mm.
Chauliognathus texanus Fender. Tex.

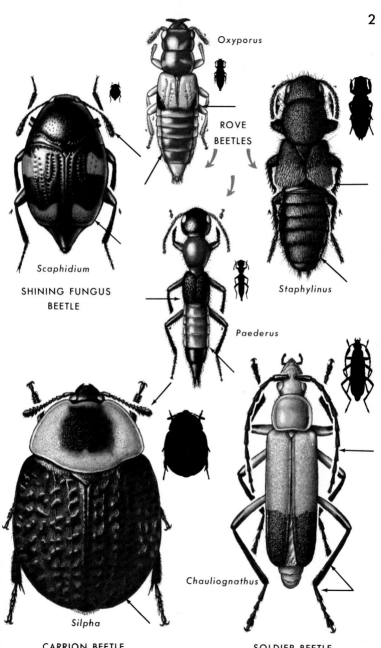

2

Oxyporus

ROVE
BEETLES

Scaphidium

SHINING FUNGUS
BEETLE

Paederus

Staphylinus

Silpha

CARRION BEETLE

Chauliognathus

SOLDIER BEETLE

PLATE 3

Soft-winged Flower Beetles, Dermestid Beetle, Lightningbug, and Others

SOFT-WINGED FLOWER BEETLES,
Family Melyridae   **p. 211**
In e. U.S. species, body nearly always widest *toward the rear*. Elytra usually *soft, loosely* covering abdomen. Pronotum usually wider than it is long. Antennae *sawtoothed* or *threadlike*. 1.5–7 mm.

    Collops bipunctatus Say. Kans. to sw. U.S.

    Anthocomus bipunctatus (Harr.). E. U.S.

DERMESTID BEETLES, Family Dermestidae   **p. 192**
Body *robust* and elongate to nearly *round*. Head more or less *concealed* from above, often with a median *ocellus*. Antennae *short*, each with a 3-segmented club; each antenna often fits into groove below side of pronotum. Body often covered with *scales* or *hair* (as shown). 1–12 mm.

    Novelsis varicolor (Jayne). W. U.S.

LIGHTNINGBUGS, Family Lampyridae   **p. 188**
Head *concealed* from above by *flattened* pronotum. Pronotum as wide (or nearly so) as elytra. Sides of body often nearly parallel, both ends *rounded; soft-bodied.* Antennae *threadlike* or *sawtoothed.* 1–2 abdominal segments often luminescent. 4.5–20 mm.

    Photinus frigidus Oliv. Newfoundland.

CHECKERED BEETLES, Family Cleridae   **p. 208**
Body covered with *bristly hairs;* nearly always elongate-narrow. Head *wide*—usually as wide as or wider than pronotum. Often attractively *marked* with red, orange, yellow, or blue (as shown). 1.8–24 mm (most 3–10 mm).

    Chariessa elegans Horn. Tex., Ore., Calif.

NET-WINGED BEETLES, Family Lycidae   **p. 186**
Elytra sculptured with a network of *lengthwise ridges* and less distinct *cross-ridges* (sculpturing weak in a few species). Elytra nearly always *broadest toward rear,* extending *loosely* beyond body. Body *soft.* Head more or less *concealed* from above. Antennae long; sawtoothed or threadlike. 3–18.5 mm (usually over 6 mm).

    Lycostomus sanguineus Gorh. Sw. U.S.

BARK-GNAWING BEETLES, Family Trogositidae   **p. 207**
Each antenna ends in a *club* with 3 segments that nearly always *extend* laterally. Body usually *cylindrical* to *flattened.* Head nearly as broad as pronotum. Body with a distinct *division* between pronotum and elytra; usually 5–15 mm.

    Temnochila chlorodia (Manner.). W. N. America.

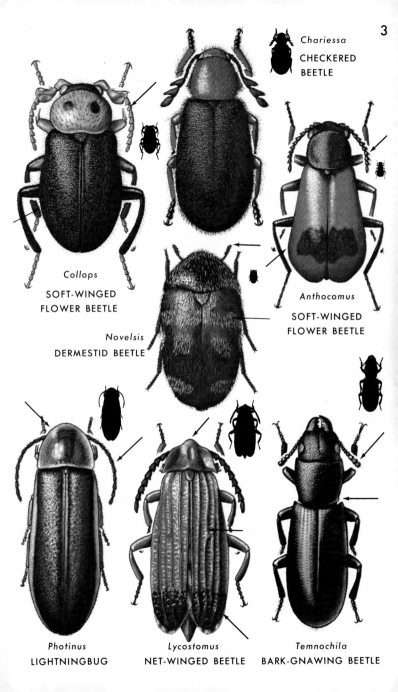

3

Chariessa
CHECKERED BEETLE

Collops
SOFT-WINGED
FLOWER BEETLE

Novelsis
DERMESTID BEETLE

Anthocomus
SOFT-WINGED
FLOWER BEETLE

Photinus
LIGHTNINGBUG

Lycostomus
NET-WINGED BEETLE

Temnochila
BARK-GNAWING BEETLE

PLATE 4

Metallic Wood-boring Beetles and Click Beetles

METALLIC WOOD-BORING BEETLES,
Family Buprestidae **p. 165**
Color distinctive — nearly always *metallic* or *bronzed,* especially on *ventral* surface. Body usually *shiny,* dorsal surface frequently *metallic.* Body with or without hairs, sometimes with yellow or red markings. Tips of elytra often pointed, elytral sides nearly parallel (body thus somewhat bullet-shaped). Antennae *short; sawtoothed,* threadlike, or comblike. First 3 abdominal segments fused at middle. Hard-bodied. 2–40 mm (most 5–20 mm).

SCULPTURED BUPRESTIDS, Subfamily Buprestinae p. 166
Some of our largest and most attractive buprestids. Some are serious pests.
Thrincopyge alacris LeC. Sw. U.S.
Anthaxia quercata (Fab.) E. U.S.
Buprestis aurulenta L. W. N. America.
Chalcophora georgiana LeC. Se. U.S.

CLICK BEETLES, Family Elateridae **p. 172**
Form distinctive — front of body *loosely* joins back of body and can be moved. Rear corners of pronotum nearly always extend backward. Body elongate-narrow, often nearly parallel-sided; each end rounded, often with tips of elytra bluntly pointed. Prosternum with an elongate *lobe* that fits into a depression in mesosternum (which allows beetle to click); front edge of prosternum nearly always *lobed.* Antennae close to eyes; nearly always *sawtoothed,* sometimes comblike (as shown). Usually brown or black, sometimes with light markings. Tarsi 5-5-5. 1.5–45 mm (most 3–20 mm).
Hemirhipus fascicularis (Fab.). E. U.S. to Tex.
Chalcolepidius rectus Casey. Ariz.

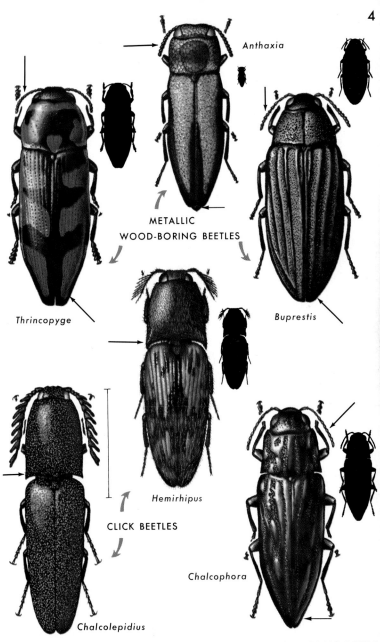

4

Anthaxia

METALLIC
WOOD-BORING BEETLES

Thrincopyge

Buprestis

Hemirhipus

CLICK BEETLES

Chalcolepidius

Chalcophora

METALLIC WOOD-BORING BEETLE

PLATE 5

Handsome Fungus Beetles, Lady Beetles, and Pleasing Fungus Beetles

HANDSOME FUNGUS BEETLES,
Family Endomychidae   p. 237
Form of prothorax usually distinctive, with *2 lengthwise grooves* at base; front corners more or less *extend* along both sides of head. Each antenna ends in a loose, 3-segmented *club.* Usually black, with red or orange (as shown). Dorsal surface shiny, usually hairless. Body oval or oblong. 1–10 mm (usually 4–8 mm). Tarsi apparently 3-3-3, actually 4-4-4.
> *Mycetina perpulchra* (Newm.) Much of U.S.
> *Phymaphora pulchella* (Newm.). E. U.S.

LADY or LADYBIRD BEETLES,
Family Coccinellidae   p. 231
Form and antennae distinctive: Broadly *oval* to nearly *circular;* dorsal surface strongly *convex,* ventral surface usually *flat.* Antennae short, usually *very short;* each with 8–11 segments, including a *weak club* of 3–6 segments. Pronotum short. Tarsi apparently 3-3-3, actually 4-4-4. Head partly or completely *concealed* from above. Color varies from yellow, red, or orange with black markings to black with yellow, orange, or red markings; some are entirely black. 0.8–10 mm.

> BLACK-SPOTTED LADY BEETLES, Tribe Coccinellini   p. 235
> *Anatis ocellata* (L.). E. U.S.
> *Agrabia cyanoptera* (Muls.). Sw. U.S.

PLEASING FUNGUS BEETLES, Family Erotylidae   p. 226
Elongate-oval to broadly oval. Ground color *black,* often with *red, orange,* or *yellow* markings (as shown); usually shiny, hairless. Each antenna ends in an *abrupt, broad, flat club* of 3 (rarely 4–5) segments. Elytra usually finely striate. Tarsi 5-5-5. 2.5–22 mm.
> *Triplax festiva* Lac. E. U.S. to Tex.
> *Cypherotylus californicus* Lac. Kans. and Wyo. to Mexico.

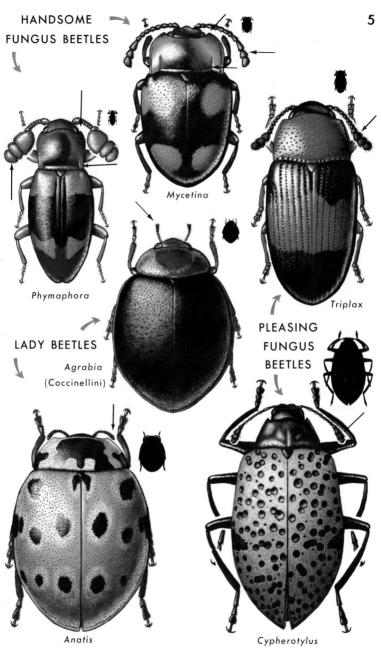

5

HANDSOME FUNGUS BEETLES

Mycetina

Phymaphora

LADY BEETLES

Agrabia
(Coccinellini)

PLEASING FUNGUS BEETLES

Triplax

Anatis
(Coccinellini)

Cypherotylus

PLATE 6

Blister Beetles

BLISTER BEETLES, Family Meloidae   **p. 270**
Head and body form distinctive: Head *broad,* usually nearly *rectangular* from above; head nearly always *wider* than pronotum, with a short *neck.* Pronotum *narrow.* Elytra wider at base than pronotum. Body nearly always *slender* and elongate, rarely oval. Body *soft, leathery.* Elytra *loosely* covering abdomen and nearly always *rolled* (arched over body); sometimes short, exposing abdomen. Antennae threadlike or beadlike; middle segments infrequently enlarged. Legs long, slender. Usually black, brown, or gray, sometimes brightly colored; often covered with fine hairs. Tarsi 5-5-4; each claw with teeth or a slender lobe.

    Cysteodemus wislizeni LeC. Tex. to Ariz.

    Tegrodera erosa Lec. S. Calif.

    Pyrota invita Horn. Tex.

    Eupompha fissiceps LeC. Tex.

    NUTTALL BLISTER BEETLE, *Lytta nuttalli Say.*
Cen. U.S. to Canada.

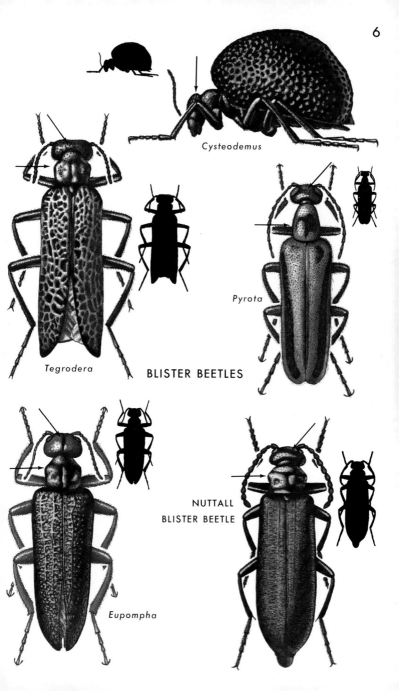

6

Cysteodemus

Tegrodera

Pyrota

BLISTER BEETLES

Eupompha

NUTTALL
BLISTER BEETLE

PLATE 7

Scarab Beetles (1), Stag Beetle, Death-watch Beetle, and Darkling Beetle

SCARAB BEETLES, Family Scarabaeidae   **p. 138**
Each antenna ends in a *lamellate* club of 3–4 (rarely up to 7) segments, with lobes that can be *closed tightly*. Whole antenna consists of 8–11 segments. Body form variable — oval to elongate, usually stout and heavy-bodied. Tarsi 5-5-5. 2–62 mm (usually 2–20 mm).

DUNG BEETLES AND TUMBLEBUGS,
Subfamily Scarabaeinae   p. 139
Hind legs located far back on body — usually closer to tip of abdomen than to middle legs.
Phanaeus igneus Mac. Se. U.S.

JUNE BEETLES, CHAFERS, AND OTHERS,
Subfamily Melolonthinae   p. 143
Tarsal claws often toothed or bilobed. Bases of antennae usually concealed from above.
TENLINED JUNE BEETLE, *Polyphylla decemlineata* (Say). Cen. to sw. U.S.

STAG BEETLES, Family Lucanidae   **p. 135**
Antennae distinctive: Each with 10 segments, ending in a comblike club of 3–4 segments that *cannot* be held together; antennae often *elbowed* (as shown). Mandibles of ♂ (shown) often *large* to very large. Body elongate-robust; medium-sized to very large, 8–60 mm. Red-brown to black. Tarsi 5-5-5.
GIANT STAG BEETLE, *Lucanus elaphus* Fab. Se. U.S. to Okla.

DEATH-WATCH BEETLES, Family Anobiidae   **p. 199**
Prothorax usually *hoodlike* — nearly always *enclosing* head and *concealing* it from above. Last 3 segments of each antenna usually *lengthened* and *expanded*, or simply lengthened — club *not symmetrical*. Body shape varies from elongate-cylindrical to oval or nearly round. Head, legs, and antennae moderately to highly *contractile*. Most often light brown to black. Tarsi 5-5-5. 1.19–mm.
Utobium marmoratum Fish. W. U.S.

DARKLING BEETLES, Family Tenebrionidae   **p. 249**
A variable group, usually recognizable by 5-5-4 tarsi, notched eyes, and form of antennae. Each eye nearly always *notched* by a *frontal ridge*. Antennae usually *threadlike, beadlike,* or weakly *clubbed;* each usually 11-segmented; insertion *concealed* from above. Most often dull black or brown, sometimes with red (as shown). 2–35 mm.

TYPICAL DARKLING BEETLES,
Subfamily Tenebrioninae   p. 252
Nearly all darkling beetles in e. U.S. belong to this subfamily.
Platydema ellipticum Fab. E. U.S.

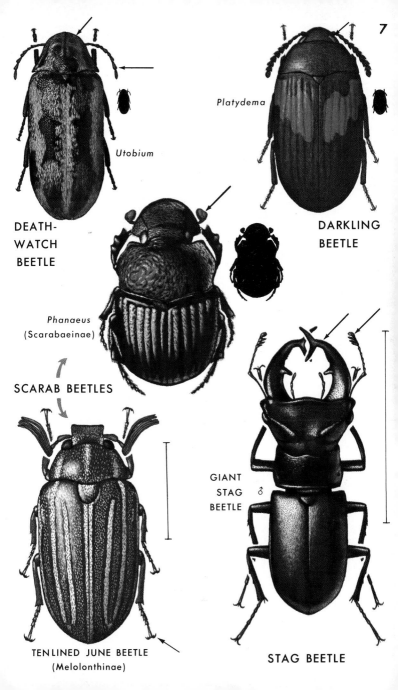

7

DEATH-WATCH BEETLE

Utobium

DARKLING BEETLE

Platydema

Phanaeus (Scarabaeinae)

SCARAB BEETLES

TENLINED JUNE BEETLE (Melolonthinae)

GIANT STAG BEETLE ♂

STAG BEETLE

PLATE 8

Scarab Beetles (2)

SCARAB BEETLES, Family Scarabaeidae p. 138
Antennae distinctive — each one ends in a *lamellate club* of 3–4 (rarely up to 7) segments; segments expanded laterally into oval or elongate lobes that can be *closed tightly;* each antenna has 8–11 segments. Body form variable—usually stout and heavy-bodied, oval to elongate. Tarsi 5-5-5. 2–62 mm (most 2–20 mm).

SHINING LEAF CHAFERS, Subfamily Rutelinae p. 144
Claws, especially on hind legs, of unequal length. Adults feed on foliage and fruits; larvae feed on plant roots. Some adults are very colorful; a number are important pests.
Plusiotis gloriosa LeC. Ariz. to Tex.

RHINOCEROS BEETLES AND OTHERS,
Subfamily Dynastinae p. 147
Some species are among the largest beetles in N. America; males often have horns on the head and/or the pronotum (as shown).
EASTERN HERCULES BEETLE, *Dynastes tityus* (L). Se. U.S.

FLOWER BEETLES AND OTHERS,
Subfamily Cetoniinae p. 147
Many are found on flowers where they feed on pollen; some occur under bark or in rotting wood; a few live in ant nests. Larvae feed on plant roots, on organic material in soil, or in decaying trees.
GREEN JUNE BEETLE, *Cotinis nitida* (L). Se. U.S.
Trigonopeltastes delta (Forst.) Se. U.S.
Gymnetis sallei Schaum. Sw. U.S.

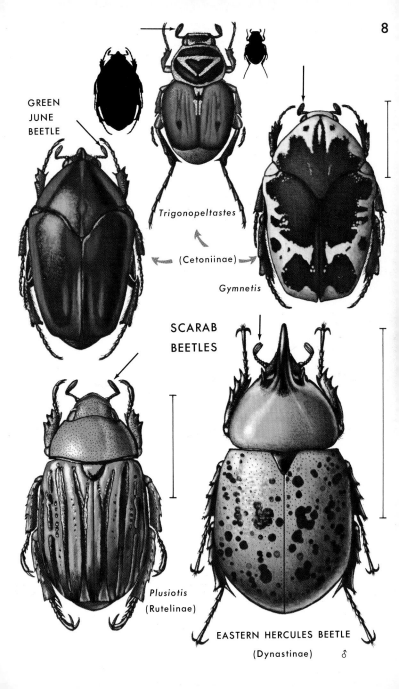

8

GREEN
JUNE
BEETLE

Trigonopeltastes

(Cetoniinae)

Gymnetis

SCARAB
BEETLES

Plusiotis
(Rutelinae)

EASTERN HERCULES BEETLE
(Dynastinae) ♂

PLATE 9

Long-horned Beetles (1)

LONG-HORNED BEETLES, Family Cerambycidae   p. 279
Antennae long — each one nearly always *at least half* as long as body, often *approaching* length of body, sometimes *longer* than body. Body usually robust, with a broad-shouldered appearance. Eyes usually *notched;* base of each antenna often inserted in notch. 2–60 mm (usually 10–25 mm). Tarsi nearly always appear to be 4-4-4, actually 5-5-5, rarely obviously 5-5-5.

FLOWER LONG-HORNS, Subfamily Lepturinae   p. 283
Shape of body and pronotum often distinctive: Pronotum often bell-shaped (broad at base, narrowed toward head); elytra tapered toward rear, making body appear *broad-shouldered*. Face slanting forward or nearly vertical, and last segment of maxillary palp blunt or straight across at tip. Slender, elongate shape of body (especially posteriorly constricted head and anteriorly narrowed pronotum) helps these beetles extract nectar and pollen.
Anthophylax cyanea (Hald.). Ne. U.S.
Desmoceris auripennis Chev. Calif., Nev.

ROUND-NECKED LONG-HORNS,
Subfamily Cerambycinae   p. 284
Pronotum usually rounded and widest at about middle, sometimes enlarged at middle. Last segment of maxillary palp blunt or straight across, face slanted forward or nearly vertical. The largest subfamily of long-horned beetles; including some of the most attractive of all beetles.
Rosalia funebris Mots. Alaska to N.M.
Dryobius sexfasciatus (Say). Cen. U.S.

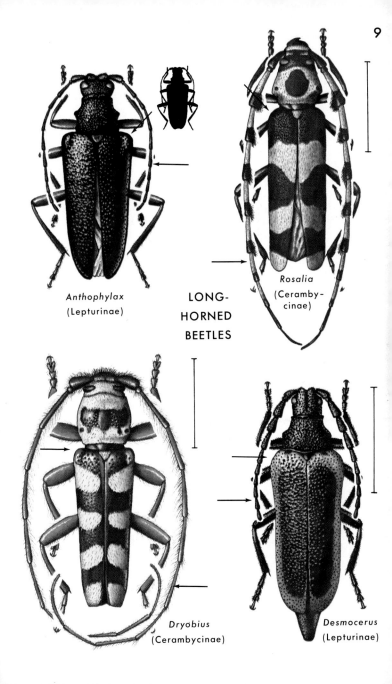

9

Anthophylax
(Lepturinae)

LONG-
HORNED
BEETLES

Rosalia
(Ceramby-
cinae)

Dryobius
(Cerambycinae)

Desmocerus
(Lepturinae)

PLATE 10
Long-horned Beetles (2)

LONG-HORNED BEETLES, Family Cerambycidae   **p. 279**
Antennae long—each one nearly always *at least half* as long as body, often *approaching* length of body, sometimes *longer* than body. Body usually *robust,* with a *broad-shouldered* appearance. Eyes usually *notched;* base of each antenna often inserted in notch. 2–60 mm (usually 10–25 mm). Tarsi nearly always appear to be 4-4-4, actually 5-5-5, rarely obviously 5-5-5.

    FLOWER LONG-HORNS, Subfamily Lepturinae   p. 283
    Shape of body and pronotum often distinctive: Pronotum often bell-shaped (broad at base, narrowed toward head); elytra tapered toward rear, making body appear *broad-shouldered.* Face slanting forward or nearly vertical, and last segment of maxillary palp blunt or straight across at tip. Slender, elongate shape of body (especially posteriorly constricted head and anteriorly narrowed pronotum) helps these beetles extract nectar and pollen.
    Evodinus monticola (Rand.). N. U.S. and Canada.

    ROUND-NECKED LONG-HORNS,
    Subfamily Cerambycinae   p. 284
    Pronotum usually rounded and widest at about middle, sometimes enlarged. Last segment of maxillary palp blunt or straight across, face slanted forward or nearly vertical. The largest subfamily of long-horned beetles, including some of the most attractive of all beetles.
    Dendrobias peninsularis Casey. S. Calif.
    SUGAR MAPLE BORER, *Glycobius speciosus* (Say). N. U.S.
    Plinthocoelium suaveolens (L.). Se. U.S.

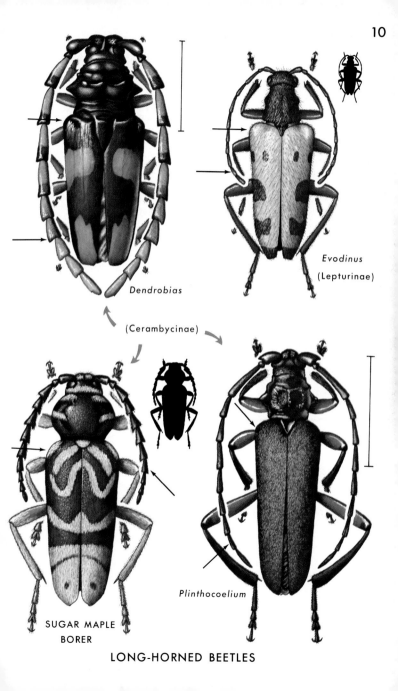

10

Dendrobias

Evodinus
(Lepturinae)

(Cerambycinae)

SUGAR MAPLE
BORER

Plinthocoelium

LONG-HORNED BEETLES

PLATE 11

Long-horned Beetle (3), Leaf Beetles (1)

LONG-HORNED BEETLES, Family Cerambycidae   **p. 279**
Antennae long—each one nearly always *at least half* as long as body, often *approaching* length of body, sometimes *longer* than body. Body usually *robust* and with a *broad-shouldered* appearance. Eyes usually *notched;* base of each antenna often inserted in notch. 2–60 mm (usually 10–25 mm). Tarsi nearly always appear to be 4-4-4, actually 5-5-5, rarely obviously 5-5-5.

> FLAT-FACED LONG-HORNS, Subfamily Lamiinae   p. 287
> Front of head nearly flat — vertical to slanting backward; last segment of maxillary palp pointed. Often covered with fine hairs in a variegated or irregular pattern (as shown).
> ROUND-HEADED APPLE TREE BORER, *Saperda candida* Fab. E. U.S.

LEAF BEETLES, Family Chrysomelidae   **p. 289**
Family difficult to characterize — members are very diverse in form, with no distinctive characters in common. Some subfamilies are distinctive in appearance or characters. Many are similar to long-horns but antennae shorter—each one nearly always *less than half* as long as body. Eyes usually not notched. Tarsi appear to be 4-4-4, actually 5-5-5 (4th segment very small). 1–16 mm (rarely over 12 mm).

> LONG-HORNED LEAF BEETLES,
> Subfamily Donaciinae   p. 290
> Elongate, moderately large (5.5–12 mm); usually dark with a metallic luster. Antennae *long*. No lateral margin on prothorax. Hind legs often enlarged (as shown).
> *Donacia aequalis* Say. E. U.S.

> CYLINDRICAL LEAF BEETLES,
> Subfamily Cryptocephalinae   p. 293
> Robust, nearly cylindrical. Head disklike and *withdrawn* into prothorax. Last abdominal segment often visible beyond elytra (as shown). 2–7.1 mm.
> *Cryptocephalus gibbicollis* Hald. E. U.S.

> BROAD-SHOULDERED LEAF BEETLES,
> Subfamily Chrysomelinae   p. 294
> Most oval to nearly circular, strongly convex above. Third tarsal segment not bilobed.
> *Calligrapha lunata* (Fab.) Ne. U.S. to Colo.

> SKELETONIZING LEAF BEETLES,
> Subfamily Galerucinae   p. 296
> Body form fairly consistent: Moderately elongate, moderately flattened. Head clearly visible from above. Pronotum somewhat narrower than elytra at base, with a distinct *lateral margin*. Elytra usually broadest toward rear. 3–16 mm.
> WESTERN CORN ROOTWORM, *Diabrotica virgifera* LeC. Cen. to sw. U.S.

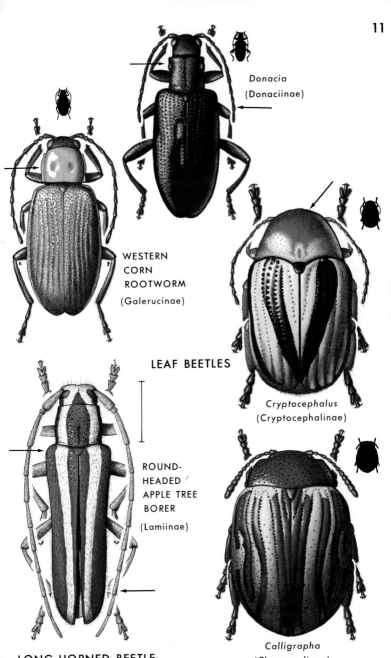

11

Donacia
(Donaciinae)

WESTERN
CORN
ROOTWORM
(Galerucinae)

LEAF BEETLES

Cryptocephalus
(Cryptocephalinae)

ROUND-
HEADED
APPLE TREE
BORER
(Lamiinae)

LONG-HORNED BEETLE

Calligrapha
(Chrysomelinae)

PLATE 12

Leaf Beetles (2), Snout Beetle, Seed Beetle

LEAF BEETLES, Family Chrysomelidae   **p. 289**
Family members very diverse in form, with no distinctive characters in common. Some subfamilies are distinctive. Many resemble long-horns but antennae shorter — nearly always *less than half* as long as body. Eyes usually not notched. Tarsi apparently 4-4-4, actually 5-5-5 (4th segment very small). 1–16 mm (rarely over 12 mm).

> SHINING LEAF BEETLES, Subfamily Criocerinae   p. 291
> Similar in appearance to long-horned beetles, but body bright and shiny; 3.2–7.5 mm.
> CEREAL LEAF BEETLE, *Oulema melanopus* (L.). Ne. U.S.

> SKELETONIZING LEAF BEETLES,
> Subfamily Galerucinae   p. 296
> Body form fairly consistent: Moderately elongate, moderately flattened. Head clearly visible from above. Pronotum somewhat narrower than elytra at base, with a distinct *lateral margin*. Elytra usually broadest toward rear. 3–16 mm.
> BEAN LEAF BEETLE, *Cerotoma trifurcata* (Forst.).
> E. N. America.

> LEAF-MINING LEAF BEETLES, Subfamily Hispinae   p. 302
> Mouth parts small and in different position on head from those of most other leaf beetles. Most have characteristic *sculpturing* on elytra (as shown)—usually distinct *ridges* bordering rows of punctures.
> *Octotoma marginicollis* Horn. Sw. U.S.

> TORTOISE BEETLES, Subfamily Cassidinae   p. 309
> Shape turtlelike — body oval to nearly circular; *sides* of pronotum and elytra often *extended* and *thin*. Mouth parts small and in a different position on head from those of most other leaf beetles. 4–13 mm.
> GOLDEN TORTOISE BEETLE, *Metriona bicolor* (Fab.).
> E. U.S. to Calif. Golden color exists in living beetles only.

SNOUT BEETLES, Family Curculionidae   **p. 309**
Snout nearly always *well-developed* — broad and flat (as shown) or (usually) very elongate and narrow. Each antenna ends in a *club* of 3 segments; antennae usually elbowed. Body often covered with scales. Tarsi apparently 4-4-4, actually 5-5-5. 0.6–35 mm (most under 10 mm).

> BROAD-NOSED WEEVILS, Subfamily Leptopiinae   p. 310
> Lobes extending from front edge of prothorax and partially covering eyes.
> *Eudiagogus rosenschoeldi* Fahr. Se. U.S.

SEED BEETLES, Family Bruchidae   **p. 304**
Body often *egg-shaped* — usually broadest toward rear or near middle; head with a short *beak*. Hind femora *enlarged*. Antennae clubbed, sawtoothed, or *comblike* (as shown). Eyes *notched* in front. 1–8 mm.
> *Megacerus discoidus* (Say). Ne. U.S. to Colo.

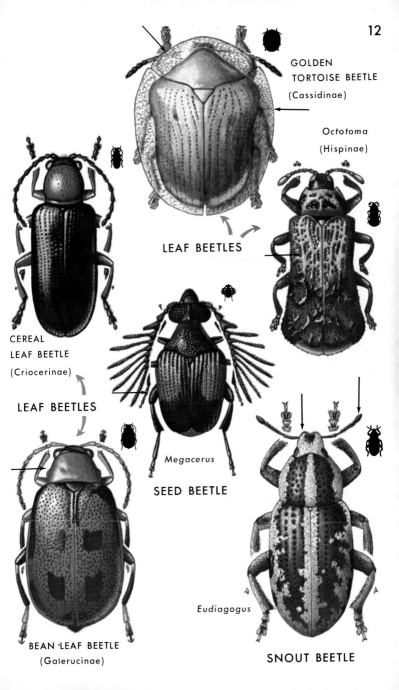

12

GOLDEN
TORTOISE BEETLE
(Cassidinae)

Octotoma
(Hispinae)

LEAF BEETLES

CEREAL
LEAF BEETLE
(Criocerinae)

LEAF BEETLES

Megacerus

SEED BEETLE

BEAN LEAF BEETLE
(Galerucinae)

Eudiagogus

SNOUT BEETLE

RARE CLICK BEETLES:
Family Cerophytidae

Identification. Distinctive for hind trochanters and body form: Hind trochanters very *long* — nearly as long as femora. Head partly visible from above. Sides of pronotum *rounded,* lacking a distinct margin, hind angles *pointed.* Elytra have impressed *striae.* Each antenna 11-segmented, *comblike* in ♂ (Fig. 71), *sawtoothed* in ♀; head protrudes between antennae. Claws *comblike.* Tarsi 5-5-5. 5.5–8.5 mm.

Similar families. The hind trochanters and body form distinguish rare click beetles. Beetles otherwise similar include: (1) click beetles (p. 172); (2) false click beetles (p. 179); (3) cebrionid beetles (p. 171); (4) perothopid beetles (p. 179); (5) death-watch beetles (p. 199); (6) soft-bodied plant beetles (p. 152); (7) false darkling beetles (p. 264); (8) Texas beetles (p. 159); (9) darkling beetles (p. 249); and (10) comb-clawed beetles (p. 256).

Range and numbers. 1 genus and 2 species; 1 occurs in ne. U.S., the other in Calif.

Habits and examples. Larvae are unknown. Adults are found in rotting wood, beneath dead bark, and on foliage. The e. U.S. species, *Cerophytum pulsator* (Hald.), 7.5–8.5 mm, is mostly black with reddish palps and tarsi. Its body is covered with moderately dense yellowish hairs.

Collecting methods. In the rare instances when these beetles have been collected they were swept from foliage or taken from rotting wood or under dead bark.

THROSCID BEETLES: Family Throscidae

Identification. Form and usually antennae distinctive — these beetles look like small, stout click beetles (p. 172). Hind angles of pronotum *extend* backward, smoothly joining sides of elytra. Body nearly always widest at *humeri;* in a few species sides of elytra are nearly parallel. Each antenna usually (in 19 of 27 species) ends in a *3-segmented club;* antennae sometimes *sawtoothed,* rarely threadlike. Dorsal surface covered with light-colored hairs. Union of prothorax and body not loose and flexible — as a result, these beetles are not able to click. Most are brown, some black, infrequently with red markings. Elytra usually striate. 1.6–5 mm.

Similar families. (1) Click beetles (p. 172) — generally larger; union of prothorax to body loose, able to click; antennae never clubbed. (2) False click beetles (p. 179) — often larger; often widest at pronotum; antennae never clubbed. (3) Some metallic wood-boring beetles (p. 165) are similar but antennae sawtoothed; most metallic, especially ventrally. (4) Biphyllid beetles (p. 240) — hind angles of pronotum not extended. (5) Fruitworm beetles (p.

240) — tarsi lobed. (6) Silken fungus beetles (p. 222) — hind angles of pronotum not extended. (7) Eucinetid beetles (p. 151) — antennae threadlike. (8) Small carrion beetles (p. 122) — antennal club usually 5-segmented.

Range and numbers. 4 genera and 27 species in N. America; most in e. U.S.

Habits. Adults are most common on flowers and foliage. Larvae live in litter or rotting wood; they are believed to be carnivorous.

Collecting methods. These beetles are usually collected by beating or sweeping low vegetation during late afternoon or evening on warm spring and early summer days. They are also attracted to lights. Sometimes they are found in Berlese samples of forest litter gathered in cold weather.

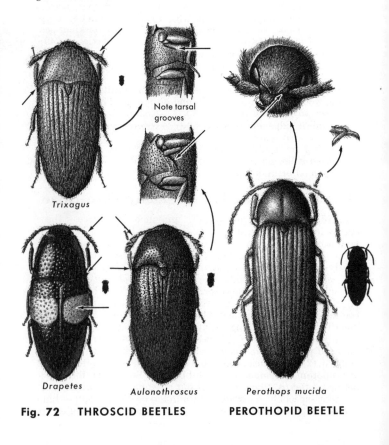

Note tarsal grooves

Trixagus

Drapetes   *Aulonothroscus*

Perothops mucida

Fig. 72   THROSCID BEETLES   PEROTHOPID BEETLE

Examples. In e. U.S. members of *Aulonothroscus* (14 species; e. U.S. to Tex., 1 w. U.S.) and *Trixagus* (5 species; 3 e. U.S., 2 w. U.S.) are most common. *Aulonothroscus* species have *long, deep tarsal grooves* on the metasternum; *Trixagus* species have *short, shallow* tarsal grooves (see Fig. 72). All species have clubbed antennae; most are 3–4 mm long. The 7 *Drapetes* species (e. U.S. to Ariz.) have *sawtoothed* antennae. Most are around 4 mm long and black; a few have red markings.

PEROTHOPID BEETLES:
Family Perothopidae

Identification. Very similar to click beetles and false click beetles. Antennae *threadlike*, arising *between* eyes, not close to eyes. Prothorax *movable.* Claws *comblike.* Sides of body nearly parallel; elytra striate. Covered with moderately dense, short, bristling hairs. Tarsi 5-5-5. Brown to dark brown. Prosternum not lobed in front. 10–25 mm.

Similar families. (1) Click beetles (p. 172) — prosternum lobed in front; antennae close to eyes; claws infrequently comblike. (2) False click beetles (p. 179) — prothorax not free and movable; claws not comblike. (3) Texas beetles (p. 159) — antennae sawtoothed from 5th segment to tip. (4) Rare click beetles (p. 177) — antennae comblike or sawtoothed. (5) Soft-bodied plant beetles (p. 152) — claws not comblike.

Range and numbers. 1 genus containing 3 species; 1 in e. U.S., 2 in Calif.

Habits and examples. Larvae are unknown and little is known about habits of adults. The single e. U.S. species, *Perothops mucida* (Gyll.), 11–18 mm, has been collected only on old beech and young apple trees. Groups of 1 Calif. species, *P. witticki* LeC. (very similar to *P. mucida*), gather on Calif. live oaks. At one site about 30 miles south of San Diego, over 500 adult beetles dropped from a single tree during a 3-day period, but none were found on nearby trees.

Collecting methods. Species are rarely collected. In e. U.S., look on old beech and young apple trees. In Calif. look for large groups of beetles gathered on or near mature oak trees, especially during May and June.

FALSE CLICK BEETLES:
Family Eucnemidae

Identification. Very similar to click beetles: body elongate-narrow, nearly parallel-sided to (often) *broadest* at pronotum and *tapering* toward rear. Clicking (flipping) ability poorly developed. Front edge of prosternum *straight across* (not lobed). Head often strongly convex. Antennae not close to eyes; each 11-segmented, sawtoothed from 3rd or 4th segment to tip, beadlike, threadlike, comblike, or fan-shaped. Elytra striate. Tarsi 5-5-5. 3–18 mm, usually 3–10 mm.

Similar families. (1) Click beetles (p. 172) — prosternum lobed at front; union of prothorax with body loose, able to click; body usually parallel-sided or widest at prothorax. (2) Perothopid beetles (p. 179) — tarsal claws comblike, union of prothorax and body loose. (3) Soft-bodied plant beetles (p. 152) — hind angles of pronotum not elongate. (4) Throscid beetles (p. 177) — each antenna usually ends in a 3-segmented club. (5) Texas beetles (p. 159) — antennae sawtoothed from 5th segment to tip. (6) Metallic wood-boring beetles (p. 165) — nearly all look metallic on ventral surfaces. (7) Rare click beetles (p. 177) — hind trochanters very long. (8) Lizard beetles (p. 224) — antennae clubbed.

Range and numbers. The 27 genera contain 67 species; most in e. U.S.

Habits. These are sometimes called cross-wood borers because larvae cut characteristic mines across grain of wood. They bore into various hardwoods; wood is generally somewhat rotted, so damage is of no economic importance. Larvae look like buprestid larvae, but the cutting edges of their mandibles are on the outside surfaces. In adults of a few species the union of prothorax and mesothorax is loose enough to allow them to click and flip, like click beetles. Some false click beetles quiver their antennae constantly (see *Dirhagus,* Fig. 73) — a habit not found in click beetles.

Collecting methods. Collected infrequently — not nearly as common as the click beetles that many strongly resemble. False click beetles are most often beaten or swept from vegetation (sometimes that of host trees); some are found under bark of host trees. A few fly to lights.

Examples. *Fornax* species (10 species; e. U.S.) strongly resemble click beetles; length is 5–16 mm. The 3 *Isorhipis* species (4–7 mm; ne. U.S. to Ga.) are mostly black with orange to light brown at base of elytra. Antennae of ♀ are sawtoothed; those of ♂ are comblike to fan-shaped. *I. obliqua* (Say) has been reared from branches of sugar maple, beech, and ironwood trees. Adults often feign death. They can spring an inch or more into the air. The 4 *Melasis* species (6–8 mm; much of N. America) have distinctly flattened tibiae. *M. pectinicornis* Melsh. occurs from Md. to Tex. Most of the 8 *Dirhagus* species (3–6.5 mm; e. U.S. to Tex.) have sawtoothed antennae, but sometimes ♂ antennae are comblike. In *D. humeralis* (Say) elytra are red at base. Other species of *Dirhagus* are entirely black or dark brown. The 6 *Nematodes* species (e. U.S. to Tex.; 6–9 mm) differ from most false click beetles in having threadlike antennae. *Dromaeolus* is the largest genus, with 11 species (3.5–8.5 mm; widely distributed). Their antennae are threadlike to slightly sawtoothed.

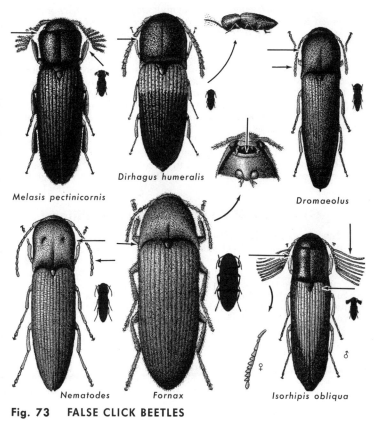

Melasis pectinicornis

Dirhagus humeralis

Dromaeolus

Nematodes

Fornax

Isorhipis obliqua

Fig. 73   FALSE CLICK BEETLES

Superfamily Cantharoidea

In these beetles the elytra are leathery and flexible, and the body is generally soft. Often medium-sized.

TELEGEUSID BEETLES:
Family Telegeusidae

Identification. Very similar to many rove beetles (p. 110), but form and exposed flying wings are distinctive: Body elongate, *nar-*

row. Elytra *short,* exposing part of abdomen; flying wings *not concealed* beneath elytra. Palps often greatly *enlarged.* Eyes large. Antennae short and *threadlike;* each 11-segmented. Tarsi 5-5-5. 5–8 mm. Found only in Ariz.

Similar families. (1) Rove beetles (p. 110) have flying wings concealed beneath the elytra. (2) Some soldier beetles (p. 183) are similar but antennae long. (3) Similar species of long-horned beetles (p. 279) have long antennae. (4) Checkered beetles (p. 208) have bristling hairs; antennae usually clubbed.

Range and numbers. The single genus contains 2 species that occur only in Ariz.

Habits and examples. Very little is known about these beetles' habits. Larvae have not yet been discovered.

Collecting methods. In the infrequent instances when these have been collected, they have usually been attracted to lights.

GLOWWORMS: Family Phengodidae

Identification. Males distinctive for antennae and mandibles: Antennae *long,* each *12-segmented, feathery;* mandibles *long, slender, prominent.* Elytra sometimes *short,* exposing most of flying wings. Tarsi 5-5-5. 4.5–20 mm. Females *larviform* — resemble larvae but have compound eyes.

Similar families. Only beetles with similar antennae can be confused with adult males of this family — see: (1) Wedge-shaped beetles (p. 268) — end of abdomen blunt. (2) Fire-colored beetles (p. 260) — tarsi 5-5-4.

Range and numbers. 6 genera and 25 species in N. America; most in sw. U.S.

Habits. Larvae and females are found in leaf litter, under logs, beneath bark, or other objects on ground; most larvae are strongly luminescent — the source of the common name for this family. Larvae feed on soft-bodied insects and other small organisms; they are sometimes quite large and may reach 65 mm (over 1½ in.). Adult females are larviform but have compound eyes; larvae have simple eyes.

Collecting methods. Collected infrequently. Males fly to lights summer to fall. For females look beneath logs, under dead bark, and in leaf litter.

Examples. *Phengodes,* with 10 species, and *Zarhipis,* with 8 species, are the largest genera. *Phengodes* species are widely distributed, with 7 species in sw. U.S.; *Zarhipis* species occur in Calif. In *Phengodes* species tip of each elytron is distinctly narrower than base, and most of flying wings are usually exposed. In *Zarhipis* tip of each elytron is less pointed than in *Phengodes. Phengodes plumosa* (Oliv.), 11–12 mm, occurs over much of e. U.S. In fall it is attracted to lights.

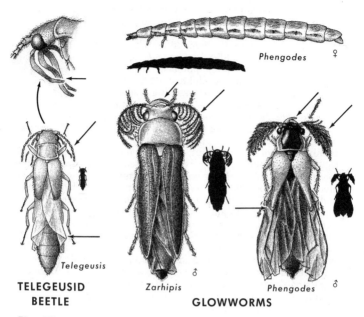

Phengodes ♀

Telegeusis

TELEGEUSID BEETLE

Zarhipis ♂

GLOWWORMS

Phengodes ♂

Fig. 74

SOLDIER BEETLES: Family Cantharidae
(Figs. 75, 76; see also Pl. 2)

Identification. Body elongate, *soft,* somewhat *flattened,* sides nearly parallel. Legs and antennae *long,* slender; antennae thread-like, rarely sawtoothed or comblike. Elytra *loosely* cover abdomen; over ⅓ of species (usually 1–5 mm) have short elytra, exposing wings and abdomen. Head usually visible from above; pronotum not distinctly extended over head. Usually black or brown; often with red, orange, or yellow on pronotum; some are mostly yellow and with black markings on elytra. Tarsi 5-5-5; 4th segment lobed underneath. 1–15 mm.

Similar families. (1) Lightningbugs (p. 188) — pronotum extends over head, concealing it from above; abdomen often has light organs. (2) Net-winged beetles (p. 186) — a network of raised lines on elytra. (3) Glowworms (p. 182) — antennae feathery. (4) Blister beetles (p. 270) — body cylindrical, head nearly square and with a distinct neck; tarsi 5-5-4. (5) Some long-horned beetles (p. 279) are similar but tarsi apparently 4-4-4. (6) False blister beetles (p. 262) — no distinct margin on sides of pronotum; tarsi 5-5-4. (7) Fire-colored beetles (p. 260) — tarsi 5-5-4; antennae sawtoothed, comblike, or feathery. (8) Some soft-winged flower beetles (p. 211) are similar to some soldier beetles (*Silis* species — see p. 187) but sides of pronotum never notched. (9) Checkered beetles (p. 208) — antennae usually clubbed. (10) Ship-timber beetles (p. 214) — very elongate; antennae short, sawtoothed. (11) Micromalthid beetles (p. 81) — 1.5–2.5 mm long; antennae short, beadlike. (12) Telegeusid beetles (p. 181) — antennae short.

Range and numbers. 16 genera and 455 species; widely distributed in N. America.

Habits. Adults are abundant on flowers and foliage, where they feed on nectar, pollen, or other insects (often aphids); insect-eating species are beneficial. Most larvae are carnivorous (some are omnivorous) and usually live on damp ground, beneath objects, or under loose bark. Larvae generally eat other soft-bodied insects, such as small caterpillars, maggots, and grasshopper eggs; a few feed on plants such as grains, potatoes, and celery. Most larvae are covered with dense (often dark) bristles that make them look velvety.

Collecting methods. Adults are common and readily collected on leaves or flowers with a sweep net, an umbrella, or by hand. Some smaller species are captured most often by beating or sweeping foliage in shady or moist areas, or by sweeping grasses and low vegetation in boggy areas or near streams.

Examples. Some of the 18 *Chauliognathus* species (see also Pl. 2) are abundant on flowers, including goldenrod, linden, wild hydrangea, and milkweed. They are usually large (8–14 mm long) and yellow or orange-yellow (rarely red) with black markings (sometimes absent); head is large and prominent. *C. pennsylvanicus* DeG. (e. U.S. to Tex.; 9–12 mm) is abundant on goldenrod and related plants in fall. *Trypherus latipennis* (Germar) (e. U.S.; 6–7 mm long) is 1 of 4 species in the genus; it has very short elytra. It may be common on catnip, flowers of red haw, and foliage of various plants.

Podabrus, with 108 species (7–14 mm), is one of the 2 largest genera. These beetles resemble species in the genus *Cantharis,* but in *Podabrus* species front of pronotum is concave or straight across and does not conceal head (Fig. 75). (In *Cantharis* pronotum is rounded in front and partially conceals head.) Members of *Podabrus* are common on foliage. Many species feed on aphids or other soft-bodied insects. Some feed exclusively on aphids and are valuable in reducing populations of these pests. In arid regions, especially in mountains, most *Podabrus* species often live close to water. Adults of *P. tomentosus* (Say) feed on all kinds of aphids; they live east of the Rocky Mts. and are 9–12 mm long. Larvae live in soil and are covered with pink, velvety hair. The 56 *Cantharis* species (widely distributed; 4–14 mm) usually live on foliage; habits of many are similar to those of *Podabrus* species.

The 13 *Polemius* species (widely distributed) are medium-sized (6–8 mm) and have flattened, more or less sawtoothed antennae. *Polemius* species are uncommon, but may be found on plants in moist areas. In the 80 *Silis* species (widely distributed; 3–6 mm)

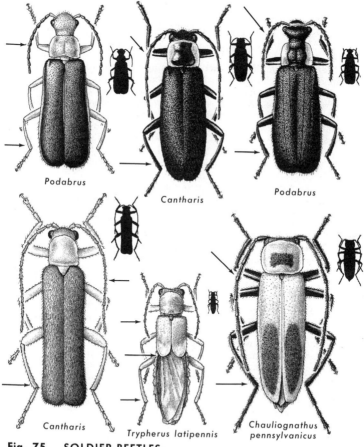

Podabrus

Cantharis

Podabrus

Cantharis

Trypherus latipennis

Chauliognathus pennsylvanicus

Fig. 75   SOLDIER BEETLES

sides of *pronotum* are *strongly notched* and most of head is concealed from above. *Silis* species are nearly always black (sometimes brown) with a red to yellow pronotum; antennae are long and sawtoothed. These beetles are common on foliage. *Malthodes* is the largest genus, with 130 species (1–5 mm; widely distributed — many in w. U.S.). Elytra are usually *short, exposing* flying wings. Most are collected on leaves in moist shady areas. Each *Malthodes* species is usually adapted to a precise habitat, and is rarely found elsewhere. Species are most often distinguished by form of tip of abdomen in ♂.

NET-WINGED BEETLES: Family Lycidae
(Fig. 76; see also Pl. 3)

Identification. Elytral sculpturing and form distinctive: Elytra have a network of lengthwise *ridges* and less distinct *cross-ridges* (sculpturing is weakly developed in a few species). Elytra nearly always *broadest toward rear* and extending *loosely* beyond body margins. Body *soft*. Head more or less *concealed from above*, sometimes with a beak. Sides of pronotum compressed, surface also flattened. Antennae long, often flattened, nearly always *sawtoothed* or *threadlike*. Usually black, often with red or orange markings, sometimes almost entirely red or orange. Tarsi 5-5-5. 3–19 mm — usually over 6 mm long.

Similar families. (1) Lightningbugs (p. 188) — elytra lack network of ridges; last 2–3 abdominal segments often yellow and luminous. (2) Soldier beetles (p. 183) — elytra lack network of ridges; head usually clearly visible from above. (3) Glowworms (p. 182) — elytra lack network of ridges; body short; antennae feathery. (4) Some leaf beetles (Hispinae, p. 302) are similar but antennae short, often weakly clubbed; body hard. (5) Reticulated beetles (p. 80) — head prominent from above.

Range and numbers. 17 genera and 78 species in N. America; most in w. U.S.

Habits. Adults are active in daytime on foliage, flowers, or tree trunks, usually in dense woods or moist places. Some are predaceous, others are believed to feed on decaying vegetation. Larvae are carnivorous and live under bark.

Collecting methods. Sweeping or beating vegetation in densely wooded areas is most productive; a few may be found under logs. Some fly to lights. Net-winged beetles are fairly common in e. U.S.; locally abundant in sw. U.S.

Examples. *Plateros* is the largest genus with 32 species (widely distributed, 4–10.5 mm). Usually black with dull orange markings on pronotum. *Plateros* species can be identified by ♂ characters only; a ♀ can be identified to species only if captured while mating with an identifiable ♂. The largest (8.5–19 mm) and most attrac-

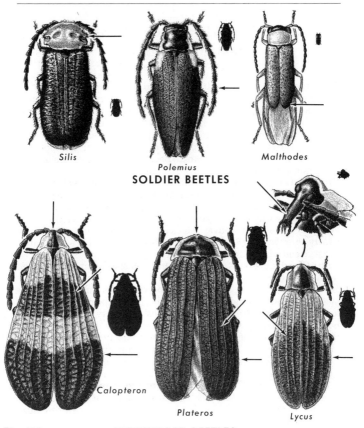

Silis

Polemius

SOLDIER BEETLES

Malthodes

Calopteron

Plateros

Lycus

Fig. 76   NET-WINGED BEETLES

tive net-winged beetles are the 3 species of *Calopteron*. All are
found from e. U.S. nearly to Rocky Mts. They are mostly black
with yellow-orange markings on elytra and sides of pronotum. *C.
reticulatum* (Fab.), 11–19 mm, is our largest species. It has light
markings at base of elytra and in a broad band across the middle.
C. discrepans (Newm.), 9.5–15 mm, is very similar to *C. reticulatum*. In *C. terminale* (Say), 8.5–16 mm, the elytra are mostly
yellow-orange, with black only at tip. The 12 *Lycus* species (usually 8–10 mm) occur in e. to sw. U.S.; they have *beaks* that are as
long as the beaks of many snout beetles (see Figs. 76 and 135).

LIGHTNINGBUGS or FIREFLIES:
Family Lampyridae
(Figs. 77, 78; see also Pl. 3)

Identification. Form distinctive: Head *concealed* from above by *flattened* pronotum (head often extended in life), pronotum nearly as wide as elytra; body *soft,* flattened, often with nearly *parallel sides,* both ends *rounded.* Elytra *loosely* covering body; ♀ sometimes short-winged or wingless. Antennae threadlike to saw-toothed, rarely with lateral projections. Often 1 or 2 abdominal segments are luminescent. Most species are brown or black with light markings. Tarsi 5-5-5. 4.5–20 mm.

Similar families. (1) Net-winged beetles (p. 186) — elytra with network of distinct lengthwise ridges and less distinct cross-ridges. (2) Soldier beetles (p. 183) — head clearly visible from above; sometimes with short elytra. (3) Glowworms (p. 182) — head clearly visible from above; feathery antennae; elytra short, abruptly narrowed. (4) Ship-timber beetles (p. 214) — antennae short; head visible from above.

Range and numbers. 20 genera and 136 species in N. America; most in e. U.S.

Habits. This family is quite well-known for its luminescent species. All larvae and most adults produce light. The process is chemical and nearly 100% efficient — almost no energy is given off as heat; even the eggs of some species glow faintly. Luminescent abdominal segments of adults are ivory or glazed in appearance when not glowing. In most N. American fireflies flashing plays an important role in courtship and is the means by which the sexes recognize each other. In common species the ♂ flashes in flight and is then attracted to answering flashes of the ♀ on the ground. In these species the ♂ often has very large eyes. Each species has a distinctive pattern of flashes, and a beetle specialist can recognize most species solely by the number, duration, and interval between flashes. Some females answer flashes of males of other species, then subdue and eat any ♂ that is attracted to them; this is termed aggressive mimicry. Species that do not flash or that have weakly developed flash organs are generally active in daytime. Many females are fully winged (as are nearly all males), but some have short wings or none at all and look like larvae. These larviform females have eyes that are compound (containing 200 or more facets), not simple, as in larvae. Larvae feed on smaller insects, insect larvae, snails, and slugs. Food of most adults is not known. Larvae and most adults are nocturnal; in the daytime these beetles may be found clinging to foliage, tree trunks, or branches. Species typically breed in damp areas near swamps, marshes, or rivers.

Collecting methods: Many lightningbugs (nearly always males) are readily collected at night with an aerial net or by hand when they are flashing. With much effort wingless females of some species can be found on the ground when they answer flashing of a ♂. Some species that do not flash can sometimes be found during the day — look on trunks and branches of trees during spring and summer and on flowers in fall. Those that flash at night rest in the daytime on foliage (usually in or near moist areas) where they can be captured in a sweep net. Males of those species that flash are readily collected, but flightless females are much less easily collected; in fact, some species are known from ♂ specimens only. Fireflies rarely fly to lights.

Examples. The 16 *Pyractomena* species (8–15 mm) live in e. U.S. In these species the pronotum bears a more or less distinct median ridge. The light organs are well-developed in both sexes; those of ♂ occupy the entire 5th and 6th abdominal segments, those of ♀ are at the sides of the segments, and the middle of each segment is dark or dusky. The 3 *Lucidota* species (e. U.S.; 5–11 mm) are distinctive for their flattened, non-sawtoothed antennae that gradually become narrower toward the tips. Light organs are weakly developed; in the ♀ they are marked by yellow spots on the last ventral segment and in the ♂ by yellow areas on the last 2 ventral segments. These species are active in daytime and are found in shady places. The 4 *Ellychnia* species (widely distributed; 5–14 mm) have no light organs; they are active during the day and are sometimes common on tree trunks in spring or on goldenrod and asters in autumn.

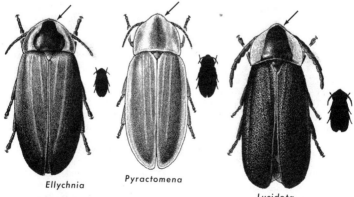

Ellychnia

Pyractomena

Lucidota

Fig. 77   **LIGHTNINGBUGS**

Each of the 20 species of *Photuris* (e. U.S. to Kans. and Tex.) has a distinctive courtship signal. The intervals between these flashes are an important factor in attracting a ♂ to a ♀; a ♀ can sometimes be attracted by a flashlight mimicking the males' flashes. Light organs generally occupy 5th and 6th abdominal segments. One species, *P. fairchildi* Barber, shows some variation in its flash pattern — the number of flashes often increases as a ♂ approaches an answering ♀. Females of this species are aggressive mimics, often answering flash signals of ♂ fireflies of *Pyractomena* and *Photinus*. The 28 *Photinus* species range over the same areas as *Photuris* species and are often similar in appearance. Members of these 2 genera are the most readily collected fireflies. The 2 genera can be distinguished by the form of the side of each elytron (Fig. 78): In *Photuris* species the lateral margin of each elytron is incomplete at the base, whereas in *Photinus* species the margin is complete and distinct at the base. Light organs of *Photinus* species are always larger in ♂ than in ♀; in ♂ they occupy the entire ventral abdominal segments behind the 4th segment; in ♀ they occur just in the middle of the ventral segments.

Superfamily Dermestoidea

These are nearly always small; antennae clubbed.

TOOTH-NECKED FUNGUS BEETLES:
Family Derodontidae

Identification. Head with a pair of *ocelli-like* tubercles, sometimes large, prominent. Each antenna ends in a loose, 3-segmented *club*. Elytra widest before tip, with striae consisting of rows of punctures that are usually *large* and *close together*. Some species (4 of 9) have prominent "teeth" along side of pronotum; in 1 species the sides (lateral margins) of pronotum are expanded. Brown, sometimes with dark markings. Hair absent or (in 3 species) bristling. 1.8–6 mm.

Similar families. (1) Silken fungus beetles (p. 222) have no elytral striae and no ocelli-like tubercles on the head. (2) Hairy fungus beetles (p. 242) have no ocelli-like tubercles. (3) Fruitworm beetles (p. 240) have no elytral striae. (4) Cerylonid beetles (p. 228) have a strong antennal club.

Range and numbers. 3 genera and 9 species in N. America; in ne. and w. U.S.

Habits. Adults and larvae of some species live together (sometimes in large numbers) under loose bark or on fungi; they apparently feed on fungi. One species (*Laricobius erichsonii*) preys on aphids.

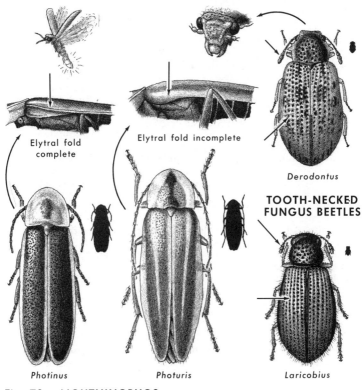

Elytral fold complete

Elytral fold incomplete

Derodontus

TOOTH-NECKED FUNGUS BEETLES

Photinus

Photuris

Laricobius

Fig. 78 LIGHTNINGBUGS

Collecting methods. Collected infrequently. Look under loose bark and on fungi; one species may be swept from foliage.

Examples. The 4 *Derodontus* species (2.5–3 mm) are the source of the common name for the family — in this genus the sides of the pronotum are toothed. These beetles lack dorsal hairs and have prominent elytral striae. One species occurs in ne. U.S., the other from Alaska to B.C. *Laricobius erichsonii* Rosenh. has been imported from Europe and released among aphid-infested firs in N.B. Its larvae feed on aphid eggs; adults are active on warm sunny days. The 4 *Laricobius* species have dorsal hairs.

WOUNDED-TREE BEETLES:
Family Nosodendridae

Identification. Body *oval.* Head *visible* from above; dorsal surface *convex; black.* Elytra with rows of short hair *tufts* that are easily rubbed off. Head directed forward. Antennal *club* abrupt, 3-segmented. Tibiae broadened toward end. Tarsi 5-5-5. 4–6 mm.
Similar families. (1) Sap beetles (p. 215) — abdomen nearly always exposed; tibiae not expanded. (2) Pleasing fungus beetles (p. 226) — elytra striate. (3) Pill beetles (p. 155) — head directed downward; antennae threadlike or gradually clubbed. (4) Chelonariid beetles (p. 159) — head concealed. (5) Dermestid beetles (p. 192) — tibiae not expanded, head directed downward. (6) Death-watch beetles (p. 199) — antennal club asymmetrical (lopsided) if present. (7) Round fungus beetles (p. 124) — antennal club weak; elytra often striate. (8) Monommid beetles (p. 245) — elytra striate.
Range and numbers. 1 genus, containing 2 species; 1 in ne. U.S. to Kans., 1 along Pacific Coast and in Idaho.
Habits. Adults and larvae live on oozing wounds of trees (often elms, alders, and oaks in e. U.S., firs and oaks in w. U.S.) that are infected with microorganisms, called slime fluxes. Adults are believed to be carnivorous; larvae might be also.
Collecting methods. Slime fluxes are marked by a black stain on trees, caused by oozing sap. Look carefully in the wettest part of the wound for concealed adults. These beetles can be moderately common there. Some are also found on carrion.
Examples. *Nosodendron californicum* Horn (Pacific Coast and Idaho; not shown) occurs in fir and oak slime fluxes. In cold parts of its range, this beetle is often found in sap-exuding frost cracks. The greatest numbers of adults may be found in the wet mass of needles and litter at the base of a frost crack. *N. unicolor* Say (ne. U.S.) is fairly common in slime fluxes of oaks, elms, alders, and other hardwoods; it also occurs on carrion, but not commonly.

DERMESTID BEETLES:
Family Dermestidae
(Figs. 79, 80; see also Pl. 3)

Identification. Body *elongate-robust* to nearly *circular;* head more or less *concealed* from above, directed downward, often with a median *ocellus.* Antennae *short, clubbed* — club usually abrupt and consisting of 3 segments; antennae often fit into *grooves* below each side of pronotum. Often covered with *scales* or *hair* that form a pattern. Body usually brown to black. Tarsi 5-5-5. 1–12 mm. The **Odd Beetle** (p. 194) departs greatly from this description.

Similar families. No other beetles of this form have an *ocellus*. (1) Death-watch beetles (p. 199) — antennae longer; if clubbed, club is asymmetrical (lopsided). (2) Fungus weevils (p. 307) have a beak. (3) Seed beetles (p. 304) have a beak and an exposed pygidium. (4) Pill beetles (p. 155) — each antenna, if clubbed, ends in a gradual club. (5) Fruitworm beetles (p. 240) — tarsal segments 2 and 3 have lobes beneath. (6) Marsh beetles (p. 149) — antennae threadlike to weakly sawtoothed. (7) Some false darkling beetles (p. 264) are similar but their antennae are threadlike. (8) Wounded-tree beetles (p. 192) — tibiae expanded; head directed forward. (9) Chelonariid beetles (p. 159) — antennae sawtoothed. (10) Eucinetid beetles (p. 151) — antennae threadlike. (11) Small carrion beetles (p. 122) — loose, gradual antennal club. (12) Monommid beetles (p. 245) — elytra striate.

Range and numbers. 15 genera and about 123 species, widely distributed in N. America.

Habits. Dermestid beetles are sometimes called skin beetles, for they are primarily scavengers that feed on dried skin and other soft remains of animals, such as fur, feathers, wool, leather, and hides. They also eat carpets, silk, dried meats, dead insects, and stuffed animals, and some feed on cork, seeds, grain, or cereal products. A few species are very troublesome pests in insect collections; a collection that is not protected by a fumigant can be totally destroyed. The larvae of these beetles cause hundreds of millions of dollars worth of damage to animal and plant materials each year.

Nosodendron unicolor

WOUNDED-TREE BEETLE

BLACK LARDER BEETLE

LARDER BEETLE

DERMESTID BEETLES

Fig. 79

Some small dermestids are found in bee or wasp nests, where they feed on old pollen stores or on dried remains of bees or wasps. Some live in bird nests and eat old feathers, or in mammal nests, where they feed on hair or fur. A few prey on wasp and bee larvae or eat spider eggs. Adults of many smaller species occur on various flowers, where they feed on pollen and nectar; they often feign death when disturbed. Larvae are hairy and most have 1 or more dense tufts of hair. Larvae of certain dermestids are used in museums to clean dried skin, fur, muscles, etc. from bones to be added to collections — dermestids do this job better than any other means available.

Collecting methods. Many smaller species are common on various flowers, primarily in spring, and can be swept or collected by hand. Some dermestid beetles (especially *Dermestes* species) are common on old dried animal carcasses. Check the inside of windows in houses or buildings for dermestids in spring — their presence will not only provide an opportunity to collect specimens, but will also indicate an infestation indoors, usually in carpets. A few species can be found in mammal or bird nests, but larvae are more common in these situations than adults. Adults fly to lights.

Examples. The 15 *Dermestes* species (widely distributed) include the largest species in this family (5–12 mm); they are typically black, often with gray hairs. The **Larder Beetle,** *D. lardarius* L., and the **Black Larder Beetle,** *D. ater* DeG., are pests found in dried meats, cheese, and other foods of animal origin, or on hides and furs. Both species may be common and numerous in dried remains of dead animals; they occur worldwide. The **Odd Beetle,** *Thylodrias contractus* Mots., 2.5–3 mm, is highly unusual in appearance. The ♂ is clearly beetlelike, but the ♀ looks more like a larva than an adult. Larviform adults occur in other families (such as glowworms, p. 182) — a larviform adult differs from a true larva in having compound eyes, not ocelli. The 4 *Orphilus* species (2–3 mm) are widely distributed. They are black and differ from typical dermestids in lacking hairs and scales on dorsal surface.

The 9 *Attagenus* species (widely distributed) are brown to black and sparsely covered with hairs. In these beetles the antennal club is 3-segmented, and in the ♂ length of last segment of club exceeds combined length of 2 preceding segments. In some areas the **Black Carpet Beetle,** *A. megatoma* (Fab.), 3–5 mm, is the most destructive household dermestid. The 12 *Anthrenus* species (widely distributed; 1.8–4 mm long) are distinctive for the flat, colored scales that often form a pattern on their broad bodies. The **Buffalo Carpet Beetle,** *A. scrophulariae* (L.), 2.2–3.5 mm, occurs worldwide and is probably the best-known dermestid. Its larvae feed on woollen fabrics, dried animal products, dried insects, and other museum specimens. Adults emerge in spring and are common on flowers and inside windows of buildings containing infested articles. The 9 *Novelsis* species (Pl. 3) occur in Tex. and west of the Rocky Mts.

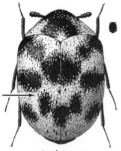

Anthrenus

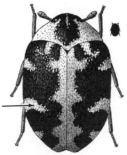

BUFFALO CARPET BEETLE

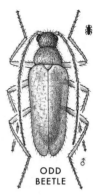

ODD BEETLE

Orphilus

Megatoma variegata

Cryptorhopalum

Larva

Trogoderma

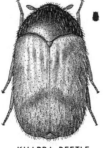

KHAPRA BEETLE

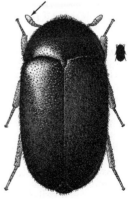

BLACK CARPET BEETLE

Fig. 80   **DERMESTID BEETLES**

Segments of antennal club are loosely joined, not compact as in most dermestids.

The 15 *Trogoderma* species (2–5 mm; widely distributed) have an antennal club of 3–8 segments; club is symmetrical, comblike, or even fan-shaped. These beetles frequently have light markings and light hairs on a dark background. Some live on plant material as well as on animal remains. The **Khapra Beetle,** *T. granarium* Everts, is a foreign pest that has been accidentally introduced at various points in U.S. When an infestation is found the U.S. Department of Agriculture spares no expense to eradicate it, for potentially this beetle is a highly injurious pest. Attempts at eradication are complicated by the larva's habit of crawling into tight spaces, making it difficult to reach with insecticides. Larvae are most common in cereal products but also in animal products.

Cryptorhopalum is the largest genus in the family, with 32 species; they are light brown to black, usually 2–3 mm long, and are widely distributed. Antennal club consists of 2 segments, with next to last segment longer than last one. *Anthrenus* species are similar but have *flat scales* on dorsal surface; members of *Cryptorhopalum* have hairs (which are sometimes light and form a vague pattern) but never have scales (Fig. 80). No species of *Cryptorhopalum* are pests. All 9 species of *Megatoma* occur in w. U.S. Dorsal surface frequently bears light markings. Larvae of *M. variegata* Horn feed on moth egg masses.

Superfamily Bostrichoidea

These beetles are often wood-borers; nearly always small; tarsi 5-5-5.

SPIDER BEETLES: Family Ptinidae

Identification. Form and characters distinctive: More or less *spiderlike;* elytra usually *oval,* sometimes elongate and nearly *parallel-sided,* infrequently *globular.* Thorax *narrower* than elytra. Legs and antennae usually *long, thin,* and covered with dense, light *hairs.* Head usually *concealed* from above, with no neck. Antennae inserted *close* together, threadlike, rarely with a 1-segmented club. Elytra usually covered with hairs or scales; striate, not shiny — in 3 species the elytra are hairless, non-striate, and shiny. 1–5 mm.

Similar families. (1) Some death-watch beetles (p. 199) are similar but their antennae are inserted farther apart (Fig. 82). (2) Antlike flower beetles (p. 276) and (3) antlike leaf beetles (p. 278) — head visible from above, with a neck. (4) Grass-root beetles (p. 130) —head visible; hairs sparse or absent. (5) Antlike stone beetles (p. 128) — head visible; antennal club 3- or 4-segmented.

Range and numbers. 10 genera and about 50 species in N. America; most in sw. U.S.

Habits. Larvae and adults are scavengers that feed on a wide variety of dead, dried animal and vegetable materials. In nature these beetles most frequently occur in nests of mammals, birds, and bees, on carrion, or wherever organic refuse accumulates. Some species are minor pests in warehouses, homes, mills, or museums, where they generally feed on grain, seeds, grain meal, flour, feathers, fishmeal, skins, drugs, roots, dried fruit, dried carrion, and sometimes wood. The spider beetles that are pests on stored materials are readily transported in commerce and are frequently introduced into new areas as a result; about 16 of our species have been introduced from other areas.

Collecting methods. Species that live indoors are collected most readily — look in stored organic materials or in organic debris. Outdoor species are uncommon — look in mammal, bird, or bee nests, and on dry carrion. Some fly to lights.

Examples. The 2 species of *Mezium* (1.5–3.5 mm) occur from e. U.S. to Tex.; elytra are round, smooth, and shiny. Both have dense, light-colored *hairs* on head, thorax, and appendages. *M. affine* Boield. (not shown) occurs in houses, warehouses, and granaries. It feeds on seeds and various kinds of animal and vegetable remains, including dead insects. The **American Spider Beetle,** *M. americanum* Lap., is found in houses, warehouses, granaries, and mills,

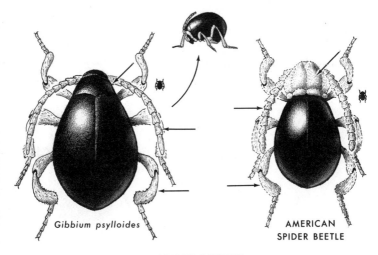

Gibbium psylloides   AMERICAN
                              SPIDER BEETLE

Fig. 81   **SPIDER BEETLES**

and feeds on seeds, grains, pepper, and other stored food. *Gibbium psylloides* (Czemp.), 2.3–2.8 mm, is similar to the 2 species of *Mezium* but has no hairs on head and pronotum; it is widely distributed. This beetle occurs in houses, warehouses, mills, granaries, bakeries, etc. It feeds on seeds, pepper, wheat bran, stale bread, decayed animal and vegetable refuse, cereals, leather, and other materials. *Mezium* and *Gibbium* species are rarely found outdoors.

The 35 *Ptinus* species (2–5 mm) are widely distributed but most are found from Tex. to sw. U.S. In most species both sexes have elytra that are similar in form and elongate to oblong. However, in about ⅓ of these species, elytra are elongate with nearly parallel sides in ♂; but in ♀ elytra are distinctly oval. The **White-marked Spider Beetle**, *P. fur* (L.) — widely distributed and 2.6–3.6 mm long — is generally the most common member of the genus *Ptinus*. It occurs both indoors and outdoors, and feeds on a wide variety of plant and animal materials, including insect specimens, wasp combs, feathers, skins, stuffed birds, dried plants, seeds, ginger, cacao, dates, pepper, bread, flour, cereals, grain, grain sacks, and

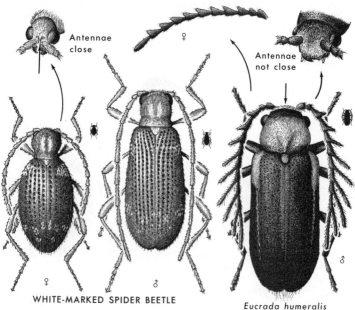

Antennae close

♀

Antennae not close

♀   ♂

WHITE-MARKED SPIDER BEETLE

Eucrada humeralis

♂

Fig. 82   SPIDER BEETLES   **DEATH-WATCH BEETLE**

even papered canvas partitions. Though it feeds on a wide variety of materials, this beetle is almost never a major pest, for egg output of ♀ is small and the developmental period of the larvae is comparatively long — each larva undergoes a long resting period before pupating. (Major pests typically build up large populations in a short period of time.)

Because spider beetle populations in stored material are rarely large, comparatively little food material is eaten, and little stored material is contaminated with silk and cocoons of pupated larvae. Larvae cause the most damage when they leave food material and bore through paper, cardboard, or wood containers or cloth sacking material in search of a pupation site.

DEATH-WATCH BEETLES:
Family Anobiidae
(see also Pl. 7)

Identification. Prothorax usually *hoodlike* — nearly always *enclosing head* and *concealing it* from above. Last 3 segments of each antenna are usually *lengthened* and *expanded,* or simply lengthened; club *not symmetrical.* Antennae sometimes sawtoothed, infrequently comblike, rarely threadlike. Body shape varies from elongate-cylindrical to oval or nearly spherical. Head and appendages moderately to highly *contractile* — appendages often can be retracted into hollows or grooves in body. Femora retract into *grooves* in hind coxae, most often light brown to black. Tarsi 5-5-5. 1.1–9 mm.

Similar families. (1) Branch-and-twig borers (p. 202) have short antennae, with a compact club. (2) Ptilodactylid beetles (p. 158) — scutellum heart-shaped; tarsi lobed. (3) Chelonariid beetles (p. 159) — 2nd and 3rd segments of each antenna enlarged, 5th–10th segments sawtoothed. (4) Rare click beetles (p. 177) — hind trochanters very long. In some beetles that are otherwise similar antennal club is symmetrical — see (5) dermestid beetles (p. 192); (6) bark-and-ambrosia beetles (p. 326); (7) pill beetles (p. 155); (8) minute tree-fungus beetles (p. 243); (9) fruitworm beetles (p. 240); and (10) dry-fungus beetles (p. 219).

Range and numbers. Widespread throughout N. America — about ⅔ of species in sw. U.S. 53 genera and 310 species.

Habits. Two species **(Drugstore Beetle** and **Cigarette Beetle)** are serious pests that feed on various stored organic materials, including drugs, tobacco, seeds, spices, cereal products, and leather. Larvae of many species bore into dead hardwoods and softwoods. Some of these — such as the **Furniture Beetle** and the **Death-watch Beetle,** *Xestobium rufovillosum* (De G.) — damage woodwork and structural wood of buildings. Larvae of some species feed in fungi, others in cones or twigs of conifers. A few eat seeds or tree bark. Certain wood-boring species produce a tapping sound by striking their mandibles against the walls of the tunnel as they burrow. Superstitious persons have interpreted the sound as a sign of coming death — this is the source of the common name for this family of beetles.

Collecting methods. In most collecting these beetles are encountered infrequently and in small numbers. In e. N. America sweeping or beating vegetation in dense woods or at edges of woods will yield some specimens (usually compact-bodied anobiids). Mature woods with much dead wood and fungi are most productive. Examine the catch in your net closely — these beetles usually withdraw their appendages and stay motionless when disturbed, so they are easily overlooked. Death-watch beetles may be found in numbers on foliage of dogwood and nearby plants. In one instance 2 collectors on 4 visits to a small collecting site were able to collect 120 specimens (representing 4 genera, 6 species) largely from dogwood foliage by hand-picking for a total of 1 hour, 20 minutes. Adults can be reared from larval host material (usually wood, fungi, bark, or seeds); they are also attracted to lights at night, but rarely in large numbers.

Examples. Larvae of *Eucrada humeralis* (Melsh.) bore beneath bark of dead oaks. Their tunnels lie halfway in wood and halfway in bark; little damage to wood results, so this species is of little economic importance. Before pupating each larva bores at an angle into bark close to surface. It spins a cocoon (a habit of only a few death-watch beetle larvae) and pupates. After emerging from the cocoon (generally in spring), adult gnaws an exit hole through bark to surface. Adults have an orange spot on each humerus. Form of antennae differs in sexes — comblike in ♂; sawtoothed in ♀ (Fig. 82).

Ernobius mollis (L.), not shown, occurs in e. U.S. and is widely distributed throughout the world. Larvae live primarily in bark of pines, but also in bark of spruce, larch, and fir trees; they may bore into wood underneath. They usually feed in seasoned wood, but also in recently felled trees. Sexes differ in that antennae are longer in ♂ than in ♀. The **Drugstore Beetle,** *Stegobium paniceum* (L.), feeds on a great variety of stored materials, including some that are extremely bitter or even poisonous to humans. Because the Drugstore Beetle and Cigarette Beetle are both often found in stored products, they are sometimes confused with each other, in spite of numerous differences. The best way to distinguish them is by studying the form of the antennae and the sculpturing on the elytra. The **Cigarette Beetle,** *Lasioderma serricorne* (F.), feeds on a great variety of dried stored materials, though it is best known as a pest of dried tobacco.

Trichodesma species (7 in N. America) are often quite attractive; they have tufts of *bristles* and a dense covering of *hair,* sometimes arranged in a pattern. Larvae bore into twigs and wood,

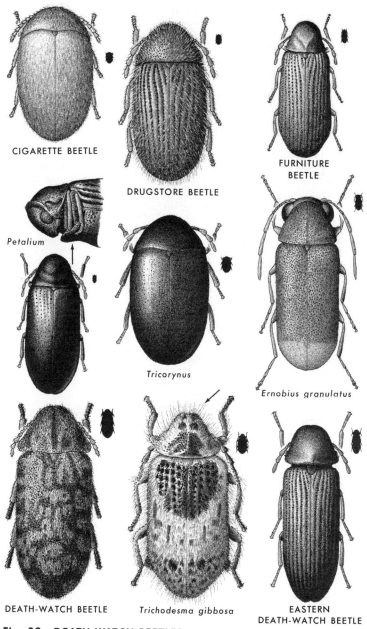

CIGARETTE BEETLE

DRUGSTORE BEETLE

FURNITURE BEETLE

Petalium

Tricorynus

Ernobius granulatus

DEATH-WATCH BEETLE

Trichodesma gibbosa

EASTERN DEATH-WATCH BEETLE

Fig. 83 **DEATH-WATCH BEETLES**

and may damage joists and studs in buildings. Of the 2 species occurring in e. U.S., *T. gibbosa* (Say) is more common. The **Furniture Beetle,** *Anobium punctatum* (DeG.), lives in dead or dying parts of trees or in fence posts outdoors. Damage done under these conditions is generally negligible, but when this beetle attacks old furniture, paneling, flooring, or structural wood, it is a serious pest. In a few years furniture or woodwork can be almost completely reduced to powder. First evidence of an attack is usually a small round exit hole left by adult; powdery frass formed by larvae may fall from this hole.

The **Eastern Death-watch Beetle,** *Hemicoelus carinatus* (Say), is the most common wood-damaging anobiid in e. N. America. Larvae bore into dead hardwood and softwood and may damage woodwork and structural wood of buildings. *Tricorynus* is the largest genus in this family, with 82 species. *T. confusus* (Fall), the most common species, eats a wide variety of foods and has been found in tobacco warehouses, where it could become a serious pest. The 23 *Petalium* species are distinctive for the broad lobe formed by front part of metasternum (Fig. 83).

The most distinctive character of the 8 *Ptilinus* species is the strongly comblike ♂ antennae; ♀ antennae are sawtoothed. Front of pronotum is *toothed* in both sexes — a character found in no other genus in this family. Larvae bore into hardwoods and may damage woodwork or structural members. *P. ruficornis* Say is the second most common wood-eating death-watch beetle in ne. N. America.

Many death-watch beetles are highly contractile but this characteristic is more highly developed in *Caenocara* species **(puffball beetles)** than in others. These beetles are common, though they are often overlooked or ignored due to their small size (1.5–2.5 mm) and their habit of lying still when disturbed, then suddenly flying off. In some species of *Dorcatoma* (such as *D. pallicornis* LeC.) the ♂ antennae are enlarged.

BRANCH-AND-TWIG BORERS:
Family Bostrichidae

Identification. Two general forms: (1) Most (53 of 60 species) are broadly to narrowly *cylindrical;* elytra parallel-sided; pronotum usually with *rasplike teeth* at front, pronotum as wide as head but not enclosing it; head bent down, nearly to completely *concealed* from above. (2) In 7 species (Subfamily Psoinae, most in w. U.S.) body flattened; head clearly visible from above. Antennal club of 3–4 segments, often enlarged to 1 side. Tarsi 5-5-5, 1st segment often small. Nearly always 2–24 mm, 1 w. species reaches 52 mm (up to 2 in.).

Similar families. (1) Some death-watch beetles (*Ptilinus* species,

p. 202) — antennae sawtoothed to fan-shaped. (2) Bark-and-ambrosia beetles (p. 326) — antennal club compact, seemingly of 1 segment. (3) Minute tree-fungus beetles (p. 243) and (4) dry-fungus beetles (p. 219) — antennal club symmetrical.

Range and numbers. The 60 species (18 genera) occur nearly throughout N. America, but most live in sw. U.S.

Habits. Some of these beetles are very destructive — they damage stored vegetable products such as dried roots and grains, and bore

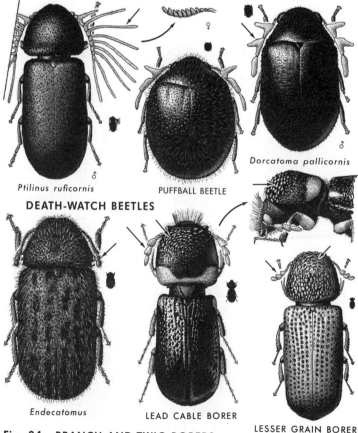

Ptilinus ruficornis   PUFFBALL BEETLE   *Dorcatoma pallicornis*

DEATH-WATCH BEETLES

Endecatomus   LEAD CABLE BORER   LESSER GRAIN BORER

Fig. 84   BRANCH-AND-TWIG BORERS

into a variety of wood and bamboo products. Larvae do most of the damage. Many species have been widely distributed by commerce. In addition, some can kill weakened trees; others tunnel into green shoots of plants. Two species bore into woody fungi. Tropical species are especially destructive, for they damage felled timber.

Collecting methods. Collecting at lights is the best method; these beetles are moderately common there. Some adults can also be captured with an aerial net during spring flights. Those that feed on fungi are sometimes common on host. Wood- or bark-borers are not collected often on trees, for they are usually con-

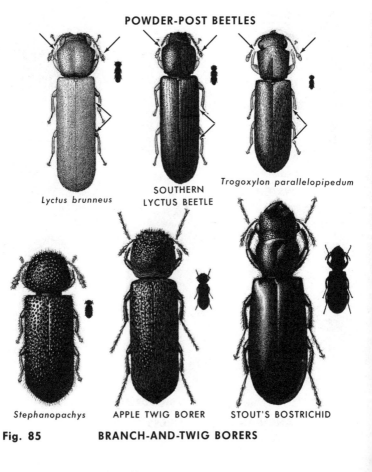

POWDER-POST BEETLES

Lyctus brunneus

SOUTHERN
LYCTUS BEETLE

Trogoxylon parallelopipedum

Stephanopachys

APPLE TWIG BORER

STOUT'S BOSTRICHID

Fig. 85   **BRANCH-AND-TWIG BORERS**

cealed in host. These beetles may be reared from infested material. **Examples.** The **Lesser Grain Borer,** *Rhyzopertha dominica* (F.), is the only species of the genus. In spite of its small size (2–3 mm) it is one of the most destructive beetles attacking grain in this country. Both adults and larvae damage grain; they do the most harm in s. U.S. They can cut into the tough seed coat of sound grain, thus opening the way for other grain-eating pests that are not able to do this. *Scobicia declivis* (LeC.), 5–7.5 mm, known as the **Lead Cable Borer** in w. U.S., is notorious for boring into lead-sheathed telephone cables. When water enters the tunnel the cable short-circuits; repairing this requires cutting out cable, splicing and insulating wires, and resheathing them — a very costly procedure. This beetle normally feeds in various hardwoods, and can kill a tree. The 5 other species of *Scobicia* are widely distributed. The **Apple Twig Borer,** *Amphicerus bicaudatus* (Say), 6–11.5 mm, e. U.S., also bores into telephone cables but normally feeds in dying branches of shade and fruit trees. The 2 *Endecatomus* species (3–5 mm) are unlike most branch-and-twig borers in appearance and habits. They bore into woody fungi and are fairly common; adults hibernate. The **Giant Palm-boring Beetle,** *Dinapate wrightii* Horn (not shown), is a remarkable species. It looks like species of the genus *Amphicerus,* but grows very large — 33–52 mm ($1\frac{1}{4}$–2 in.), compared to 2–24 mm for all other branch-and-twig borers. It feeds on California fan palms in dry regions at low altitudes. Although an infestation may kill a tree, there is little danger that this beetle will wipe out our fan palms. The 9 species of *Stephanopachys* (2.5–6.5 mm) make it the largest genus in this family. Larvae bore in bark, wood, or cones of pines and firs. **Stout's Bostrichid,** *Polycaon stoutii* LeC.(10–24 mm; Calif. and Ore.) belongs to the subfamily Psoinae. Larvae bore in various hardwoods; adults may emerge from polished table tops after chewing their way through the native hardwoods underneath the veneer.

POWDER-POST BEETLES: Family Lyctidae

Identification. Form characteristic: Body elongate, *narrow, flattened,* nearly parallel-sided. Head, pronotum, and elytra roughly *equal* in width; pronotum somewhat *wider* at front. Elytra often with *rows* of hairs. Antennal club *2-segmented.* Mandibles usually visible from above. Dorsal surface hairy. Reddish brown to black. 1–7 mm long.

Similar families. (1) Some flat bark beetles (p. 219) are similar but their antennae are usually long and threadlike — sometimes ending in a 2-, 3-, or 4-segmented club. (2) Cylindrical bark beetles (p. 246) and (3) cerylonid beetles (p. 228) have mandibles concealed from above; often lack hairs. (4) Rhizophagid beetles (p. 217) — tip of abdomen visible beyond elytra. (5) Smaller darkling beetles (p. 249) are similar but most have a gradual antennal club;

tarsi always 5-5-4, not 5-5-5. (6) False tiger beetles (p. 260) — antennal club 3-segmented.

Range and numbers. Only 3 genera and 11 species in N. America; widely distributed.

Habits. Larvae and adults bore in dry seasoned wood and can be highly injurious. They primarily infest sapwood of various hardwoods but also bore in pith of vines and dried roots of herbaceous plants. They can severely damage tool handles, gun stocks, joints, beams, flooring, and any stored lumber materials that have not been painted, varnished, or shellacked. Damage (holes) caused by larvae is usually more unsightly than structural, but if a species bores for years in the same material, an appreciable to nearly complete loss of strength can occur. Due to their wood-boring habits many species are transported in commerce. Their common name refers to the dry powdery frass that often falls from holes left behind in wood surface where adults have emerged.

Collecting methods. Infrequently captured in the field; collected in numbers only if you have access to infested stored wood. These beetles are sometimes found in dead twigs or branches but build up the greatest populations in stored seasoned wood that has not been painted or varnished.

Examples. The largest genus is *Lyctus* with 7 species (widely distributed; 1.7–7 mm). In e. U.S. the most harmful of these species is the **Southern Lyctus Beetle,** *L. planicollis* LeC., 4–6 mm. *Lyctus brunneus* (Steph.) is also a pest. Females lay eggs only within open (unsealed) pores of seasoned hardwoods — usually hickory, ash, and oak, but also many others. Larval food consists primarily of starch, which is more abundant in sapwood than in heartwood. As wood becomes seasoned, the starch in it becomes more suitable for larval nutrition. Each ♀ lays many eggs, and tunneling of generations of larvae may result in near-total destruction of wood, with only a thin outer shell remaining. Any material that seals wood pores (paint, varnish, shellac) can prevent this damage. Life cycles of different species of *Lyctus* are markedly similar and show only minor differences. All pass the winter as larvae in wood, and pupate in early spring. In late spring adults emerge and females look for suitable wood for egg-laying. In heated buildings larval development may continue all year round. The 3 *Trogoxylon* species, 2.2–4.3 mm, have habits similar to those of *Lyctus* species. *T. parallelopipedum* (Melsh.), 2.5–4.3 mm, is highly injurious in e. U.S. Yearly losses from powder-post beetles are estimated at about $18 million. In addition to the monetary loss, powder-post damage can also be a menace to life and limb — if a wooden ladder is weakened, for example.

Superfamily Cleroidea

These beetles are small to medium-sized; usually soft-bodied.

BARK-GNAWING BEETLES:
Family Trogositidae
(Figs. 86, 87; see also Pl. 3)

Identification. Each antenna ends in a 3-segmented *club,* club segments nearly always *enlarged* to 1 side. Two body forms: 1) Most are *cylindrical* to *flattened,* head nearly as broad as pronotum, pronotum and elytra *separated* by a narrow "waist"; body smooth, hairless, more or less shiny; black, sometimes brown, infrequently with metallic green (45 species, common in e. U.S.). 2) The rest (13 species, common in w. U.S.) are *oval* or *elliptical* and *flattened;* head about ½ as broad as pronotum; surfaces *sculptured;* black or brown, nearly lusterless; pronotum and elytra *meeting closely.* Tarsi 5-5-5, 1st segment very short. 2.3–22 mm, most 5–15 mm.

Similar families. (1) Ground beetles (especially *Scarites* species and *Clivina* species, p. 88) — antennae threadlike. (2) Some cylin-

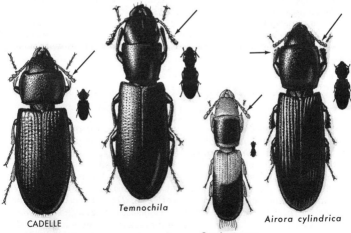

CADELLE

Temnochila

Corticotomus

Airora cylindrica

Fig. 86 BARK-GNAWING BEETLES

drical bark beetles (p. 246) are similar to small cylindrical bark-gnawing beetles but have mandibles that are concealed from above.

Range and numbers. The 13 genera include 55 species; most in w. U.S.

Habits. Most adults and larvae prey on wood-eating insects or their eggs, so they are considered beneficial. Some feed on rotting plant material or fungi. One species is a worldwide pest in granaries.

Collecting methods. In e. U.S. *Tenebroides* and *Airora* species are common at night — examine dead trees, logs, and stumps with a flashlight. In daytime look beneath bark of dead trees, logs, and stumps; look on fungi for broad, flat species (common only in w. U.S.).

Examples. Most of the 10 *Temnochila* species (6–20 mm; see Pl. 3) occur in e. U.S. Handle them carefully — the larger species can inflict painful bites. *T. virescens* (Fab.) eats bark beetles and wood-borers in galleries and on wood surfaces. The 3 *Airora* species (3.2–15 mm; 1 in e. U.S., 2 in w. U.S.) are similar to *Temnochila* species but all their tibiae are spiny; in *Temnochila* species just the front tibiae are spiny. *A. cylindrica* (Serv.) is common in e. U.S. on dead trees, logs, and stumps at night. *Tenebroides* is the largest genus with 18 species (most in e. U.S.; 3.2–12 mm); some feed on bark beetles. The **Cadelle,** *T. mauritanicus* (L.), 6.5–10 mm, feeds on grains and cereal products as a larva and as an adult. The 6 *Corticotomus* species (3 in e. U.S., 3 in w. U.S.) at 2.3–5.3 mm are our smallest bark-gnawing beetles. They are similar in form to certain cylindrical bark beetles (p. 246), but differ in having mandibles that are visible from above. The broad and flat species (including the 3 *Ostoma* species; 5–12 mm) are usually found on fungi or under dead bark. More common in w. than in e. U.S.

CHECKERED BEETLES: Family Cleridae
(Figs. 87, 88; see also Pl. 3)

Identification. Body covered with *bristly hairs;* nearly always elongate-narrow; *head wide* — usually as wide as or wider than pronotum; *pronotum* narrower than elytra, often nearly *cylindrical,* with a distinct margin in a few species. Often *marked* with red, orange, yellow, or blue. Antennae clubbed, sawtoothed, or thread-like. Tarsi 5-5-5. 1.8–24 mm (most 3–10 mm).

Similar families. (1) Pedilid beetles (p. 274); (2) antlike flower beetles (p. 276); and (3) antlike leaf beetles (p. 278) have a constriction ("neck") between head and pronotum that is not present in checkered beetles. (4) Some soft-winged flower beetles (p. 211) are similar but pronotum is margined; antennae usually saw-

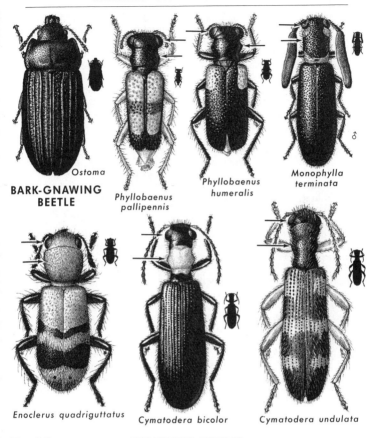

Ostoma

**BARK-GNAWING
BEETLE**

Phyllobaenus
pallipennis

Phyllobaenus
humeralis

Monophylla
terminata

Enoclerus quadriguttatus

Cymatodera bicolor

Cymatodera undulata

Fig. 87 **CHECKERED BEETLES**

toothed. (5) Micromalthid beetles (p. 81) — antennae beadlike. (6) False tiger beetles (p. 260) — head directed forward, not downward. (7) Telegeusid beetles (p. 181) lack bristly hairs; live only in Ariz. and Calif. (8) Smaller soldier beetles (p. 183) — antennae long and threadlike.

Range and numbers. Throughout N. America but most in sw. U.S.; 35 genera and 261 species.

Habits. This family is very important for attacking wood-boring beetles. In some cases their predatory feeding habits may suppress a serious outbreak of bark beetles. Adults typically prey on adult bark beetles; some eat pollen. Larvae usually eat eggs, larvae, and adults of wood-boring beetles in galleries — mostly bark beetles and long-horned beetles. A few species are scavengers. One, the **Red-legged Ham Beetle,** *Necrobia rufipes* (DeG.), is a pest of foodstuffs and may be found in spoiled meat products.

Collecting methods. May be collected with moderate frequency by sweeping and beating foliage. Some are common on bark of trees that are dying from bark beetle attacks. A few species are attracted to lights. Collect pollen-feeding species on flowers.

Examples. *Monophylla terminata* (Say), 4–7 mm, is distinctive for *expanded last segment* of each antenna (larger in ♂ than in ♀). Such an antenna appears burdensome, but the enlarged segment is thin and easily managed. This beetle preys on wood-boring beetles, including branch-and-twig borers, powder-post beetles, and death-watch beetles in dry dead wood. The largest genus is *Cymatodera* (61 species; 4–20 mm); most species live in sw. U.S. *Cymatodera* species have a distinctive elongate form and a narrow thorax with curved sides. *C. bicolor* (Say), 5.5–10 mm, is an important predator in e. U.S. on long-horned beetle and metallic wood-boring beetle larvae. Each larva searches out and devours larval borers in their tunnels. The 40 *Enoclerus* species (5–14 mm) are among our most colorful checkered beetles; they often have red, yellow, white, and dark markings, which form an attractive pattern. *E. quadriguttatus* (Oliv.), 4.5–7 mm, feeds on bark beetles in dying pine trees. Adults are common on bark of infested trees, where they catch and eat many adult beetles. Larvae are found in bark beetle brood chambers, where they feed on bark beetle larvae. The 58 *Phyllobaenus* species (3–8 mm) typically have short antennae, each with last segment slightly enlarged. Some are common on foliage, particularly of blackberry bushes. A few species, such as *P. pallipennis,* have short elytra that do not cover abdomen (Fig. 87).

The **Red-legged Ham Beetle,** *Necrobia rufipes* (DeG.), 3.5–6 mm, is widely distributed in this country and is a minor pest in cured meats, cheese, and other foods of animal origin; it sometimes feeds on dermestid larvae. The other 2 *Necrobia* species feed on remains of dead animals. *Chariessa pilosa* (Forst.), 7.5–13 mm, is common in e. U.S.; larvae feed on a variety of wood-boring larvae in various hardwoods. Each larva feeds for 2 seasons before pupating in spring, usually in gallery of a wood-borer. Adults are active throughout the summer, and feed on many adult insects. Last 3 antennal segments are larger in ♂ than in ♀. Light markings at side of thorax are yellow to orange. *Zenodosus sanguineus* (Say) (4.5–6.5 mm), the sole member of the genus, is red-brown with bright red elytra. It lives on the trunk or under bark of dead trees infested with small wood-boring insects. Adults overwinter under bark. *Phlogistosternus dislocatus* (Say) is active in daytime and

CHECKERED BEETLES

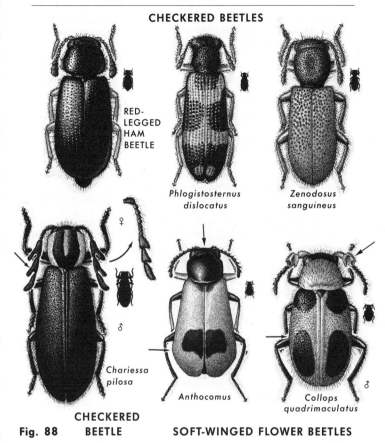

RED-
LEGGED
HAM
BEETLE

*Phlogistosternus
dislocatus*

*Zenodosus
sanguineus*

♀

♂

*Chariessa
pilosa*

Anthocomus

*Collops
quadrimaculatus* ♂

Fig. 88   CHECKERED
BEETLE   SOFT-WINGED FLOWER BEETLES

found primarily on dead branches of oak; it is 3.5–6 mm long. It is believed to prey on a wide variety of wood-boring insects, for it has been found on branches infested with various boring insects.

SOFT-WINGED FLOWER BEETLES: Family Melyridae
(Figs. 88, 89; see also Pl. 3)

Identification. Form and characters often distinctive: In e. U.S. species body is nearly always widest *toward rear,* less distinctly so in most w. U.S. species. Elytra usually *soft* and *loosely* covering abdomen; abdomen sometimes exposed beyond elytra. Pronotum usually *wider* than it is long; head more or less *concealed* from above. Antennae *sawtoothed* or *threadlike,* rarely comblike or fan-shaped. Legs usually long and slender. Black, blue, or green, often with red, yellow, or orange. Often covered with moderately dense erect hairs. Tarsi 5-5-5. 1.5-7 mm.

Similar families. (1) Some soldier beetles (*Silis* species, Fig. 76, p. 187) are similar but sides of pronotum notched. (2) Some leaf beetles (Subfamily Galerucinae, p. 296) are similar but antennae threadlike; tarsi apparently 4-4-4. (3) Some checkered beetles (p. 208) are similar but antennae usually clubbed, sometimes sawtoothed or threadlike; head (at eyes) often as wide as or wider than pronotum. (4) Micromalthid beetles (p. 81) have beadlike antennae and no margin on thorax; length 1.5-2.5 mm.

Range and numbers. 47 genera and about 502 species; most in w. U.S., with many species in Calif.

Habits. Adults are common on foliage or flowers and mostly prey on other insects that visit flowers; some species eat pollen. Larvae are carnivorous or are scavengers on dead animal material; many occur under bark of dead trees or in leaf litter. Some feed on bark beetles, their larvae, or eggs. About ⅓ of adults have extensible vesicles (sacs) at side of body — these are believed to be scent organs used in defense.

Collecting methods. Moderately common. Sweep or beat vegetation or flowers; some fly to lights. A few are found on the ground near plants.

Examples. To *Collops* (Pl. 3) belong some of the largest species of the family; the 28 species (4-7 mm) in this genus are widely distributed but many live in w. U.S. Each antenna is apparently 10-segmented, but is actually 11-segmented — 2nd segment is very small and concealed. Segments near base of antennae are often greatly *expanded in males* (Fig. 88); ♂ apparently uses these to clasp antennae of ♀ during mating. *C. quadrimaculatus* (Fab.), 4-6 mm, occurs in e. U.S. to Ariz.; often common. A couple of w. U.S. species are highly beneficial for preying on insect pests that eat alfalfa. Some of the 35 *Anthocomus* species also reach 7 mm — 3 species occur in e. U.S., the others in w. U.S., with most in Calif. Some live in galleries of wood-boring beetles. The 31 *Attalus* species are generally 1.5-3.5 mm long and occur in e. and sw. U.S. In males (Fig. 89) 2nd segment of front tarsus overlaps 3rd segment and is grooved underneath. In e. U.S., species of this genus are collected more frequently than members of other genera. In males of the 5 *Hypebaeus* species (1.5-2.5 mm; 4 in e. U.S., 1 in w. U.S.) elytra are elongate and curved at tips; these beetles are moderately common. All but 1 of the 22 species of *Dasytes* live in sw. U.S. In these beetles pronotum has roughly sculptured areas on sides; hairs are occasionally bristling. *Trichochrous* (2-4.5 mm) is

Fig. 89

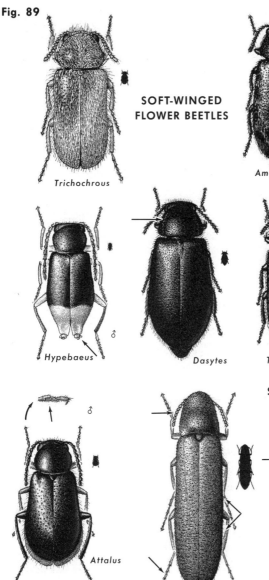

SOFT-WINGED FLOWER BEETLES

Trichochrous

Amecocerus

Hypebaeus ♂

Dasytes

Trichochrous

♂

SOFT-WINGED FLOWER BEETLE

Attalus ♂

CHESTNUT TIMBERWORM

SHIP-TIMBER BEETLES

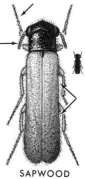

SAPWOOD TIMBERWORM

easily the largest genus in this family, with 126 species. All live in w. U.S., most in sw. In *Trichochrous* species, hairs lie flat on dorsal surface but are erect along edges of body. All 74 *Amecocerus* species are found in w. U.S. Sides of pronotum are minutely sawtoothed; species often have light hairs that form a pattern (Fig. 89).

Superfamily Lymexylonoidea

This superfamily includes a single family of rare beetles.

SHIP-TIMBER BEETLES:
Family Lymexylonidae

Identification. Body form and antennae distinctive: Body elongate, very *narrow*, with *nearly parallel sides.* Antennae *short,* segments *expanded.* Tarsi *long.* Elytra weakly *ribbed.* Light brown to dark brown. Maxillary palps fan-shaped in ♂. Tarsi 5-5-5. 10–13.5 mm.

Similar families. Only certain members of the following families are similar: (1) Soldier beetles (p. 183) have long, threadlike antennae. (2) Lightningbugs (p. 188) — head concealed from above. (3) Blister beetles (p. 270) — antennae threadlike. (4) Some long-horned beetles (especially some Lepturinae, p. 283) — antennae threadlike, usually long.

Range and numbers. Only 3 genera, each with 1 species; 2 species in e. U.S., 1 in sw. U.S.

Habits. Larvae are wood-borers in sapwood and heartwood of dead chestnut, oak, and other hardwoods. Adults live in decaying wood, on tree trunks, or under bark; they are uncommon to rare.

Collecting methods. Rarely collected. Species are nocturnal so examination of chestnut, oak, and other trees at night may yield adults. Try rearing adults from material known to be infested. These beetles come to lights, but infrequently.

Examples. The **Chestnut Timberworm,** *Melittomma sericeum* (Harr.), 11–13.5 mm, was a destructive pest when chestnut trees were common; it caused worm holes in 50–90% of chestnut logs, and ruined wood for many purposes. Also feeds in oak. Adults are rarely seen, but larval damage is still common where chestnut trees exist. Eggs are laid on damaged trees — the same wound may be used for years. Larval damage is easily recognized by the increasing size of the darkly stained holes as the larvae grow and expand their tunnels. The **Sapwood Timberworm,** *Hylecoetus lugubris* Say, 10–12 mm, feeds in sapwood of poplar, birch, and tulip trees.

Superfamily Cucujoidea

These beetles are generally small. Most have clubbed antennae.

SAP BEETLES: Family Nitidulidae

Identification. Antennal club *abrupt* and *3-segmented,* nearly always *ball-like.* Body shape varies — usually *elongate-robust* to broadly oval, infrequently long and slender with short elytra that expose most of abdomen. Elytra usually non-striate. Front coxae strongly transverse (not round). Usually 1–3 abdominal segments are *exposed* beyond elytra. Dull black to yellowish brown, sometimes with yellow or orange. Tarsi 5-5-5; segments 1–3 more or less dilated, 4th segment small, tarsi rarely 4-4-4. 1–12 mm.

Similar families. (1) Pleasing fungus beetles (p. 226) — abdomen never exposed beyond elytra; elytra striate. (2) Wounded-tree beetles (p. 192) — tibiae expanded; abdomen not exposed beyond elytra; segments of antennal club loose. (3) Pill beetles (p. 155) — antennae threadlike or gradually clubbed, club of 3–7 segments. (4) Some leaf beetles (Subfamily Cassidinae, p. 302) resemble certain sap beetles, but head concealed from above and antennae threadlike to gradually clubbed. (5) Soft-bodied plant beetles (p. 152) — antennae sawtoothed. (6) Marsh beetles (p. 149) — antennae threadlike to sawtoothed; head usually concealed from above; elytra never short. (7) Shining mold beetles (p. 225) — antennal club less compact; dorsal surface shiny. (8) Minute fungus beetles (p. 229) — pronotum usually expanded and concealing head; antennal club not ball-like. (9) Round fungus beetles (p. 124) — antennal club gradual; elytra striate. (10) Dermestid beetles (p. 192) have scales or hairs. (11) Hairy fungus beetles (p. 242) have short hair and a loose antennal club.

Range and numbers. 37 genera and over 177 species in N. America; widely distributed.

Collecting methods. Common and readily collected in the right habitats. Examine sap flows and rotting fruit and vegetation. Those on flowers can be collected by sweeping or hand-picking; inspect animal carcasses for those that feed on dead tissues. Malt or molasses traps (p. 23) are an excellent way to collect these beetles. Some fly to lights.

Examples. *Glischrochilus* species (9; 4–12 mm; widely distributed) are black and often attractively marked with yellow or yellow-orange. They are common in fallen fruit and rotting melons, but also in fungi and damaged corn. Some species may be vectors of oak wilt fungus — a serious disease that kills many trees. The largest genus is *Carpophilus* (1.5–4.5 mm), with 32 widely distributed species; some are economically important as pests. The

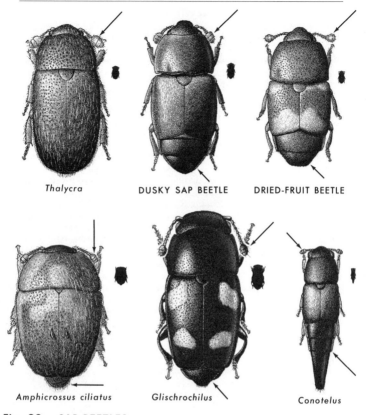

Thalycra DUSKY SAP BEETLE DRIED-FRUIT BEETLE

Amphicrossus ciliatus *Glischrochilus* *Conotelus*

Fig. 90 SAP BEETLES

Dusky Sap Beetle, *C. lugubris* Murr., 2.8–4.2 mm, is one of the most common sap beetles in much of N. America. It is attracted to a wide variety of overripe fruits and fermenting vegetable matter and feeds on corn, especially sweet corn. It is common on corn damaged by the **Corn Earworm** (a caterpillar), but also infests undamaged ears. Not all larvae in ears of corn are removed by cannery washing, so inspection and trimming of corn is essential to prevent larval fragments in corn foodstuffs. Only in the last 20 years or so has this beetle become a corn pest. Mechanized farming may have played a role in this. To make husking by machine easier, new varieties of corn have been bred with loose husks, which make it easy for these beetles to get to the corn kernels; the new corn-picking machines also leave many ears behind that serve as a larval food supply. The **Dried-fruit Beetle,** *C. hemipterus* (L.), 2.1–3.9 mm, is occasionally found in damaged corn but is more common in rotting peaches, apples, melons, and other fruits. This beetle occurs nearly worldwide. In Calif. this species and 2 other less common sap beetles are serious pests of figs and dates. The amount of fruit that is actually eaten by the adults and larvae is insignificant, but much more is soiled by their droppings, so much time, effort, and money must be spent to insure that dates and figs are fit to eat. These beetles also carry mold and souring organisms that can destroy over $\frac{1}{2}$ a date crop when humidity is unusually high.

The 4 *Conotelus* species (usually 3–4 mm) are unique for their strong resemblance to rove beetles but they can be readily distinguished from them by their clubbed antennae. *Conotelus* species occur on flowers; an eastern species is common on morning glory. The 14 species of *Thalycra* are infrequently collected; habits of only 2 species are partially known and may indicate the reason for their apparent rarity. These 2 species have been collected while feeding on fungi of the genus *Rhizopogon;* this fungus rarely appears above surface of ground and usually grows 3 in. deep in sandy soil, under needles and other litter in woods where coniferous trees are common. *Thalycra* species may be attracted to malt traps. *Amphicrossus ciliatus* (Oliv.), 3.5–4.5 mm, is one of the most compact sap beetles. This beetle is hairy and is found on fungi, in rotting fruit and melons, and in sap flows. *Phenolia grossa* (Fab.) resembles tortoise beetles (p. 302) but no tortoise beetle has an antennal club that is ball-like, as in this species (Fig. 91). *P. grossa* occurs on fungi; body length is 6.5–8 mm.

RHIZOPHAGID BEETLES:
Family Rhizophagidae

Identification. Characters distinctive: Body *elongate-narrow,* sides usually nearly parallel; last abdominal segment *exposed* beyond elytra; each antenna has 10 segments and a club of *1–2 segments* (3-segmented in 1 species), last segment *ball-like,* appearing to consist of *2* segments. Head clearly visible from above. Dorsal surface either shiny (with sparse hairs, if any) or dull, with distinct bristling hairs. 1.5–3 mm.

Similar families. In most beetles of similar size, form, and antennal club tip of abdomen is not exposed; those most easily confused are: (1) cylindrical bark beetles (p. 246); (2) powder-post beetles (p. 205); (3) cerylonid beetles (p. 228); and (4) minute brown scavenger beetles (p. 239).

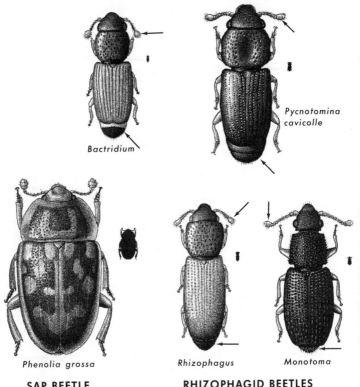

Bactridium

Pycnotomina cavicolle

Phenolia grossa

Rhizophagus

Monotoma

SAP BEETLE   **RHIZOPHAGID BEETLES**

Fig. 91

Range and numbers. 11 genera and 56 species, widely distributed in N. America.

Habits. Most occur under dead bark, in rotten wood, or in rotting plant material; some feed on wood-boring insects. A few live in ant nests; species of 1 genus may be found on carrion.

Collecting methods. Look closely beneath bark and in rotting wood. Some species are attracted in good numbers to molasses traps in dense woods. A few are attracted to lights. Most are collected infrequently.

Examples. The 14 *Rhizophagus* species (most in e. U.S.) are elongate-narrow, with nearly cylindrical bodies and dorsal surfaces that are shiny and nearly hairless. They are brown to black and some have light markings. *Monotoma* is the largest genus with 16 species; they are widely distributed. Usually head and thorax are densely punctured and elytra have rows of punctures, each with a stout hair. Body surfaces are rough and easily become coated with foreign matter. Pronotum typically has sharp corners. Head is narrowed behind eyes to form a short neck. Six of the 8 species in the genus *Bactridium* occur in e. U.S. In these beetles the head is not narrowed into a neck. The single species of *Pycnotomina* — *P. cavicolle* (Horn), ne. U.S. — may be collected in large numbers in molasses traps in dense woods. Body of this beetle is broader than that of most other species in this family; it is red-brown with a hairless and shiny dorsal surface. Pronotum has a broad, flat area down the middle.

DRY-FUNGUS BEETLES:
Family Sphindidae

Identification. Body *cylindrical,* sides nearly parallel; elytra more or less clearly *striate,* often with distinct *hairs.* Pronotum convex, as wide as elytra. Each antenna ends in a gradual, symmetrical, 3-segmented *club.* Head partially visible from above. 1.5–3 mm.
Similar families. (1) Minute tree-fungus beetles (p. 243) — elytra usually not striate; often with short, erect, stiff hairs. (2) Branch-and-twig borers (p. 202) — antennal club asymmetrical. (3) Bark-and-ambrosia beetles (p. 326) — antennal club apparently 1-segmented and usually ball-like. (4) Death-watch beetles (p. 199) — antennal club asymmetrical (segments lopsided).
Range and numbers. 3 genera and 6 species in N. America; 5 in e. U.S. (1 of which ranges into Colo.) and 1 just in Calif.
Habits and examples. Little is known about these beetles. Adults and larvae occur in slime molds on dead trees, logs, and stumps. Slime molds last for only a few days, so development of beetle, by necessity, is very rapid. *Sphindus americanus* LeC. (much of e. U.S.; 2–2.5 mm) is the most readily collected species in its area. Pronotum is quite strongly convex in this beetle (Fig. 92); in other dry-fungus beetles it is less convex.
Collecting methods. Examine dead trees, logs, and stumps for slime molds in which these beetles are found. (A slime mold looks like a smooth mound of dry, powdery fungus.) Dry-fungus beetles are collected infrequently but can be abundant if located.

FLAT BARK BEETLES: Family Cucujidae

Identification. These beetles are distinctive for their body form, which is usually *greatly flattened.* Dorsal surface usually hairless — only 6 of 88 species have short, sparse hairs. Antennae usually

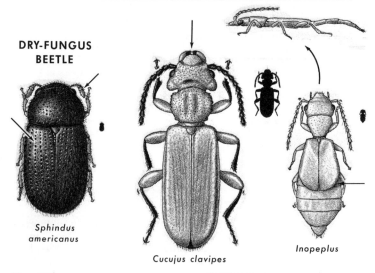

DRY-FUNGUS BEETLE

Sphindus americanus

Cucujus clavipes

Inopeplus

Fig. 92   **FLAT BARK BEETLES**

beadlike or *threadlike* and *long,* sometimes short and ending in a gradual 2- to 4-segmented club. Mandibles point forward. Usually light brown to dark brown. Elytra usually *striate.* Tarsi 5-5-5, sometimes apparently 5-5-4. 1.3–14 mm.

Similar families. (1) Powder-post beetles (p. 205) — antennae short, club 2-segmented. (2) Wrinkled bark beetles (p. 82) — thorax with deep grooves. (3) Rhizophagid beetles (p. 217) — abdomen exposed beyond elytra. (4) Cylindrical bark beetles (p. 246) — antennal club abrupt, 2- or 3-segmented; tarsi 4-4-4 or 3-3-3. (5) Silken fungus beetles (p. 222) — antennal club loose, 3-segmented; body usually hairy. (6) Certain darkling beetles (p. 249) are similar but their antennal insertions are concealed from above. (7) False tiger beetles (p. 260) — antennal club 3-segmented. (8) Some narrow-waisted bark beetles (p. 259) are similar, but pronotum lacks lateral margin. (9) In flattened species of bark-gnawing beetles (p. 207) antennal club is abrupt.

Range and numbers. 23 genera and 88 species, widely distributed in N. America.

Habits. Most probably feed on dead plant or animal material; some prey on insects. A few feed in groups in stored materials, such as grains, dried fruits, tobacco, nuts, and cereals. Adults and larvae of strongly flattened species typically live under bark of trees.

Fig. 93

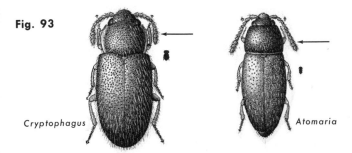

Cryptophagus

Atomaria

SILKEN FUNGUS BEETLES

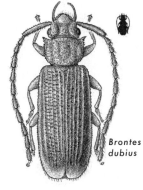

SAW-TOOTHED
GRAIN BEETLE

Brontes dubius

SQUARE-NECKED
GRAIN BEETLE

FLAT BARK BEETLES

Telephanus velox

Catogenus rufus

Laemophloeus

Collecting methods. Look beneath loose bark of dead trees, stumps, and logs or in decaying plant materials; some live in stored plant materials. One common species *(Telephanus velox)* lives on the ground.

Examples. *Cucujus clavipes* Fab. (10–14 mm; much of N. America) is the largest and most striking species; it is very flat and bright red. Most common beneath bark of dead ash and poplar. The 2 *Inopeplus* species (e. U.S. to Tex.) are distinctive for their *short elytra,* which expose most of the abdomen. The **Saw-toothed Grain Beetle,** *Oryzaephilus surinamensis* (L.), about 2.5 mm long, is named for the *teeth* at the side of its thorax (Fig. 93) and its habit of feeding on grain; it occurs worldwide. *Cathartus quadricollis* (Guer.), 2.4–3 mm, the **Square-necked Grain Beetle,** has similar habits, but lacks teeth on its thorax; it is common in s. U.S. *Catogenus rufus* (Fab.) varies greatly in size (5–11.5 mm); it is often common in e. U.S. and may hibernate in groups. *Laemophloeus* (1.5–4 mm) is the largest genus, with 42 species (widely distributed). They are typically quite flat and often have ridges on the sides of the pronotum.

Brontes dubius Fab. (4.5–5.5 mm; e. U.S. and Calif.) is common beneath dead bark in e. U.S.; *Brontes* has only 2 species. Unlike most flat bark beetles, *Telephanus velox* Hald. (3.8–4.5 mm; e. U.S.) lives on the ground; it is also atypical in appearance (see Fig. 93). There are 2 species in *Telephanus.*

SILKEN FUNGUS BEETLES:
Family Cryptophagidae

Identification. Body robust, oval to elongate-oval. Each antenna ends in a *loose,* 3-segmented club. Pronotum often has *depressions* at base, sometimes *irregular* margins on sides. Elytra lack striae. Yellow-brown to red-brown, sometimes with dark markings, rarely dark overall. Often covered with *silky* hairs. 0.8–5 mm, most 1–3 mm.

Similar families. (1) Hairy fungus beetles (p. 242) — over $\frac{2}{3}$ have light markings on dark elytra. (2) Cylindrical bark beetles (p. 246) often have an antennal club but it is 2-segmented; hairs coarse or absent. (3) Cerylonid beetles (p. 228) — antennal club 2-segmented; often hairless above. (4) Flat bark beetles (p. 219) — antennae usually not clubbed. (5) In fruitworm beetles (p. 240) 2nd and 3rd tarsal segments are lobed underneath. (6) Tooth-necked fungus beetles (p. 190) have prominent grooves on elytra. (7) Minute brown scavenger beetles (p. 239) have grooves on elytra. (8) Small carrion beetles (p. 122) — each antenna usually ends in a loose, gradual, 5-segmented club. (9) Some false darkling beetles (p. 264) are similar but have no antennal club or a weak, gradual one. (10) Throscid beetles (p. 177) — hind margins of pronotum

Fig. 93

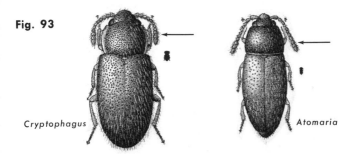

Cryptophagus   *Atomaria*

SILKEN FUNGUS BEETLES

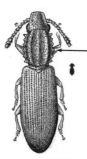

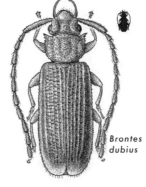

SAW-TOOTHED
GRAIN BEETLE

*Brontes
dubius*

SQUARE-NECKED
GRAIN BEETLE

FLAT BARK BEETLES

Telephanus velox   *Catogenus rufus*   *Laemophloeus*

Collecting methods. Look beneath loose bark of dead trees, stumps, and logs or in decaying plant materials; some live in stored plant materials. One common species *(Telephanus velox)* lives on the ground.

Examples. *Cucujus clavipes* Fab. (10–14 mm; much of N. America) is the largest and most striking species; it is very flat and bright red. Most common beneath bark of dead ash and poplar. The 2 *Inopeplus* species (e. U.S. to Tex.) are distinctive for their *short elytra,* which expose most of the abdomen. The **Saw-toothed Grain Beetle,** *Oryzaephilus surinamensis* (L.), about 2.5 mm long, is named for the *teeth* at the side of its thorax (Fig. 93) and its habit of feeding on grain; it occurs worldwide. *Cathartus quadricollis* (Guer.), 2.4–3 mm, the **Square-necked Grain Beetle,** has similar habits, but lacks teeth on its thorax; it is common in s. U.S. *Catogenus rufus* (Fab.) varies greatly in size (5–11.5 mm); it is often common in e. U.S. and may hibernate in groups. *Laemophloeus* (1.5–4 mm) is the largest genus, with 42 species (widely distributed). They are typically quite flat and often have ridges on the sides of the pronotum.

Brontes dubius Fab. (4.5–5.5 mm; e. U.S. and Calif.) is common beneath dead bark in e. U.S.; *Brontes* has only 2 species. Unlike most flat bark beetles, *Telephanus velox* Hald. (3.8–4.5 mm; e. U.S.) lives on the ground; it is also atypical in appearance (see Fig. 93). There are 2 species in *Telephanus.*

SILKEN FUNGUS BEETLES:
Family Cryptophagidae

Identification. Body robust, oval to elongate-oval. Each antenna ends in a *loose,* 3-segmented club. Pronotum often has *depressions* at base, sometimes *irregular* margins on sides. Elytra lack striae. Yellow-brown to red-brown, sometimes with dark markings, rarely dark overall. Often covered with *silky* hairs. 0.8–5 mm, most 1–3 mm.

Similar families. (1) Hairy fungus beetles (p. 242) — over ⅔ have light markings on dark elytra. (2) Cylindrical bark beetles (p. 246) often have an antennal club but it is 2-segmented; hairs coarse or absent. (3) Cerylonid beetles (p. 228) — antennal club 2-segmented; often hairless above. (4) Flat bark beetles (p. 219) — antennae usually not clubbed. (5) In fruitworm beetles (p. 240) 2nd and 3rd tarsal segments are lobed underneath. (6) Tooth-necked fungus beetles (p. 190) have prominent grooves on elytra. (7) Minute brown scavenger beetles (p. 239) have grooves on elytra. (8) Small carrion beetles (p. 122) — each antenna usually ends in a loose, gradual, 5-segmented club. (9) Some false darkling beetles (p. 264) are similar but have no antennal club or a weak, gradual one. (10) Throscid beetles (p. 177) — hind margins of pronotum extend backward. (11) Biphyllid beetles (p. 240) have lines on abdomen. (12) Variegated mud-loving beetles (p. 161) — antennae short, sawtoothed. (13) In some darkling beetles (p. 249) antennal insertions are concealed.

Range and numbers. 22 genera and 166 species, widely distributed in N. America.

Habits. Larvae and adults generally occur on mold, fleshy fungi, and in decayed vegetation but are sometimes found in nests of bees and wasps. These beetles probably are scavengers. Some are found on moldy stored products but feed only on mold.

Collecting methods. Most common on molds or moldy materials, on fungi, and in decaying vegetation. Look in any habitat

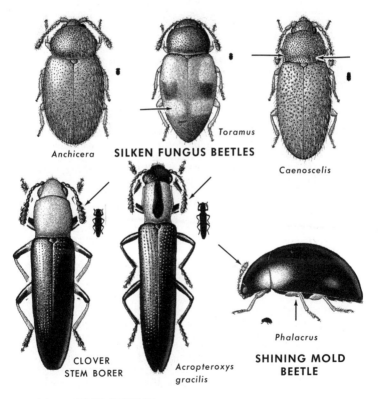

Anchicera   **SILKEN FUNGUS BEETLES**   *Toramus*

Caenoscelis

CLOVER STEM BORER   *Acropteroxys gracilis*   *Phalacrus*

SHINING MOLD BEETLE

Fig. 94   LIZARD BEETLES

where molds or fungi occur: rotting wood, vegetable debris, animal nests, or under dead bark. Some may be swept or beaten from foliage. Members of the genus *Cryptophagus* are sometimes found on carrion.

Examples. In the 40 *Cryptophagus* species (the largest genus; widely distributed) front edge of pronotum is thickened and toothed. These beetles are 1.5–4.5 mm long and reddish brown to black. They feed on fungi (including large fungi) and molds in bird, mammal, and insect nests, in stored food, and under bark. Some live on needles of coniferous trees; a few are found on carrion. The 35 *Atomaria* species (widely distributed; 0.8–2 mm) are sparsely hairy and shiny; they may be common. They are typically more elongate than most silken fungus beetles, as are the 13 species of *Caenoscelis* (1.5–2 mm; widely distributed). *Caenoscelis* species have double margins on each side of the thorax and are quite hairy. They can be collected beneath dead bark or by sifting organic material (see p. 22). The 5 *Toramus* species occur from e. U.S. to sw. U.S.; they often have elytral markings. The 27 *Anchicera* species (widely distributed; 0.8–1.8 mm) resemble *Toramus* species but their antennal insertions are close together; insertions are far apart in *Toramus*.

LIZARD BEETLES: Family Languriidae

Identification. Form distinctive: Body *very elongate-slender,* nearly *parallel-sided;* elytra, pronotum, and head nearly *equal* in width. Antennal club *4- or 5-segmented.* Shining black or blue-black; pronotum (and sometimes head and elytra) reddish, orange, or yellow. Tarsi 5-5-5. 3–16 mm.

Similar families. Some members of other families are similar but readily distinguished. (1) Metallic wood-boring beetles (notably *Agrilus* species, p. 168) are often metallic, especially on ventral surface. (2) Click beetles (p. 172) and (3) false click beetles (p. 179) — never black with red, orange, or yellow; antennae saw-toothed. (4) False darkling beetles (p. 264) — never black with red, orange, or yellow; antennae threadlike; tarsi 5-5-4. (5) Primitive weevils (p. 308) have a beak.

Range and numbers. Nearly throughout N. America, but most in s. U.S.; 4 genera and 17 species.

Habits. Larvae feed in stems of a variety of plants. Adults feed on pollen and are found on flowers and leaves of host plants.

Collecting methods. Sweep host plants. Except for 2 common species, lizard beetles are collected infrequently.

Examples. The **Clover Stem Borer,** *Languria mozardi* Latr., 4–9 mm, is a minor pest of red clover and alfalfa and also feeds on other clovers and weeds; it is widely distributed. Larvae are slender, and tunnel in stems of host plants. Only 1 generation in n. U.S. but up to 3 in sw. U.S. Adults overwinter. *Acropteroxys gracilis*

(Newm.), 6–12 mm, breeds in the dead pith of ragweed and in stems of nettle and chicory; adults occur on larval hosts and other plants, such as wild rose and Jersey tea.

SHINING MOLD BEETLES:
Family Phalacridae

Identification. *Broad* and *oval,* dorsal surface very *convex,* ventral surface *flat* (Fig. 94). Elytra usually have fine *grooves* near suture; *shiny.* Most are *black or brown,* some are partly or entirely orange. Antennae moderate in length, each with an oval 3-segmented *club.* Femora *enlarged* and *flattened,* widest at middle. Dorsal surface lacks hairs. 1–3 mm.

Similar families. (1) Lady beetles (p. 231) — antennae very short, club weak, of 3–6 segments; many small black species have hairs. (2) Pleasing fungus beetles (p. 226) are rarely as convex; often black with red, yellow, or orange. (3) Water scavenger beetles (p. 104) — maxillary palps very long; body usually over 3 mm long. (4) Round fungus beetles (p. 124) — antennal club of 3–5 segments; tibiae often expanded and spiny. (5) Some sap beetles (p. 215) are similar but antennal club ball-like; elytra not shiny. (6) Minute beetles (p. 149) can partially roll themselves up. (7) Minute fungus beetles (p. 229) lack grooves on elytra; pronotum often extends over head. (8) Marsh beetles (p. 149) — antennae threadlike, sawtoothed, or (rarely) clubbed.

Range and numbers. Widely distributed; 13 genera and about 122 species.

Habits. Adults of *Olibrus* species are found primarily on flowers or foliage; larvae most often live in heads of flowers. Adults and larvae of other species live on fungi with powdery spore masses, such as smuts and rusts.

Collecting methods. Common on flowers and foliage — sweeping will produce many specimens. Look on smutty plants, moldy vegetation, and on branches that have blown down. Many hibernate as adults, and can be sifted from ground litter in spring. Often common at lights.

Examples. In the 25 *Phalacrus* species (most in w. U.S.) the antennae are inserted under a frontal ridge with their bases concealed from above, and each elytron has one groove near the suture (Fig. 95). *P. politus* Melsh., the **Smut Beetle** (black, 1.8–2.2 mm), is common in much of e. U.S. In early spring it is found on leaves of skunk cabbage, sedges, and arum. Members of the 3 following genera differ from *Phalacrus* in that bases of their antennae are not concealed. The 28 *Olibrus* species are widely distributed. Each elytron has 1–2 grooves near the suture. *O. semistriatus* LeC. (brown; 1.8–2.2 mm) occurs from e. U.S. to Ariz. on flowers of thoroughwort and goldenrod. Most of the 20 *Acylomus* species

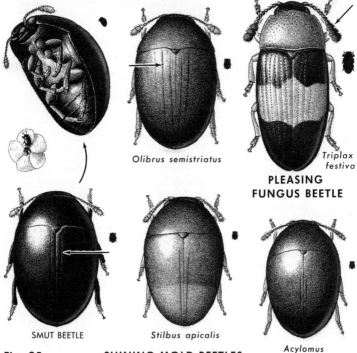

Olibrus semistriatus

Triplax
festiva

**PLEASING
FUNGUS BEETLE**

SMUT BEETLE

Stilbus apicalis

Acylomus

Fig. 95   SHINING MOLD BEETLES

occur in e. U.S. to Tex. In males the hind tibiae are expanded, with large spurs. The 34 species of *Stilbus* make it the largest genus in the family; most occur in e. U.S. They are usually black or reddish brown with light tips on their elytra. *S. apicalis* (Melsh.) occurs over much of N. America; it is dark brown to black and 2–2.3 mm long. It is commonly swept from grasses and comes to lights in large numbers.

PLEASING FUNGUS BEETLES:
Family Erotylidae
(Figs. 95, 96; see also Pl. 5)

Identification. Elongate-oval to broadly oval. *Black,* often with *red, orange,* or *yellow* markings. Body *shiny* and *hairless.* Each antenna ends in an *abrupt,* 3-segmented, *broad, flat* club, which is rarely 4- or 5-segmented. Elytra usually finely striate. Tarsi 5-5-5. 2.5–22 mm.

Similar families. (1) Handsome fungus beetles (p. 237) — front angles of pronotum extended; tarsi apparently 3-3-3. (2) Some sap beetles (p. 215) are similar but elytra short, never striate. (3) Wounded-tree beetles (p. 192) — black overall; elytra with hairs and no striae. (4) Some leaf beetles (Subfamilies Eumolpinae, p. 293, and Chrysomelinae, p. 294) — antennae threadlike to gradually clubbed. (5) Chelonariid beetles (p. 159) — head concealed from above. (6) Lady beetles (p. 231) — antennal club weak. (7) Eucinetid beetles (p. 151) — antennae threadlike. (8) Round fungus beetles (p. 124) — black, rarely with light markings. (9) Monommid beetles (p. 245) — black to partly red-brown; antennae inserted into cavities. (10) Some darkling beetles (p. 249) — no abrupt antennal club.

Range and numbers. Over $\frac{2}{3}$ of the 50 species in this family occur in e. U.S.; there are 10 genera.

Habits. Poorly known — only a few species have been studied. Nearly all feed on fungi; 1 species feeds on rotten wood. Larvae and adults occur in fungi, beneath dead bark, or in rotten wood. Nearly all are active at night. Those species that feed on fungi may be helpful — some of these fungi cause heart-rot in trees.

Collecting methods. Most species are uncommon, but on occasion you may find one in numbers. Look on or near hard and soft fungi, especially at night. For future collecting, try to leave fungi undamaged. Search under bark and in cavities in rotten wood, or in rotten stumps. Two species come to lights.

Examples. The 2 largest genera are *Triplax* (18 species; 2.3–6.5 mm; widely distributed) and *Tritoma* (13 species; 2.6–5.6 mm; e. N. America). In *Triplax* species body usually more elongate than in *Tritoma* species; most *Triplax* species have a margin at base of elytra that is not present in *Tritoma* species. *Triplax* species favor soft bracket fungi; more than 1 species may occur on a fungus. *T. festiva* Lac. (see Pl. 5) is a common species; it is 4.5–6.5 mm long and occurs from e. U.S. to Tex. *Tritoma* species eat toadstools or soft fungi on logs, and are not found in the large numbers typical of *Triplax;* usually only a few are found on a fungus. *Tritoma biguttata* (Say) is 2.7–4.4 mm long, occurs in e. U.S., and is the most common species in this genus.

Megalodacne heros (Say), 14–22 mm, occurs from e. U.S. to Rocky Mts.; its habits are well-known. It is nocturnal and spends the day congregating in sheltered spots at or near its feeding grounds (such as in fungi, in decaying wood, or under loose bark). At dusk these beetles travel to feed, usually on soft, velvety fungi, but also on harder fungi. A second species of *Megalodacne* has a similar distribution but is smaller (10–15 mm). *Ischyrus quadripunctatus* (Oliv.) also occurs in groups on fungi from e. U.S. to

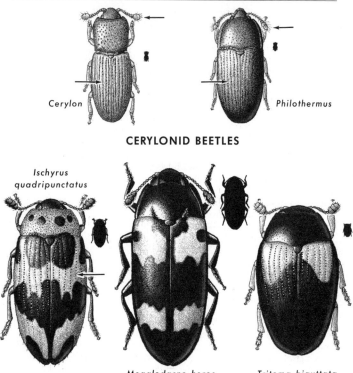

Cerylon

Philothermus

CERYLONID BEETLES

Ischyrus
quadripunctatus

Megalodacne heros

Tritoma biguttata

Fig. 96   PLEASING FUNGUS BEETLES

Rocky Mts. It has a distinctive *color pattern* with yellow markings on a black background; it is 5–8 mm long. There are 3 other species in *Ischyrus* — 1 in Fla., 2 in Ariz.

CERYLONID BEETLES: Family Cerylonidae

Identification. Difficult to characterize: Usually elongate-robust, somewhat flattened, sometimes oval. Head visible from above; antennal insertions exposed. Dorsal surface hairless and shiny. Elytra nearly always *striate*. Antennal club *1- or 2-segmented, abrupt.* Red-brown. 1–3 mm.

Similar families. (1) Nearly all cylindrical bark beetles (p. 246) differ in being either markedly cylindrical and shiny, or flattened and not shiny — see Fig. 105. (2) Powder-post beetles (p. 205) are hairy; sides of body nearly parallel; mandibles prominent. (3) Hairy fungus beetles (p. 242) are robust, hairy, and usually have a distinct color pattern. (4) Rhizophagid beetles (p. 217) — tip of abdomen exposed beyond elytra. (5) Minute brown scavenger beetles (p. 239) are usually hairy — if hairless, then pronotum is narrow. (6) Tooth-necked fungus beetles (p. 190) differ in form (compare Figs. 78 and 96) and have a weak antennal club. (7) Smaller handsome fungus beetles (p. 237) are often similar but each antenna is 3-segmented; no elytral striae. (8) Certain smaller darkling beetles (p. 249) can be confused with these beetles but they usually have a weak antennal club or one with 3 segments. **Range and numbers.** 10 genera and 18 species, widely distributed in N. America. **Habits and examples.** Cerylonid beetles are most common in forest litter and under bark; some occur in ant nests; 1 species is found in materials stored in granaries and warehouses. Most (if not all) eat fungi. The 5 *Cerylon* species (widely distributed; 2.2–3 mm) make this the largest genus; it is the only one in the family with more than 3 species. The lack of a lateral margin on the pronotum distinguishes this group. The 3 *Philothermus* species (1.6–2.3 mm) differ from *Cerylon* species in having a distinct margin on the pronotum. Other species in the family are oval to nearly round, and are quite uncommon. **Collecting methods.** Use a Berlese funnel on leaf litter and rotten wood; also look closely beneath dead bark. Often common.

MINUTE FUNGUS BEETLES:
Family Corylophidae

Identification. In most (over $\frac{2}{3}$) of these beetles pronotum is *extended* into a sharp *margin* over head, *concealing* it from above (sometimes head is partially visible from above). Often very small — 0.5–2.2 mm. Body oval. Antennae clubbed, club usually of *3 segments*. Usually brown or black, but sometimes with light brown or orange to red markings; infrequently entirely light brown. **Similar families.** Numerous families have similar species, but with exception of (1) some marsh beetles (p. 149) with threadlike antennae, none have a pronotum that extends over the head. Other similar families follow: (2) Shining mold beetles (p. 225) — elytra usually with weak striae; antennae longer. (3) Small lady beetles (p. 231) — antennae very short, club weak. (4) Feather-winged beetles (p. 126) — head usually visible from above, and fringed wings often visible beyond elytra; antennae longer. (5) Minute beetles (p. 149) can partially roll themselves up. (6) Round fungus beetles (p. 124) that do not roll up usually have striae on elytra. (7) In minute bog beetles (p. 102) pronotum is narrow; occur only in Tex., s. Calif., and Wash. (8) Sap beetles (p. 215) may be similar but antennal club ball-like. (9) In pill beetles (p. 155) ventral surface generally convex, not flat. (10) Certain minute brown scavenger beetles (p. 239) are similar but elytra usually striate.

Range and numbers. 11 genera and 61 species in N. America; nearly $\frac{2}{3}$ live in e. U.S.

Habits. Adults usually live in rotting plant material, under bark, sometimes in dung, rarely on carrion; they probably eat mold.

Collecting methods. Look under dead bark and in rotting stumps or plant material, or in dung or carrion.

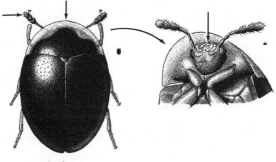

Bathona

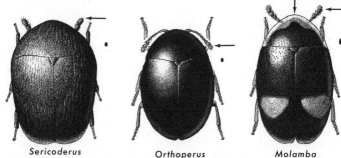

Sericoderus   *Orthoperus*   *Molamba*

Fig. 97   MINUTE FUNGUS BEETLES

Examples. The *Orthoperus* species (6 e. U.S., 7 w. U.S.), at 0.5–1 mm, are among the smallest of all beetles. The 10 species of *Molamba* and 4 of *Bathona* (widely distributed) are more typical of the family than *Orthoperus* in having a *shelflike* pronotum that extends over the head (Fig. 97); they are usually dark brown with light markings. In the 5 *Sericoderus* species (3 e. U.S., 2 w. U.S.) pronotum is less distinctly shelflike than in species of *Molamba* and *Bathona*.

LADY or LADYBIRD BEETLES:
Family Coccinellidae
(Figs. 98–100; see also Pl. 5)

Identification. Shape and antennae distinctive: Broadly *oval* to nearly *round;* dorsal surface strongly *convex,* ventral surface usually *flat.* Antennae short to (usually) *very short,* with 8–11 segments, and with a *weak club* of 3–6 segments. Pronotum *short.* Head partly to completely *concealed* from above. Often bright yellow, red, or orange with black markings or black with yellow, orange, or red markings; sometimes entirely black. Tarsi apparently 3-3-3, actually 4-4-4 (3rd segment minute; see Fig. 98). 0.8–10 mm.
Similar families. Most beetles have much longer antennae. (1) Shining mold beetles (p. 225) — antennal club distinct, tarsi apparently 4-4-4, actually 5-5-5; no distinct markings. (2) Certain leaf beetles are similar (Chrysomelinae, p. 294) but tarsi apparently 4-4-4, actually 5-5-5. (3) Handsome fungus beetles (p. 237) — front angles of pronotum elongated. (4) Pleasing fungus beetles (p. 226) — antennal club abrupt. (5) Marsh beetles (p. 149) — antennae threadlike or sawtoothed. (6) Minute fungus beetles (p. 229) — antennal club distinct. (7) Round fungus beetles (p. 124) — antennal club distinct and elytra often striate.
Range and numbers. 46 genera and 400 or so species, widely distributed.
Habits. Easily the most beneficial of all beetles; some are abundant and well-known. Most adults and larvae (except for 6 species) prey on soft-bodied insects — typically aphids and scale insects — but sometimes eat insect eggs, mites, and small larvae. Adults and larvae of each species have similar habits and are generally found on plants where their food is abundant. They act as a natural control on aphids and scales and play a major role in holding down outbreaks; some have been very important in biological control of pests. Only 3 species feed on plants; 3 others feed on fungus spores. Each larva looks like a tiny fat alligator — typically blackish, often with numerous spines; some larvae are spotted or banded with red or yellow. Larvae of some species secrete a white waxy substance that makes them look like the mealybugs on which they

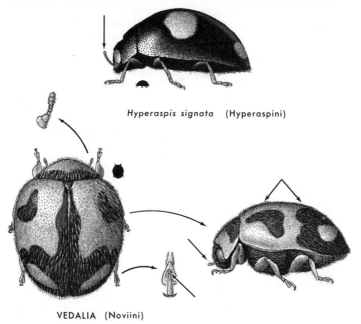

Hyperaspis signata   (Hyperaspini)

VEDALIA   (Noviini)

Fig. 98   **LADY BEETLES**

feed. A grown larva attaches itself by its tail to a branch or leaf and pupates, emerging as an adult some days later. When disturbed, a few adults (such as those of the genus *Epilachna*) force blood from their leg joints; this sticky fluid traps enemies such as ants.

Collecting methods. Readily collected by beating or sweeping foliage, especially that infested with aphids, scales, and mealybugs. In w. U.S. adults may congregate for hibernation, either in canyons or on hillsides. In other parts of the country some species hibernate in groups under loose bark or in other sheltered locations.

Subfamilies and tribes. There are 2 subfamilies of lady beetles: The first 8 tribes below belong to subfamily Coccinellinae; the last tribe belongs to Subfamily Epilachninae.

AUSTRALIAN LADY BEETLES Tribe Noviini
The classic example of successful biological control involves the

Vedalia, *Rodolia cardinalis* (Muls.). It was the first insect successfully introduced into any country to prey on an injurious insect. This beetle is red with variable black markings and is 2.5–3.5 mm. It was introduced from Australia to control the Cottony-cushion Scale, a small inactive insect that sucks sap from leaves and twigs of citrus trees. The scale was first found in California in 1872. Within 15 years it had spread over the entire citrus-producing area of the state, and threatened to wipe out the industry. No means of control was known. The situation was so bad that some growers gave up and destroyed their trees. Because the scale was believed to be from Australia, an entomologist was sent there to find its natural enemies. He discovered the Vedalia, which fed eagerly on the scale eggs and larvae. The first shipment of 28 beetles arrived in Calif. in 1888. Later shipments followed until 514 beetles were imported. In less than 2 years the Vedalia brought the scale under complete control.

YELLOW-SPOTTED LADY BEETLES Tribe Hyperaspini

The 73 species of *Hyperaspis* are widely distributed and 1.5–4.2 mm long. Predominantly black; most species have well-defined orange to deep red markings — usually *spots,* sometimes stripes. Species are separated largely by color pattern. *H. signata* (Oliv.) is one of the larger (2.7–3.7 mm) and more common species; it occurs from N.Y. to Fla. and Tex. The **Lateral Lady Beetle,** *H. lateralis* Muls., is a common and effective predator on various mealybugs, particularly the Redwood Mealybug, which feeds on Monterey cypress. This lady beetle occurs in sw. U.S. to Mont. Its larvae are covered with waxy strands.

MINUTE LADY BEETLES Tribe Microweisini

The 5 *Microweisea* species are among our smallest lady beetles; they occur in e. U.S., Tex., and Calif. They have a fine, oblique line on each front angle of pronotum. *M. misella* (LeC.) is black and 0.8–1 mm long; occurs in much of N. America. It is a common and effective predator on San Jose scale in N.M., Ariz., Calif., and Ore.

DUSKY LADY BEETLES Tribe Scymnini

Scymnus, with about 94 species (widely distributed), is the largest genus of the family. *Scymnus* species are 1.4–3 mm long, usually black (sometimes with light markings) and are often hairy. Adults and larvae feed on mealybugs, scale insects, aphids, red spiders, mites, and other plant-feeding organisms. Larvae are usually covered with white wax and are often mistaken for mealybugs. *S. americanus* Muls. (not shown) is one of the more common species from e. U.S. to Colo.; it eats aphids. Black with brownish yellow on head, abdomen, and tip of elytra; 2.4–2.7 mm. *S. socer* LeC. is common in se. U.S.; 1.6–2.1 mm. Black with reddish yellow on head, pronotum, tip of elytra, and much of abdomen. *S. socer,* like

Scymnus socer
(Scymnini)

Microweisea misella
(Microweisini)

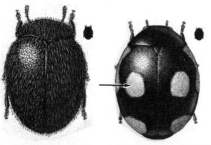

BLACK LADY BEETLE   LATERAL LADY BEETLE   MEALYBUG DESTROYER
(Coccidulini)   (Hyperaspini)   (Scymnini)

Fig. 99   **LADY BEETLES**

some other species, can be identified only after examination of ♂ genitalia. The **Mealybug Destroyer,** *Cryptolaemus montrouzieri* Muls., was introduced into Calif. from Australia in 1892. This shiny black beetle with reddish markings is 3–3.5 mm long. It is reared in large numbers in insectaries in Ventura County, Calif. and released into citrus groves where it effectively controls mealybugs. Insectary workers refer to these beetles as "crypts" — a name derived by shortening their generic name.

SINGULAR LADY BEETLES Tribe Coccidulini
This tribe is named for the technical characters of these beetles, which are unusual for this family. The **Black Lady Beetle** *Rhizobius ventralis* (Erich.), was introduced into Calif. from Australia in 1892; it destroys Black Scale. Adults are 2–2.5 mm long, shiny or velvety black with reddish abdomen. This beetle is also a valuable

predator on mealybugs, Brown Apricot Scale, and other soft scales. When young, larvae feed on scale eggs, and later on immature scales.

BLACK-SPOTTED LADY BEETLES
Tribe Coccinellini   **(Fig. 100; see also Pl. 5)**
The 18 *Hippodamia* species (widely distributed; 4–8 mm) are orange with black spots or stripes. A species often shows considerable variation in markings on pronotum and elytra. These are among the more elongate lady beetles; most are very similar in shape. The **Convergent Lady Beetle,** *H. convergens* Guér., is one of the most abundant and beneficial species; its common name refers to the *converging light markings* on its pronotum. This beetle occurs over much of N. America. Adults and larvae feed on aphids and on eggs and larvae of various insects. Studies show that each larva eats about 25 aphids per day, and each adult about 56 aphids per day. During late fall in some parts of w. U.S., particularly in the Sierra Nevada and Pacific Coast mountain ranges of Calif., adults assemble in great numbers in warm spots in canyons to hibernate. At high elevation these beetles are buried under snow. When spring arrives they return to the valleys below.

The **Two-spotted Lady Beetle,** *Adalia bipunctata* (L.), is one of the most familiar of all insects, partly due to its habit of entering houses in fall; it is often seen emerging in spring. Mostly orange with black and white markings; 4–5 mm long; it feeds on aphids. The 13 species of *Coccinella* (4–7.5 mm; widely distributed) are yellow to red, usually with black spots or bands; some are very abundant. The **California Lady Beetle,** *C. californica* Mann., has no elytral markings. Adults feed on aphids and commonly assemble on mountains for hibernation. The **Spotted Lady Beetle,** *Coleomegilla fuscilabris* (Muls.), is very common in much of N. America. It is red to pink with black markings, and is 4–7 mm long. All 4 species of this genus feed on aphids.

POLISHED LADY BEETLES Tribe Synonychini
The **Ashy Gray Lady Beetle,** *Olla abdominalis* (Say), the only N. American member of this genus, is found in most of U.S. Typically pale yellow with many black spots; 4–6 mm. Adults and larvae devour walnut aphids and other aphids. Easily one of the most important lady beetles in controlling aphids in Calif.

RED-SPOTTED LADY BEETLES Tribe Chilocorini
The **Twice-stabbed Lady Beetle,** *Chilocorus stigma* (Say), is named for the *2 red spots* on its black elytra; abdomen also red; length 4–5 mm. Larvae are black with a yellow band across middle and are covered with many long branched spines. Adults and larvae feed extensively on many species of scales. Abundant throughout N. America. The **Variable Lady Beetle,** *Exochomus margini-*

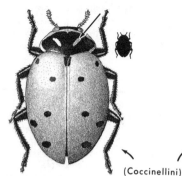

CONVERGENT LADY BEETLE
(Coccinellini)

TWO-SPOTTED
LADY BEETLE

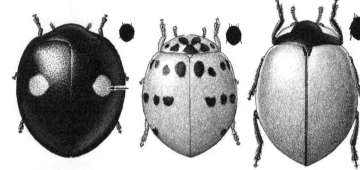

TWICE-STABBED
LADY BEETLE
(Chilocorini)

ASHY GRAY LADY BEETLE
(Synonychini)

CALIFORNIA
LADY BEETLE
(Coccinellini)

SPOTTED LADY BEETLE
(Coccinellini)

MEXICAN BEAN BEETLE
(Epilachnini)

VARIABLE LADY BEETLE
(Chilocorini)

Fig. 100   **LADY BEETLES**

pennis LeC., is shiny black with variable red markings and is about 3 mm long; it feeds on numerous scales. One of only 6 species in the genus *Exochomus;* they are widely distributed.

LEAF-EATING LADY BEETLES Tribe Epilachnini

Although most lady beetles are helpful, 2 leaf-eating species in the genus *Epilachna* (3 N. American species; e. and sw. U.S.) are considered the "black sheep" of the family because they eat crops. At 6–10 mm, these are among the largest lady beetles in N. America. They are yellow to dirty yellow with black spots. The **Mexican Bean Beetle,** *E. varivestis* Muls., is the more serious pest. Its original range was Mexico or the sw. U.S., but in 1920 it was found in Ala. and has since spread throughout the e. U.S. It commonly damages beans (especially bush, pole, and lima beans) and also harms soybeans. It also feeds on cowpeas, ladino clover, and beggartick. Adults and larvae feed on underside of leaves, leaving only a lacy network behind. If these pests are present in large numbers they will also eat the pods and stems of these crops. Eggs usually develop into adults in 1 month; there are 1–4 generations a year, depending upon the climate. Larvae are spiny and yellow to orange. Experience with Mexican Bean Beetle offers an example of a biological control project that failed. In the 1920s a wasp parasite of the beetle was found in central Mexico; thousands were released in this country. The parasite multiplied rapidly in the field, and it appeared that the Mexican Bean Beetle was about to be controlled. Unfortunately, the following spring not a single one of these wasps was found. Evidently this wasp is adapted only to tropical or subtropical habitats, and cannot survive in temperate areas. The other injurious species of *Epilachna* — the **Squash Beetle,** *E. borealis* (Fab.) (not shown) — differs from the Mexican Bean Beetle in having 7 (not 8) spots on each elytron. Found in e. and s. U.S.; it sometimes destroys squash, pumpkin, and gourds.

HANDSOME FUNGUS BEETLES:
Family Endomychidae
(Fig. 101; see also Pl. 5)

Identification. Form of pronotum usually distinctive: Pronotum has 2 *lengthwise grooves* at base; front margins of pronotum more or less extend along each side of head. Antennae end in a loose, *3-segmented club.* Usually *black* with *red* or *orange.* Usually no hairs on dorsal surface, *shiny.* Elytra lack striae. Body oval or oblong. 1–10 mm, usually 4–8. Tarsi apparently 3-3-3, actually 4-4-4. **Similar families.** (1) In lady beetles (p. 231) antennae are very short with a weak club; front margins of pronotum never elongate. (2) Pleasing fungus beetles (p. 226) — front margins of pronotum not elongate; elytra usually striate. (3) Cerylonid beetles (p.

228) — never black; elytra striate. (4) Some leaf beetles (some Eumolpinae, p. 293, and some Chrysomelinae, p. 294) are similar, but tarsi apparently 4-4-4, actually 5-5-5.

Range and numbers. 17 genera and 35 species in N. America; about $\frac{2}{3}$ occur in e. U.S.

Habits. Larvae typically feed in fungi in woodlands; adults are found in fungi, rotten wood, or in decayed fruit; infrequently in dung or decayed animal carcasses. Adults often overwinter underneath objects on ground, sometimes in groups.

Collecting methods. Examine fungi, decayed fruit, and look beneath dead bark. Sometimes in dung or on carrion.

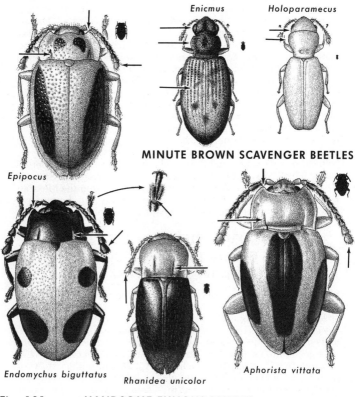

Enicmus

Holoparamecus

MINUTE BROWN SCAVENGER BEETLES

Epipocus

Endomychus biguttatus

Rhanidea unicolor

Aphorista vittata

Fig. 101   HANDSOME FUNGUS BEETLES

Examples. *Aphorista vittata* (Fab.), at 5.5–6.3 mm, is one of the larger e. U.S. species, and is moderately common; 1 of just 3 species in genus. *Rhanidea unicolor* (Zieg.), 3.5 mm, is as common in e. U.S. as any species; it occurs in rotting wood, beneath bark, and sometimes on flowers of thoroughwort in fall. *Phymaphora pulchella* Newm. (Pl. 5) is 3.8 mm long and is fairly common beneath bark; ♂ has greatly swollen antennal club. *Epipocus* is the largest genus, with 6 species; they range from se. U.S. to Tex. *Endomychus biguttatus* Say (3.5–4.2 mm; ne. to w. U.S.) is somewhat common. Like some other species in this family, it hibernates underneath logs or dead leaves.

MINUTE BROWN SCAVENGER BEETLES:
Family Lathridiidae

Identification. Usually recognizable by body form: Elytra *elongate-oval,* widest at middle, usually *rounded* at humeri. Pronotum nearly always *narrower* than elytra, often nearly *round* (from above); in some species sides are nearly parallel or widest at front. Head *prominent,* often nearly as wide as pronotum. Antennal club with 2 or 3 segments. Elytra usually striate. Red-brown to brown, rarely black. Dorsal surface sometimes hairy. 1–3 mm.

Similar families. (1) Silken fungus beetles (p. 222) and (2) hairy fungus beetles (p. 242) — often larger (0.8–6 mm); pronotum usually as wide as base of elytra. (3) Tooth-necked fungus beetles (p. 190) — antennal club weak; large punctures on elytra. (4) Cerylonid beetles (p. 228) — pronotum nearly as wide as base of elytra. (5) Rhizophagid beetles (p. 217) — elytra short.

Range and numbers. 16 genera and 108 species; widely distributed in N. America.

Habits. Adults and larvae feed on molds on plant and animal matter. Presence of these beetles on shipments or stores of grains, cheeses, hay, packing materials, bulbs, orchids, or other plant material indicates that mold or mildew is present. Some adults are found on vegetation or flowers.

Collecting methods. Collected fairly often by sweeping vegetation, often of conifers and nearby plants. Look on moldy plant or animal materials, under dead bark, in rotten wood, and under logs; sifting moldy leaves or plant debris may be productive. Species with rounded pronotum are most common. Some fly to lights.

Examples. The 6 *Holoparamecus* species occur in e. to sw. U.S. Antennal club 2-segmented; pronotum narrower at rear; elytra widest before middle and lack punctures; length is 1–1.4 mm. The 22 species of *Enicmus* (widely distributed) and the 5 species of *Lathridius* (widely distributed) have a narrow pronotum, but pronotum of *Enicmus* lacks ridges while that of *Lathridius* is *ridged.* The 27 species of *Corticaria* (widely distributed) and the 21 species

of *Melanophthalma* (21; widely distributed) have a rounded pronotum. They are often swept from vegetation and flowers. Species
of these 2 genera look very similar.

BIPHYLLID BEETLES: Family Biphyllidae

Identification. Dorsal surface hairy — some hairs lie flat, others
are somewhat or fully erect, forming lengthwise *rows* on pronotum
and elytra. First abdominal segment has *oblique lines*. Dark
brown. Body more or less flattened; head visible from above.
Elytra have more or less distinct *striae*. Antennal club with *3 segments*. 2–3.5 mm.
Similar families. (1) Silken fungus beetles (p. 222) and (2) hairy
fungus beetles (p. 242) have no lines on abdomen. (3) Fruitworm
beetles (p. 240) — often larger at 2.7–4.4 mm; hairs lie flat. (4)
Some false darkling beetles (p. 264) are similar but antennal club
weak or absent. (5) Throscid beetles (p. 177) — hind margins of
pronotum extended.
Range and numbers. Only 2 genera and 4 species in N. America;
in e. to sw. U.S.
Habits and examples. Found in fungi and under decaying bark.
Diplocoelus brunneus LeC. (1 of 3 species of genus) occurs in ne.
U.S. Adults have been collected on fungi on beech and maple trees
and sifted from dead leaves at base of trees.
Collecting methods. Infrequently collected. Look on fungi or
beneath dead bark; sometimes sifted from organic material.

FRUITWORM BEETLES: Family Byturidae

Identification. Form and tarsal lobes distinctive: Body *robust;*
sides of elytra nearly parallel; head mostly *concealed* from above;
2nd and 3rd tarsal segments *lobed* beneath. Hairs moderately long
and dense, usually uniform in color, sometimes (in 1 w. U.S. species) forming patches. Each antenna ends in a *3-segmented club*.
Elytra covered with punctures, not striate. Tarsal claws with a
large tooth at base. 2.7–4.4 mm.
Similar families. Most similar beetles have no tarsal lobes, or
segments 1–4 are lobed beneath. Antennae often very different —
see: (1) Dermestid beetles (p. 192). (2) Soft-bodied plant beetles (p.
152) — may have tarsal segments 1–4 lobed beneath. (3) Silken
fungus beetles (p. 222). (4) Hairy fungus beetles (p. 242). (5)
Death-watch beetles (p. 199). (6) Throscid beetles (p. 177). (7)
Biphyllid beetles (p. 240) have abdominal lines. (8) Comb-clawed
beetles (p. 256). (9) Tooth-necked fungus beetles (p. 190). (10) Variegated mud-loving beetles (p. 161).
Range and numbers. 2 genera and 5 species; 4 widely distributed, 1 in Calif. and Ore.
Habits. Adults and larvae of the 4 species of *Byturus* are impor-

Fig. 102   MINUTE BROWN SCAVENGER BEETLES

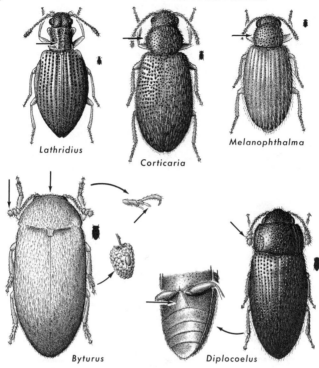

Lathridius

Corticaria

Melanophthalma

Byturus

Diplocoelus

FRUITWORM BEETLE   **BIPHYLLID BEETLE**

tant pests of blackberries, raspberries, and loganberries; they also feed on avens. In spring adults feed on young leaves and blossoms, which reduces the amount of fruit formed. Larvae penetrate flower buds and developing fruits, often causing them to fall off or decay. Larval activity makes fruit wormy and unmarketable. A w. U.S. species has been reared from male catkins on oaks; adults are found on oak trees.

Collecting methods. Common on host plants (see above). Hand-pick adults from foliage of berry bushes or use a beating umbrella (see p. 14); thorns of these plants can rip or snag a sweep net.

Examples. Common species include the **Western Raspberry Fruitworm,** *Byturus bakeri* Barber; the **Eastern Raspberry**

Fruitworm, *B. rubi* Barber; and the **Common Raspberry Fruitworm,** *B. unicolor* Say. Adults emerge from soil in April and May, feed and lay eggs on blossom clusters, and later on developing berries. Larvae eat blossoms and young fruits; they grow to nearly ⅓ in. Mature larvae burrow into soil to pupate. Pupae transform into adults during summer but do not emerge from soil until following spring. Adults also occur on flowers other than those of common host plants. *Byturellus grisescens* (Jayne) is found in Calif. and Ore.; it does not feed on berries.

HAIRY FUNGUS BEETLES:
Family Mycetophagidae

Identification. Most species are *dark brown,* often with orange or yellowish *markings* on elytra; some are uniformly dark brown.

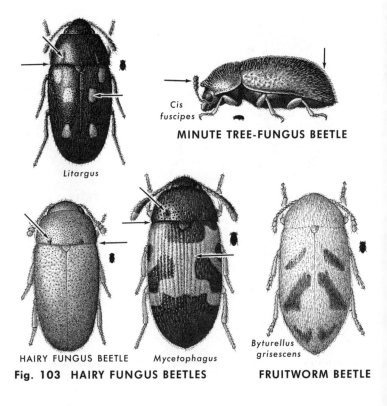

Litargus

Cis
fuscipes

MINUTE TREE-FUNGUS BEETLE

HAIRY FUNGUS BEETLE   *Mycetophagus*

Byturellus grisescens

Fig. 103   HAIRY FUNGUS BEETLES   **FRUITWORM BEETLE**

Sides of pronotum nearly always smoothly *continuous* with sides of elytra; often with a pair of *depressions* on pronotun. Usually with distinct *hairs*. Antennae vary — in some, last 5 segments enlarge gradually into a loose club; in others, last 2–4 segments form an abrupt, loose club. Elytra often striate. 1– 6.3 mm.

Similar families. (1) Fruitworm beetles (p. 240) differ in having distinct tarsal lobes. (2) Small carrion beetles (p. 122) are orange with small eyes and a weak antennal club. (3) Silken fungus beetles (p. 222) — color rarely the same; pronotum usually widest at middle. (4) Some flat bark beetles (p. 219) are similar in shape but lack light markings. (5) Some comb-clawed beetles (p. 256) are similar but antennae threadlike or sawtoothed. (6) Variegated mud-loving beetles (p. 161) — antennae sawtoothed. (7) Biphyllid beetles (p. 240) have abdominal lines; never have light markings. (8) Cerylonid beetles (p. 228) — color uniform; often hairless. (9) Minute brown scavenger beetles (p. 239) — pronotum narrower than elytra.

Range and numbers. 5 genera and 26 species in N. America; about $\frac{2}{3}$ occur in e. U.S.

Habits. Apparently feed on fungi. Larvae live in fungi or in plant material with fungi.

Collecting methods. Look in decaying fungi, under dead bark bearing fungi, in shelf fungi, or in moldy vegetable material; sometimes on carrion. These beetles may fly to lights. Adults often move fast and are hard to catch. Moderately common.

Examples. The 15 *Mycetophagus* species (most e. U.S.; 3.1–6.3 mm) are dark brown to black and have 2 depressions at base of pronotum; most have orange or yellow markings. The 6 *Litargus* species (widely distributed) are similar in color but are 1.8–4.5 mm long and more broadly oval. Pronotum often has 2 depressions. The **Hairy Fungus Beetle,** *Typhaea stercorea* (L.), is 2.3–2.7 mm and reddish brown to dark brown. It occurs over much of U.S., sometimes indoors, and is the only member of that genus.

MINUTE TREE-FUNGUS BEETLES:
Family Ciidae

Identification. Elongate, *cylindrical;* head more or less *concealed from above.* Antennae short, each with 8–10 segments; antennal club loose, symmetrical, with 2–3 segments. Usually brown, sometimes black; usually covered with erect *bristles* that often reflect light; sometimes hairless. Pronotum and head sometimes have horns; eyes round. 0.5–6 mm.

Similar families. (1) In branch-and-twig borers (p. 202) and (2) death-watch beetles (p. 199) antennal club is not symmetrical. (3) In bark-and-ambrosia beetles (p. 326) antennal club is large (apparently consisting of 1 segment); eyes elongate. (4)

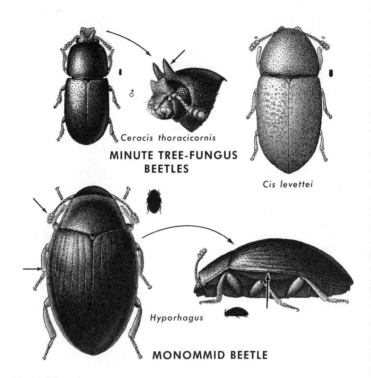

Ceracis thoracicornis
MINUTE TREE-FUNGUS BEETLES

Cis levettei

Hyporhagus
MONOMMID BEETLE

Fig. 104

Dry-fungus beetles (p. 219) lack erect bristles; antennal club solid; elytra striate.

Range and numbers. 13 genera and 85 species; widely distributed, but most in se. U.S.

Habits. Adults and larvae are found together on over 100 species of wood-rotting fungi (most often *Polyporus* fungi). *Polyporus* fungi are fairly small fungi that form many thin, overlapping shelves, sometimes in great masses on dead trees and logs. Some beetles occur in much thicker shelf fungi (*Fomes* and *Ganoderma* fungi).

Collecting methods. Collected only if you examine host fungi, then can be taken in fair to large numbers. Look for *Polyporus,*

Ganoderma, and *Fomes* fungi; beetles are usually found in tunnels they bore in these fungi. Easily reared from infested fungi. **Examples.** *Cis* is the largest genus, with 43 species. Males of some species in this and other genera have small to large horns on head and pronotum. *C. fuscipes* Mellie is widely distributed and often parthenogenetic — some populations consist only of females; this beetle lives in *Polyporus* fungi. Genus *Ceracis* (20 species) is similar to *Cis* but tip of front tibia has spines (in *Cis* species, tibia has 1 or no spines). *Ceracis thoracicornis* (Zieg.) lives in more than 20 different fungi in e. U.S.

MONOMMID BEETLES:
Family Monommidae

Identification. Form and antennae distinctive: Body *oval,* widest near *middle.* Elytra finely *striate.* Eyes not visible from above. Ventral surface of prothorax has a groove on each side in which entire antenna (except basal segments) fits. Head, thorax, and elytra have distinct *margins.* Tibiae *flattened.* Each antenna ends in a 2- or 3-segmented *club.* Head prognathous. Black to partly red-brown. Dorsal surface lacks hairs. Tarsi 5-5-4. 5–12 mm.
Similar families. (1) In pleasing fungus beetles (p. 226) antennal club is larger; no margin on head. (2) Hister beetles (p. 132) — tip of abdomen visible beyond elytra; antennae elbowed. (3) Certain false darkling beetles (p. 264) are similar but hairy, with no distinct antennal club. (4) Wounded-tree beetles (p. 192) — elytra smooth; eyes visible from above. (5) Some darkling beetles (p. 249) are similar, but eyes visible from above and antennae weakly clubbed. (6) Dermestid beetles (p. 192) that are similar have hairs or scales on dorsal surface; head concealed from above. (7) Pill beetles (p. 155) — either head directed downward (hypognathous) and antennae threadlike, or dorsal surface covered with hairs or scales. (8) Chelonariid beetles (p. 159) — head concealed from above. (9) Death-watch beetles (p. 199) of similar shape have an asymmetrical antennal club.
Range and numbers. The 5 species (2 genera) occur in Fla., Ala., Ark., S.C., and Tex. to Calif.
Habits. Larvae bore into stalks of agave and yucca and are found under bark of logs. Adults generally occur on foliage or in debris.
Collecting methods. Look for adults on grass or foliage, beneath dead cacti or in leaf litter; 1 s. Fla. species occurs on dead twigs.
Examples. The 4 *Hyporhagus* species occur in se. U.S., Ark., and Tex. to s. Calif.; they have a 3-segmented antennal club. The 1 *Aspathines* species (s. Fla.; not shown) has a 2-segmented antennal club.

CYLINDRICAL BARK BEETLES:
Family Colydiidae

Identification. Body form variable. Most species are *elongate,* more or less *flattened,* with sides of body nearly parallel. Surfaces not *shiny,* densely sculptured; often covered with hairs or scales that may form a linear pattern. In a few species body is *broad* with *flattened* sides. Some species are elongate and *cylindrical* (sometimes markedly so), more or less shiny, hairless dorsally. Family characters follow: Antennal club *abrupt* in most species, with 1, 2, or 3 segments; antennae not clubbed in a few species. Pronotum often has *ridges* or *grooves.* Front and middle coxae *rounded.* Black or brown, infrequently with markings. Tarsi 4-4-4. 1.7–13 mm, most 2–8 mm.

Similar families. (1) Some smaller darkling beetles (p. 249) are similar but tarsi 5-5-4; antennal club gradual. (2) In rhizophagid beetles (p. 217) short elytra expose tip of abdomen. (3) Powderpost beetles (p. 205) — mandibles prominent from above (in cylindrical bark beetles mandibles nearly always concealed from above). (4) Wrinkled bark beetles (p. 82) — antennae beadlike, not clubbed. (5) Many flat bark beetles (p. 219) are similar but tarsi 5-5-5, sometimes apparently 5-5-4; antennae beadlike, threadlike, or clubbed. (6) Cerylonid beetles (p. 228) — elytra never have scales or ridges; body rarely over 2 mm long. (7) Pinhole borers (p. 325) — antennal club ball-like, 1-segmented. (8) Sap beetles (p. 215) — antennal club ball-like.

Range and numbers. 29 genera and 92 species, widely distributed in N. America.

Habits. Both larvae and adults are most common under bark, in galleries of wood-boring insects, or in fungi. As is typical of concealed beetles, habits are not well-known. Many seem to feed on fungus; others probably prey on wood-boring larvae; a few parasitize larvae or pupae of wood-boring beetles; some are scavengers. In general these beetles are beneficial.

Collecting methods. Most species are collected infrequently. Look under dead bark in fall or spring when beetles are hibernating in groups. Some are found in dead trees infested with borers; others may occur in dry fungi. Some fly to lights.

Examples. The 5 *Aulonium* species (3 e. U.S. to Tex., 2 w. U.S.; 3.7–5.5 mm) can be distinguished from one another by sculpturing on pronotum alone; in 3 species this sculpturing differs in sexes. 2 species are scavengers in bark beetle-infested trees. The 21 *Lasconotus* species (widely distributed; most 2–3 mm) have an antennal club of 3 segments; 2 species in this genus have habits similar to those of members of *Aulonium. Lasconotus* is easily the largest genus of the family. The 9 *Bitoma* species (widely distrib-

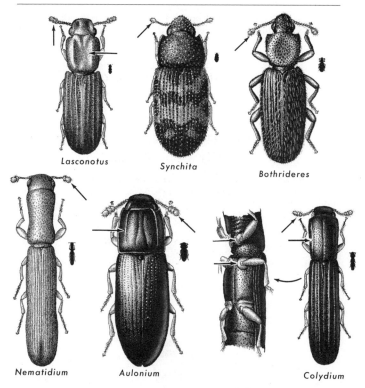

Lasconotus   Synchita

Bothrideres

Nematidium   Aulonium

Colydium

Fig. 105   **CYLINDRICAL BARK BEETLES**

uted; 2–3.5 mm; not shown) are similar to *Lasconotus* species but
have an antennal club composed of 2 segments. *Synchita fuliginosa*
Melsh. lives on tree bark infested with fungi, especially chestnut
trees infested with *Endothia* fungus; adults eat fungus. There are 4
other species in the genus *Synchita*. The markedly elongate and
slender cylindrical bark beetles, such as the 4 species of *Colydium*
and the 1 of *Nematidium,* are typically found in galleries of ambrosia beetles, weevils, and other borers. The long, cylindrical
shape of these beetles is believed to be an adaptation for living in
tunnels of wood-borers, on which they feed. In some species the
legs can be partially retracted into hollows in the body (Fig. 105),
which allows the beetle to crawl into a tunnel only slightly wider
than itself. *Bothrideres geminatus* (Say), 3–4.5 mm, is an e. U.S.

species that feeds on wood-borers in hardwood trees. The 5 other *Bothrideres* species are widely distributed. Larvae of *B. geminatus* are predaceous or parasitic.

Superfamily Tenebrionoidea

These beetles are usually medium-sized; antennae usually thread-like, tarsi 5-5-4.

FALSE LONG-HORNED BEETLES: Family Cephaloidae

Identification. Form similar to that of many true long-horned beetles (p. 279), but each tarsal claw has a membranous, ventral *lobe;* claws in 6 of 10 species *comblike.* Antennae 11-segmented, threadlike but with last segment slightly *enlarged.* Body elongate, narrow. Pronotum usually lacks lateral margin, broadest at base; head elongate, with a *neck.* Legs long, slender; tarsi 5-5-4. Body covered with fine hairs. 8–20 mm.

Similar families. (1) Long-horned beetles (p. 279) — tarsi apparently 4-4-4, actually 5-5-5, claws not lobed. (2) False blister beetles (p. 262) — pronotum widest at front; next to last tarsal segment

Fig. 106

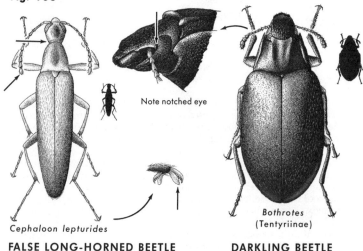

Note notched eye

Cephaloon lepturides

FALSE LONG-HORNED BEETLE

Bothrotes
(Tentyriinae)

DARKLING BEETLE

broad; hairy below. (3) Blister beetles (p. 270) — head broad, directed downward, usually wider than pronotum; pronotum often widest near middle. (4) Pedilid beetles (p. 274) — pronotum widest at middle; claws not lobed. (5) Cebrionid beetles (p. 171) — mandibles prominent; 20–25 mm.

Range and numbers. 4 genera and 10 species; 4 in w. U.S., 6 in e. U.S.

Habits. Little is known of adults' habits; most often collected on flowers or foliage. Larvae of 5 species have been found in decaying wood of coniferous and hardwood trees in forests.

Collecting methods. Usually swept from flowers or foliage; rarely collected.

Examples. The genus *Cephaloon* contains 6 species; they occur in e. and nw. U.S. *Cephaloon lepturides* Newm., about 8–9 mm, is the most common ne. U.S. species. Color varies — usually brown with orange appendages, elytra and pronotum may also be orange. In *C. lepturides* the claws are comblike and lobe of each claw is stout. In the other e. U.S. species of *Cephaloon* the claws are comblike but lobe of each claw is narrow and curving.

DARKLING BEETLES:
Family Tenebrionidae
(Figs. 106–109; see also Pl. 7)

Identification. Body shape varies widely within this family, but most family members can be recognized by 5-5-4 tarsi, notched eyes, and form of antennae. Eyes nearly always *notched* by a *frontal ridge.* Each antenna usually 11-segmented, *threadlike, beadlike,* or *slightly clubbed;* insertion *concealed* from above. Most often dull black or brown, sometimes with red. 2–35 mm (up to $1\frac{3}{8}$ in.)

Similar families. (1) False darkling beetles (p. 264) — 1st segment of hind tarsus longer than any other, pronotum often has 2 impressions at base. (2) Comb-clawed beetles (p. 256) — tarsal claws comblike. (3) Ground beetles (p. 86) — tarsi 5-5-5; 1st abdominal segment divided by hind coxae. (4) Pleasing fungus beetles (p. 226) resemble some darkling beetles but each antenna ends in an abrupt club. (5) Cerylonid beetles (p. 228), (6) cylindrical bark beetles (p. 246), and (7) powder-post beetles (p. 205) resemble some small darkling beetles but in these other groups antennae end in a distinct club. (8) Trout-stream beetles (p. 94) — similar to a few darkling beetles but tarsi 5-5-5; habitat is w. U.S. streams. (9) Monommid beetles (p. 245) — eyes concealed from above.

Range and numbers. The 5th largest family of beetles, with about 180 genera and 1300 species; most in w. U.S.

Habits. A very conspicuous part of the insect fauna in desert regions of w. U.S. Commonly found under objects on ground; habits are similar to those of ground beetles (p. 86). Over 1100 species found in w. U.S.; only about 140 in e. U.S. Adults and larvae live in a variety of terrestrial habitats: in rotting wood; under logs and stones; in termite and ant nests; on plant materials; in houses; in fungi; in debris. Nearly all of these beetles are scavengers on decaying vegetation, animal dung, seeds, and cereals; some feed on living plant roots, tubers, or flowers. A few are pests in stored cereals, seeds, and other materials. Some feed in fruiting bodies of fungi. Larvae are cylindrical and hard-bodied, and are called false wireworms because they often resemble click beetle larvae (wireworms). Most adults are nocturnal, but some are active in daytime. Very little is known about most species for very few of them are economically important as pests.

Collecting methods. In e. U.S. most are readily captured in daytime beneath bark or on fungi, and at night on dead trees, logs, or stumps; some are common. A few are found on carrion; some fly to lights. In w. U.S. most common (sometimes abundant) beneath objects on ground or under dead bark. They make up a much larger portion of beetle fauna in w. U.S. than in e. U.S.

Subfamilies. All 3 of the N. American subfamilies are described below.

SUBFAMILY TENTYRIINAE   Figs. 106, 107

Nearly all the 300 or so species occur in desert regions of sw. U.S. The 2 *Bothrotes* species (9–15 mm) occur in s. to sw. U.S. ♀ typically has strong ridges or depressions on pronotum. In the 54 *Metoponium* species (sw. U.S.; about 5–9 mm) ventral surface of tarsi is covered with numerous long, stiff *bristles*. The **Small Darkling Ground Beetle,** *M. abnorme* (LeC.), damages buds of grapevines, bark of young grapefruit trees, and fruit of strawberries and tomatoes in s. Calif. and Ariz. All 11 *Triorophus* species (most 6–9 mm) occur in sw. U.S. In these beetles and members of similar genera the elytra curve inward and hug the side of body.

SUBFAMILY ASIDINAE   Fig. 107

All but 1 of the 380 or so species occur in sw. U.S. The **Ironclad Beetle,** *Phloeodes pustulosus* LeC. (not shown), is 15–23 mm long, flattened, and very rough on top. The dorsal surface of this beetle is so hard that it will sometimes bend a pin point. Adults occur under bark of dead trees, logs, and stumps; and sometimes overwinter in groups. They eat woody fungi and probably decayed wood. This is the most common of the 8 species in this genus; all occur in Calif. The 14 *Araeoschizus* species (sw. U.S.; usually 3–5 mm) have *cuplike* antennal segments; antennae are usually scaly. The genus *Nyctoporis* contains 8 species, all in Calif.; length is 8–16 mm. One species, *N. carinata* LeC. (13–16 mm) has been

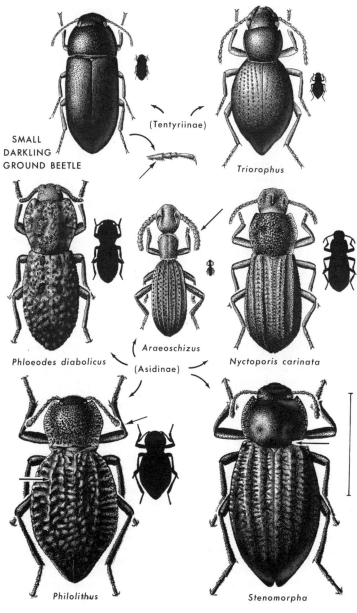

SMALL DARKLING GROUND BEETLE

(Tentyriinae)

Triorophus

Phloeodes diabolicus

Araeoschizus

(Asidinae)

Nyctoporis carinata

Philolithus

Stenomorpha

Fig. 107   **DARKLING BEETLES**

found feeding on stored grain used as animal feed. It could become a pest if it becomes well-adapted to grain. The 29 species of *Philolithus* (8–24 mm) occur from sw. U.S. to Wash. In these beetles the 10th antennal segment is *enlarged* and more or less encloses the smaller 11th segment; most also have 1–2 strong *ridges* on each elytron. The genus *Stenomorpha* (about 15–33 mm) is one of the larger genera with 62 species; found primarily in sw. U.S., but their range extends to Ore., Colo., and Nebr. In these beetles base of prothorax is more or less *broadly lobed* and sides are curving (Fig. 107).

TYPICAL DARKLING BEETLES   (see also Pl. 7)
Subfamily Tenebrioninae
Easily the largest subfamily, with about 700 species — nearly all darkling beetles in e. U.S. belong to this group. *Eleodes,* with over 100 species (all in w. U.S.), is one of the largest genera in the family. These darkling beetles are 10–35 mm long and most have smooth, more or less shiny surfaces. Some are economically important; in their area these larvae (false wireworms) are second only to true wireworms as pests of newly planted wheat and corn. Though wheat is their preferred food, they also eat other grasses, cotton, legumes, sugar beets, and garden crops. Sprouting seeds and seedlings are eaten by larvae; adults sometimes feed on foliage and stems; greatest damage occurs in fall. Original food of *Eleodes* species was roots and seeds of native plants, but since land has been turned over to agriculture, they are left with little to eat but crops, primarily wheat. These beetles typically occur in semiarid and desert areas, sometimes in large numbers; they normally hide beneath objects during day. During migration (spring to early summer) they travel by night and day and are quite conspicuous. A distinctive habit is the ridiculous position these beetles assume when fleeing; the abdomen is elevated about 45° from ground, so the beetle appears to be standing on its head as it runs (Fig. 108). At the same time it gives off a fluid with an offensive odor. *E. tricostata* (Say) (about 18 mm long) is one of the most common and widespread false wireworms in wheat-growing regions. *E. armata* LeC. has teeth on its femora, as do certain other species.

The 34 species of *Eusattus* (6–14 mm) are found from sw. U.S. to Kans. and Colo. They are wingless, as are members of the genus *Coniontis. Coniontis* species (over 100; most 8–16 mm) are found primarily in sw. U.S., usually under stones, logs, and debris; some are quite common. These beetles are somewhat cylindrical, elongate, smooth, and black or bluish. In s. Calif. some are minor pests that feed on young tomatoes, lima beans, and sugar beets. The small darkling ground beetles — genus *Blapstinus* (52 species; 3–8 mm; widely distributed) — have recently become pests in w. U.S. They attack many plants, usually girdling them at soil surface. Young tomatoes, peppers, cotton, strawberries, cucumbers, grapes, and hop plants are damaged.

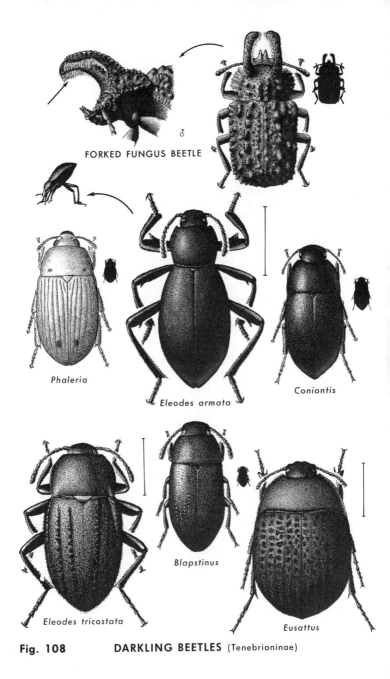

FORKED FUNGUS BEETLE

♂

Phaleria

Eleodes armata

Coniontis

Eleodes tricostata

Blapstinus

Eusattus

Fig. 108   DARKLING BEETLES (Tenebrioninae)

The 8 *Phaleria* species (2–7 mm) occur from e. to w. U.S., but primarily in s. U.S.; they are broad-bodied and generally light in color. The **Forked Fungus Beetle,** *Bolitotherus cornutus* (Panz.) — only member of the genus — lives only in e. U.S. It is one of the most interesting species in the family for its unusual form (Fig. 108). It is 10–12 mm long and very robust; dorsal surface is covered with coarse sculpturing, with little or no gloss. The ♂ has a pair of stout, forward-pointing *horns.* This beetle is active at night. During day larvae and adults are found in hard shelf fungi or in crevices in bark to which fungi are attached. It is especially common on beech and maple trees and logs. When disturbed these beetles remain motionless, and may be overlooked because they are well-camouflaged. The 3 *Diaperis* species (e. U.S. to Calif.; about 5–6 mm) resemble lady beetles (p. 231) in form and color but their antennae are much longer. Most often found under bark and in fungi, and sometimes live in groups. The 16 species of *Platydema* (e. and s. U.S.; Fig. 109, see also Pl. 7) resemble pleasing fungus beetles (p. 226), but have a more gradual antennal club. Length varies from 3–7 mm. Generally found under bark and in fungi. The **Red-horned Grain Beetle,** *P. ruficorne* Sturm, is sometimes abundant in shelled corn in Mo., Ill., and Iowa. It is usually found on damp and moldy grain.

Two species of the genus *Tribolium* (6 species), the **Confused Flour Beetle,** *T. confusum* Jacq. Duval, 4.5–5 mm, and the **Red Flour Beetle,** *T. castaneum* (Herbst), not shown, 4–4.5 mm, are serious pests. They are found throughout the world and feed primarily on milled grain products, grain dust, and broken kernels. The Confused Flour Beetle is the most abundant and harmful insect pest in flour mills in N. America. In temperate regions it predominates over the Red Flour Beetle, which is better adjusted to subtropical climates. The 2 beetles are similar in size, color, and texture of dorsal surface. They are most readily distinguished by the segments of the antennal club, which increase gradually in size in Confused Flour Beetle, but are abruptly larger than preceding segments in Red Flour Beetle. Development from egg to adult takes about 4 weeks in warm habitats; development is retarded by cool temperatures and lack of preferred food.

Alobates pennsylvanica (DeG.) is 19–24 mm long and is ungainly and slow-moving. It is one of the most common darkling beetles in the e. U.S. In daytime it is found under loose bark of dead trees, logs, or stumps, but is most readily collected in these places at night. The 2 *Tenebrio* species (11–16 mm) are known as mealworms, and are found worldwide in grains and cereal products. Larvae of the **Yellow Mealworm,** *T. molitor* L. (adult, 13–16 mm), and the **Dark Mealworm,** *T. obscurus* Fab. (adult, 14–17 mm; not shown) are the largest beetle larvae found in these materials; they are well over 1 in. long when full grown and look much like wireworms. They are seldom found in homes, but are numer-

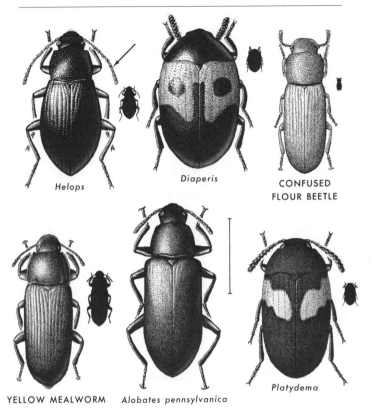

Helops

Diaperis

CONFUSED
FLOUR BEETLE

YELLOW MEALWORM

Alobates pennsylvanica

Platydema

Fig. 109 **DARKLING BEETLES** (Tenebrioninae)

ous in neglected grains and milled products that accumulate in dark corners or in places where livestock feed is stored. These beetles are adapted to moist habitats and may be found under bark of dead trees. Larvae of both species are frequently reared as food for captive animals and as fishbait. The Dark Mealworm adult is generally black; the Yellow Mealworm adult is generally dark red-brown. The 40 *Helops* species (4–19 mm) are widely distributed. In these beetles the outer antennal segments are very slightly enlarged, tarsi are slender, and metasternum is flattened in front.

LONG-JOINTED BARK BEETLES:
Family Lagriidae

Identification. Antennae and form distinctive: Antennae *thread-like*, last segment very *elongate*. Body slender; pronotum much *narrower than elytra;* elytra widest before *tip*. Tarsi 5-5-4; next to last segment *broad*. Brown to black, often shiny, sometimes metallic green or with green or blue highlights. Long-legged. 6–15 mm.
Similar families. Some members of the following families resemble these beetles, but none of them have threadlike antennae with the last segment elongate. See: (1) ground beetles (p. 86); (2) pedilid beetles (p. 274); (3) false blister beetles (p. 262); and (4) false tiger beetles (p. 260).
Range and numbers. 2 genera and 21 species in N. America; widely distributed.
Habits and examples. Adults feed on foliage at night; during the day they are concealed. Larvae feed on leaf litter or foliage and are found in stumps and under dead bark. The 3 species of *Arthromacra* occur in e. U.S. The 18 *Statira* species are found in e. to sw. U.S. The 2 genera differ as follows: *Arthromacra* species (9–15 mm) have small (not prominent) eyes, and elytra with many coarse punctures that are not clearly in rows. *Statira* species (6–14 mm) have large, prominent eyes and distinctly striate elytra with rows of punctures in shallow grooves.
Collecting methods. In daytime look beneath dead bark and in rotting wood; at night sweep foliage. Collected fairly often. They come to lights at night.

COMB-CLAWED BEETLES:
Family Alleculidae

Identification. The only distinctive character of this family is the *comblike tarsal claws*. Body elongate-robust to elongate-narrow. Often covered with fine silky hairs. Eyes *notched*. Light brown to black, infrequently with elytral markings. Antennae usually threadlike or sawtoothed, rarely comblike. Tarsi 5-5-4. 4–15 mm.
Similar families. Other beetles with comblike tarsal claws (not included below) rarely have same body form; none of those with similar form also have comblike tarsal claws. Those with similar form are: (1) darkling beetles (p. 249); (2) false darkling beetles (p. 264); (3) fruitworm beetles (p. 240); (4) soft-bodied plant beetles (p. 152); (5) hairy fungus beetles (p. 242); (6) ptilodactylid beetles (p. 158); and (7) narrow-waisted bark beetles (p. 259).
Range and numbers. 18 genera and 177 species in N. America; about ⅔ in w. U.S.
Habits. Adults occur on foliage, flowers, or under bark; some (es-

pecially *Hymenorus* species) may be common. Most adults are believed to feed on pollen; sometimes found in groups on flowers.
Larvae look like wireworms and are found in rotting wood, leaf
litter, fungi, or beneath dead bark; they are believed to feed on
decaying plants. Larvae may live together in a cavity in decayed
wood, or in dead areas of living trees. Some larvae are found
around roots of plants, others in ant, termite, and bird nests; none
are harmful.

Collecting methods. Sweep low vegetation or flowers, or look

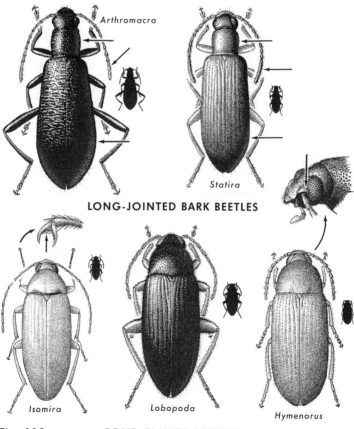

LONG-JOINTED BARK BEETLES

Arthromacra

Statira

Isomira

Lobopoda

Hymenorus

Fig. 110   **COMB-CLAWED BEETLES**

beneath dead bark. Many species are found on dead trees or logs at night; some fly to lights. Comb-clawed beetles frequently run away rapidly, trying to escape. Specimens collected must be pinned carefully; body is often fragile.

Examples. *Hymenorus* is easily the largest genus with about 100 species (most in sw. U.S.); these comb-clawed beetles are collected more often than species of other genera. Adults are light to dark brown or black, and usually 4–9 mm long. Species within this genus look very much alike and are difficult to identify; they are

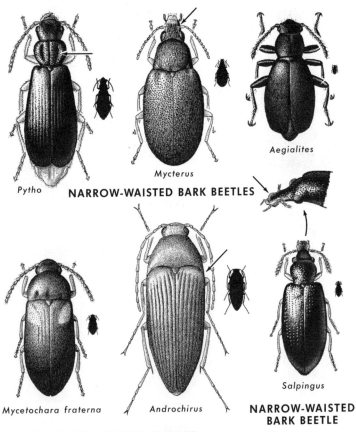

Pytho

Mycterus

Aegialites

NARROW-WAISTED BARK BEETLES

Mycetochara fraterna

Androchirus

Salpingus

NARROW-WAISTED BARK BEETLE

Fig. 111 COMB-CLAWED BEETLES

also quite fragile and must be handled carefully. Common in sw. U.S., with many species in Ariz. Larvae infest decaying softwoods (such as pine and cedar) and hardwoods (such as oak, chestnut, and willow). Also found in knots in living trees; a few live in ant and termite nests. The 24 *Mycetochara* species (4–8 mm; widely distributed) are generally dark brown to black; many have red on humeri. Generally feed on fungi and often found under bark. Antennae are usually shorter and stouter than those of other comb-clawed beetles. Larvae of *M. fraterna* (Say) infest decaying oak logs and rotting heartwood in living trees. The 12 *Isomira* species (3.5–7.7 mm; widely distributed) occur on foliage or flowers of low plants. They are light to dark brown; their only distinctive character is their slender, threadlike antennae (see Fig. 110). The 6 species of *Lobopoda* (widely distributed) are dark brown to black and 6–13 mm; adults generally live under bark in dead wood, bracket fungi, flowers, algae, lichens, or nests. The 2 *Androchirus* species occur in e. U.S.; body is gray-black to black; legs and antennae are long and slender. Eyes are weakly notched; in most comb-clawed beetles they are deeply notched. Hind angles of pronotum extend backward.

NARROW-WAISTED BARK BEETLES:
Family Salpingidae

Identification. Difficult to characterize. Body elongate-oblong to elongate with nearly parallel sides. Head *prominent,* sometimes with a *beak* (in 9 species). Antennae threadlike, somewhat beadlike, or sawtoothed, sometimes with a slight club. Pronotum usually with no margin, or (rarely) with a slight margin; usually narrowed at base. Tarsi 5-5-4. 2–21 mm.

Similar families. (1) Ground beetles (p. 86) — tarsi 5-5-5. (2) Snout beetles (p. 309) are often similar to narrow-waisted bark beetles with a beak but tarsi apparently 4-4-4. (3) Comb-clawed beetles (p. 256) — tarsal claws comblike. (4) Fungus weevils (p. 307) — antennae distinctly clubbed.

Range and numbers. 12 genera and 34 species in N. America; many either in Canada and n. U.S. or in sw. U.S.

Habits. Usually found under bark of conifers, beneath objects, in detritus, or on flowering plants. Adult feeding habits are unknown; larvae are carnivorous and sometimes found in galleries of wood-boring insects. Three rare species are found in intertidal zone along the W. Coast.

Collecting methods. Rarely collected. May be swept from foliage or captured on flowers; look beneath dead bark of conifers, or in detritus. Some fly to lights.

Examples. Members of the genus *Pytho* (6 species; most 10–15 mm) occur in Canada and n. U.S. Dorsal surface lacks distinct hairs; pronotum is flat, with 2 shallow *depressions,* and sides are curving; elytra are striate. Of the 5 *Mycterus* species, 1 occurs in e. U.S., 4 in w. U.S. Their shape and beak make them hard to distinguish from certain snout beetles (p. 309). The 3 *Salpingus* species (Canada and n. U.S.) have a *very long beak* (Fig. 111). The flattened body of the 3 small species of *Aegialites* allows them to live in rock crevices in the barnacle zone along the Pacific Coast; 2 species are found in Calif., 1 in Canada.

FIRE-COLORED BEETLES:
Family Pyrochroidae

Identification. Shape, size, antennae, and color distinctive: Elytra elongate, widest *at rear;* pronotum *narrower, oval* or nearly square, with no margin; 4.5–19 mm, most 8–19 mm. Antennae long, *sawtoothed, comblike,* or *feathery,* rarely threadlike. Often elytra black and head and pronotum *red* (sometimes orange); entire body red, orange, or yellowish in a few species. Head with a neck. Tarsi 5-5-4. Legs long and thin.

Similar families. Nearly all similar beetles have threadlike antennae — see: (1) soldier beetles (p. 183); (2) long-horned beetles (p. 279); (3) false blister beetles (p. 262); (4) pedilid beetles (p. 274); and (5) blister beetles (p. 270).

Range and numbers. Only 4 genera and 15 species in N. America; widely distributed.

Habits. Larvae eat wood and fungi and are often found under bark of recently killed trees; sometimes in decayed wood. Adults may be found on leaves but are primarily nocturnal (usually hidden in daytime).

Collecting methods. Adults may be common on dead trees, stumps, or logs at night. Infrequently found on foliage, beneath bark, or in other hiding places; they may fly to lights. Some are attracted to fermented beer or molasses.

Examples. Of the species found in e. U.S., the 3 *Dendroides* species (6 in U.S.) and the 2 *Neopyrochroa* species (4 in U.S.) are most common. *Dendroides* species (7-18 mm) have large eyes that nearly touch at top of head in ♂; in ♀ eyes are more widely separated. Antennae are feathery in ♂; comblike in ♀. *Neopyrochroa* species (11–19 mm) have eyes at top of head separated by width of an eye or more. Antennae are sawtoothed in ♀; comblike in ♂. Head of ♂ unusual — looks almost skull-like (see close-up in Fig. 112).

FALSE TIGER BEETLES: Family Othniidae

Identification. Similar to tiger beetles (p. 83). Body *slender;* head *wide* (as wide as pronotum), and directed forward; elytra nearly parallel-sided. Each antenna ends in a 3-segmented *club.*

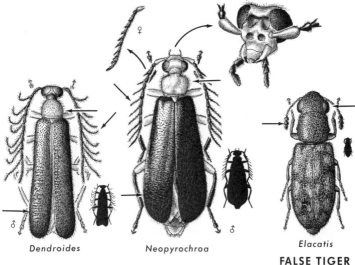

Dendroides   *Neopyrochroa*   *Elacatis*

FALSE TIGER BEETLE

Fig. 112   FIRE-COLORED BEETLES

Brown to dark brown. Covered with moderately dense hairs. Tarsi 5-5-4. 5–9 mm.

Similar families. (1) Tiger beetles (p. 83) — antennae threadlike; length 6–40 mm. (2) Checkered beetles (p. 208) — head directed downward. (3) Powder-post beetles (p. 205) — antennal club 2-segmented. (4) Long-jointed bark beetles (p. 256) — antennae threadlike, last segment very long. (5) Some flat bark beetles (p. 219) are similar but have threadlike antennae. (6) Certain ant-like flower beetles (p. 276) are similar, but have head with a distinct neck.

Range and numbers. 1 genus, containing 5 species — 1 is found in Va., the other 4 occur from Nebr. to Calif.

Habits and examples. Larvae and adults are found in rotting leaves, in cacti, or under bark of trees; adults may also be found on foliage. Little is known about habits of adults and larvae — adults are believed to be carnivorous; larvae are probably scavengers. *Elacatis fasciatus* (Bland), from Va., may be found on dead pines infested with **Southern Pine Beetle** (p. 329). A w. U.S. species occurs on trees killed by bark beetles.

Collecting methods. Sweep or beat foliage, look beneath bark, in rotting plant material, or in cacti. Uncommon to rare.

FALSE BLISTER BEETLES:
Family Oedemeridae

Identification. Body elongate-*slender and soft.* Pronotum *rounded,* with no lateral margin; *widest at front, narrower* than elytra at base; sometimes with *depressions.* Elytra often finely *ridged.* Antennae threadlike, slightly sawtoothed in a few species. Usually light-colored, some with yellow, red, or orange. Tarsi 5-5-4; next to last segment broad, hairy. 5–23 mm.

Similar families. (1) Blister beetles (p. 270) — head broad, with a narrow neck; head usually wider than pronotum. (2) Long-horned beetles (p. 279) — tarsi apparently 4-4-4, actually 5-5-5; pronotum often widest at base. (3) False long-horned beetles (p. 248) — claws comblike, lobed; pronotum widest at base. (4) Fire-colored beetles (p. 260) — antennae sawtoothed, comblike, or feathery. (5) Soldier beetles (p. 183) — pronotum margined; tarsi 5-5-5. (6) Pedilid beetles (p. 274) — head with a neck.

Range and numbers. 17 genera and 53 species widely distributed in N. America.

Habits. Most larvae feed in moist decaying wood, particularly of conifers; some can survive in wood that is completely submerged underwater. May be found in logs, stumps, and roots; 1 occurs in wood infested with dry rot. Adults are often attracted to flowers, such as those of palms, dogbane, willow, and Russian thistle; they eat pollen. Sometimes found on foliage.

Collecting methods. The **Wharf Borer** is most common under driftwood along beaches of Atlantic Coast or Great Lakes, but may also fly in daylight. In e. U.S. adults of many species are common on spring flowers, particularly of willow or wild plum trees. Most fly to lights at night, but rarely in numbers. The best collecting at lights is in areas where larval food is abundant, such as along beaches or in moist areas with fallen wood. Some species can be swept from dune plants.

Examples. The **Wharf Borer,** *Nacerdes melanura* (L). (not shown; 8–12 mm), is an introduced species and is the only pest of any economic importance in this family. On occasion it damages wharves, pilings, and wood in moist places. Wood-rotting fungi are usually present in wood it infests. Genus *Xanthochroa* includes 6 species found in se. U.S. and on W. Coast. Larvae live in rotting or moist wood; adults are 8–14 mm long. *Oxacis,* with 17 species (5–13 mm), is the largest genus in the family; found in s. U.S. Most *Oxacis* species are uncommon and little is known about the habits of their larvae. Larvae of *O. laeta* (Water.) feed in driftwood from salt water; adults are found on coconut palm buds in Fla. The 9 species of *Oxycopis* (5–12 mm) occur in e. and s. U.S. Larvae live in rotting hardwoods and softwoods, and in roots of various plants.

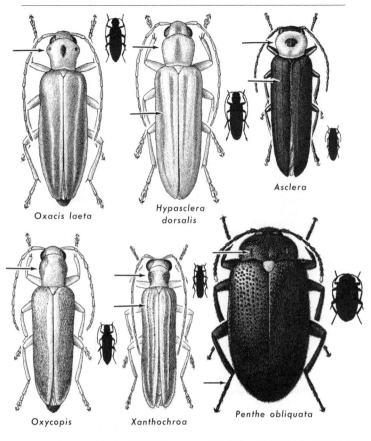

Oxacis laeta

Hypasclera
dorsalis

Asclera

Oxycopis

Xanthochroa

Penthe obliquata

FALSE BLISTER BEETLES **FALSE DARKLING BEETLE**

Fig. 113

The 8 *Hypasclera* species (5–15 mm) are found in e. and s. U.S. Two species, *H. dorsalis* (Melsh.), 8–14 mm; and *H. pleuralis* (LeC.), not shown, 6–9 mm; live in rotting driftwood along ocean beaches. In e. U.S. the 6 species of *Asclera* (5–9 mm; widely distributed) are common on willow flowers in spring. Most are black with an orange pronotum, and have fine ridges on the elytra.

FALSE DARKLING BEETLES:
Family Melandryidae

Identification. Hard to recognize. Pronotum usually has 2 *depressions* near base (Fig. 113). First segment of each hind tarsus *longer than any other segment*. Nearly always dark brown to black; a few have red, orange, or yellow markings. Antennae threadlike, sometimes clubbed, rarely sawtoothed. Body shape varies — elongate-oval (usually) to elongate-narrow. Tarsi 5-5-4. 2–20 mm.

Similar families. (1) Darkling beetles (p. 249) — eyes notched; 1st segment of hind tarsus not as long; a few have depressions on pronotum. (2) Comb-clawed beetles (p. 256) — tarsal claws comblike. (3) Tumbling flower beetles (p. 266) — body arched; abdomen pointed. (4) Ground beetles (p. 86), (5) soft-bodied plant beetles (p. 152), and (6) false click beetles (p. 179) — tarsi 5-5-5. (7) Rare click beetles (p. 177) — hind trochanters long. (8) Dermestid beetles (p. 192) — antennal club abrupt. (9) Click beetles (p. 172) can click; tarsi 5-5-5. (10) Small carrion beetles (p. 122) — antennal club usually 5-segmented.

Range and numbers. 50 genera and 95 species in N. America; most in e. U.S.

Habits. Adults live under bark, in fungi, or on foliage or flowers. Larvae live under bark in dry wood, fungi, or decaying logs or stumps; a few live in forest litter; some are carnivorous, others eat plant material.

Collecting methods. Some small, elongate species are frequently swept from leaves or flowers. Larger species are often found under bark or in rotting logs or stumps. Some of these are common on dead trees, logs, and stumps at night; a few are found on carrion. Some fly to lights. A few are fragile and easily damaged when handled or pinned.

Examples. The 2 *Penthe* species (10 –14 mm; e. U.S. to Tex.) are common on woody fungi and beneath loose bark; they sometimes overwinter in groups beneath logs. *P. obliquata* (Fab.) has an orange scutellum; in *P. pimelia* (Fab.), not shown, the scutellum is black. The 5 *Eustrophinus* species (widely distributed; 4–7 mm) are broad-bodied and convex above; they are often common on fungi or beneath bark of fungus-covered logs or stumps. The 2 *Dircaea* species (ne. U.S.; 7–11 mm) have distinctive wavy *orange markings* on their elytra and a narrow-elongate body. They may be found under bark, but are more readily collected at night on dead trees. These beetles must be handled and pinned carefully — body is quite fragile. The 7 *Melandrya* species (1 in Calif., most in e. U.S.) are among the larger species of the family. *M. striata* Say is 7.5–15 mm long and is common under bark.

The following smaller species (usually 2–5 mm) are common on foliage and generally resemble tumbling flower beetles (below): The 4 *Canifa* species (e. U.S.) are quite common; they are light to dark brown, with fine punctures, and a sharp lateral margin on the rear of the pronotum. Their eyes are *deeply notched* (Fig. 114). The 10 species of *Anaspis* (widely distributed) are similar to those of *Canifa,* but are less common in e. U.S. Unlike *Canifa* species, their eyes are *slightly notched,* and their antennae are *gradually enlarged* at tip.

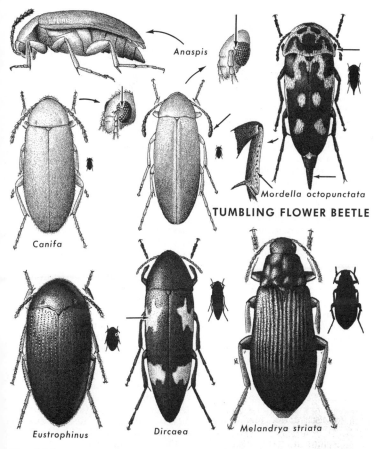

Anaspis

Mordella octopunctata

TUMBLING FLOWER BEETLE

Canifa

Eustrophinus

Dircaea

Melandrya striata

Fig. 114   **FALSE DARKLING BEETLES**

Superfamily Melooidea

Small to medium-sized, often soft-bodied; antennae often thread-like.

TUMBLING FLOWER BEETLES:
Family Mordellidae

Identification. Distinctive for body form and behavior: Body *humpbacked,* more or less *wedge-shaped,* broadest *at front;* head is bent *downward,* attached *ventrally;* abdomen *pointed, extending* beyond elytra. Hind legs *enlarged.* These beetles *kick* and *tumble* about when disturbed. Black or gray, some brown; hairy, light patches of hair sometimes form a pattern. Antennae short to moderate, threadlike, sawtoothed, or clubbed. Tarsal claws often bilobed or comblike. 1.5–15 mm, usually 3–8 mm. Tarsi 5-5-4.

Similar families. (1) Some false darkling beetles (p. 264) are similar but abdomen never distinctly pointed. (2) Some wedge-shaped beetles (p. 268) are similar but tip of abdomen blunt.

Range and numbers. Only 6 genera with 204 species in N. America; widely distributed.

Habits. Few beetles are so distinctive in appearance and behavior. Their habit of jumping and tumbling about when captured is comical, but often results in their escape. They also fly readily. Common on flowers and foliage; sometimes on dead trees or logs. Larvae occur in dead or dying hardwoods, in pith of weeds, or in bracket fungi; they are believed to eat the plant materials.

Collecting methods. A common and conspicuous beetle on flowers; can be picked off by hand or swept with a net. Use care, for these beetles can be elusive (see above). Some can be reared from dead wood; a few fly to lights.

Examples. Most of the species you will catch belong to either the genus *Mordella* (24 species; widely distributed; 3–8 mm) or *Mordellistena* (about 150 species; widely distributed; 2–4 mm, rarely to 5 mm). These genera may be distinguished by shape of their antennae and *sculpturing* of their hind legs. In *Mordella* species, antennae are strongly sawtoothed to clubbed and each hind tibia has *tubercles* — but no distinct ridges — on outer surface, near tip (Fig. 114). In *Mordellistena* species, antennae are usually threadlike, sometimes slightly sawtoothed, and each hind *tibia* has 1–6 short, more or less *oblique ridges* on outer surface (see close-up in Fig. 115); tarsal segments may also bear ridges. The number and arrangement of the tibial and tarsal ridges are useful in identifying species. For clarity the close-up in Fig. 115 shows the tibial ridges on a light-colored beetle, but most *Mordellistena* species are black,

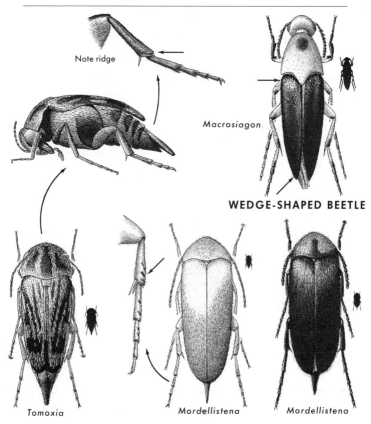

Note ridge

Macrosiagon

WEDGE-SHAPED BEETLE

Tomoxia   Mordellistena   Mordellistena

Fig. 115   TUMBLING FLOWER BEETLES

with less distinct ridges. Most are solid black, but some have red, orange, or yellow markings. *Mordella* species are also usually black, but some have a pattern of light-colored hairs on their elytra. *M. octopunctata* Fab. (6–7 mm) is found on flowers of Jersey tea in much of U.S.; its larvae live in rotten oak. The 9 species of *Tomoxia* (widely distributed; most 4–13 mm) have slightly sawtoothed antennae and have a fine *ridge* along the outer edge of each rear tibia.

WEDGE-SHAPED BEETLES:
Family Rhipiphoridae

Identification. Two distinctive forms: (1) Most species are broadly *wedge-shaped* (broadest at *abdomen*), with very *short* and *scalelike* elytra that expose hind wings and most of abdomen (Fig. 116). (2) Some have a long body (widest near *humeri*) with *long, pointed* elytra that conceal abdomen (Fig. 115). In both forms abdomen is *blunt;* head directed downward. Antennae sawtoothed in ♀; comblike, somewhat feathery, or fan-shaped in ♂. Most are black. Tarsi 5-5-4. 3.5–15 mm.

Similar families. (1) Twisted-winged parasites (p. 269) resemble wedge-shaped beetles with short elytra, but eyes stalked; abdomen pointed; wings fanlike. (2) Tumbling flower beetles (p. 266) look like wedge-shaped beetles with long elytra, but antennae thread-like; abdomen pointed. (3) Certain false darkling beetles (p. 264) are similar, but antennae threadlike; abdomen pointed. (4) Glow-worms (p. 182) — tarsi 5-5-5.

Range and numbers. 5 genera and 50 species in N. America; widely distributed.

Habits. As larvae, all are parasites of wasps and bees — first larval stages are spent as an internal parasite, and later stages are spent as an external parasite. (These habits are rare for beetles). Adults are free-living; females are found on flowers where they lay eggs. **Collecting methods.** Sweep flowers or examine them closely. Females are more likely to be caught because of their habit of laying eggs on flowers; males are collected infrequently. Most of these beetles are uncommon to rare, partly because of their short lifespan.

Examples. The 11 species of *Macrosiagon* (most in e. U.S.; 3.5–12 mm) are parasitic on wasp larvae. Adults are often dark with orange markings.

Rhipiphorus, with 36 species (most in w. U.S.; 4–11 mm), is the largest genus. Habits of 9 species are known; all are parasitic on bee larvae. *R. smithi* Linsley and MacSwain, 4–7 mm, occurs in San Joaquin Valley of California and parasitizes larvae of a ground-nesting bee that lives in groups. Host bee nests in flat, hard-packed ground near its principal pollen source, alkali mallow. Adults of *R. smithi* are short-lived — males live less than 1 day. Males emerge first; females emerge 15 minutes to 1 hour later, and immediately attract all males close by. Evidently scent of ♀ is a sex attractant — complexity of ♂ antennae supports this view. When a ♂ has mated with a ♀, other males lose interest and fly away.

After it has mated, ♀ flies off in search of alkali mallow on which to lay eggs. ♀ deposits her eggs (about 9 at a time) in various spots on the smaller buds. Each ♀ lays over 800 eggs. Eggs hatch as flower opens; 1st instar larva has well-developed legs and is quite active. When a bee visits flower, the beetle larva attaches itself to the bee, and is carried to its nest. Larva seeks out a bee egg and feeds on the bee larva when it hatches. The beetle larva overwinters in this stage; 1st instar larva completes development the following spring, and leaves the body of its host, which is still alive. Beetle larva spends 2nd–6th instars outside host (bee larva), feeding on it; form of beetle larva changes greatly during this period. Until about last 2 days of feeding, the beetle larva's host remains alive. Pupal stage of this beetle lasts about 2 weeks.

TWISTED-WINGED PARASITES:
Family Stylopidae

Identification. Males distinctive: *Flylike,* with a *wide* head and *protruding* eyes; antennae *fan-shaped* or *comblike,* with 4–7 segments; pronotum *small;* elytra *very small, clublike;* flying wings large and fanlike; prominent — never concealed. Females usually larviform. Black to brown. 0.5–4 mm.

Scientists disagree on status of this group; many researchers recognize it as a separate order (Strepsiptera) because these insects

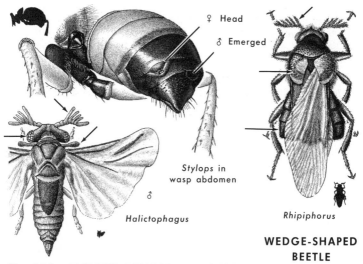

♀ Head

♂ Emerged

Stylops in wasp abdomen

♂

Halictophagus

Rhipiphorus

WEDGE-SHAPED BEETLE

Fig. 116   TWISTED-WINGED PARASITES

look so different from other beetles, even those to which they are believed to be related.

Similar families. (1) Certain wedge-shaped beetles (p. 268) are somewhat similar, but head much smaller, and abdomen wide at tip.

Range and numbers. 11 genera and 56 species in N. America; most in e. U.S.

Habits. Larvae and adult females of many species are parasitic on other insects, such as grasshoppers, spittlebugs, planthoppers, leaf-hoppers, treehoppers, or bees and wasps. The sexes differ in form and behavior; males are free-living and have wings; females lack wings and (often) legs, and, when parasitic, do not leave their hosts. (Some females have legs and are free-living.) Hosts are not always killed, but are generally injured, with misshapen abdomen; ♂ injures host more often than does ♀. An emerged ♂ seeks out a partially exposed ♀ (which is still feeding in her host) and mates with her. The ♀ produces many (1,000–5,000) tiny, active, and legged larvae that leave the original host and enter a new host's body, where they become legless and wormlike, and feed inside that host. A larva must find an insect of the right species to continue its life; survival rate is low.

Collecting methods. Winged males are rarely found by most collectors; larviform females are found on their hosts, where they spend their entire lives. Best way to collect males is by collecting hosts and rearing adults, or by using trapped parasitized hosts to attract males that come to mate with females in host. Bees and wasps are most readily collected (by sweeping flowers) and are easiest to recognize as hosts, because of the distorted shape of their abdomens when parasites are present. (Parasites cause slight to prominent distortion of some abdominal segments, usually those visible dorsally in the rear half of abdomen.) Head of the parasite is usually visible (see Fig. 116).

Examples. The 21 species of *Stylops* (easily the largest genus) are widely distributed but most occur in e. U.S.; they parasitize certain common wild bees. Each antenna is 6-segmented. The 13 *Halictophagus* species (widely distributed) parasitize leafhoppers, treehoppers, spittlebugs, and pygmy grasshoppers. In these species the antennae have 7 segments.

BLISTER BEETLES: Family Meloidae
(Figs. 117, 118; see also Pl. 6)

Identification. Head and body form distinctive: Head *broad,* usually somewhat *rectangular* (from above), nearly always *wider than pronotum,* with a short *neck.* Pronotum *narrow;* elytra wider at base than pronotum. *Elongate-slender,* rarely oval. Body *soft, leathery.* Elytra *loosely* cover abdomen and nearly always *rolled;*

sometimes short, exposing abdomen. Antennae threadlike or beadlike; intermediate segments sometimes enlarged. Legs long, slender. Usually black, brown, or gray, sometimes brightly colored. Tarsi 5-5-4. 3–30 mm, usually 10–20 mm.

Similar families. Similar beetles rarely have head wider than pronotum. (1) Soldier beetles (p. 183) — tarsi 5-5-5; elytra usually lie flat over abdomen, not rolled. (2) False blister beetles (p. 262) — head lacks a neck. (3) Fire-colored beetles (p. 260) — antennae sawtoothed to comblike. (4) False long-horned beetles (p. 248) — head narrow. (5) Ship-timber beetles (p. 214) — antennae short, sawtoothed. (6) Pedilid beetles (p. 274) — elytra closely cover abdomen; head rounded; pronotum long.

Range and numbers. 26 genera and over 335 species; most in sw. U.S.

Habits. This family is quite unusual, for larvae of many species are beneficial but adults are injurious, although in some species the reverse is true. Adults of most species feed on foliage or flowers; some are pests on potatoes, tomatoes, beets, or other vegetables, certain flowers, and ornamentals. *Epicauta* larvae eat eggs of grasshoppers. All others live in bee nests and feed on eggs, larvae, and stored food. Larvae undergo great changes in body form during development. When disturbed, blister beetles exhibit "reflex bleeding" — they emit blood from knee joints and other parts of the body. This liquid can raise blisters on the skin, giving these beetles their common name. The blood (containing cantharidin)

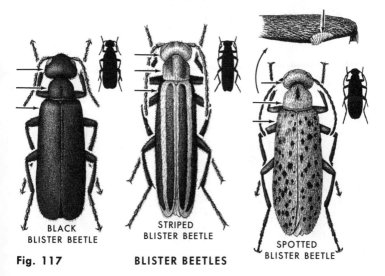

BLACK
BLISTER BEETLE

STRIPED
BLISTER BEETLE

SPOTTED
BLISTER BEETLE

Fig. 117   **BLISTER BEETLES**

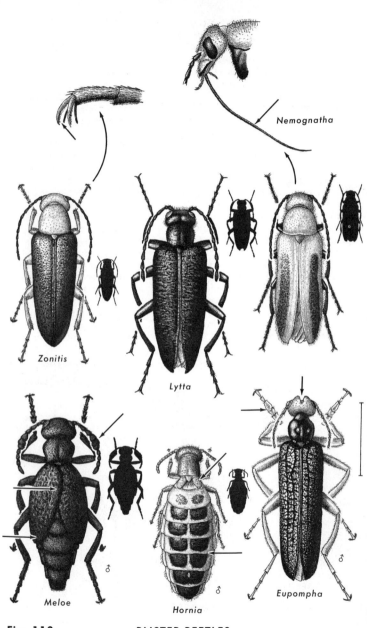

Nemognatha

Zonitis

Lytta

Meloe ♂

Hornia ♂

Eupompha ♂

Fig. 118 **BLISTER BEETLES**

deters some of their predators (such as birds and ground beetles), though other predators (such as mantids and robber flies) are not bothered by it.

Collecting methods. Most are collected infrequently, though some may be locally abundant, appearing suddenly and leaving as suddenly. Sweep or beat foliage or flowers. Some species appear seasonally — a few are found only in spring, many only in summer, others only in fall. Some have been found only at lights.

Examples. The over 100 species of *Epicauta* (widely distributed; most 4–18 mm) make this the largest genus; some are pests. These blister beetles have a patch of *silky* hairs underneath the front femur (Fig. 117). Some of the most common species are the **Margined Blister Beetle,** *E. pestifera* Werner (not shown); the **Striped Blister Beetle,** *E. vittata* (Fab.); the **Spotted Blister Beetle,** *E. maculata* (Say); and the **Black Blister Beetle,** *E. pennsylvanica* (DeG.). These beetles damage many vegetables, flowers, and ornamentals, and often eat alfalfa and sugar beets. Some species are known as **Old-Fashioned Potato Beetles** when they eat potatoes. Adults appear about midsummer; typically the entire population emerges in a short period of time and can do much damage before noticed; adults usually feed in groups. Larvae of *Epicauta* species are beneficial for eating grasshopper eggs. Populations of these blister beetles fluctuate with the populations of the grasshoppers on which they feed. Females lay eggs in soil, and young larvae search out grasshopper eggs when they hatch. One larva is able to destroy an egg pod of 30–40 eggs. As it grows, the larva changes greatly. When it first hatches it has well-developed legs, but as it feeds its body becomes more robust while its head and legs get smaller. With each following molt it changes more, until by the 6th instar its legs and mouth parts are rudimentary and its body segmentation is indistinct. The last instar is smaller but has larger legs. Pupa overwinters; there is 1 generation a year.

The 3 *Hornia* species (Calif., cen. and e. U.S.) are rarely collected because they live underground. Adults overwinter in a chamber near ground-nesting bees; mating and egg-laying occur in this chamber. A young larva crawls to the surface, attaches to a bee, and rides to a new nest. The remainder of its development takes place underground. These beetles have *very small elytra;* their abdomens are *enlarged and membranous* and they lack flying wings. The 20 *Meloe* species (12–30 mm) also lack flying wings; their elytra are *small* and *overlap* at the base. They are found on the ground or low foliage. When disturbed, they feign death and exude a thick oily substance from their leg joints, which gives them the name oil beetles. Larvae live in bee nests and feed on bee eggs and stored food. Males are generally smaller than females and sometimes have *greatly modified* antennae.

The 68 species of *Lytta* (7–27 mm; most w. U.S.; Fig. 118, Pl. 6) have habits similar to *Epicauta* species in that adults are sometimes pests on various plants, but larvae live in bee nests. Adults lack the patch of hair on the front femur found in *Epicauta* species. The 28 species of *Nemognatha* (most w. U.S.; 5.5–15 mm) feed on nectar and pollen of various flowers. Females lay eggs on flowers; larvae attach themselves to bees when they visit flowers and are then carried to bee nests where they eat bee eggs and stored food. Adults may be somewhat beneficial for pollinating host plants, although plants are of little commercial value. Larvae are harmful for destruction of bees, some of which pollinate commercial crops. Some species of *Nemognatha* are abundant in favorable seasons, and may be important in reducing numbers of host bees. This situation of adults being beneficial and larvae being harmful is a complete reversal of the pattern in *Epicauta* species.

The 14 *Zonitis* species, 6.5–13 mm, are similar in habits to those of *Nemognatha*. The galeae of the species of *Nemognatha* and of some of *Zonitis* and *Gnathium* (5 species) are greatly *elongated* to form a *sucking tube*, which is sometimes nearly as long as the body (Fig. 118). They use the tube to suck nectar from flowers. Species of these genera also have *comblike* tarsal claws; most blister beetles have cleft or simple claws. As a rule, species of *Nemognatha,* *Zonitis*, and *Gnathium* are partially or entirely brown, orange, or yellow, and often vary in color. Most other blister beetles are dark or gray and are not as variable in color. In males of some *Eupompha* species (9 species, w. U.S.; Fig. 118, Pl. 6) head is *deeply notched* at tip and front tarsi are enlarged. Blister beetles of e. U.S. are generally dull in color, but western species are often very colorful (see Pl. 6).

PEDILID BEETLES: Family Pedilidae

Identification. Similar to antlike flower beetles (p. 276), but body more *elongate,* usually larger *(4–15 mm).* Each eye nearly always has a *notch* next to the antenna. Head narrowed at base into a *neck.* Pronotum *oval* or *oval-elongate,* with no lateral margins. Antennae long, threadlike, sometimes sawtoothed. Tarsi 5-5-4. Black or brown, sometimes with pale or red markings.

Similar families. (1) Antlike flower beetles (p. 276) — nearly always smaller (1.7–4.3 mm); eyes not notched. (2) Some leaf beetles (Orsodacninae, p. 291) and some (3) long-horned beetles (p. 279) are similar, but have no neck; tarsi apparently 4-4-4. (4) Checkered beetles (p. 208) — no neck; have bristles. (5) Long-jointed bark beetles (p. 256) — last antennal segment very elongate. (6) Blister beetles (p. 270) — elytra loosely cover abdomen. (7) Fire-colored beetles (p. 260) — antennae sawtoothed or comblike. (8) False blister beetles (p. 262) — no neck. (9) Grassroot beetles (p. 130) — elytra oval; hair sparse or absent. (10) Antlike leaf beetles (p. 278) — 1.5–3 mm. (11) False long-horned beetles (p. 248) — pronotum widest at base.

Range and numbers. The 7 genera include 57 species; about 40 species occur only in w. U.S.

Habits. Larvae live in vegetable debris, often in very moist areas, and even in sand along seashore. Little is known about their habits. Adults are usually found on flowers and also on foliage, often in damp areas.

Collecting methods. Look on flowers of false indigo, osage orange, and red haw. Sweep foliage in moist areas or near water, particularly foliage of mayapples, horseweeds, willows, maples,

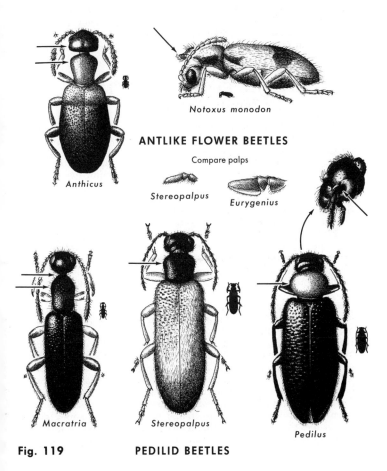

Notoxus monodon

ANTLIKE FLOWER BEETLES

Anthicus

Compare palps

Stereopalpus
Eurygenius

Macratria
Stereopalpus
Pedilus

Fig. 119   **PEDILID BEETLES**

buckeyes, and alders. Some species are common on foliage near small streams. Some fly to lights.

Examples. The 4 *Macratria* species (ne. U.S. and Tex.; 4–5 mm) have a *narrow* neck in comparison with other pedilids, and are among the few species with eyes that are not notched. The 8 species of *Eurygenius* (e. U.S., Tex., and Calif.; about 10–12 mm) and the 11 species of *Stereopalpus* (e. and w. U.S.; 7–10 mm) have gray, sometimes patchy hair; in both genera pronotum is narrow at tip and margined at base. In *Eurygenius* species, last segment of maxillary palp is *triangular;* in *Stereopalpus* species last segment is long and pointed (Fig. 119). *Pedilus,* with 30 species, is the largest genus; about ⅔ occur in w. U.S.; length is 4–8 mm. They are black or brown and not densely hairy. Prothorax is often nearly *round* to broadest in front. Some are common on mayapple foliage.

ANTLIKE FLOWER BEETLES:
Family Anthicidae

Identification. Shape and form characteristic: Head as *wide as pronotum,* with a narrow *neck.* Pronotum widest *at front,* constricted at base, with no lateral margin. Elytra elongate-oblong to elongate and nearly parallel-sided. Legs moderately long. Pronotum (in about ⅓ of species) has a large *horn* extending over head. Antennae threadlike to weakly clubbed. Eyes not notched. Hairs moderately dense. Abdominal segments not fused. 1.7–4.3 mm.

Similar families. (1) Pedilid beetles (p. 274) — 4–15 mm; eyes almost always notched next to antennae. (2) Antlike leaf beetles (p. 278) — eyes notched; first 2 abdominal segments fused. (3) Antlike stone beetles (p. 128) — antennal club loose, 3-4-segmented. (4) Grass-root beetles (p. 130) — no distinct hairs; 3.4–6 mm. Other similar beetles lack a neck — see: (5) Some leaf beetles (Orsodacninae and Criocerinae, p. 291), 3.2–12 mm; (6) checkered beetles (p. 208); (7) flat bark beetles (p. 219); (8) spider beetles (p. 196); and (9) false tiger beetles (p. 260).

Range and numbers. 16 genera and about 140 species; about ⅔ of species in w. U.S.

Habits. Larvae live in soil and in decayed vegetation on ground; little is known about their habits. Adults generally live under objects on the ground. Many species are apparently scavengers. Adults feed on dead insects; larvae are assumed to have similar habits. One species preys on dobsonfly eggs.

Collecting methods. Many are collected at lights. Some are swept from foliage; others are found under boards, stones, etc. Sometimes these beetles are found on carrion. A few species live on coastal beaches, dunes, and alkali flats. In spring, scatter boards over the ground in grassy areas and look underneath them early in the morning; these and other beetles apparently hide there to escape night chill. In arid regions these beetles are most numerous in stream valleys. Certain species of *Anthicus* and *Notoxus* are attracted to dead blister beetles — consider using them as bait.

Examples. The 38 species of *Anthicus* (widely distributed; 1.7–4.3 mm) make it the second largest genus in the family. Base of the head is often truncate. The little known about these beetles indicates that they are scavengers — adults feed on dead insects; larvae probably eat dead insects and soil fungi. Larvae of *A. heroicus* Casey eat dobsonfly egg masses. Forty-five of 48 species of antlike flower beetles that have a large *pronotal horn* extending over their head belong to the genus *Notoxus* (widely distributed); some are

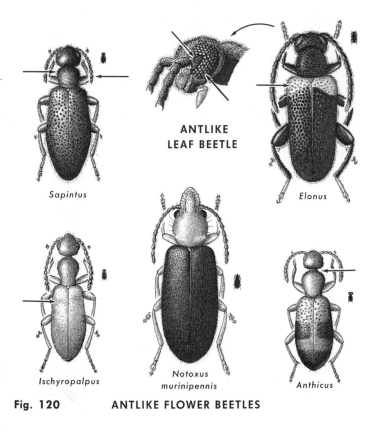

ANTLIKE
LEAF BEETLE

Sapintus

Elonus

Ischyropalpus

*Notoxus
murinipennis*

Anthicus

Fig. 120   **ANTLIKE FLOWER BEETLES**

common. *N. monodon* Fab. (e. U.S. to Tex.) is one of our most common antlike flower beetles. *N. monodon* and many other *Notoxus* species bear elytral markings, but *N. murinipennis* (LeC.) is reddish yellow with dark elytra. It is common in e. ⅓ of U.S. The **Fruit Notoxus,** *N. constrictus* Casey (not shown), is common in orchards of Calif. Adults often feed on damaged fruit and on cut fruit that is being dried — adults have been found on apples, apricots, cherries, peaches, plums, prunes, and young eggplants. Larvae do not feed on fruit.

The other 3 species of antlike flower beetles with a pronotal horn belong to the genus *Mecynotarsus* (not shown), and differ from *Notoxus* species in that the length of the 1st segment of the hind tarsus exceeds the length of the remaining segments combined (in *Notoxus* that segment is not longer than the remaining segments). In *Sapintus* (9 species; widely distributed) pronotum is *unusually small,* with sinuate (arched) sides behind its middle. These beetles are usually a uniform color; their antennae have an *abrupt but weak* 3-segmented club (Fig. 120). The 13 species of *Ischyropalpus* (widely distributed, many in sw. U.S.) often have a transverse impression and sparse *hairs* on their elytra; length is 2–3 mm. Body is usually brown with part of the elytra darker brown.

ANTLIKE LEAF BEETLES:
Family Euglenidae

Identification. Similar to antlike flower beetles, but eyes *notched* and *coarsely faceted* (Fig. 120); first 2 abdominal segments *fused.* Elytra often light overall or with light *markings.* Often covered with dense, erect *hairs.* Pronotum *oval,* with no margin; head wide, nearly always arched or *truncate* at base, with a distinct *neck.* Antennae threadlike to gradually clubbed or comblike (in some males); each 11-segmented. Tarsi 5-5-4; 1st segment usually long. 1.5–3 mm.
Similar families. (1) Antlike flower beetles (p. 276) — eyes not notched; 1st 2 abdominal segments not fused. (2) Pedilid beetles (p. 274) are larger (4–15 mm). (3) Some leaf beetles (Orsodacninae and Criocerinae, p. 291) are similar but are 3.2–12 mm long and have no neck. The following have no neck: (4) false tiger beetles (p. 260); (5) checkered beetles (p. 208); and (6) soldier beetles (p. 183).
Range and numbers. 13 genera and 39 species; about ⅔ in e. U.S.
Habits. Larvae have been found in litter and rotten wood. Adults typically occur on foliage, but also on flowers.
Collecting methods. Found with moderate frequency by beating or sweeping vegetation; most common in moist areas.
Examples. The 3 *Elonus* species occur from e. U.S. to Tex. In these beetles base of head is deeply arched and antennae are thick

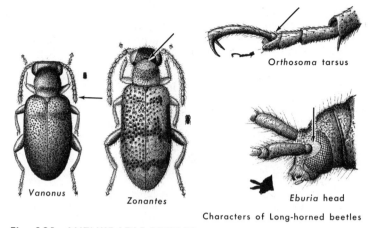

Orthosoma tarsus

Vanonus

Zonantes

Eburia head

Characters of Long-horned beetles

Fig. 121 ANTLIKE LEAF BEETLES

and nearly cylindrical. The 8 species of *Zonantes* occur from e. U.S. to Tex. They differ from members of *Elonus* in that head is *truncate* (not arched) at base, and body hairs are stiff and not matted. In e. U.S. *Zonantes* species are collected much more often than other antlike leaf beetles. Most of the 10 *Vanonus* species (the largest genus) occur in e. U.S.; 1 lives in Calif. Each antenna ends in a gradual club; body is dark with no markings; body hairs are very short.

Superfamily Chrysomeloidea

Tarsi apparently 4-4-4, actually 5-5-5; usually small to medium-sized. All are plant-feeders — some are pests.

LONG-HORNED BEETLES:
Family Cerambycidae
(Figs. 121-125; see also Pls. 9-11)

Identification. Each antenna nearly always at least *half as long as body,* often *approaching* length of body, sometimes *longer* than body. Body usually *robust* and *broad-shouldered.* Eyes usually *notched;* each antenna often inserted in notch (Fig. 121). 2–60 mm (up to $2\frac{3}{8}$ in.), usually 10–25 mm (up to 1 in.). Tarsi apparently 4-4-4, actually 5-5-5 (4th segment usually minute; Fig. 121), rarely obviously 5-5-5.

Similar families. (1) In some leaf beetles (Donaciinae, p. 290) pronotum is nearly always broadest at front; in other leaf beetles (Orsodacninae and Criocerinae, p. 291) — antennae short, body 3.2–12 mm long; in still others (Galerucinae, p. 296) — elytra usually widest at rear; rarely over 10 mm long. (2) False blister beetles (p. 262) — tarsi 5-5-4. (3) False long-horned beetles (p. 248) — claws comblike; tarsi 5-5-4. (4) Soldier beetles (p. 183) —tarsi clearly 5-5-5. (5) Cebrionid beetles (p. 171) — mandibles enlarged; hind angles of pronotum extended. (6) Pedilid beetles (p. 274) have a neck; tarsi 5-5-4. (7) Fire-colored beetles (p. 260) — antennae sawtoothed to feathery.

Range and numbers. The 6th largest family of beetles in N. America, with over 290 genera and 1100 species; widely distributed.

Habits. All are plant-feeders. Most larvae (often called round-headed borers) eat solid tissues of various plants, usually wood of trees; some feed on roots. Condition of host wood varies from living to dry and seasoned or thoroughly decayed. Some can cause serious defects in lumber, and even totally destroy timber for commercial purposes. Much damage results from feeding in recently felled trees before they are sawed. These beetles play an important role in forest ecology, however, by aiding in the decomposition of dead and dying trees.

The larvae of most species have strict feeding requirements for normal development. Most larvae live beneath bark of trees, and usually bore into wood to feed, then bore into bark to pupate. Some adults eat nothing; those that do feed generally do so on flowers (pollen, stamens, nectar), bark, leaves, pine needles and cones, sap, fruit, roots, and fungi. Flower-feeding adults usually visit many different blossoms, but some visit only certain species of flowers. These beetles help pollinate some plants and are the most important of all beetles in plant pollination.

Collecting methods. The bright colors and handsome appearance of many long-horned beetles make this family a favorite with collectors. Though this is a large family with many species that are abundant (presumably, at least) in nature, these beetles are not usually collected as easily as other beetles with more prominent habits, such as leaf beetles and ground beetles. Exceptions include those long-horned beetles that are attracted to various flowers (mostly flower long-horns and some round-necked long-horns — see below) and others (such as the **Red Milkweed Beetle**) that are common on a certain host plant. In e. U.S., flowers of various species of *Viburnum* attract many long-horns; these plants bloom in the spring. In w. U.S. flowers of *Caenothus* and *Rhus* attract many species of long-horns. Sweeping and beating foliage in a variety of

habitats will produce specimens, but usually in small numbers. In spring check cordwood piles for emerging adults. Rearing specimens from infested wood may provide species that are not easily collected. Many species are attracted to lights. Some are attracted to baits such as fermented molasses (see p. 23). Handle long-horns (especially large ones) carefully — they bite.
Subfamilies. Six of the 7 subfamilies are discussed below; the subfamily excluded here contains 2 species that are not widely distributed.

ABERRANT LONG-HORNS Subfamily Parandrinae
Similar to certain stag beetles (p. 135), but antennae not clubbed; or to certain darkling beetles (p. 249), but tarsi obviously 5-5-5 (not 5-5-4). The body shape; *broad, margined* pronotum; and tarsi that are obviously 5-5-5 (Fig. 122) are a combination of characters in these beetles that is unique among long-horned beetles. The 3 species in this subfamily belong to the genus *Parandra* and are found from e. to sw. U.S. *P. brunnea* (Fab.), 9–18 mm, may harm mature shade trees. The ♀ lays eggs on exposed wood on tree trunks; trees extensively damaged by boring may blow over in a wind. Adults are active at night, and may be captured with a flashlight at tree bases, logs, or stumps.

TOOTH-NECKED LONG-HORNS Subfamily Prioninae
These are our largest long-horns (22–60 mm — nearly 1-2⅜ in.); they are distinctive for their *toothed pronotal margin* (Fig. 122) as well as their size. In the genus *Prionus,* males are generally smaller than females, and have longer and more fully developed antennae. The **Tile-horned Prionus,** *P. imbricornis* (L.), 22–47 mm, is found nearly throughout e. U.S. It is probably the most harmful species in this subfamily, although an accurate estimate of damage it causes is nearly impossible because it lives underground. Larvae feed in roots of living oaks, chestnuts, and other hardwoods, and will completely hollow out large roots, often severing them. Larvae move from root to root by tunneling through ground. Hollowed roots may be filled with pelletlike excrement from larvae, coarse fibers, and earth. The Tile-horned Prionus is most common where trees grow under unfavorable conditions, such as in parks where the ground is packed, on hilly slopes, or in pastures. Over some years the trees may die limb by limb. The **Ponderous Borer,** *Ergates spiculatus* LeC., the largest w. U.S. beetle (about 60 mm — up to 2⅜ in.), feeds in Douglas fir and pines, and damages felled logs and telephone poles; it occurs throughout w. U.S. The **Brown Prionid,** *Orthosoma brunneum* (Forst.), 22–40 mm, occurs nearly throughout e. U.S. Larvae feed in groups in coniferous or hardwood trees that have been dead for several years; they make extensive excavations that are tightly packed with coarse frass. Cross-ties, telephone poles, and structural timbers in moist areas are also subject to damage.

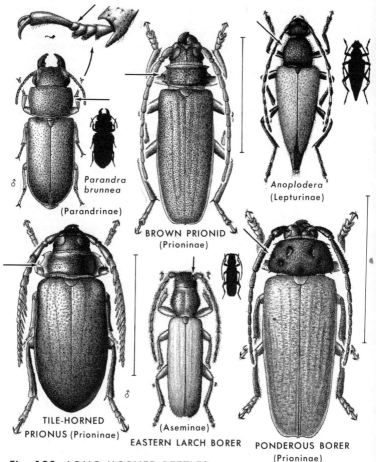

Parandra
brunnea
(Parandrinae)

BROWN PRIONID
(Prioninae)

Anoplodera
(Lepturinae)

TILE-HORNED
PRIONUS (Prioninae)

(Aseminae)
EASTERN LARCH BORER

PONDEROUS BORER
(Prioninae)

Fig. 122 LONG-HORNED BEETLES

SUBFAMILY ASEMINAE

The 22 species are difficult to distinguish from the round-necked
long-horns (p. 284; with about 450 species). The **Eastern Larch
Borer,** *Tetropium cinnamopterum* Kirby, 12–14 mm, feeds in living and dying conifers, especially larch trees. In adults the eyes are
completely *divided* into an upper and a lower part, and joined by a
linelike bridge.

FLOWER LONG-HORNS   (Figs. 122, 123;
Subfamily Lepturinae   see also Pls. 9 and 10)

Members of this group are often distinctive for their *bell-shaped pronotum* (which is narrow at front, broad at base) and for their broad-shouldered appearance, with elytra that taper in back. This subfamily includes about 250 species in N. America. Many are readily collected due to their flower-feeding habits. Flower long-horns differ from flat-faced long-horns (Lamiinae, p. 288) in that their face *slants forward* or is *nearly vertical,* and the last segment of each maxillary palp is blunt or straight across at the tip. In flat-faced long-horns, the face is vertical or slants backward, and the tip of each maxillary palp is pointed. Some flower long-horns resemble round-necked long-horns (Cerambycinae p. 284); but base of each antenna is not surrounded by the eye, as is usually the case in Cerambycinae (see *Eburia,* Fig. 121). The narrow form; elongate, posteriorly constricted head; and anteriorly narrowed pronotum of flower long-horns are adaptations that help these beetles extract nectar and pollen from flowers.

Members of the largest genus, *Anoplodera* (57 species; typically 7-20 mm) and those of *Leptura* (25 species; most 8-30 mm), and *Typocerus* (16 species, usually 9-14 mm; not shown) are attracted to flowers, and are usually similar in form. Some have yellow or red markings on a dark background, or black markings on a yellow or red background. They are active, fly well, and can evade a careless or slow collector. Larvae feed in dead, usually moist wood, and show little preference for a particular host. Adults continue to lay eggs in favorable wood, such as poles or cross-ties, until the host is completely destroyed. The **Chestnut Bark Borer,** *Anoplodera nitens* (Forst.), not shown, 10-15 mm, is black with golden yellow bands. Larvae feed in moist, thick bark at base and in crotches of living chestnut and oak in e. U.S. Rarely does this injure the tree, but large patches of bark can be destroyed. Wounds made by this beetle allowed spores of chestnut blight disease to enter chestnut trees; this beetle thus played a role in the rapid destruction of these trees.

The 7 slender and distinctive species of *Strangalia* (most 9-14 mm) breed in a variety of trees, usually hardwoods, and are often common on wild roses. *Cortodera* is one of the largest genera with 20 species (usually 6-10 mm), which are found on many flowers. *C. longicornis* (Kirby) varies in color from black overall to black with brownish elytral stripes. The **Oak Bark Scaler,** *Encyclops coerulea* (Say), 7-9.5 mm, is bright greenish blue. Larvae bore in outer bark of living white oaks and other hardwoods. This makes portions of bark peel off but does not damage wood, so this beetle is not considered a pest.

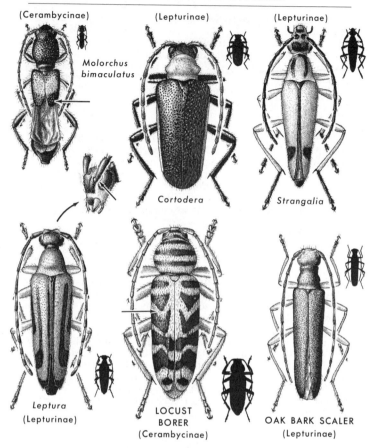

(Cerambycinae)   (Lepturinae)   (Lepturinae)

Molorchus
bimaculatus

Cortodera   Strangalia

Leptura   LOCUST   OAK BARK SCALER
(Lepturinae)   BORER   (Lepturinae)
                     (Cerambycinae)

Fig. 123   LONG-HORNED BEETLES

ROUND-NECKED LONG-HORNS   (Figs. 123, 124;
Subfamily Cerambycinae   see also Pls. 9, 10)
Pronotum is usually rounded and widest at about middle. For
characters that distinguish this group from flower long-horns
(Lepturinae), see above. Round-necked long-horns differ from
flat-faced long-horns (below) in that the last segment of each maxillary palp is blunt or straight across (not pointed) and the face is
slanted forward or nearly vertical (not vertical or slanting back-

ward). This is the largest subfamily of long-horned beetles, with about 450 species, including some of the most attractive of all beetles.

Molorchus bimaculatus Say, 5–7 mm, has short elytra as do certain other long-horns; its larvae eat dead wood of redbud, dogwood, sweet gum, and other trees. The **Locust Borer,** *Megacyllene robiniae* (Forst.), 12–18 mm, is strikingly marked with narrow *yellow bands on black elytra*. It is common on goldenrod in fall and injures black and yellow locust trees. Larval boring in bark and sapwood of healthy trees stunts their growth; trees may be killed and wood made worthless for posts and poles. The **Painted Hickory Borer,** *M. caryae* (Gahan), not shown, 12–20 mm, is so similar to the Locust Borer that they are best distinguished by the time of year when adults emerge — Locust Borer in fall; Painted Hickory Borer in spring. Larvae of the Painted Hickory Borer feed in many hardwoods. *Psyrassa unicolor* (Rand.), 8–12 mm, is much narrower than most round-necked long-horns. It prunes small branches from living beeches, oaks, and other trees.

Local outbreaks of the **Oak Twig Pruner,** *Elaphidionoides villosus* (Fab.), 10–17 mm, are common; young trees may be deformed, but older ones are not usually damaged. Adults fly when oak leaves form and lay eggs in bark of twigs and small branches. When mature, each larva severs twig from inside, leaving only bark as support, then moves up twig, plugging tunnel behind it. The first high wind causes damaged twig to fall, and the larva (still inside) is usually protected during winter by a blanket of snow. Species of *Euderces* (6 in N. America; 4–9 mm) are among the smallest of our long-horns. They are antlike and are often attractively marked. Larvae feed in dead branches of chestnuts, hickories, oaks, redbuds, hackberries, and other trees.

The **Red-headed Ash Borer,** *Neoclytus acuminatus* (Fab.), 6–18 mm, is reddish brown to brown with yellow *cross-bands* on its elytra. It is often common. There is only 1 generation in n. U.S., but more in s. U.S., with some overlapping of generations. When red maples blossom, adults fly to ash logs and lay eggs in bark crevices. When they hatch, larvae completely honeycomb sapwood, causing serious damage to ash logs left in woods or stored with their bark on. The **Banded Ash Borer,** *N. caprea* (Say), not shown, 12–20 mm, has a cross-band of yellowish white on front of its thorax, and 4 bands on its elytra (first 2 bands meet and almost form circles). Habits of this beetle are similar to those of the Red-headed Ash Borer.

The **Elm Bark Borer,** *Physocnemum brevilineum* (Say), 12–16 mm, is bluish black with 3 short, raised, *whitish lines* on each elytron (Fig. 124). Adults deposit eggs beneath bark scales of living elm trees in late summer. Larvae mine into cambium, sometimes causing bark to fall off, and exposing wood to attack by other insects. This beetle may play a role in transmitting the

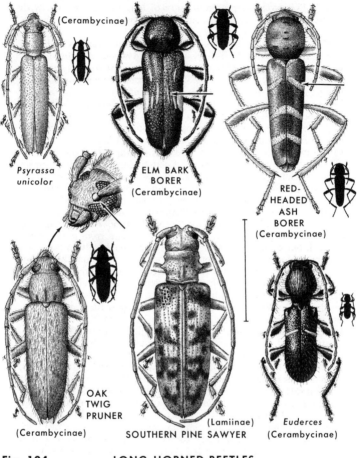

(Cerambycinae)

Psyrassa unicolor

ELM BARK BORER (Cerambycinae)

RED-HEADED ASH BORER (Cerambycinae)

OAK TWIG PRUNER (Cerambycinae)

(Lamiinae) SOUTHERN PINE SAWYER

Euderces (Cerambycinae)

Fig. 124   **LONG-HORNED BEETLES**

causal agent of Dutch Elm Disease, but this has not been proven. Attack by the **Elm Borer,** *Saperda tridentata* Oliv. (p. 289), may follow damage by this species. The **Cypress Bark Borer,** *Physocnemum andreae* Hald. (not shown; about 20 mm long) is reddish brown with a white arc on each elytron. Larvae damage felled and girdled cypress trees in s. U.S.

The **Sugar Maple Borer,** *Glycobius speciosus* (Say), is a strikingly attractive beetle — see Pl. 10. Unfortunately, it is the worst enemy of sugar maple trees in some areas. This beetle is 23–27 mm long. Its larvae feed between bark and wood of healthy trees, and may kill large limbs or entire trees. Scattered dead limbs and dead bark, or naked scars on branches and trunk (especially near base of large limbs) are evidence of these borers.

FLAT-FACED LONG-HORNS
Subfamily Lamiinae

(Figs. 124, 125;
see also Pl. 11)

Members of this subfamily are recognizable by their nearly *flat face* that is vertical or slanting backward, and by the pointed last segment of each *maxillary palp* (Fig. 125). Species in this subfamily often have hairs forming variegated or irregular patterns. This is the second largest subfamily, with over 300 species.

The 11 *Monochamus* species are known as sawyer beetles and are responsible for much damage to dying, recently killed, and felled conifers throughout most of U.S. Adults (13–32 mm) eat needles of conifers or bark of twigs; each antenna is frequently twice as long as the body. The **Southern Pine Sawyer,** *M. titillator* (Fab.), is especially harmful to felled trees. Severe storms that uproot many trees provide favorable breeding conditions for this beetle. It varies in length from 16–32 mm; the antennae are much longer in ♂ than in ♀. The 7 species of *Goes* are known as trunk-borers, for their larvae bore into trunks or branches of living hardwoods, making mines through heartwood and exuding fibrous frass. Adults are 10–30 mm long and prettily blotched or spotted. When chestnut trees bloom, adults emerge and feed on bark of young hardwood twigs and females lay eggs. Each ♀ gnaws oval pits through bark of hardwoods and lays an egg between wood and inner bark. Newly hatched larva, after entering wood, extends mine upward and deep into heartwood. Larvae need 2–4 years to develop. Rarely does larval damage kill a tree, for larvae do most of their feeding in solid wood, so growing tissue is undamaged. Nonetheless, wood defects can be serious; in some areas hardly an oak can be cut that does not show abandoned larval mines. One species — the **Oak Sapling Borer,** *G. tesselatus* (Hald.), not shown (about 25 mm) — kills many oak saplings by cutting them off at the base. When mature trees are damaged, secondary insects such as carpenter ants and wood-destroying fungi can enter trees.

Larvae of *Hippopsis lemniscata* (Fab.) feed in living ragweed and daisy fleabane; adults are 10–13 mm long. Adults are found on ragweed in midsummer; this is the only species of the genus. Larvae of *Dorcaschema wildii* Uhler (adults 15–22 mm long) feed in living branches of mulberry and osage orange; repeated infestations may kill host. Adults are found on infested branches in midsummer. Some of the most handsome beetles belong to the genus *Saperda* (8 species), which also includes some of the most injurious long-horns. The **Round-headed Apple Tree Borer,** *S. candida* Fab. (see Pl. 11) is an important pest of fruit trees and ornamentals in e. U.S.; it is 15–20 mm long. Its chief hosts are apple, pear, quince, peach, and cherry trees. Females lay eggs on trunks, seldom over 2–3 feet above the ground. Young trees may be killed the

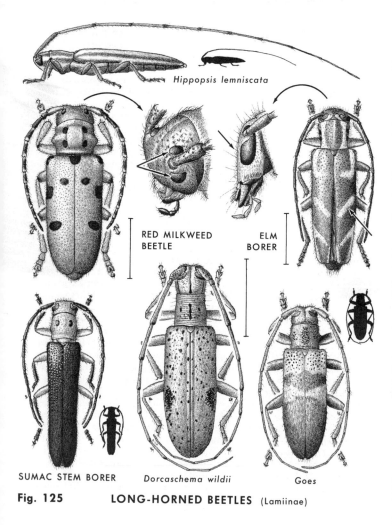

Hippopsis lemniscata

RED MILKWEED BEETLE

ELM BORER

SUMAC STEM BORER   *Dorcaschema wildii*   *Goes*

Fig. 125   **LONG-HORNED BEETLES** (Lamiinae)

1st year; larger trees may live 2–3 years, to be blown over eventually due to trunk weakening.

The **Elm Borer**, *Saperda tridentata* Oliv., is densely clothed with gray hairs and has lengthwise and diagonal *bands of orange* on its pronotum and elytra; it is 9–17 mm long. Elm trees are its only host; attacks are generally confined to unhealthy trees. Thinning of top foliage and scattered dead limbs indicate the presence of this beetle. Infested trees die slowly as beetles work from top down; usually it takes 3 years for Elm Borers to kill a tree. Outbreaks of the **Poplar Borer**, *S. calcarata* Say (not shown; 25–31 mm) are always local. It frequently feeds in unhealthy trees or trees damaged by insects; it attacks various cottonwoods, poplars, and willows throughout most of U.S. Larvae work in trunk and larger limbs; infested trees are marked by coarse, excelsiorlike shreds of wood and frass pushed out of tunnels. Larvae require 2–3 years to develop. Because *Saperda* larvae feed deep within a tree and are protected by bark and wood, control of these beetles is nearly impossible.

Species of *Oberea* (25 in N. America; 8–19 mm) are distinctive for their cylindrical form, with the elytra slightly narrowed at the middle. Nearly all species are pests; they typically bore into twigs and branches of hardwoods and bushes. Examples are the **Sumac Stem Borer**, *O. ocellata* Hald., 13–14 mm, and the **Rhododendron Stem Borer**, *O. myops* Hald., 8–16 mm (not shown). The species of *Tetraopes* (13 in N. America; 5–17 mm long) are red with black markings and are distinctive for having each *compound eye divided,* so there appear to be 4 eyes, not 2 (Fig. 125). Each species is found only on 1 or more species of milkweed; adults are most common when the plant is blooming. The **Red Milkweed Beetle,** *T. tetrophthalmus* (Forst.), 9–14 mm, is one of the most common species; both larvae and adults feed on milkweed.

LEAF BEETLES: Family Chrysomelidae
(Figs. 126–132; see also Pls. 11, 12)

Identification. Cannot be readily characterized; family members are very diverse in form and have no distinctive characters in common. Some subfamilies are distinctive in appearance or characters (see below). Many are similar to long-horned beetles (p. 279) but each antenna nearly always less than *half* as long as body. Eyes usually not notched. Tarsi apparently 4-4-4, actually 5-5-5, 4th segment small (Fig. 126). 1–16 mm, rarely over 12 mm.
Similar families. See subfamily treatments.
Range and numbers. The 4th largest family, after snout beetles (Curculionidae), rove beetles (Staphylinidae), and ground beetles (Carabidae); widely distributed. About 175 genera and 1474 species in N. America.

Habits. As the common name implies, these beetles occur on vegetation. Both larvae and adults feed on living plants, infrequently on plant remains. Most species eat herbaceous plants; larvae usually feed on roots, adults on leaves. A few larvae and adults eat leaves of woody plants; a very few mine these leaves. Most (with notable exception of certain crop pests) feed only on particular plants; host plants of many are not known.

Collecting methods. These are very common, and their habit of feeding on foliage makes them as easy to collect in large numbers as any family of beetles. Sweeping or beating foliage is the best collecting method. Many more leaf beetles occur on weeds and bushes than on trees, so open weedy areas are most productive. Few feed on trees. Collecting in a wide variety of habitats will produce the greatest number of different species. Hand-pick those that are crop pests to avoid damaging plants. Some fly to lights at night.

Subfamilies. 16 in N. America; 4 rare ones are excluded from this guide.

LONG-HORNED LEAF BEETLES   (Fig. 126;
Subfamily Donaciinae   see also Pl. 11)

These are elongate, 5.5–12 mm, usually dark-colored, and have a metallic luster. Antennae *long;* pronotum *lacks* a lateral margin; and hind legs are often *enlarged.* Of the 49 species in N. America,

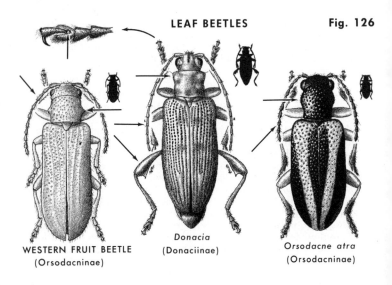

LEAF BEETLES   Fig. 126

WESTERN FRUIT BEETLE
(Orsodacninae)

Donacia
(Donaciinae)

Orsodacne atra
(Orsodacninae)

31 belong to the genus *Donacia*. They are similar to some long-horns (p. 279), but few long-horns have a pronotum that is nearly parallel-sided or widest in front (as in these beetles). Larvae feed in submerged portions of aquatic plants; tip of abdomen bears 2 spines, each with a spiracle. Larvae bury these spines in stems of plants and breathe oxygen from plant vessels. Adults live on exposed parts of host plants. They are active and fast-flying, and are often very difficult to capture. In adults, almost entire ventral surface of body bears a dense pile of fine hairs; this holds a thin film of air and allows ♀ to breathe while laying eggs on host plants under water.

PUNCTATE LEAF BEETLES Subfamily Orsodacninae

These are also similar to long-horns, but have short antennae. Some resemble antlike flower beetles (p. 276) and pedilid beetles (p. 274) but members of both of those families have a neck (these leaf beetles do not). Elongate; light brown to black; *no lateral margin* on pronotum; 4–12 mm long. Only 10 species in N. America. Larvae feed on roots and adults on flowers and foliage. *Orsodacne atra* (Ahr.), the only species of the genus, is highly variable in color — entirely black to black with brown spots or stripes to entirely brown. It is found on willow flowers in spring. The genus *Syneta* has 8 species; one, the **Western Fruit Beetle,** *S. albida* LeC., is injurious to orchard trees in Pacific Northwest. Apple and pear trees are chief hosts; adults eat leaves, buds, flowers, and fruit; larvae feed on roots.

SHINING LEAF BEETLES   (Fig. 127;
Subfamily Criocerinae   see also Pl. 12)

These, again, are similar to long-horns, but body surfaces are shiny, and in 23 of 26 species pronotum is *narrowed at middle;* in the other 3 species the sides are rounded. All lack a lateral margin on pronotum; body length is 3.2–7.5 mm. Somewhat similar to antlike flower beetles (p. 276) and pedilid beetles (p. 274) but with no neck. The **Asparagus Beetle,** *Crioceris asparagi* (L.), feeds on asparagus as larva and adult, as does the **Spotted Asparagus Beetle,** *C. duodecimpunctata* (L.). Both species were accidentally introduced from Europe, but *C. asparagi* is now more widespread. The **Cereal Leaf Beetle,** *Oulema melanopus* (L.), Pl. 12, was also an accidental introduction from Europe, and is potentially a serious pest of cereal crops. The **Threelined Potato Beetle,** *Lema trilinea* White, is sometimes found on potato plants but is more common on weeds. Members of *Lema* (23 species) have tarsal claws that *touch at base* (see close-up in Fig. 127).

SHORT-HORNED LEAF BEETLES Subfamily Clytrinae

Distinctive for short, sawtoothed antennae. Body generally nearly cylindrical, stout, elongate-robust to broad and oval; 2–10 mm

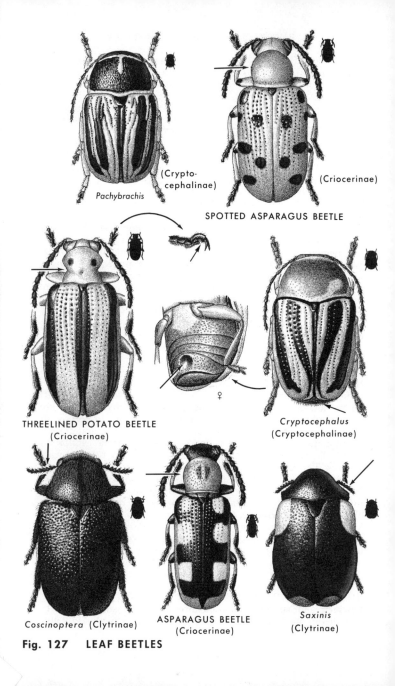

(Crypto-cephalinae)

Pachybrachis

(Criocerinae)

SPOTTED ASPARAGUS BEETLE

THREELINED POTATO BEETLE
(Criocerinae)

♀

Cryptocephalus
(Cryptocephalinae)

Coscinoptera (Clytrinae)

ASPARAGUS BEETLE
(Criocerinae)

Saxinis
(Clytrinae)

Fig. 127   LEAF BEETLES

long. Similar to cylindrical leaf beetles (below), but they have threadlike antennae. In N. America, 9 genera and about 40 species. Larvae of this subfamily and of the next 2 subfamilies are often known as casebearers, for they surround themselves with a case made of their excrement and debris. Little is known about larval feeding habits — larvae of nearly all short-horned leaf beetles and cylindrical leaf beetles occur on or in ground, so investigations of their habits are very difficult. Some are known to eat detritus and humus. Larvae of a few species are found in nests of ants. Adult short-horned leaf beetles are found on young shoots of leguminous plants; in extremely arid regions they congregate on nectar sources. Two of the largest genera in this subfamily are *Coscinoptera* (8 species) and *Saxinis* (10 species).

CYLINDRICAL LEAF BEETLES   (Fig. 127;
Subfamily Cryptocephalinae   **see also Pl. 11)**
Body robust, nearly cylindrical. Head disklike; can be withdrawn into prothorax. Last abdominal segment often visible beyond elytra; body 2–7.1 mm long. Short-horned leaf beetles (above) are similar but antennae sawtoothed, not threadlike. Habits of only a few of the more than 250 species are known, but adults are most often collected on leaves, flowers, or fruits. Adults of the large genus *Pachybrachis* (about 150 species; 2–5.5 mm) are extremely difficult to identify, for their diagnostic characters consist primarily of color and color pattern, both of which often vary within a species. In the related genus *Cryptocephalus* (71 species; 2–7.5 mm; see Pl. 11), the color patterns are so constant and distinctive that most species can be identified by the color pattern on their elytra alone. Sexes of *Cryptocephalus* are distinguished by form of 5th abdominal segment — ♀ has a round, deep depression (Fig. 127); ♂ has no depression.

WARTY LEAF BEETLES Subfamily Chlamisinae
The 35 or so species (5 genera) are readily separated from nearly all other beetles by their appearance. They bear what look like coarse warts of various sizes and fine sculpturing (Fig. 128). In addition, they are broad-bodied, 1.8–6.1 mm long, have a sawtoothed elytral suture, and are usually metallic in color. These beetles are easily mistaken for caterpillar droppings. Even after a collector thinks he has learned to recognize them, he can still be fooled — occasionally in collections there are caterpillar droppings that have been mounted and labeled, right along with specimens of warty leaf beetles. Larvae feed on foliage and are protected by the case they construct; adults also occur on foliage. The largest genus is *Neochlamisus* with 16 species (2.8–4.9 mm).

OVAL LEAF BEETLES Subfamily Eumolpinae
Body elongate-robust to oval. Some resemble certain broad-bodied

leaf beetles (below), but have a deeply bilobed 3rd tarsal segment (Fig. 128). (That segment is not bilobed in the next subfamily.) Most are dark, though some are light or patterned and a few are iridescent; length is 3–11 mm. Families with similar members include pleasing fungus beetles (p. 226), handsome fungus beetles (p. 237), and certain darkling beetles (p. 249). More than 150 species belong to this subfamily (Eumolpinae). Larvae live in the soil and feed on roots of various plants; they may badly damage strawberries, raspberries, roses, grapes, and other plants. The **Strawberry Rootworm,** *Paria fragariae* Wilcox, is widely distributed in the U.S.; it also feeds on raspberries, blackberries, roses, and other plants. The 23 species of *Colaspis* (4–9 mm) generally have double rows of punctures on their elytra. The **Grape Colaspis,** *C. brunnea* (Fab.), is the most common member of the genus. The **Rose Leaf Beetle,** *Nodonota puncticollis* (Say), is common in n. U.S., and is found on a variety of plants. Seven species belong to the genus. Nine of the 13 species of *Myochrous* (4–7 mm; widely distributed) are distinctive for the *3 teeth* at each side of the pronotum; these beetles are typically dull brown with brown or gray scales.

BROAD-BODIED LEAF BEETLES   **(Figs. 128, 129;**
Subfamily Chrysomelinae   **see also Pl. 11)**
Most of the 136 species are *oval to nearly circular* (dorsal view) and strongly convex above (lateral view), but some (such as *Chrysomela* species) are elongate-robust. Some oval leaf beetles (above) are similarly rounded, but in that group the 3rd tarsal segment is deeply bilobed (it is not in this subfamily). Similar families include pleasing fungus beetles (p. 226), handsome fungus beetles (p. 237), some lady beetles (p. 231), and certain darkling beetles (p. 249). Both adults and larvae feed on foliage or flowers of various plants; adults are 3–14 mm long.

The **Colorado Potato Beetle,** *Leptinotarsa decemlineata* (Say), not shown, 5.5–11 mm, was first collected by Thomas Say in about 1822; it then fed on sandbur — a weed related to the potato plant — in eastern and southern Colo. and was of no economic importance. After the potato plant was introduced into the habitat of this beetle, it thrived on the new host plant, and has since spread to nearly all potato-growing areas. This beetle was once the major pest of potatoes, but insecticides are effective and now the Colorado Potato Beetle is rarely a problem. The 10 black stripes on the elytra are the basis for the species name, *decemlineata*. The **False Potato Beetle,** *L. juncta* (Germ.), is quite similar, but differs in that the rows of punctures on the elytra are regular (irregular in *decemlineata*). Twelve species belong to the genus *Leptinotarsa*. The genera *Calligrapha* (36 widely distributed species; see Pl. 11) and *Zygogramma* (13 species, widely distributed) are similar in form, size (4–10 mm), and often in color. Many species bear a pattern of spots and lines; some have lines only. These 2 genera are

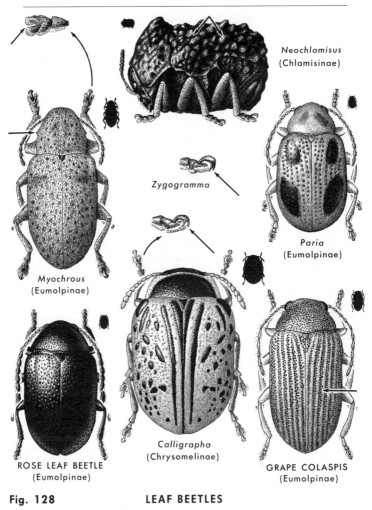

Neochlamisus
(Chlamisinae)

Zygogramma

Myochrous
(Eumolpinae)

Paria
(Eumolpinae)

ROSE LEAF BEETLE
(Eumolpinae)

Calligrapha
(Chrysomelinae)

GRAPE COLASPIS
(Eumolpinae)

Fig. 128   **LEAF BEETLES**

easily distinguished by their tarsal claws, which are separated at the base in species of *Calligrapha* but are nearly touching at the base in *Zygogramma* (Fig. 128). *Chrysomela* species (17 in N. America; Fig. 129) are often common and injurious on willows, poplars, and alders. Most bear broad spots or spots and stripes on their elytra, but a few lack markings. Early in this century, when basket willows were grown in N.Y., these beetles were serious pests. Willows are not now grown for commercial products, so damage caused by these beetles is of little importance. The **Cottonwood Leaf Beetle,** *C. scripta* Fab., is the most common species in the genus (found nearly throughout N. America). The **Klamathweed Beetles,** *Chrysolina quadrigemina* (Suff.) and *C. hyperici* (Forst.) have been introduced into w. U.S. for control of Klamathweed, a nuisance plant that displaces desirable range plants and is poisonous to livestock. These beetles have nearly eliminated this weed as a problem. The 9 species of *Phaedon* (3–5 mm; widely distributed) are among the smallest members of this subfamily.

SKELETONIZING LEAF BEETLES   **(Figs. 129, 130;**
Subfamily Galerucinae   **see also Pls. 11, 12)**
Some of these resemble shining leaf beetles (Criocerinae, p. 291) but pronotum is broad and has a distinct lateral margin; see figures for long-horned beetles (p. 279), soft-winged flower beetles (p. 211), water-penny beetles (p. 156), and checkered beetles (p. 208). Body form is fairly consistent for the 212 species: head clearly visible from above, pronotum somewhat narrower than elytra at base, and elytra broadest at rear; length 3–16 mm.

Most of the 10 species of *Diabrotica* (widely distributed; Fig. 129, Pl. 11) have a pair of *depressions* on the pronotum; 4 species are major pests. *D. undecimpunctata* Mann. has 2 common names: the **Spotted Cucumber Beetle** and the **Southern Corn Rootworm.** It occurs throughout U.S. e. of Rocky Mts., and is most injurious to corn and cucumbers, but will feed on over 200 other plants. Because of this beetle's abundance and the variety of plants it damages, it is one of our 10 worst insect pests. In addition to root damage (by larvae) and foliage damage (by adults), it transmits causative agent of cucurbit wilt and bacterial wilt (Stewart's disease). In the **Northern Corn Rootworm,** *D. longicornis* (Say), the elytra are not clearly spotted and have fairly distinct parallel ridges. This beetle is one of the major pests of corn in the corn belt. Adults feed on foliage and silk of growing corn, reducing the number of kernels formed. Larvae feed almost exclusively on roots of corn, and usually die if corn is not available. These food requirements and the fact that the eggs of this beetle overwinter make rotation of crops an effective control for this pest.

The **Elm Leaf Beetle,** *Pyrrhalta luteola* (Mull.), 5–7 mm, is found on elms throughout N. America. Adults and larvae feed on leaves; the larva skeletonizes lower surface of leaves and the adult eats small holes in leaves. Severe defoliation weakens trees and makes them vulnerable to attack by other insects. Adults overwinter and frequently enter buildings (houses, barns, sheds, etc.) in fall to seek shelter. Their presence indoors may be annoying, but they do no damage there. Genus *Pyrrhalta* contains 16 widely distributed species. The **Striped Cucumber Beetle,** *Acalymma vitatum* (Fab.), 5-6.5 mm, feeds on cucumbers, squash, muskmelons, cantaloupes, watermelons, and pumpkins. When seedlings push through soil, adults feed on them, cutting off their stems and cotyledons; larvae and adults also feed on larger plants, often destroying them. Adults also transmit causative agent of bacterial wilt; infection by this bacterium can cause more damage than the beetle does. The 5 species of *Acalymma* are distinctive for the 3 dark stripes and closely spaced *rows of punctures* on the elytra.

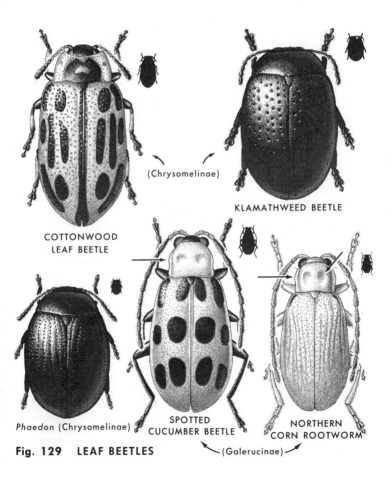

(Chrysomelinae)

KLAMATHWEED BEETLE

COTTONWOOD
LEAF BEETLE

Phaedon (Chrysomelinae)

SPOTTED
CUCUMBER BEETLE

NORTHERN
CORN ROOTWORM

Fig. 129   LEAF BEETLES

(Galerucinae)

Trirhabda species (about 25 in N. America; widely distributed) resemble the **Elm Leaf Beetle,** but are 5–12 mm long (compared to 5–7 mm) and have 1 median and 2 lateral dark stripes on the eltyra. *T. bacharidis* (Weber), 7.5–12 mm, feeds on the shrubby plant groundseltree, which is found along the Atlantic Coast, and can build up large populations on this host, resulting in great foliage damage. This plant is unimportant to man, so this beetle is not considered a pest. Twenty of 25 species in the genus *Scelolyperus* occur in w. U.S.; they are 3–7 mm long. Their shape is uniform and in all species at least the head and elytra are dark. The 15 *Monoxia* species are known in w. U.S. as alkali bugs, for most of them feed on desert and salt marsh plants such as goosefoots, wormwoods, and mugworts. Adults range from 2–5.3 mm in length.

FLEA BEETLES Subfamily Alticinae
Common name of this group of beetles refers to their jumping ability. Hind femora (which contains leaping muscles) moderately to greatly enlarged. This is the most distinctive character, but members of other families also have enlarged femora: seed beetles (p. 304); some marsh beetles (p. 149); some snout beetles (flea weevils, p. 320); and some antlike leaf beetles (p. 276). Shining leaf beetles (p. 291) and some long-horned leaf beetles (p. 279) also have enlarged hind femora, but lack a margin on pronotum. This subfamily (Alticinae) is easily the largest subfamily of leaf beetles, with about 370 species in N. America. Adults feed on foliage, often chew small round holes that make a leaf look as if tiny shot had been fired through it. Most larvae feed on roots, but some feed on foliage. Certain species are very injurious. Length is 1–8.5 mm.

Chaetocnema species (about 30 in N. America) are 1–3.3 mm, generally black, and have striate elytra. The hind tibiae are *deeply notched* and have a *row of bristles*. Adults eat tiny holes in leaves and larvae feed on roots. Four species are important pests on corn, sorghums, broom corn, small grains, and other plants. The **Corn Flea Beetle,** *C. pulicaria* Melsh., is a major pest that harbors bacteria over the winter that cause corn wilt and spreads it during the growing season. Feeding habits of the adult **Sweetpotato Flea Beetle,** *C. confinis* Crotch (not shown), are unlike those of other flea beetles — this beetle chews shallow irregular channels into both leaf surfaces but does not puncture the leaf. Adults may destroy so many young plants that replanting is necessary.

The 12 species of *Epitrix* are similar in size and appearance to *Chaetocnema* species, but have *bristling* body hairs and hind tibiae that are not notched. Five species seriously damage tobacco, potato plants, and eggplant. Larvae of some species, such as the **Tuber Flea Beetle,** *E. tuberis* Gentner, scar surface of potatoes or bore into them, causing discoloration; this results in waste when potatoes are pared, or may make potatoes rot in storage.

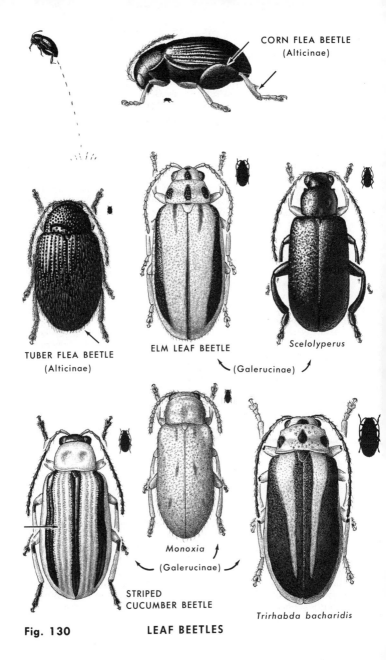

CORN FLEA BEETLE
(Alticinae)

TUBER FLEA BEETLE
(Alticinae)

ELM LEAF BEETLE

Scelolyperus

(Galerucinae)

Monoxia

(Galerucinae)

STRIPED
CUCUMBER BEETLE

Trirhabda bacharidis

Fig. 130   LEAF BEETLES

Altica species (about 65; found nearly throughout N. America) have hind femora that are *less enlarged* than in most flea beetles. Body length is 2-6 mm. These beetles are generally black, and often have blue or green reflections. Base of pronotum generally bears a *transverse groove* that varies from distinct to almost completely absent. Body shape of these species varies only slightly. The **Grape Flea Beetle,** *A. chalybea* Illig. (not shown), occurs throughout the Mississippi R. valley and eastward. In addition to eating leaves of wild and cultivated grapes, it feeds on Virginia creeper, plum, apple, pear, quince, beech, and elm trees. Both adults and larvae feed on foliage. The **Alder Flea Beetle,** *A. ambiens* LeC., at 5-6 mm, is one of the largest species of *Altica*. Dorsal surface shows cobalt blue to greenish blue reflections. This beetle occurs over much of U.S. and is normally scarce; it periodically builds up tremendous numbers that defoliate many alders.

Blepharida rhois (Forst.) — the only species of the genus — is one of our largest flea beetles (at 5.6-5.7 mm) and greatly resembles species of broad-bodied leaf beetles (Figs. 128, 129). It can be readily separated from them by its enlarged hind femora (none of the broad-bodied leaf beetles have hind femora as large). This flea beetle is found on sumac and is not a pest.

The **Pale-striped Flea Beetle,** *Systena blanda* (Melsh.), occurs nearly throughout N. America and is the most common of the 20 species of the genus; color is somewhat variable. It feeds on corn, tomatoes, peas, beans, peanuts, oats, cotton, and strawberry plants. About half the species of *Systena* are brown or black with light stripes. Some are entirely black; others are light overall. The *Phyllotreta* species (about 40 in N. America) are similar to *Systena* species in form and color, but are usually smaller (*Phyllotreta* — 1.8-3.5 mm; *Systena* — 3-6 mm). In *Phyllotreta* species with yellowish elytral stripes (about half the species), stripes are wavy, not straight as in most *Systena* species. Most *Phyllotreta* species that do not have stripes are dark overall, but a few have light spots. The 4 pest species in this genus feed on horseradish, cabbage, turnips, radishes, flowers, and herbs.

The **Alligatorweed Flea Beetle,** *Agasicles hygrophila* Selman and Vogt, is similar in form to *Systena* species. A U.S. Department of Agriculture entomologist, George Vogt, discovered this beetle in S. America and introduced it into se. U.S. to control alligatorweed, a plant that clogs waterways. The beetle has proven very effective at this task.

The 38 *Longitarsus* species are distinctive for the elongate 1st tarsal segment of the hind legs (about ½ as long as tarsus). Most are light brown (a few are black) and 1-3 mm long. Most of the 33 species of *Disonycha* feed on weeds and none are economically important. They are distinctive for their large size (4.8-8.5 mm), usually striped elytra, and slightly *angular* hind corners of pronotum. The *Kuschelina* species (27 in N. America; 4.7-8.9 mm) are

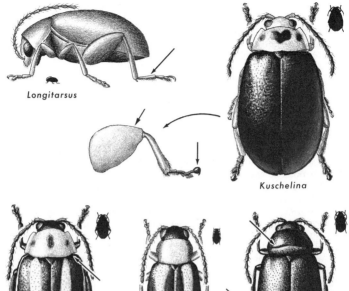

Longitarsus

Kuschelina

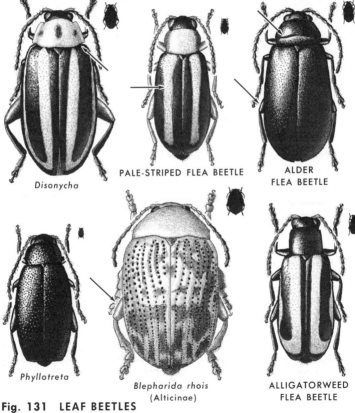

Disonycha

PALE-STRIPED FLEA BEETLE

ALDER
FLEA BEETLE

Phyllotreta

Blepharida rhois
(Alticinae)

ALLIGATORWEED
FLEA BEETLE

Fig. 131 LEAF BEETLES

similar to *Disonycha* in size and frequently in color but do not have angular hind corners on pronotum. *Inflated last tarsal segment* of hind legs is characteristic (see close-up in Fig. 131).

LEAF-MINING LEAF BEETLES   (see also Pl. 12)
Subfamily Hispinae

Unlike all other leaf beetles, the species of this subfamily and of the next subfamily (tortoise beetles, below) have *small mouth parts* and a head that slants backward. Adults in 60 of the 64 species in this subfamily have characteristic *sculpturing* on elytra: generally distinct ridges border rows of punctures. Reticulated beetles (p. 80) and net-winged beetles (p. 186) are somewhat similar but can be readily distinguished from these leaf beetles — see Figs. 24 and 76. These leaf beetles are usually wedge-shaped and widest toward the rear, but some species are elongate and nearly parallel-sided. As implied by their common name, larvae mine leaves, feeding between upper and lower surfaces. The **Locust Leaf Miner,** *Odontota dorsalis* (Thunb.), 6–6.5 mm, sometimes extensively defoliates locust trees; larvae do much of the damage, and sometimes a single mine will kill a leaf. Heavy defoliation comes late in growing season and as a rule does not seriously damage a tree, but makes it look burned and unsightly. The **Basswood Leaf Miner,** *Baliosus ruber* (Web.), a reddish yellow beetle with dark markings, is about the same size as the **Locust Leaf Miner;** it lives on basswood and oak leaves. The largest genus in this subfamily is *Anisostena,* with 13 species (widely distributed).

TORTOISE BEETLES   (see also Pl. 12)
Subfamily Cassidinae

These beetles are distinctive for their turtlelike shape: Body *oval* to nearly circular, often with *protruding thin margins* on pronotum and elytra. Head is largely or completely *concealed from above.* Thirty-five species (4–13 mm) are found in N. America. Certain members of other families — such as some sap beetles (p. 215) and bark-gnawing beetles (p. 207) — resemble these. Larvae and adults of various tortoise beetles feed on foliage of sweet potato plants, morning glory, and bindweed; they may cause considerable damage. Larvae are flat, spiny, and have a forked appendage at tip of abdomen to which are attached cast skins, debris, and excrement; this is held over body much like a parasol. When a larva is approached by a predator such as an ant, the larva forces this material into the predator's face; the enemy usually looks elsewhere for a meal if it is still hungry.

The **Argus Tortoise Beetle,** *Chelymorpha cassidea* (Fab.), 9.5–11.5 mm, resembles many broad-bodied leaf beetles (p. 294), but has small mouth parts and a head that slants backward (in broad-bodied leaf beetles mouth parts are normal in size and head

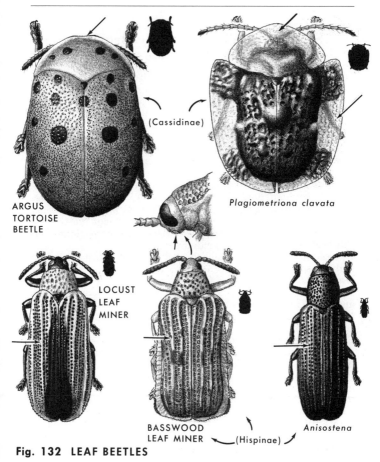

(Cassidinae)

ARGUS
TORTOISE
BEETLE

Plagiometriona clavata

LOCUST
LEAF
MINER

BASSWOOD
LEAF MINER   (Hispinae)   *Anisostena*

Fig. 132 LEAF BEETLES

is directed downward, not diagonally backward). There are 3 species of *Chelymorpha* in N. America. The **Golden Tortoise Beetle,**
Metriona bicolor (Fab.) — see Pl. 12 — shows transient golden reflections only when it is alive; after death this beetle fades and
looks dull yellow-orange. *Plagiometriona clavata* (Fab.), e. U.S. to
Ariz., is a fairly common species; it is 7–7.5 mm long. *P. clavata* is
the only member of the genus and is easily recognized due to its
color pattern.

SEED BEETLES: Family Bruchidae
(Figs. 133, 134; see also Pl. 12)

Identification. Shape and characters distinctive: Body often *egg-shaped,* usually broadest toward the rear or at the middle. Head often *concealed* from above, prolonged into a *short* or very short, *broad beak.* Hind femora *enlarged,* nearly always with large *teeth* on lower margin. Each antenna ends in a *club* of 6–7 segments, or is sawtoothed, sometimes comblike. Eyes *notched* in front. Elytra striate; nearly always *exposing* tip of abdomen. Black or brown, sometimes with red markings, often with brown or gray hairs. 1–8 mm.

Similar families. (1) Fungus weevils (p. 307) — beak nearly always larger; antennal club 3-segmented. (2) Some leaf beetles (subfamilies Eumolpinae, p. 293, and Alticinae, p. 298) are similar but have no pygidium and no beak. (3) Snout beetles (p. 309) — beak larger; antennal club 3-segmented; no pygidium. (4) Pill beetles (p. 155) — no pygidium.

Range and numbers. Found throughout N. America; 20 genera and 107 species.

Habits. Larvae eat seeds of various plants; some are quite injurious to stored beans and peas. Adults are most common in flowers and on foliage; some jump or feign death when disturbed.

Collecting methods. Sweeping foliage is most effective. Some adults feed on flowers — use a sweep net or pick them off by hand. Some species may be reared from seeds and seedpods collected in the field. Moderately common on foliage and flowers.

Examples. The **Pea Weevil,** *Bruchus pisorum* (L.), 4–5 mm, and the **Bean Weevil,** *Acanthoscelides obtectus* (Say), 2.5–4 mm, are major pests of peas and beans, and have spread worldwide. The **Pea Weevil** feeds on all varieties of edible and field peas. Adults usually hibernate in field crop remnants, stored peas, or dried pea plants. With arrival of warm weather beetles are attracted to blooming peas, where they feed and lay eggs. When a larva hatches it tunnels into pod and enters pea, where development is completed in about 6 weeks. During its development larva eats center of pea, destroying it or making it unfit for consumption. The genus *Bruchus* contains 3 species; they are distinctive for having a tooth on lateral margin of pronotum.

Acanthoscelides is easily the largest genus, with 56 species. The most harmful species, the **Bean Weevil,** is a pest of only stored beans in n. U.S., but in s. and sw. U.S. it also infests beans in fields. Unlike the Pea Weevil, it reinfests (also lays eggs on) stored beans. This weevil feeds in variety of beans, peas, and seeds of other plants. Larvae partially to completely destroy seeds. In heavy infestations, a dozen beetles may emerge from a single seed.

There are 1–2 generations per year outdoors, but 6 or more indoors.

There are 4 species in *Callosobruchus*. The **Cowpea Weevil,** *C. maculatus* (Fab.), 2.5–4 mm, is primarily a pest of cowpeas but also feeds in beans and seeds of other plants. It occurs in s. U.S. and Calif., but has been found in seeds shipped to n. U.S. Development from larva to adult takes place entirely inside seeds. Infested cowpeas and beans are unfit as food, and may be unsuitable for planting. The adult Cowpea Weevil looks like the Bean Weevil, but has a large black spot on the side of each elytron and darker markings at the rear. The **Southern Cowpea Weevil,** *C. chinensis*

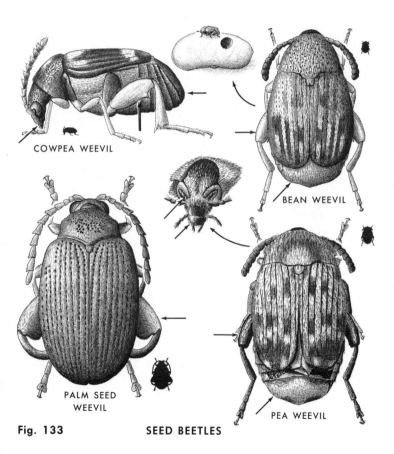

COWPEA WEEVIL

BEAN WEEVIL

PALM SEED WEEVIL

PEA WEEVIL

Fig. 133   **SEED BEETLES**

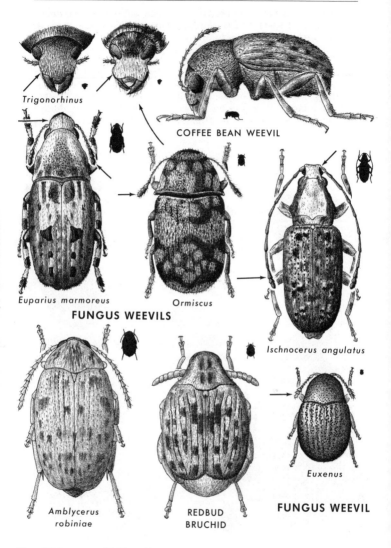

Trigonorhinus

COFFEE BEAN WEEVIL

Euparius marmoreus   *Ormiscus*

FUNGUS WEEVILS

Ischnocerus angulatus

Amblycerus robiniae   REDBUD BRUCHID

Euxenus

FUNGUS WEEVIL

Fig. 134   **SEED BEETLES**

(L.), not shown, feeds on same hosts as Cowpea Weevil but is a little smaller (2.2–3 mm) and has different markings; the ♂ has comblike antennae.

The **Palm Seed Weevil,** *Caryobruchus gleditsiae* (L.), at 5–8 mm, is one of the largest seed beetles; it jumps well. It is found from N.C. south to Fla. and w. to Tex. and is sometimes abundant. Larvae develop in palm seeds and keep them from germinating well. The **Redbud Bruchid,** *Gibbobruchus mimus* (Say), is an attractive and common species. It is found on oxeye daisy, thoroughworts, joe-pyeweed, and other plants from Ont. to Kans. and Tex. The ♂ of *Megacerus discoidus* (Say) has comblike antennae (see Pl. 12); its black and red pattern is quite attractive. *Megacerus* includes 4 other species. *Amblycerus robiniae* (Fab.) is another of the larger species in this family (7-8 mm). Its larvae feed in seeds of honey locust trees; adults may be abundant on foliage. The 3 species of *Amblycerus* occur from e. U.S. to Ariz.

Superfamily Curculionoidea

In most of these beetles the head is prolonged into a distinct beak; nearly all are small. All are plant-feeders — some are pests.

FUNGUS WEEVILS: Family Anthribidae

Identification. Head with a *broad flat beak,* rarely small; antennae not elbowed, *club of 3–4 segments;* palps *visible* and *movable.* Body robust; usually brownish, very often *mottled* with patches of white, gray, brown, or straw-colored hairs. Pronotum with a sharp *margin* at base, often extending along side. Pygidium *exposed.* Tarsi apparently 4-4-4, actually 5-5-5. 0.8–15 mm.

Similar families. Other beetles with a beak are most readily confused with these — see: (1) Snout beetles (p. 309) — palps small and not movable; antenna usually elbowed; beak often elongate. (2) Seed beetles (p. 304) — antenna clubbed, sawtoothed, or comblike; club (if present) of 6–7 segments. (3) Narrow-waisted bark beetles with a beak (p. 259) have sawtoothed antennae and no exposed pygidium.

Range and numbers. The 81 species belong to 23 genera and occur throughout N. America, but most live in e. U.S.

Habits. Most are uncommon (and thus poorly known); but 1 species is economically important as a pest. Larvae feed in vegetable material; they live in twigs and branches of trees, in hard or polypore fungi, or under bark of dead and dying trees. Adults generally feed on larval host — those whose larvae feed in plant stems generally feed on pollen of the same plants. Those adults with fungus-feeding larvae usually are found on the same fungus. Those with wood-boring larvae occur on dead or dying trees or branches, and may eat bark.

Collecting methods. Most are collected infrequently. Adults are usually captured on larval food plants, including herbaceous plants, fungi, and dead trees. Beat dead or diseased branches and twigs and sweep various weeds and bushy plants. Be careful — some species recover rapidly and fly off and a few jump. Examine polypore fungi on dead trees — look for smooth gray or black (hard, charcoal-like) lumps or flat patches of fungi; many fungus weevils feed on these.

Examples. The most common species in e. U.S. is *Euparius marmoreus* (Oliv.), about 5–8 mm. Larvae and adults occur on polypore fungi. There are 4 other species in *Euparius*. The **Coffee Bean Weevil,** *Araecerus fasciculatus* (DeG.), damages many stored plant materials including seeds, dried fruits, and dry stalks. Adults of the 2 largest genera — *Ormiscus* and *Trigonorhinus* (21 species each) — are similar in appearance. Adults of *Ormiscus* occur on dead twigs, but adults of *Trigonorhinus* feed on pollen or smut spores on herbaceous plants. In species of *Ormiscus* beak *does not* become narrower from base to tip; in *Trigonorhinus* beak *narrows* from base to tip (Fig. 134). *Ischnocerus angulatus* Mart. has long antennae; it occurs in Ariz. The 2 species of *Euxenus* (0.8–1.7 mm) are among our smallest fungus weevils. Their snout is very small and they can jump.

PRIMITIVE WEEVILS: Family Brentidae

Identification. Form and beak distinctive: Body very *elongate, narrow.* Elytra striate, sides nearly parallel. Prothorax and head more or less *pear-shaped* (Fig. 135). Head with a forward-pointing *beak* that is *long and narrow* in females and some males and broad in some other males. Antennae often *beadlike,* may be weakly clubbed. Femora *enlarged* toward end. Dark brown to black; elytra often with *light stripes.* Body smooth, hairless, shiny. 5.2–42 mm (up to 1⅝ in.); most 8–18 mm.

Similar families. (1) Wrinkled bark beetles (p. 217) — no beak; pronotum grooved. (2) Some snout beetles (p. 309) are elongate but beak is directed downward (not forward). (3) Lizard beetles (p. 224) — no beak; antennae clubbed.

Range and numbers. 6 species (5 genera) in N. America; 1 in e. U.S., 3 in Fla., 1 in Tex., 1 in Calif.

Habits. These wood-borers are sometimes known as timberworms. Larval boring in solid wood often lessens value of timber.

Collecting methods. Collected infrequently during day under dead bark. Best collected in open at night with a flashlight; examine dead trees, logs, and stumps.

Examples. The **Oak Timberworm,** *Arrhenodes minutus* (Drury), ranges from e. U.S. to Kans. and Tex. It sometimes damages oak, beech, and poplar. Females lay eggs in living trees where sapwood has been exposed by a previous injury; when eggs hatch larvae bore into sound wood, forming pinhole burrows. Resulting damage to oak makes it unfit for special purposes, such as casks and barrels. ♂ is 7-22 mm; ♀ is 7-14 mm. ♂ has a short, broad beak; ♀ has a long, narrow beak (Fig. 135). *Brentus anchorago* (L.) is a tropical species also found in s. Fla. under tree bark. Size range for this species (11–42 mm) is unusually large. Both ♂ and ♀ have an elongate beak.

SNOUT BEETLES: Family Curculionidae
(Figs. 135-143; see also Pl. 12)

Identification. Snout nearly always *well-developed; broad* and *flat* to (usually) very *elongate* and *narrow* (Fig. 135). Antennal club of *3 segments,* usually compact; antennae usually *elbowed.* Palps nearly always small and *rigid,* often concealed. Body often covered with *scales.* Tarsi apparently 4-4-4, actually 5-5-5. 0.6–35 mm (up to $1\frac{3}{8}$ in.); most under 10 mm.
Similar families. Other beetles with a snout are most easily confused with these but they have straight antennae — see (1) fungus weevils (p. 309) — snout broad; palps flexible; pronotum often has a distinct margin at base. (2) Primitive weevils (p. 308) — antennae beadlike, not distinctly clubbed; beak directed forward. (3) Some narrow-waisted bark beetles (p. 259) have a beak, but tarsi 5-5-4. (4) Seed beetles (p. 304) have a short beak; antennal club of 6–7 segments, or antennae sawtoothed or comblike.
Range and numbers. Snout beetles (Curculionidae) are the second largest family of beetles in N. America but are the largest family worldwide — possibly the largest family in animal kingdom. A 1964 study of this family listed 2432 species and 375 genera.
Habits. All our species are plant-feeders; some are serious pests. Larvae feed on all parts of plants — most live inside tissues of host; a few feed externally on leaves. Larvae of broad-nosed weevils usually feed on roots; some cause galls on roots. Many larvae burrow into stems of plants; some feed in weakened trees, others in healthy trees. Many species feed under bark and in wood of dead trunks and limbs. Some are leaf-miners, others feed on dead leaves; a few feed in developing flower buds or seedpods. Fruits and nuts are hosts for some species. Adult weevils typically feed on leaves, pollen, flowers, developing fruit, or fungi; a few burrow into wood. Adults may feed on a plant different from the host on which the larva feeds. Some species feed on underwater plants throughout their life cycle. Parthenogenesis occurs in some groups, with no males ever having been discovered.
Collecting methods. Sweeping and beating foliage are most effective. Weevils often favor young, rapid growing plants and those

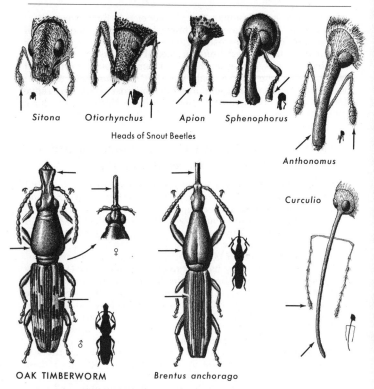

Sitona   *Otiorhynchus*   *Apion*   *Sphenophorus*

Heads of Snout Beetles

Anthonomus

Curculio

OAK TIMBERWORM   *Brentus anchorago*

Fig. 135   **PRIMITIVE WEEVILS**

flowering or fruiting; they are also more common in moist areas than in dry areas. Dead limbs or trees may yield specimens of wood-infesting forms. Many species are nocturnal and best collected at night by sweeping or beating. Some species come to lights. A few adults can be captured on aquatic plants with an aquatic net. Adults typically play dead when disturbed, and may be overlooked.

Subfamilies: 42 subfamilies are recognized; 28 are included below. Small and uncommon subfamilies are excluded from this guide.

BROAD-NOSED WEEVILS Subfamily Brachyrhininae
These 99 species and those of following 3 subfamilies are com-

monly known as broad-nosed weevils; this name refers to their short, broad snout. Some other weevils also have short snouts, but most weevils have elongate snouts. Many larvae feed on plant roots. Adults feed on leaves of various plants. Some adults (especially in deserts) are active only at night. Members of the genus *Otiorhynchus* (5–8.5 mm) are known as root weevils; some of the 8 species (all from Europe) are plant pests. All look alike. These beetles are flightless and no males are known. Damage is caused by larvae eating roots and adults eating leaves.

The **Alfalfa Snout Beetle,** *O. ligustici* (L.), feeds on alfalfa and other legumes. This species has spread little since it was first recorded in N.Y. in 1933. The **Strawberry Root Weevil,** *O. ovatus* (L.), not shown, and the **Black Vine Weevil,** *O. sulcatus* (Fab.), not shown, are also pests; their life histories are similar. Most individuals overwinter in soil as nearly grown larvae, pupate in spring, and emerge in June as adults. As an example of the destructiveness of these pests, larvae of the Strawberry Root Weevil killed 75,000 young hemlock and several thousand blue spruce seedlings near Hartford, Conn. in 1934. The **European Snout Beetle,** *Phyllobius oblongus* (L.), was first collected at Rochester, N.Y., in 1923, and has spread as far west as Ohio. It feeds on a wide variety of hardwoods, including elm, maple, willow, cottonwood, pear, apple, and plum trees. Adults feed on leaves and young shoots of host trees; they may be common in neglected orchards.

EUROPEAN
SNOUT BEETLE
(Brachyrhininae)

ALFALFA SNOUT BEETLE
(Brachyrhininae)

SWEET-CLOVER WEEVIL
(Thylacitinae)

Fig. 136   **SNOUT BEETLES**

BROAD-NOSED WEEVILS Subfamily Thylacitinae
About 100 species belong to this subfamily. The **Sweet-clover Weevil**, *Sitona cylindricollis* Fahr., is found from ne. U.S. to Neb. Clover is damaged when adults eat crescent-shaped areas from leaves and larvae eat roots. If abundant, adults can destroy seedling sweet clover. Adults overwinter in soil and lay eggs in spring. One commonly used control for this pest consists of plowing under mature plants as "green manure"; if operation is timed correctly it will kill up to 85% of new generation eggs and young larvae. The **Clover Root Curculio,** *S. hispidulus* (Fab.), not shown, is 3–5 mm long. Adults feed on sweet and red clover and many other legumes; larvae seriously damage root systems. The genus *Sitona* contains 17 widely distributed species.

The 4 N. American species of *Graphognathus* (introduced from Argentina) are known as **white-fringed beetles;** they are 9–12 mm long. They badly damage field and garden crops and ornamental plants. Larvae feed on roots and do most of damage; affected plants usually turn yellow, wilt, and die. Adults (all females; no males known) feed on leaves but do little damage. These beetles cannot move any distance on their own, for larvae have no legs and adults cannot fly. They are spread by movement of plants, crops, nursery stock, or agricultural implements. In this way they have spread from Fla. (where they were first introduced in 1936) north to Va. and west to La. These beetles are most abundant in well-drained, sandy loam. Damage is spotty — injury to a crop may be slight in one field and destruction almost total in a nearby field.

BROAD-NOSED WEEVILS   **(Fig. 137;**
Subfamily Leptopiinae   **see also Pl. 12)**
In the 148 species in this subfamily and 3 species in the next subfamily the *front lobes* of the *prothorax* partially *cover* the *eyes* (Fig. 137). Species are primarily western. Adults are generally found on various trees, shrubs, and other plants; larvae of some species feed on roots. The 3 largest genera, *Ophryastes, Dyslobus* (not shown), and *Panscopus* all have 25–30 species; members of the first 2 genera occur just in w. U.S., those of the last genus are widely distributed. None are important pests.

ORIENTAL BROAD-NOSED WEEVILS
Subfamily Eremninae
All 3 species occur in e. U.S. and have been introduced from Japan. The **Asiatic Oak Weevil,** *Cyrtepistomus castaneus* (Roel.), is common on foliage of oak and other trees.

UNDERWATER WEEVILS Subfamily Cylindrorhininae
Many of the 84 species in this subfamily breed in aquatic or semi-aquatic plants; adults are found near water. Members of *Listro-*

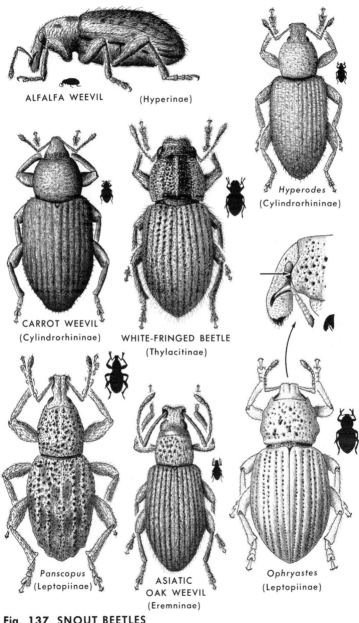

ALFALFA WEEVIL (Hyperinae)

Hyperodes (Cylindrorhininae)

CARROT WEEVIL (Cylindrorhininae)

WHITE-FRINGED BEETLE (Thylacitinae)

Panscopus (Leptopiinae)

ASIATIC OAK WEEVIL (Eremninae)

Ophryastes (Leptopiinae)

Fig. 137 SNOUT BEETLES

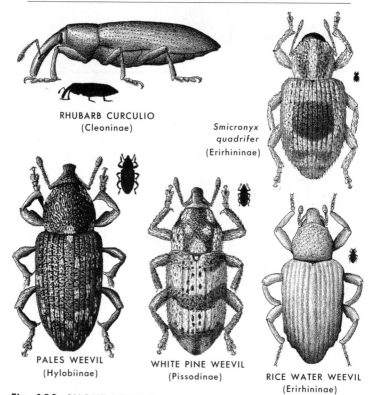

RHUBARB CURCULIO
(Cleoninae)

*Smicronyx
quadrifer*
(Erirhininae)

PALES WEEVIL
(Hylobiinae)

WHITE PINE WEEVIL
(Pissodinae)

RICE WATER WEEVIL
(Erirhininae)

Fig. 138 SNOUT BEETLES

notus (28 species; 4.2–14 mm) and *Hyperodes* (48 species; 2.3–5.5 mm) have similar habits; most feed on sedges, arrowhead, and knotweed. The **Carrot Weevil** (also known as the **Parsley Weevil**), *L. oregonensis* (LeC.), sometimes damages carrots and parsley, but also feeds on celery, parsnips, and dill. It ranges from Va. and N.Y. to Iowa. Larvae do most damage by boring into roots and stems. The **Vegetable Weevil**, *Listroderes costirostris obliquus* (Klug), not shown, occurs in the Gulf states and Calif. It attacks potatoes, tomatoes, turnips, carrots, and other vegetables. Larvae and adults feed, usually at night, on buds, foliage, and roots; plants may be cut off at ground level. There are 2 species in *Listroderes*.

CLOVER and ALFALFA WEEVILS Subfamily Hyperinae
All 7 species belong to the genus *Hypera;* 4 are pests. The **Alfalfa Weevil,** *H. postica* (Gyll.), is a European insect first found in Utah about 1904 that has since spread through much of N. America. It is mostly a pest of first-growth alfalfa, and may cause tremendous damage. Adults and larvae feed on young-growth alfalfa, lowering its value as a crop or preventing production of seed. The larva of this species is unusual for feeding externally on leaves and stems. Severe winters kill many overwintering eggs and reduce populations of this pest.

CYLINDRICAL WEEVILS Subfamily Cleoninae
This subfamily includes about 68 N. American species, with 28 belonging to the genus *Lixus. Lixus* species are often large for weevils; they range in size from 6.5–15 mm. The **Rhubarb Curculio,** *L. concavus* Say (10–15 mm), is one of the largest snout beetles in e. U.S. Larvae bore in stems of dock and sunflowers. Adults normally feed on these plants, but may eat and lay eggs on rhubarb plants. Larvae almost never develop in rhubarb, however, so damage to this plant is generally minor. Elimination of dock from vicinity of rhubarb plants is an effective control for this pest.

PINE WEEVILS Subfamily Hylobiinae
Only 21 species in N. America — 2 are important pests of forest trees. The **Pales Weevil,** *Hylobius pales* (Herbst), 7–10 mm, injures coniferous seedlings, especially of white pine. Larvae feed in trunks of dead and dying pines. Mass cutting of many trees followed by planting of seedlings encourages damage: Beetles emerging from old stumps feed on tender bark of saplings and at bases of seedlings; they can kill an entire planting. Damage can be avoided by waiting 2 years after cutting to replant.

CONIFER WEEVILS Subfamily Pissodinae
The single genus, *Pissodes,* contains 33 species (3.7–9.1 mm). Some damage conifers; larvae feed primarily on terminal shoots, but will feed on trunks or roots. The **White Pine Weevil,** *P. strobi* (Peck), is the worst pest of white pine in e. U.S. It occurs over entire range of eastern white pine, its most frequent host; it also feeds on jack pine, pitch pine, and other conifers. Eggs are laid on terminal leader (uppermost shoot) of a tree; larva enters leader and bores downward, killing that shoot. A lateral branch then becomes the leader. This produces a tree with a distinct bend in trunk that makes it useless for timber. To date, there is no effective control method for this weevil that is not prohibitive in cost. Most natural stands of white pine now consist of forked and crooked trees that are almost worthless; many planted stands are little better. Loss of tree value in last half century amounts to millions of dollars. Western species of *Pissodes* have similar habits, and are potentially as damaging.

MARSH WEEVILS Subfamily Erirhininae
This subfamily includes 176 species. Many larvae feed in aquatic plants; adults are often found near water. The **Rice Water Weevil,** *Lissorhoptrus oryzophilus* Kuschel, 2.8–3.2 mm, is a native beetle found from New England to the Gulf states. It normally feeds on semiaquatic grasses, but also eats rice in s. U.S. Larvae eat roots of young plants; adults feed on leaves. Largest genus is *Smicronyx,* with 68 species (widely distributed; 1.8–3.5 mm). Larvae feed in seeds and stems of assorted herbaceous plants. One species, *S. quadrifer* Casey, 2.2–2.5 mm, feeds in stems of dodder, a parasitic plant, and consistently moves from dodder into stems of dodder's host plant — an unusual feeding pattern among plant-feeding insects.

NEW YORK WEEVIL Subfamily Ithycerinae
The single species in this subfamily, *Ithycerus noveboracensis* (Forst.), is one of our largest weevils at 12–18 mm; it occurs in e. U.S. Adults gnaw on tender bark and eat buds of various hardwoods, such as oak, hickory, and beech trees; this may kill or weaken twigs, causing them to break in a strong wind. Larvae also feed on twigs.

SWEET-POTATO WEEVIL Subfamily Cyladinae
The only species in this subfamily, *Cylas formicarius elegantulus* (Sum.), 5–6 mm, is readily recognized by its antlike form and red and blue color. This weevil is found from S.C. and Fla. west to Tex., and is the worst pest of sweet potato plants where it occurs. Larvae bore into vines and through roots and tubers, killing plants and making tubers unmarketable; they will also feed on stored potatoes. There may be as many as 8 generations per year.

PEAR-SHAPED WEEVILS Subfamily Apioninae
All but 2 of 127 species belong to the genus *Apion;* length varies from 1.4–3.2 mm. These are very common and are generally recognizable by their pear-shaped body and straight (non-elbowed) antennae. Snout varies from short to very long, and is typically longer in ♀ than in ♂. Larvae feed within seeds of various plants or on leaves and stems, causing galls. Adults generally feed on leaves and produce small circular holes. The **Hollyhock Weevil,** *A. longirostre* Oliv., feeds only on hollyhock and occurs throughout much of n. U.S. Adults feed on leaves and larvae feed in seed embryos. Snout of this species is unusually long for a member of this genus (Fig. 139).

LEAF-ROLLING WEEVILS Subfamily Attelabinae
The 8 species in this subfamily (all *Attelabus* species, 3–6 mm) are markedly broad-bodied and have a short snout. Females of some species cut leaves and form them into neat, solid rolls; a single larva develops inside each roll. Larvae of some species feed in fruit

or buds. Some members of the next subfamily are quite similar in appearance to these weevils; they can be distinguished by microscopic examination of the mandibles.

LEAF and BUD WEEVILS   Subfamily Rhynchitinae
Forty-three weevils belong to this subfamily; their snout is usually long. The 8 *Eugnamptus* species (2.7–4.7 mm) mine leaves of various hardwoods; other species feed in buds, fruits, and nuts. Largest

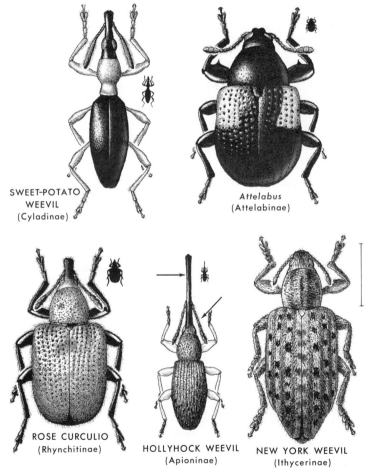

SWEET-POTATO
WEEVIL
(Cyladinae)

Attelabus
(Attelabinae)

ROSE CURCULIO
(Rhynchitinae)

HOLLYHOCK WEEVIL
(Apioninae)

NEW YORK WEEVIL
(Ithycerinae)

Fig. 139 SNOUT BEETLES

genus is *Rhynchites* (1.8–6.5 mm) with 29 species (widely distributed). The **Rose Curculio,** *R. bicolor* (Fab.), 5–6.5 mm, is a minor pest of roses; its larvae feed in fruits. Adults eat holes in buds of wild and cultivated roses; bud either dies or produces petals riddled with holes. This species is particularly destructive in cold regions.

ANTLIKE WEEVILS Subfamily Myrmecinae
Thirty-two of the 36 species in this subfamily belong to the genus *Myrmex*. *Myrmex* species (1.9–5 mm) are long-legged and have an oval thorax that is *narrowed* at the base. One species develops in galls formed on oaks and another in stems of mistletoe. Larvae of a third species feed in dead and dying twigs of sycamores killed by sycamore blight; adults feed on fruit.

WEDGE-SHAPED BARK WEEVILS Subfamily Magdalinae
Twenty-five of the 30 species in this group are members of *Magdalis*. *Magdalis* species (2.5–6 mm) usually have small *teeth* on front margins of pronotum. Nine species in e. U.S. feed in broken branches or dead or dying trees. The **Red Elm Bark Weevil,** *M. armicollis* (Say), 3.5–6 mm, may help spread Dutch elm disease by weakening trees, making them more susceptible to the disease.

ACORN and NUT WEEVILS Subfamily Curculioninae
All 44 species in this group belong to the genus *Curculio*. They are medium-sized with an elongate-oval body and a very long snout. Color varies from brown to brown and gray, often with a mottled pattern. In females of some species the snout is much longer than the body. All species look quite similar. Mandibles (at tip of beak) move vertically instead of horizontally (as in other beetles) and are used by ♀ to drill holes in nuts for egg-laying. Length of beak varies — in each species it is correlated with thickness of husk and shell of nut where ♀ lays eggs. Larvae develop inside nuts and leave when mature to pupate in soil. The most harmful nut weevil is the **Pecan Weevil,** *C. caryae* (Horn). This weevil (7–9 mm) feeds in practically all hickories (pecan is a type of hickory). In s. U.S. it can destroy up to 65% of a pecan crop. Nut weevils that feed on oak may destroy 50–90% of an acorn crop, and are harmful to reforestation.

FRUIT and SEED WEEVILS Subfamily Anthonominae
Some of the 166 species in this subfamily are pests. Larvae typically feed in fruit and seeds of various trees and plants. To the genus *Anthonomus* belong 116 species, including the worst pest of the family, if not of all N. American beetles. The **Boll Weevil,** *A. grandis grandis* Boh., is a notorious pest. Adults are 4–7.5 mm long. Some regard this weevil as the most destructive insect pest in N. America, for it causes $200–$300 million worth of damage

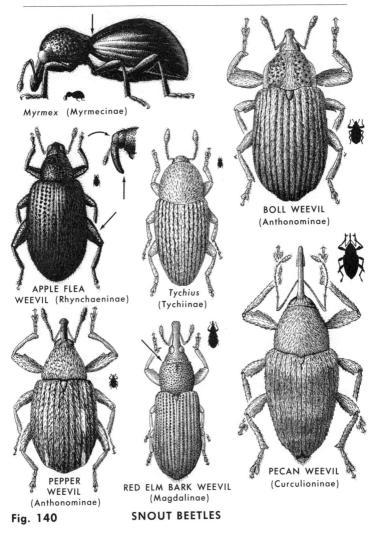

Myrmex (Myrmecinae)

APPLE FLEA
WEEVIL (Rhynchaeninae)

Tychius
(Tychiinae)

BOLL WEEVIL
(Anthonominae)

PEPPER
WEEVIL
(Anthonominae)

RED ELM BARK WEEVIL
(Magdalinae)

PECAN WEEVIL
(Curculioninae)

Fig. 140   **SNOUT BEETLES**

yearly to cotton, and makes its cultivation unprofitable in some
areas. Control of this beetle is one of the worst problems encountered by farmers and scientists in this country. Insecticides used to
kill the Boll Weevil have caused much of the chemical pollution

in the cotton belt. The Boll Weevil was first reported in this country in 1892 in s. Tex., and has since spread to nearly all cotton-growing areas. Females lay eggs in flower buds, or squares, as they are called. Larval feeding kills a bud, so it will never flower or produce cotton. With no control, most if not all cotton bolls are destroyed, and the crop is a failure. After feeding for 7–12 days, larvae pupate; there are several generations per year. Even with wide use of chemical controls, the beetle destroys roughly 10% of each crop, or over $200 million worth of cotton yearly. The **Pepper Weevil,** *A. eugenii* Cano, and the **Strawberry Weevil,** *A. signatus* Say, both about 2–3 mm, are also pests. Females of the latter lay eggs in strawberry blossom buds, then partly cut through stem causing bud to wilt, fall over at an angle, or fall to ground.

FLEA WEEVILS Subfamily Rhynchaeninae
These weevils have enlarged hind femora and leap the way flea beetles do. All 16 species belong to the genus *Rhynchaenus*. They are usually found on willow, elm, alder, apple, cherry, and birch trees; larvae mine leaves and adults chew holes in them, producing damage similar to that caused by flea beetles. Some adults strongly resemble flea beetles (p. 298), but are easily identified by their long beak. *R. pallicornis* (Say), the **Apple Flea Weevil,** occurs from Mo. and Ill. east to N.Y. This weevil feeds on apple, hawthorn, crab apple, and other trees, and does the most damage in the western part of its range. Larvae mine leaves and adults feed on leaves and buds.

LEGUMINOUS SEED WEEVILS Subfamily Tychiinae
The 30 species in the group generally feed inside seeds of various legumes; adults occur on flowers. Some are pests of clover — larval feeding can interfere with seed production. Ten of the species belong to the genus *Tychius;* they are 2.3–4.7 mm long.

SEEDPOD WEEVILS Subfamily Gymnaetrinae
Only 7 species (4 in the genus *Gymnaetron*) live in N. America; some are common. Larvae develop in seedpods of mullein, lobelia, toadflax, and plantain.

HIDDEN SNOUT WEEVILS Subfamily Cryptorhynchinae
The 2nd largest subfamily with 187 species. In many species the beak can be retracted into a deep groove in the sternum; most also have sculpturing on the elytra, such as striae, ridges, punctures, or tubercles (Fig. 141). Larvae of the largest genus, *Conotrachelus* (62 species; 2.5–7 mm), typically injure developing fruit. The **Plum Curculio,** *C. nenuphar* (Herbst), 4.5–6.5 mm, is often responsible for wormy peaches in e. U.S.; it does not occur west of the Rocky Mts. Fruit becomes scarred when adults feed and lay eggs; inside is damaged by larval feeding. Rupturing of skin by adult allows

brown rot fungus to enter. In addition to stone fruits, hosts include
apple, pear, quince, and related plants. With no controls, over half
a peach crop may be damaged. Adults usually drop to ground if
disturbed, which affords a means of control — a sheet can be held
beneath the tree while the tree is jarred. Beetles that fall onto the

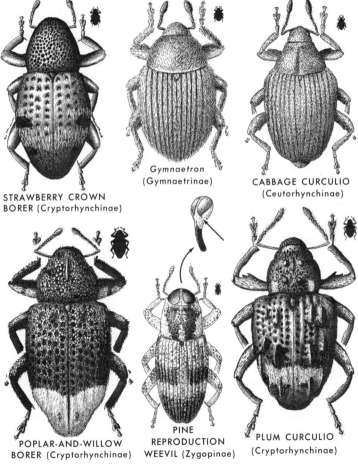

STRAWBERRY CROWN
BORER (Cryptorhynchinae)

Gymnaetron
(Gymnaetrinae)

CABBAGE CURCULIO
(Ceutorhynchinae)

POPLAR-AND-WILLOW
BORER (Cryptorhynchinae)

PINE
REPRODUCTION
WEEVIL (Zygopinae)

PLUM CURCULIO
(Cryptorhynchinae)

Fig. 141   **SNOUT BEETLES**

sheet can be destroyed. Three *Conotrachelus* species feed in acorns. One species feeds in cambium of injured trees. The **Strawberry Crown Borer,** *Tyloderma fragariae* (Riley), 3.5–4.2 mm, is generally the worst pest of strawberry plants. Flightless adults (females) damage crowns of plants by egg-laying, and eat small holes in leaves. Damage caused by larvae is worse — they hollow out the crown, which kills the plants or checks their growth. The **Poplar-and-willow Borer,** *Cryptorhynchus lapathi* (L.), 7.5–10 mm, is a European beetle that is now established in ne. and nw. U.S. Larvae feed in inner bark and outer sapwood and may girdle and kill poplar and willow trees. All poplars and willows, especially those newly planted, are susceptible. The 11 other species in this genus are pests of various hardwoods.

TWIG and STEM WEEVILS Subfamily Zygopinae
Eyes are *elongate* and pointed *ventrally* (see close-up in Fig. 141). The 37 species feed in trees or herbaceous plants. Two of the 28 species of *Cylindrocopturus* (2–4.5 mm) are pests of conifers in w. U.S. The **Pine Reproduction Weevil,** *C. eatoni* Buch., injures small ponderosa and Jeffrey pines.

MINUTE SEED WEEVILS Subfamily Ceutorhynchinae
This large group (145 N. American species) contains some pest species. Genus *Ceutorhynchus* (76 species; 1.5–3.2 mm) is widely distributed and includes the **Cabbage Curculio,** *C. rapae* Gyll., 2.7–3.2 mm. Larvae feed in stems of cabbage, cauliflower, horseradish, turnip, mustard, and peppergrass plants. The **Cabbage Seed-pod Weevil,** *C. assimilis* (Payk.), not shown, damages seed crops in Washington, including those of cabbage, turnip and rutabaga.

FLOWER WEEVILS Subfamily Baridinae
The largest subfamily of snout beetles, with over 500 N. American species; some are quite common. Flower weevils can usually be recognized by upward-extended mesepimera, which may be visible from above. The genus *Baris* includes 93 species (widely distributed; 2.2–6 mm). Larvae feed in stems and roots of plants in daisy family. The **Grape Cane Gall-maker,** *Ampeloglypter sesostris* (LeC.), 2.7–3 mm, causes gall-like swellings in grape canes, where ♀ deposits eggs. The **Grape Cane Girdler,** *A. ater* LeC., normally feeds on Virginia creeper but also attacks grapevines. Female lays eggs on stem, in a circle of feeding punctures around stem. Larval feeding and adult damage may weaken cane and cause it to break. The **Potato Stalk Borer,** *Trichobaris trinotata* (Say), 3–4 mm, feeds in stems of plants in the potato family and may destroy eggplant and potato plants; larval feeding does the most damage.

BILLBUGS and GRAIN WEEVILS
Subfamily Rhynchophorinae
The robust form, *arched pronotal margins,* and tapering elytra

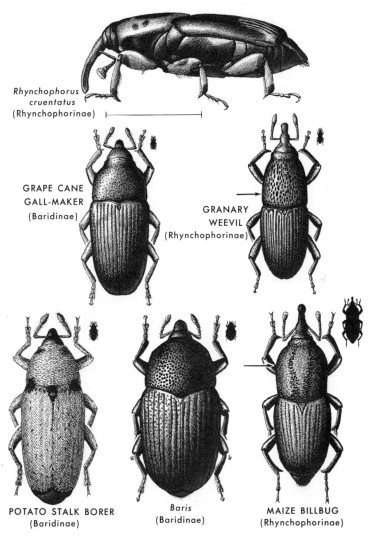

Rhynchophorus
cruentatus
(Rhynchophorinae)

GRAPE CANE
GALL-MAKER
(Baridinae)

GRANARY
WEEVIL
(Rhynchophorinae)

POTATO STALK BORER
(Baridinae)

Baris
(Baridinae)

MAIZE BILLBUG
(Rhynchophorinae)

Fig. 142   **SNOUT BEETLES**

are typical for this group of 90 species. Some are among our largest snout beetles. *Rhynchophorus cruentatus* (Fab.), 20–30 mm, feeds in trunks of cabbage palmetto and other palms; it occurs in se. U.S. (from S.C. to Fla. and La.). The **Granary Weevil,** *Sitophilus granarius* (L.), 3–4 mm, and the **Rice Weevil,** *S. oryzae* (L.), 2.1–2.8 mm (not shown), damage stored grain. The Rice Weevil is the worst insect pest of stored grain in this country. Both species bore into sound grain, opening the way for insects that cannot eat through seed coats; larvae devour inside portion of grain. Both species occur worldwide and losses are high in areas where they can breed year round. The 71 *Sphenophorus* species are called billbugs. These beetles feed on various grasses and sedges; adults (4.9–17 mm) feed on foliage and larvae bore into stalks. Some are pests of corn, small grains, peanuts, rice, and sugarcane. The **Maize Billbug,** *S. maidis* Chitt., is 10–15 mm; it damages growing corn, sometimes severely. Adults feed on leaves and stems of young plants; larvae tunnel through stalk, doing more serious damage. This billbug may completely destroy a crop in or near a field that

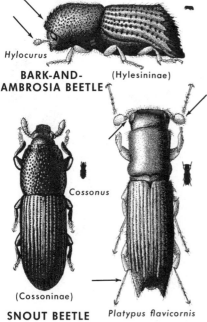

Hylocurus

BARK-AND-AMBROSIA BEETLE

(Hylesininae)

Cossonus

(Cossoninae)

SNOUT BEETLE

Fig. 143

Platypus flavicornis

PINHOLE BORER

Portion of tree limb showing Hickory Bark Beetle engraving

was infested the previous year. The **Clay-colored Billbug,** *S. aequalis aequalis* (Gyll.), 11–17 mm (not shown), also injures corn. The **Bluegrass Billbug,** *S. parvulus* Gyll., 5–6.5 mm (not shown), feeds on corn, barley, and rye in addition to bluegrass.

Billbugs are tolerant of high moisture levels and are more numerous in wet lowland areas than in dry areas. The Maize Billbug is so hardy that it can survive over 3 weeks of total submersion. Poultry are sometimes injured or killed by feeding on adult billbugs. When a turkey or chicken eats a billbug, the beetle grips the bird's tongue or throat with the spurs on its tibiae so strongly that the bird cannot dislodge it. The bird often starves to death because of its inability to swallow the beetle or normal food.

BARK WEEVILS Subfamily Cossoninae

These weevils (79 in N. America) have a short beak that is broadened at tip; body is generally elongate and black or reddish. Some species have a long curved tibial spine. Members of *Cossonus* (20 in N. America; 2.9–7 mm) are common in sapwood of dead hardwoods and conifers — often trees that have been killed by bark beetles. Species of other genera occasionally damage woodwork in buildings. Larvae of all species bore meandering galleries across wood grain and pack galleries with frass. In addition to damaging woodwork, these weevils may ruin sapwood of trees killed by bark beetles and prevent their use for timber.

PINHOLE BORERS or
AMBROSIA BEETLES:
Family Platypodidae

Identification. Shape, antennal club, and tarsi distinctive: Body very *elongate,* nearly *parallel-sided;* antennal club *large, flat, 1-segmented;* tarsi *long, slender.* Head visible from above; as *wide* as or slightly *wider* than pronotum. Thorax *constricted* near middle. Light brown to dark brown. Tarsi 5-5-5. 2–8 mm.
Similar families. (1) Bark-and-ambrosia beetles (p. 326) — tarsi not long; head not as broad. (2) Cylindrical bark beetles (p. 246) — antennal club 2- or 3-segmented; tarsi not as long.
Range and numbers. The 7 species belong to the genus *Platypus;* they occur nearly throughout U.S.
Habits. Larvae and adults bore in hardwoods and softwoods; they feed on a minute fungus (ambrosia) that grows on walls of tunnels bored by these beetles. The ambrosia fungus produces characteristic black stains in wood. These beetles seldom attack vigorous trees and typically enter trees through an injured or dying area of bark. Fermenting sap (from an unhealthy tree) is probably essential for development of ambrosial fungus that serves as their food. Although these beetles may not actually kill a tree, they undoubt-

edly hasten the death of sickly trees. More importantly, their bur-rows often ruin heartwood in trees girdled or felled in lumbering operations and make it worthless for timber. These ambrosia bee-tles are more destructive than other ambrosia beetles (see under family Scolytidae, below), for their burrows are more extensive and penetrate deep into the heartwood of trees.

Collecting methods. These beetles are easiest to collect at lights after they have left a tree to find a new host. When boring in wood they may be difficult to collect, but they repeatedly push frass from burrows and may be picked from pried-off bark. Look for piles of fine sawdust in bark crevices or on the ground under a dead or dying tree.

Examples. Wilson's Wide-headed Ambrosia Beetle, *Platypus wilsoni* Swaine (not shown), occurs in Pacific Coast region, where it feeds on firs, spruce, hemlock, and other conifers; it is the only ambrosia beetle in this area. *P. flavicornis* (Fab.), about 5 mm, is common from N.J. to se. U.S. It feeds in conifers, especially pines, and has been reported on deciduous trees. This beetle is a very energetic borer and may attack a tree in large numbers, soon ren-dering wood worthless for timber and reducing its value even for cordwood. *P. compositus* Say (not shown), about 4.5 mm, occurs throughout se. U.S. and into N.Y. and Ill. It attacks a variety of trees, primarily hardwoods, but also baldcypress. Greatest damage is to recently felled hardwoods and to girdled baldcypress. Because of these beetles, many sawmills in s. U.S. make it a rule to saw all felled hardwoods within 2 weeks.

BARK-AND-AMBROSIA BEETLES:
Family Scolytidae

Identification. Form and antennal club distinctive: Body nearly always *elongate-cylindrical.* Antennae *short, elbowed,* and nearly always ending in a *large,* nearly *round, abrupt* club; club usually of 1–3 segments, club rarely weakly lamellate. Front of pronotum often bears *teeth.* Head usually *concealed* from above, nar-rower than pronotum. Tarsi short. Brownish to black. 0.6–9 mm (most 1–5 mm).

Similar families. (1) Pinhole borers or ambrosia beetles (p. 325) have very long tarsi; head as wide as pronotum. (2) In branch-and-twig borers (p. 202) antennal club is asymmetrical, not rounded. (3) Some death-watch beetles (p. 199) are very similar but antennal club is asymmetrical, or antennae sawtoothed or comblike. (4) Some snout beetles (p. 309) are elongate-cylindrical but they have a distinct beak. (5) Minute tree-fungus beetles (p. 243) have a loose, 2- or 3-segmented antennal club. (6) Dry-fungus beetles (p. 219) have a gradual, 3-segmented club.

Range and numbers. 64 genera and 476 species in N. America; widely distributed.

Habits. Adults of most species bore through bark of a tree and tunnel galleries between bark and wood, in which they lay eggs; larvae also excavate between bark and wood, at right angles to tunnels of adults. Thus the complete work, or engraving, of these beetles consists of 2 types of tunnels — galleries for eggs, made by the adults, and larval tunnels, called mines, formed by the growing larvae. These tunnels form a pattern which is distinctive for each species (Fig. 143) and is usually very similar for members of a genus. In concentrated attack these beetles can girdle and kill a tree. For attacks on healthy trees to be successful, these beetles must infest a tree in sufficient numbers to overcome its resistance. Light attacks on living trees often fail, because the trees' flow of pitch is so plentiful that the beetles are killed or driven from their galleries. Certain chemicals in pitch are repellent or toxic to beetles. Normal infestations of bark beetles are present in nearly all mature forests, causing only a small loss (a fraction of 1%) of the timber each year. Favorable conditions can, however, lead to tremendous population increases for some species over months or years. These epidemics may be of short duration or may continue for many years, destroying much usable timber over extensive acreages.

In mature timber stands of w. U.S., these beetles are the greatest single cause of timber loss. They annually destroy 1–5 billion board feet of mature timber in our forests. Vast forest tracts in w. U.S. that consist largely of 1 kind of tree and often contain many overmature and weakened trees offer ideal conditions for certain bark beetles. (The bulk of the destruction is caused by 5 species of pine beetles discussed below.) The price of wood products, and, in time, the price we pay for a home, are increased by this damage.

Some scolytids are called ambrosia beetles. These beetles bore into the trunk of trees and their larvae mine short chambers and nourish themselves on a fungus (ambrosia) that grows in their galleries. The relationship between ambrosia beetles and the fungus on which they feed is symbiotic — both organisms (fungus and beetle) benefit from their association. These beetles can transmit causal agents of diseases to trees where they feed.

Collecting methods. These beetles typically spend nearly all their life in the host tree, and are in the open only long enough to fly from an old host tree to a new one. Because of their concealed feeding habits, these beetles may seem uncommon, but the frequency with which they are collected does not usually reflect their abundance in nature. During their flight period (usually spring or summer), bark-and-ambrosia beetles can be captured by hand, with a sweep net, or with an aerial net. Many fly in spring, and some come to lights. Rearing them from infested material is the best way to collect a variety of species; this is easiest to do with species that breed in cones, twigs, and branches. An unhealthy tree is a likely host — remove small sections of bark from the trunk. Many of these beetles breed in recently felled trees, but a tree that has been dead for some time is unlikely to yield live specimens. **Subfamilies.** All 3 are included below.

TYPICAL BARK BEETLES Subfamily Scolytinae
There are only 20 N. American species in this subfamily. The 19 species of *Scolytus* (2–5.5 mm) are readily recognized by their straight to *concave* (and sometimes ornamented) abdomen and the *curved hook* at the tip of their foretibia (see close-ups in Fig. 144). The **Smaller European Elm Bark Beetle,** *S. multistriatus* (Marsh.), 2.2–3 mm, was accidentally introduced into N. America early in this century, and has spread nearly throughout the range of elm trees. The chief danger results from its role in spreading the fungus that causes Dutch elm disease, which has nearly wiped out the American elm in many areas. This beetle shows a preference for unhealthy trees; it is not usually successful in attacking a healthy tree. Young adults emerge in May and June and fly to healthy elms where they feed on bark of young twigs; this habit makes them vectors of the disease fungus. The **Native Elm Bark Beetle,** *Hylurgopinus rufipes* (Eich.) — a member of the next subfamily (Hylesininae) — is less effective at spreading Dutch elm

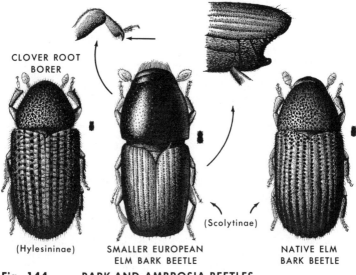

CLOVER ROOT
BORER

(Scolytinae)

(Hylesininae)   SMALLER EUROPEAN   NATIVE ELM
                  ELM BARK BEETLE   BARK BEETLE

Fig. 144   BARK-AND-AMBROSIA BEETLES

disease fungus; this beetle is 2–2.5 mm long. The **Hickory Bark Beetle,** *Scolytus quadrispinosus* Say (4–5 mm), is the worst enemy of various hickories (see engraving, Fig. 143). It has killed thousands of trees in ne. U.S. The Hickory Bark Beetle typically breeds in unhealthy trees, but when populations increase this beetle attacks perfectly healthy trees, killing hundreds in a single season.

CRENULATE BARK BEETLES Subfamily Hylesininae
The common name of this group refers to the tiny teeth along the front edge of the elytra. There are about 150 N. American species. The **Clover Root Borer,** *Hylastinus obscurus* (Marsh.), 2.2–2.5 mm, is a pest of red and mammoth clovers. Larvae tunnel throughout roots, often killing plants. Many infested plants are pulled up by mower during cutting; others are so weakened that 2nd crop is much smaller, and seed yields are lowered.

The most important tree-killers of the family (and probably of all insects) are the 14 species of pine beetles, genus *Dendroctonus* — in fact, the genus name means "tree killers." These are our largest bark beetles, at 2.5–9 mm. All of these beetles look very much alike; the head is clearly visible from above. In w. U.S. (where most pine beetles occur) annual damage to conifers amounts to many millions of dollars. Pine beetle populations are normally small, but under favorable conditions (such as forests with many weakened or damaged trees) their numbers can build up tremendously, leading to epidemics and attacks on healthy trees.

In 1942 the **Spruce Beetle,** *D. rufipennis* (Kirby), 4.4–7 mm, built up populations in spruce forests of w. Colo. With each generation, increasing hordes developed and attacked more and more trees, until more than 4 billion board feet of timber was destroyed. Flying beetles settled on an uninfested forest and killed 400,000 trees in one mass attack. It takes several hundreds or thousands of spruce beetles to overpower a healthy tree, but when they do, the tree is killed in 2 weeks to a month. Other important w. U.S. species are the **Western Pine Beetle,** *D. brevicomis* LeC. (not shown), and the **Mountain Pine Beetle,** *D. ponderosae* Hopk. (not shown). In 1917 and in 1943 the Western Pine Beetle destroyed about 25 billion board feet of ponderosa pine along the Pacific Coast. Such devastation is seldom matched by any other pest insect.

Eastern species of *Dendroctonus* are also important as pests, and include the **Southern Pine Beetle,** *D. frontalis* Zimm. (not shown; 2.5–4 mm). It can grow from egg to adult in 30–40 days, and 1 generation may result in a 10-fold increase in numbers. With 5 generations a year, this beetle can increase greatly in numbers and damage thousands of trees.

The 26 species of *Phloeosinus* (widely distributed; 1.6–4.3 mm)

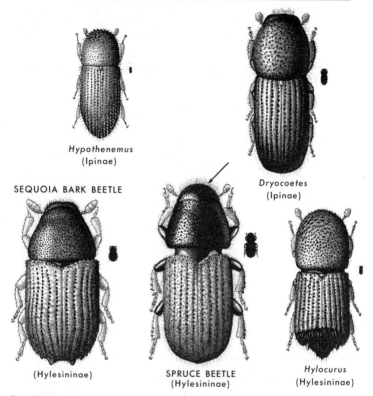

Hypothenemus
(Ipinae)

SEQUOIA BARK BEETLE

Dryocoetes
(Ipinae)

(Hylesininae)

SPRUCE BEETLE
(Hylesininae)

Hylocurus
(Hylesininae)

Fig. 145   BARK-AND-AMBROSIA BEETLES

are known as the cedar bark beetles; most are confined to cedar and cedarlike trees. They are readily distinguished from other bark beetles by their loose antennal club, the last 3 segments of which project inward. They normally breed in unhealthy trees, but on occasion build up large populations and attack healthy trees. One species, the **Sequoia Bark Beetle,** *P. sequoiae* Hopk., feeds in broken branches of giant sequoias in Calif. The genera *Hylocurus* (12 species, s. U.S., about 2–3 mm) and *Micracis* (4 species; e. and s. U.S.; not shown; 1.7–2.7 mm) are called wood-eating bark beetles. They feed in wood or pith of host, not on inner bark. In both genera, front of pronotum is distinctly roughened (Fig. 143, p. 324), and elytra are extended toward the rear. Species of *Hylocurus* and *Micracis* are most common in small or medium-sized branches.

AMBROSIA BEETLES and OTHERS Subfamily Ipinae
This is the largest subfamily of bark-and-ambrosia beetles, with about 300 species. Some species of *Hypothenemus* (20 species, most in e. U.S.; 1-1.5 mm) are very common in se. U.S. They breed in dying and dead twigs, dead bark, seeds, weeds, and dead hulls, such as cotton bolls. They are mildly beneficial in promoting decay, but are considered pests when they attack seeds and other stored vegetable products.

The 7 species of *Dryocoetes* (n. N. America; 2-4.5 mm) attack only the trunk and larger limbs of conifers and hardwoods and are most common in logs or unhealthy trees. Eastern species do not kill trees, but 1 w. U.S. species sometimes kills Alpine fir. The 6 *Pityogenes* species (widely distributed; 2-2.5 mm) are sometimes called pine engravers. Tip of elytra is concave and ornamented by *spines* (more strongly in ♂; Fig. 146) and head of ♀ is often modified. The beetles in this genus are usually of minor importance because they normally confine their attacks to limbs and twigs of weakened or felled pines. However, where an accumulation of slash (leftover branches and twigs) has produced a large population of these beetles, newly emerged beetles may find insufficient breeding material, and will attack young pines. Disposal of slash can prevent such buildups of populations. Most of the 24 species of *Ips* (2.5-6.4 mm), known as pine engraver beetles, occur in w. U.S. The distinctive concave tips of their elytra bear 3-6 pairs of *toothlike spines* (Fig. 146); the number and arrangement of the spines are different for each species. *Ips* species have habits similar to those of pine engravers in the genus *Pityogenes* (above) — they generally feed in slash or unhealthy trees. First evidence of their attack is yellow or reddish dust in bark crevices, or piles of dust around entrance holes or on ground. These beetles are injurious in w. U.S. when they build up large populations in windfalls, snowbreaks, logging and road slash, or tops of trees killed by pine beetles (*Dendroctonus* species) or other beetles. As mature forests are cut, authorities feel that this group may outrank *Dendroctonus* species in the future in destructiveness to pines. Best way to control these pests is to burn slash or pile it in the sun where it will dry out.

The **California Five-spined Ips,** *Ips confusus* (LeC.), 4.1-4.7 mm, breeds in almost any species of pine, and is destructive to saplings, poles, young trees (up to 30 in.), and tops of mature trees. The **Pine Engraver,** *I. oregoni* (Eich.), not shown, breeds in pines; it most frequently kills trees from 2-8 in. in diameter and destroys the tops of older trees.

The 18 species of *Xyleborus* (widely distributed; 1.5-3 mm) are ambrosia beetles; like other ambrosia beetles (see above) they feed on tender shoots of ambrosial fungus, which grows on walls of galleries they bore. They make very small pinholes in dying or dead wood of a wide assortment of fruit, shade, and forest trees. They do not make engravings between bark and wood that

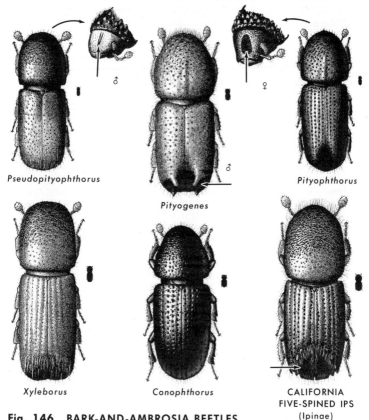

Pseudopityophthorus

Pityogenes ♂

Pityophthorus

Xyleborus

Conophthorus

CALIFORNIA
FIVE-SPINED IPS
(Ipinae)

Fig. 146 BARK-AND-AMBROSIA BEETLES

are typical of other scolytids. The chief damage associated with these beetles is the black stain from the ambrosia fungus that grows in their galleries, in sapwood of trees felled for lumber. Trees cut during flight period of these beetles will almost invariably be damaged unless used at once. Southern lumbermen know they must saw up cypress, oak, gum, and other logs felled in warm months within 2 weeks to avoid wood damage. *Conophthorus* species (about 8 species, widely distributed; most 2.6–3.8 mm) are known as cone beetles. They bore into young cones and deposit their eggs, causing cones to wither and die. Larvae feed in scales and developing seeds of wilting cones; damage to white pine cones is frequently severe. In some years 50% or more of cones may be destroyed; in limited areas destruction may approach 100%.

Nearly all species of *Pseudopityophthorus* (10 species, much of U.S.; 1-2.4 mm) breed in inner bark of various oaks, and are called oak bark beetles. In males the front of the head is ornamented with a *brush* of *long* yellowish or ashen *hairs* (see close-up in Fig. 146). Infrequently they attack and kill a weakened tree. *Pityophthorus,* with 120 species (primarily in w. U.S.), is the largest N. American genus of the family; species range in size from 1.3-3 mm. Pronotum is toothed in front; front of head is ornamented with *longer* and *more abundant hairs* in ♀ than in ♂ (see close-up in Fig. 146). Most of these beetles breed in conifers, generally in twigs or small branches; all but a few live in inner bark. Most feed only in limbs that are broken, weakened, or dying from other causes. Some may attack and kill apparently healthy twigs. Typical tunnels consist of a central breeding chamber under the bark, from which radiate several galleries, each occupied by a ♀. Eggs are laid in individual niches along galleries. When eggs hatch, larvae bore through the twig and pupate at end of mine, often in wood or pith of small twigs.

Glossary

Annotated Bibliography

Index

Glossary

The definitions below are specific for this book, and often refer just to beetles; elsewhere some terms may have additional meanings. For body parts of beetles, refer to Figs. 17 and 19 in Chapter 4.

Abdomen: The third of the 3 main body divisions (head, thorax, and abdomen). Usually covered by the elytra.

Ambrosia: The fungus grown in burrows of certain bark-and-ambrosia beetles and pinhole borers, eaten as food.

Antenna (*pl.* antennae): Feelerlike appendages located on the head, above the mouth parts. *Antennal club* — the enlarged tip (consisting of 1 or more segments) of a clubbed antenna. *Elbowed antenna* — an antenna in which the first segment is enlarged and the following segments join it at an angle.

Aphid: A small, sluggish insect that sucks plant juices; a member of the order Homoptera.

Aspirator: A device that uses suction to pick up insects.

Asymmetrical: Used to describe the symmetry of an object in which the 2 sides are not identical; lopsided.

Beak: The protruding front of the head of certain beetles; also found in bugs.

Berlese funnel: A device that uses heat to force insects from organic material. (See p. 20.)

Bilobed: Divided into 2 lobes.

Biological control: The control of a pest by using a natural enemy, such as another insect, or bacteria.

Bipectinate: Used in reference to an antenna that has lobes on both sides of segments, like a comb with teeth on both sides.

Campodeiform: Refers to a larva that is similar in form to the bristletail Campodea (see Fig. 20), that is, elongated and flattened, with well-developed legs and antennae; usually quite active.

Carnivorous: Feeding on other animals.

Carrion: The carcass of a dead animal.

Cercus (*pl.* cerci): One of a pair of appendages at the end of abdomen.

Chafer: A scarab beetle that feeds on leaves or flowers.

Chitin: An important component of the exoskeleton of insects.

337

Class: A taxonomic subdivision of a phylum or subphylum, containing 1 or more related orders.

Clubbed: Used in reference to an antenna in which the segments (or segment) at the tip are enlarged.

Cocoon: A silken case in which the pupa forms.

Complete metamorphosis: A type of insect development (typical of beetles) in which the individual passes through 4 distinct stages: egg, larva, pupa, and adult.

Compound eye: An eye composed of many individual units, each of which is marked externally by a facet; each facet looks like a portion of a sphere.

Contractile: Capable of rolling up or drawing body parts and appendages close together.

Coxa (*pl.* coxae): The basal segment of the leg.

Defoliate: To strip of leaves; a leaf-eating insect is spoken of as a defoliator. See also **chafer** and **miner.**

Detritus: An accumulation of partly to largely decomposed plant material.

Dormancy: A state of resting or inactivity.

Ectoparasite: A parasite that lives on the outer surface of its host.

Elateriform: Refers to a larva resembling a wireworm — that is, slender, heavily sclerotized, with short thoracic legs and few body hairs. (See Fig. 20.)

Elytron (*pl.* elytra): The front wing(s) of a beetle, generally thickened, leathery, or horny, and overlying the hind wings (when present) and abdomen.

Endoparasite: A parasite that lives inside its host.

Epipleuron (*pl.* epipleura): The turned-down or turned-under lateral edge of an elytron.

Eruciform: Refers to a larva that is caterpillarlike in form, that is, having a more or less cylindrical body, well-developed head, thoracic legs, and leglike abdominal structures. (See Fig. 20.)

Exarate: Refers to a pupa in which the legs are free, and not rigidly attached to the body.

Excavation: A hollowed-out portion of the body in which an appendage or other body part fits.

Exoskeleton: A type of supporting structure or skeleton that is on the outside of the body.

Facet: The external surface of an individual unit of a compound eye.

Family: A taxonomic subdivision of an order, suborder, or superfamily, containing 1 genus or (more often) a number of related genera. Family names end in *-idae.*

Femur (*pl.* femora): The 3rd leg segment, located between the trochanter and tibia.

Frass: Plant fragments (usually wood) produced by a plant-feeding insect, usually mixed with excrement.

Frons: The sclerite that is at the front of the head, above the eyes.

Galea (*pl.* galeae): The outer lobe of the maxilla of the mouth parts.

Gall: An abnormal growth of plant tissue that is produced by the presence of an insect or another organism.

Ganglion (*pl.* ganglia): An enlarged portion of a nerve containing a coordinating mass of nerve cells.

Generation: The complete life cycle of an organism, from any given stage to the same stage in the offspring.

Genus (*pl.* genera): The most important taxonomic subdivision immediately below the family level. A family consists of 1 or (more often) a number of genera. A genus consists of 1 or (more often) a group of closely related species. In a binomial or trinomial scientific name the genus name is given first and is capitalized. Generic names are Latinized and italicized.

Globular: Spherical, or nearly so.

Grub: A scarabaeiform larva. (See below.)

Head: The first of the 3 body divisions, which bears the eyes, antennae, and mouth parts.

Holometabolous: Undergoing complete metamorphosis, in which there are 4 stages — egg, larva, pupa, and adult — during development.

Humerus (*pl.* humeri): The front angle of an elytron; a shoulder-like region of the body.

Hypermetamorphosis: A type of complete metamorphosis in which larval instars differ considerably in body form. Examples occur in the blister beetles (p. 270).

Hypognathous: With the mandibles directed downward.

Hypopharynx: A median mouth-part structure located between the labium and labrum, best compared to the tongue.

Instar: The stage of an insect between successive molts. The first instar is the larval stage between hatching and the first molt.

Iridescence: An often metallic-like play of colors on a surface; these colors often vary according to the angle of the light.

Keel: An elevated ridge.

Labium: A mouth part, often compared to the lower lip.

Labrum: A mouth part that lies in front of or above the mandibles, often compared to the upper lip.

Lamellate: Refers to an antenna in which some short segments at the tip are greatly enlarged to one side.

Larva (*pl.* larvae): The immature stage of an insect (not including the egg) that undergoes complete metamorphosis; *i.e.,* the stage following the egg and preceding the pupa.

Larviform: Similar in form to a larva, as in a larviform adult female.

Leaf miner: An insect (usually the larval stage) that feeds within a leaf, between the upper and lower surfaces. Compare with **chafer.**

Mandible: One of the paired toothlike chewing structures of an insect.

Margin: A keel or ridge, such as the distinct edge on the side of a margined pronotum.

Maxilla (*pl.* maxillae): One of the paired mouth parts located immediately behind the mandibles.

Mealybug: A small, relatively inactive sucking insect, often covered with waxy secretions; a member of the order Homoptera.

Mesepimeron: The rear plate of the pleuron of the mesothorax.

Mesepipleuron: The pleuron of the mesothorax.

Mesoscutellum: The scutellum of the mesothorax; usually called simply the scutellum.

Mesosternum: The sternal portion of the mesothorax.

Mesothorax: The second or middle segment of the thorax.

Metasternum: The sternal portion of the metathorax.

Metathorax: The third or posterior segment of the thorax.

Metamorphosis: A type of development in which the individual shows distinct changes in form from one stage to the next.

Miner: A larva that makes tunnels in leaves or stems.

Molting: The shedding of the exoskeleton.

Morphology: The study of form or structure.

Naiad: The immature stage of certain insects; an aquatic nymph that breathes by means of gills.

Notum (*pl.* nota): The dorsal surface of a body segment, nearly always refers to thoracic segments, *e.g.,* the pronotum.

Ocellus (*pl.* ocelli): A simple eye of an insect, marked externally by a single facet.

Omnivorous: Eating both animal and vegetable material.

Order: A taxonomic subdivision of a class or subclass containing one family or (more often) a group of families.

Ostium (*pl.* ostia): A slitlike opening.

Paedogenesis: The production of eggs or larvae by an immature or larval stage.

Palp (*pl.* palps): One of a pair of segmented, fingerlike processes; each maxilla bears one palp, and the labium bears a pair of palps.

Parasite: An organism that lives in or on the body of another organism (its host) during at least part of its life cycle. A parasite may injure its host but generally does not kill it.

Parthenogenesis: Reproduction by eggs that develop without fertilization.

Phylum (*pl.* phyla): A major taxonomic subdivision of a kingdom. The insects belong to the phylum Arthropoda.

Pleuron (*pl.* pleura): One of the 2 lateral regions of a thoracic segment.

Pollination: The transfer of pollen from a stamen to an ovule, often done by insects.

Postnotum (*pl.* postnata): A sclerite behind the scutellum.

Predaceous: Refers to an animal that seeks out and feeds on another animal.

Prognathous: With the head horizontal or nearly so, and the mouth parts directed forward or nearly forward.

Pronotum: The dorsal sclerite of the prothorax.

Propleuron (*pl.* propleura): The lateral portion (or pleuron) of the prothorax.

Prosternum: The sternum or ventral sclerite (plate) of the prothorax.

Prothorax: The first of the 3 thoracic segments.

Punctate: Having pits or small depressions on a surface.

Pupa (*pl.* pupae): The stage between the larva and the adult in insects with complete metamorphosis.

Pupate: To transform to a pupa.

Pygidium: The last dorsal segment of the abdomen, which is exposed in some beetles.

Reticulate: With a raised networklike pattern, as on the elytra of species of net-winged beetles (p. 186).

Retractile: Capable of being pulled in.

Riffle: Part of a stream that is shallow and has broken water, usually flowing over a rocky bottom.

Scale insect: A small sucking insect, the female of which secretes waxy scales; a member of the order Homoptera.

Scarabaeiform: Refers to a sluggish, grublike larva, with a thick, cylindrical, C-shaped body and a well-developed head and thoracic legs.

Scavenger: An animal that feeds on dead plants or animals, decaying materials, or animal wastes.

Sclerite: A hardened body-wall plate of the exoskeleton, often bounded by sutures or membranous areas.

Sclerotized: Hardened.

Sculptured: With raised or impressed markings on a surface.

Scutellum: The mesoscutellum; a (usually) triangular sclerite at base of the elytra, found in nearly all beetles.

Scutum: The middle division of a thoracic notum, located just in front of the scutellum.

Segment: A subdivision of the body or an appendage, marked off by joints or articulations.

Slime flux: The area of a tree that is stained by oozing sap.

Species: A population of individuals that are able to interbreed and produce fertile offspring; the members of a species are similar to one another in structure and physiology.

Spiracle: An external opening of the tracheal or respiratory system; a breathing pore.

Spur: A movable spine; usually located at the tip of a leg segment.

Sternum (*pl.* sterna): A sclerite (plate) on the ventral side of the body, such as the prosternum or mesosternum.

Stria (*pl.* striae): A groove or impressed line or a row of punctures; beetle elytra are often striate.

Stridulate: To produce a noise by rubbing parts together.

Subfamily: A taxonomic subdivision of a family, containing a group of related tribes or genera. Subfamily names end in *-inae*.

Subspecies: A geographic race of a species. Subspecies of a species are often not sharply differentiated, and intergrade geographically; they are usually capable of some interbreeding.

Suture: An external groove or line in the body wall between sclerites; in beetles, often used in reference to the median line where the elytra meet.

Tarsal formula: A 3-part formula (such as 5-5-5) representing the number of tarsal segments on the front, middle, and hind tarsi, respectively.

Tarsus (*pl.* tarsi): The leg segment beyond the tibia, consisting of 2-5 subdivisions, the last one bearing the claws.

Teneral: Used to describe a recently molted adult, which is usually very soft-bodied and pale.

Tergum (*pl.* terga): The dorsal surface of any body segment; often used in reference to abdominal segments.

Thorax: The body region just behind the head, which bears the legs and wings.

Tibia (*pl.* tibiae): The fourth segment of a leg, between the femur and tarsus.

Trachea (*pl.* tracheae): A tube of the respiratory system of insects, ending externally in a spiracle, and branching internally to all body parts.

Transverse: Situated crosswise.

Trochanter: The second segment of a leg, located between the coxa and femur.

Truncate: Refers to a margin or edge (usually at the tip) that is straight across.

Tubercle: A small knob or raised bump.

Vermiform larva: A legless wormlike larva, lacking a well-developed head.

Vesicle: A sac or bladder, often capable of being extended.

Wireworm: An elateriform larva. (See above.)

Annotated Bibliography

Some of the books listed below are similar in scope to this Field Guide, but may illustrate or discuss species not included in this book, and thus may be useful as supplemental literature. A few provide considerably more data on particular groups than can be covered in a Field Guide. Some of the literature will allow you to carry your interest in beetles far beyond what can be achieved with general publications.

Arnett, Ross H. 1968. *The Beetles of the United States (A Manual for Identification)*. Ann Arbor: The American Entomological Institute. A necessity for the serious student of beetles; the only volume available that allows identification of all North American beetles to the genus level; includes keys to families and genera. Available from the American Entomological Institute, 5950 Warren Road, Ann Arbor, Mich. 48105.

————, N.M. Downie, and H.E. Jaques. 1980. *How to Know the Beetles*. Dubuque, Iowa: Wm. Co. Brown Co. Includes a key to families and keys within each family that lead to about 1000 species that are illustrated and discussed. Coverage of species is highly selective.

Baker, W.L. 1972. *Eastern Forest Insects*. U.S. Dept. of Agriculture, Misc. Pub. no. 1175. Essentially an update of the book by Craighead (below), but fewer families of beetles are covered. Available from the Superintendent of Documents, U.S. Government Printing Office, Washington, D.C. 20402.

Blatchley, W.S. 1910. *An Illustrated Descriptive Catalogue of the Coleoptera or Beetles (Exclusive of the Rhynchophora) Known to Occur in Indiana*. Indianapolis: Nature Publishing Co. Somewhat outdated but historically very notable — the first volume to cover nearly all beetles (weevils are in a separate book, below) occurring in a geographic area. Includes keys down to the species level with brief descriptions of each species. Few copies were printed, so it is rarely available from book dealers.

————, and C.W. Leng. 1916. *Rhynchophora or Weevils of Northeastern North America*. Indianapolis: Nature Publishing Co. Similar to Blatchley (above) but includes only weevils, and covers a wider geographic area. More copies of this book were printed, so it is usually available from book dealers.

Borror, DeLong, and Triplehorn. 1981. *An Introduction to the*

Study of Insects. 5th edition. New York: Holt, Rinehart, and Winston. Includes one of the best keys to families available. For each family there is a discussion of habits and characters.

The Coleopterists' Bulletin. A quarterly journal devoted to scientific articles (primarily taxonomic) on beetles. Of greatest interest to the advanced amateur or professional researcher. Membership in the Coleopterist's Society, including a 1-year subscription to the Bulletin, was $10.00 as of 1980. Write to The Coleopterists Society, c/o Department of Entomology, NHB 168, Smithsonian Institution, Washington, D.C. 20560.

Craighead, F.C. 1949. *Insect Enemies of Eastern Forests.* U.S. Dept. of Agriculture, Misc. Publ. no. 657. Includes considerable biological data on beetles that affect forests, either by feeding on foliage or by boring into wood. Some of the beetles discussed are beneficial for feeding on injurious insects. Fifty-two beetle families are covered; considerable text is devoted to the most harmful pests. Includes keys to genera or species of important families based on adults, larvae, or kind of damage. Order from the Superintendent of Documents, U.S. Government Printing Office, Washington, D.C. 20402.

Dillon, E.S. and L.S. Dillon. 1961. *A Manual of Common Beetles of Eastern North America.* Evanston, Illinois. Row, Peterson and Co. Includes a key to families, with partial coverage of genera and species. Most valuable for the 1100 or so drawings of common species.

Edwards, J.G. 1949. *Coleoptera or Beetles East of the Great Plains.* Ann Arbor: Edwards Brothers, Inc. Contains a lengthy key to families of beetles, with numerous illustrations. For each family there is a general discussion of habits, larval morphology, and often data on individual species.

Hatch, M.H. 1953–71. *The Beetles of the Pacific Northwest.* University of Washington Publications in Biology (Vol. 16); appeared in 5 parts. Seattle: University of Washington Press. Provides keys and descriptions for all species known from the area covered, but the format is awkward.

Usinger, R.L. 1968. *Aquatic Insects of California with Keys to North American Genera and California Species.* Berkeley and Los Angeles: University of California Press. Covers aquatic and semiaquatic beetles, with keys to genera of larger families, keys to larvae, and keys to Calif. species of each genus.

Young, F.N. 1954. *The Water Beetles of Florida.* Gainesville: University of Florida Press. Covers only the 9 families of water beetles found in Florida, but is also of some use in nearby areas.

Book Dealers

Books for which no address is given above can generally be purchased from a book dealer. Unless otherwise specified, the dealers below can supply old books and reprints as well as current literature. Current works may also be available from supply houses. Some of the more important book dealers are listed below.

The Amateur Entomological Society, Publications Agent, 137 Gleneldon Road, Streatham, London, SW 16, England. Can supply old books, current works, as well as leaflets, pamphlets, and bulletins published by the society.

Antiquariaat Junk, Dr. R. Schierenberg and Sons, Lochem, the Netherlands.

E.W. Classey, 353 Hanworth Road, Hampton, Middlesex, England.

Entomological Reprint Specialists, P.O. Box 77224, Dockweiler Station, Los Angeles, Calif. 90007.

Julian J. Nadolny, 35 Varmor Drive, New Britain, Conn. 06053.

Henry Tripp, P.O. Box 1221, Woodhaven, N. Y. 11421. A large selection of old works is available.

Wheldon and Wesley, Ltd., Lytton Lodge, Codicote, Hitchin, Herts., SG4 8TE, England.

Supply Houses

Below are listed biological supply houses that have a large variety of entomological supplies. You can write for their catalogs (all are free, except for the Turtox catalog). Compare costs — prices vary (sometimes greatly) for apparently identical items. Certain items are offered by only one or two dealers.

American Biological Supply Co., 1330 Dillon Heights Ave., Baltimore, Md. 21228

BioQuip Products, P.O. Box 61, Santa Monica, Calif. 90406

Carolina Biological Supply Co., Burlington, N.C. 27216

Turtox Cambosco, MacMillan Science Co., Inc., 8200 S. Hoyne Ave., Chicago, Ill. 60620

Ward's Natural Science Establishment, Inc., P.O. Box 1712, Rochester, N.Y. 14603

Microscope Manufacturers

Bausch and Lomb, Rochester, N.Y. 14602

Graf-Apsco Company, 5868 Broadway, Chicago, Ill. 60626

Unitron Instrument Company, Microscope Division, 66 Needham Street, Newton Highlands, Mass. 02161

Index

This index includes the names of beetles and other organisms mentioned in this guide; for the location of various subjects covered in this book, look in the Contents. Scientific names, common names, and synonyms for scientific names of families are included. Also listed are scientific names for families that are recognized in some literature as separate families, but which are not recognized as such in this guide; the family in which these groups are treated in this guide is indicated in parentheses. Numbers in **boldface** or *italics* refer to illustrations; **Pl.** before a number indicates a color plate reference; *italics* indicate a line drawing on that page in the text.

347

PICTURED KEY TO PRINCIPAL

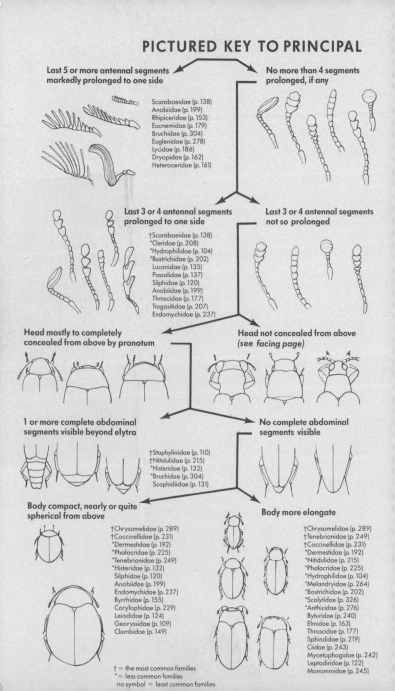

Last 5 or more antennal segments markedly prolonged to one side

Scarabaeidae (p. 138)
Anobiidae (p. 199)
Rhipiceridae (p. 153)
Eucnemidae (p. 179)
Bruchidae (p. 304)
Euglenidae (p. 278)
Lycidae (p. 186)
Dryopidae (p. 162)
Heteroceridae (p. 161)

No more than 4 segments prolonged, if any

Last 3 or 4 antennal segments prolonged to one side

†Scarabaeidae (p. 138)
*Cleridae (p. 208)
*Hydrophilidae (p. 104)
*Bostrichidae (p. 202)
Lucanidae (p. 135)
Passalidae (p. 137)
Silphidae (p. 120)
Anobiidae (p. 199)
Throscidae (p. 177)
Trogositidae (p. 207)
Endomychidae (p. 237)

Last 3 or 4 antennal segments not so prolonged

Head mostly to completely concealed from above by pronotum

Head not concealed from above
(see facing page)

1 or more complete abdominal segments visible beyond elytra

†Staphylinidae (p. 110)
†Nitidulidae (p. 215)
*Histeridae (p. 132)
*Bruchidae (p. 304)
Scaphidiidae (p. 131)

No complete abdominal segments visible

Body compact, nearly or quite spherical from above

†Chrysomelidae (p. 289)
†Coccinellidae (p. 231)
*Dermestidae (p. 192)
*Phalacridae (p. 225)
*Tenebrionidae (p. 249)
*Histeridae (p. 132)
Silphidae (p. 120)
Anobiidae (p. 199)
Endomychidae (p. 237)
Byrrhidae (p. 155)
Corylophidae (p. 229)
Leiodidae (p. 124)
Georyssidae (p. 109)
Clambidae (p. 149)

Body more elongate

†Chrysomelidae (p. 289)
†Tenebrionidae (p. 249)
†Coccinellidae (p. 231)
*Dermestidae (p. 192)
*Nitidulidae (p. 215)
*Phalacridae (p. 225)
*Hydrophilidae (p. 104)
*Melandryidae (p. 264)
*Bostrichidae (p. 202)
*Scolytidae (p. 326)
*Anthicidae (p. 276)
Byturidae (p. 240)
Elmidae (p. 163)
Throscidae (p. 177)
Sphindidae (p. 219)
Ciidae (p. 243)
Mycetophagidae (p. 242)
Leptodiridae (p. 122)
Monommidae (p. 245)

† = the most common families
* = less common families
no symbol = least common families

FAMILIES OF BEETLES

Body very narrow and elongate
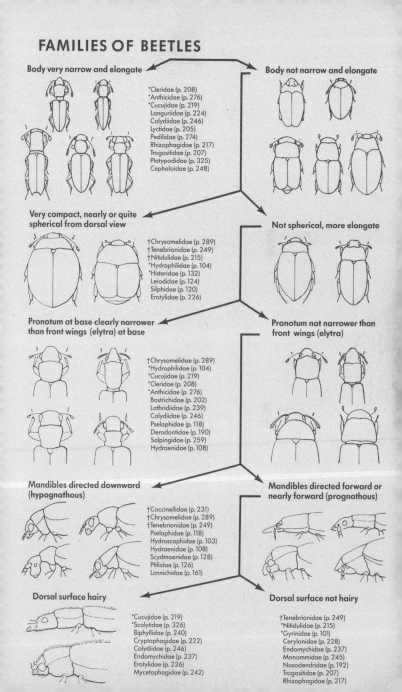

*Cleridae (p. 208)
*Anthicidae (p. 276)
*Cucujidae (p. 219)
Languriidae (p. 224)
Colydiidae (p. 246)
Lyctidae (p. 205)
Pedilidae (p. 274)
Rhizophagidae (p. 217)
Trogositidae (p. 207)
Platypodidae (p. 325)
Cephaloidae (p. 248)

Body not narrow and elongate

Very compact, nearly or quite spherical from dorsal view

†Chrysomelidae (p. 289)
†Tenebrionidae (p. 249)
†Nitidulidae (p. 215)
*Hydrophilidae (p. 104)
*Histeridae (p. 132)
Leiodidae (p. 124)
Silphidae (p. 120)
Erotylidae (p. 226)

Not spherical, more elongate

Pronotum at base clearly narrower than front wings (elytra) at base

†Chrysomelidae (p. 289)
*Hydrophilidae (p. 104)
*Cucujidae (p. 219)
*Cleridae (p. 208)
*Anthicidae (p. 276)
Bostrichidae (p. 202)
Lathridiidae (p. 239)
Colydiidae (p. 246)
Pselaphidae (p. 118)
Derodontidae (p. 190)
Salpingidae (p. 259)
Hydraenidae (p. 108)

Pronotum not narrower than front wings (elytra)

Mandibles directed downward (hypognathous)

†Coccinellidae (p. 231)
†Chrysomelidae (p. 289)
†Tenebrionidae (p. 249)
Pselaphidae (p. 118)
Hydroscaphidae (p. 103)
Hydraenidae (p. 108)
Scydmaenidae (p. 128)
Ptiliidae (p. 126)
Limnichidae (p. 161)

Mandibles directed forward or nearly forward (prognathous)

Dorsal surface hairy

*Cucujidae (p. 219)
*Scolytidae (p. 326)
Biphyllidae (p. 240)
Cryptophagidae (p. 222)
Colydiidae (p. 246)
Endomychidae (p. 237)
Erotylidae (p. 226)
Mycetophagidae (p. 242)

Dorsal surface not hairy

†Tenebrionidae (p. 249)
*Nitidulidae (p. 215)
*Gyrinidae (p. 101)
Cerylonidae (p. 228)
Endomychidae (p. 237)
Monommidae (p. 245)
Nosodendridae (p. 192)
Trogositidae (p. 207)
Rhizophagidae (p. 217)